CHRISTIAN THEOLOGY IN PRACTICE

Taken at the Collegeville Institute for Ecumenical and Cultural Research
(Fall 2010; author photo)

Christian Theology in Practice

DISCOVERING A DISCIPLINE

Bonnie J. Miller-McLemore

WILLIAM B. EERDMANS PUBLISHING COMPANY

GRAND RAPIDS, MICHIGAN / CAMBRIDGE, U.K.

Published 2012 by

Wm. B. Eerdmans Publishing Co.

2140 Oak Industrial Drive N.E., Grand Rapids, Michigan 49505 /

P.O. Box 163, Cambridge CB3 9PU U.K.

Printed in the United States of America

18 17 16 15 14 13 12   7 6 5 4 3 2 1

Library of Congress Cataloging-in-Publication Data

Miller-McLemore, Bonnie J.

Christian theology in practice: discovering a discipline /

Bonnie J. Miller-McLemore.

p.   cm.

ISBN 978-0-8028-6534-2 (pbk.: alk. paper)

1. Pastoral theology.   2. Theology, Practical.

3. Feminist theology.   I. Title.

BV4017.M52   2012

253 — dc23

2011031696

www.eerdmans.com

In Honor of
John B. Spencer (1919-1987)
Kalamazoo College
and
Don S. Browning (1934-2010)
University of Chicago Divinity School

Contents

ACKNOWLEDGMENTS   ix

INTRODUCTION
Engaging Practice: The Work of Christian Theology   1

PART I
LIVING WEB: A SUBJECT MATTER

1. The Living Web and the State of Pastoral Theology   25

2. Revisiting the Living Document and Web   46

3. Pastoral Theology as Public Theology   70

4. Practical Theology: A Definition   100

PART II
PRACTICAL WISDOM: A WAY OF KNOWING

5. A Maternal Feminist Epistemology   113

6. The Subversive Practice of Pastoral Theology   137

CONTENTS

7. The Clerical *and* the Academic Paradigm 160

8. Practical Theology, Pedagogy, and Theological Know-How 185

PART III

GENDER: A KEY CATEGORY OF ANALYSIS

9. Feminist Theory and Pastoral Theology 211

10. How Gender Studies Revolutionized Pastoral Theology 238

11. Feminist Studies in Psychology: A Resource 255

12. Pastoral Theology and the Future of Religion
and Psychological Studies 286

Index 313

Acknowledgments

With a collection spanning twenty years, it is impossible to thank everyone who contributed. I dedicate the book to John B. Spencer and Don S. Browning, undergraduate and graduate school faculty respectively, who made all the difference in my scholarly and vocational life. Both died prematurely, Dr. Spencer (as I called him then) from a brain tumor that appeared a few years before he planned to retire from Kalamazoo College and a year after I started graduate school. I still have his copy of *The Journal of Religion* containing Valerie Saiving's article "The Human Situation: A Feminine View," which he had handed to me almost as an aside with his signature etched on the top right corner. Unbeknownst to him (or did he anticipate?) and unanticipated by me, Saiving's essay had long-term impact. So did his ideas and general counsel (see pp. 36, 51). I also have Don Browning's signature and well wishes on a few of his books given to me, including his first book, *Atonement and Psychotherapy*. But his influence far outreaches the texts themselves, as this book makes evident. (His ideas appear on many pages — too many to mention.) He died at the height of an active retirement and six months before I finished this project. Celebrating his life with friends and family impressed upon me the range of his contributions and the generosity of spirit from which I benefited immensely.

I also owe thanks to more proximate colleagues who provided incentive at key moments. Over the past few years, Jim Nieman offered insight, perspective, and concrete suggestions in frank e-mails and great conversations around the edges of academic meetings (even over the din of Chicago Bear hysteria in a Michigan Avenue restaurant after a Sunday win). In fall 2008, a few years after I'd first considered the idea of this collection and run it by a few colleagues and editors, I co-taught with Ted Smith in our new doctoral curriculum in theology and practice; we read collections by Clifford Geertz and Sherry Ortner, and Ted encouraged me to get on with my plan to do my own. Ultimately, at the Collegeville Institute in Fall 2010, Don Ottenhoff and Kathleen Cahalan (backed by the wonderful staff and board of the Institute) provided exactly what was needed to turn the corner — hospitality, company, space, interest, *and* a book title. Kathleen reminds me regularly how great it feels to finish a project. No kidding. She is right about that and much else, a wisdom for which I remain grateful.

Jon Pott, Vice President and Editor-in-Chief at Eerdmans, is likely glad for these folks as well. I am grateful for his unflappable, unflagging support over the past few years as I missed deadlines. I remember one particularly important phone call that resolved my question of what to do with the introduction I had written that had turned into something else. He told me to save it for what sounded like a new book, *Practical Theology: A Manifesto* (!). "I'm not sure I want to write another book beyond this one," I answered, despite the audacious title. But he said collecting my previous work might "pave the way for future work rather than relieve you of it" and so encouraged me to push forward with the old as a springboard for the new. Behind the scenes but no less helpful, managing editor Linda Bieze guided the book through the technicalities of publication. I especially appreciated her clear, steady, supportive e-mail responses. I also thank Karen Eardley for her constant faculty assistance on details of printing, mailing, and so forth, and graduate students and research assistants Naomi Annandale, Kent Kreiselmeier, and Ira Helderman for proofreading scanned chapters, tracking down permissions, and picking up other miscellanea, such as redoing the reference style, in the midst of their own pressing research and class work. I am grateful for these and other students who raised questions that these chapters attempt to answer. They are the future for which I write. I also acknowledge two institutions that help secure that future: Vanderbilt University for employment and research leave, and the Louisville Institute for their generous Sabbatical Grant for Researchers for 2010-2011, without which I would not have had the time or space to complete this work.

Between more distant and proximate influences stand colleagues and friends too many to name here. I consider their gifts a blessing. The introductions to individual chapters recognize some of the people, events, and requests that sparked them and try to give ample credit where it is due.

Acknowledgments

I was not the only person aging as I completed the book. My parents, Gerry and John Miller, turned eighty, my kids — Chris, Matt, and Daniel — moved out of their teens and gradually vacated their upstairs bedrooms for greater adventures in the wider world, my husband Mark's red beard grayed, and our fourteen-year-old chocolate lab, Kelsey, developed arthritis, poor hearing, a drooping, drooling lip, and bad gas. For a change, there are relatively few stories in these chapters about my household and family. They should be relieved, even if this makes the book even less interesting to them than my other books. Dog and all, my family remains a steady, valued presence, enriching my life and cheering me on as they embrace their own challenges of faithful living. I am grateful for their example.

BONNIE MILLER-McLEMORE
Collegeville Institute for Ecumenical
and Cultural Research

Engaging Practice:
The Work of Christian Theology

It is living, no rather dying, suffering and facing damnation, not thinking, reading and speculating that makes a theologian.

Martin Luther, *Commentary on the First Twenty-Two Psalms*[1]

Seward Hiltner, heralded as an important forerunner of the modern discipline of pastoral theology, wrote in 1958 that the "proper study of practice" has the potential to "illuminate theological understanding itself."[2] Ever since, scholars in both pastoral and practical theology have attempted to recapture territory previously neglected in academic study — human religious experience and practice — as an essential site for theological engagement. This work has begun to redefine what theology is, how it is done, and who does it.

This book picks up and continues this cause. Its thesis is that scholarship in pastoral and practical theology has disrupted conventional theological boundaries, suggesting an expanded subject matter (Part I), alternative ways of knowing (Part II), and richer terms for analysis in doing Christian theology (Part III). This argument about theology's redefinition stands behind the book as a whole and holds together its three parts, suggesting the *living web* as theological subject matter, *practical wisdom* as a way of theological knowing, and *gender* as a critical category for understanding human situations.

---

1. Cited by Heidi Newmark, Lutheran pastor and author of a theological memoir of ministry in Harlem, in *Breathing Spaces: A Spiritual Journey in the South Bronx* (Boston: Beacon Press, 2003), p. 249.

2. Seward Hiltner, *Preface to Pastoral Theology* (Nashville: Abingdon Press, 1958), p. 47.

The Argument

Although the essays here were written over the span of twenty years, together they make a case that is greater than any one essay alone. They suggest that scholars in the academy and Christians in congregations need to expand their understanding of theology beyond its modern conflation with academic theology for the sake of Christian faith and ministry, something systematic theologian Edward Farley worried about over two decades after Hiltner in the 1980s.[3] Twenty-five years after Farley but in contrast to him and in greater alliance with Hiltner, I argue that an adequate response to theology's academic reification is *not* the re-unification of theology as "one thing," *theologia* or sapiential knowledge of God, but *recognition of its multiplicity*, or the many valuable shapes and places in which theology and wisdom of God appear. Theology is multivalent. *Academic theology* is only one kind of theology with a particular and sometimes narrow social and political location. *Theology* broadly defined is more like *liturgy*. It is the *work of the people* praising, arguing with, and turning to God in many contexts for diverse purposes.

This understanding rehabilitates Friedrich Schleiermacher's understanding, and his depiction of the tree as a metaphor for the theological enterprise in particular, an image that I believe locates theology in all its diversity. Practical theology did not emerge as an academic area in its own right until the eighteenth and nineteenth centuries, when the German Protestant theologian and father of modern theology provided a three-part conceptual infrastructure with practical theology as the "crown" and historical and philosophical theology as "trunk" and "roots" respectively. Although we commonly attribute this image to Schleiermacher, he actually deleted it from his lecture notes when he revised them for publication in response to criticism over practical theology's placement in a position of superiority. He does not include the metaphor of the tree in a final version of *Brief Outline of the Study of Theology*, his most systematic treatment of theology's organization as a positive science.[4] But U.S. pastoral theologian Jeanne Stevenson-Moessner says that we need to re-read this metaphor,

3. Edward Farley, *Theologia: The Fragmentation and Unity of Theological Education* (Philadelphia: Fortress Press, 1983).

4. Friedrich Schleiermacher, *Brief Outline of the Study of Theology* (1830), trans. Terrence N. Tice (Richmond: John Knox Press, 1970).

2

and I agree.[5] We need to move away from hierarchical interpretations, where one of the three forms of theology triumphs over the other as crown or roots, and move instead toward a more organic, ecological reading of the tree as an instance of circular and mutually interdependent movement. Just as branches, flowers, fruit, and leaves fall to the ground, where they renew the soil and roots, so also does practical theology give back to the whole rather than simply represent historical and philosophical theology's outcome, fruition, or application. In fact, in some arid ecosystems, Stevenson-Moessner points out, sap reverses its flow, absorbing moisture through the crown and sending it downward to the roots, thereby redistributing water to dry soil.[6] But whatever direction sap flows, there is a greater "equality and mutuality" among the three parts and the church as a whole than usually imagined.[7] Other practical theologians, such as Pam Couture, even judge the tree as too vertical and monolithic a metaphor to capture the complexity of contemporary theology.[8] Instead, they argue for postmodern portraits of knowledge as *rhizomatic.* Rhizomes, or plants with multiple root systems that spread horizontally, mirror the multiple, democratic, and diverse paths to Christian faith and theology. Rhizomes survive under the most adverse conditions, as does commonplace theologizing among those who sustain faith under duress.

Neither Schleiermacher nor Hiltner nor Farley nor even Reformation leader Martin Luther realized how extensive the democratization of theology might prove to be. Today, academic theologians are called to include in their consideration of theology the wider range of Christian experience and practice abounding in a variety of congregational and public contexts. Even though people have been tempted to idealize as the epitome of truth and doctrine either church theology in the first several centuries or university theology from the medieval period through modernity, no one area of theology should subsume other forms. I would even qualify Luther's hierarchy in this chapter's epigraph, which places living and suffering *over* thinking and reading, and say instead, "It is living . . . , *alongside* thinking, reading . . . that makes a theologian."

5. Jeanne Stevenson-Moessner, *Prelude to Practical Theology: Variations on Theory and Practice* (Nashville: Abingdon Press, 2008), pp. 2-3.

6. Stevenson-Moessner, *Prelude to Practical Theology,* pp. 68-69.

7. Stevenson-Moessner, *Prelude to Practical Theology,* p. 3.

8. See Pamela Couture, *Child Poverty: Love, Justice, and Social Responsibility* (St. Louis: Chalice Press, 2007), pp. 151-52. Couture credits Gilles Deleuze and Felix Guittari and cites *The Deleuze Reader,* ed. Constantin V. Boundas (New York: Columbia University Press, 1993).

In other words, the effort to redefine theology and the discovery of practical theology are not a "ruse for turning the tables," as practical theologian James Nieman rightly says, imposing a "new hierarchy" with practical, pastoral, congregational, or some other form of theology "at the peak."[9] Rather, it is an attempt to locate power at a variety of junctures in the life of Christian faith. Since theology "always occurs locally," as Nieman argues, the "challenge is to define theology broadly and flexibly enough to be recognizable across different times and places as well as various expressions of the church."[10] In addition to the widely recognized speculative and regulative roles of theology in academic and ecclesial contexts, theology has always had a "discursive" or what I would call a *practical* role with a "dynamic intent," to use Nieman's words.[11] It is action-oriented. It offers, renews, sponsors, produces, regulates, influences, and so forth. This redefinition allows us to see that practices as different and ordinary as what people wear, how we manage finances, and how we sing hymns are "also . . . assertions of theology."[12] Or, as Christian historian and lived religion scholar Charles Marsh suggests in his book on civil rights in Mississippi, this understanding allows us to ask how ordinary people and places become "theatres of complex theological drama."[13]

Since their renewal in the mid- and late twentieth century, both pastoral and practical theologies have been modern/postmodern academic disciplines dedicated to the project of greater theological inclusivity. Other people across Christian history — Luther in the sixteenth century; eighteenth- and nineteenth-century ancestors in my own tradition of Christian Church (Disciples of Christ), such as Thomas and Alexander Campbell; Hiltner in the twentieth century (partly inspired by Anton Boisen and his claim about living human documents); and liberation theologians at large — have all suggested

9. James Nieman, "Theology in the Sermon," unpublished manuscript, 2007, p. 4. He suggests instead a more "productive, inseparable relation" between the practices of local and academic theologies. So, for example, "The language of preaching is mainly performative, using words that do what they say (as when forgiveness is directly enacted by uttering 'I forgive you'). Academic theology is more reflective in form, considering from some measure of remove what has first been said performatively (as when reconciliation is extensively elaborated)."

10. James Nieman, "Attending Locally: Theologies in Congregations," *International Journal of Practical Theology* 6, no. 2 (Fall 2002): 202.

11. Nieman, "Attending Locally," p. 205.

12. Nieman, "Attending Locally," p. 206.

13. Charles Marsh, *God's Long Summer: Stories of Faith and Civil Rights* (Princeton: Princeton University Press, 1997), p. 3.

analogous shifts in theology's location and definition. Such redefinition has challenged the academy and church both then and now because it asks for a redistribution of power that we know — from the experience of addressing other endemic hierarchies like sexism, racism, and heterosexism — does not and will not come about easily.

The Idea

Practically speaking, the idea for this book arose four years ago, twenty years after I completed a doctorate in religion at the University of Chicago in an area then named Religion and Psychological Studies, when I found myself referring colleagues and students to my writings and recognized a need to make them more available. Although I did not originally write these essays with a larger argument about Christian theology in practice explicitly in mind, the connecting thread of the search for a more inclusive theology became clear when I put them together. So, two decades after searching for an academic discipline that truly grapples with theology in the midst of life, I realized I had a thesis and enough essays illustrating it to constitute a book.

Although I have been making this argument for twenty years, its path is clearer in retrospect, much like my own vocational choices. And I do not think I am finished exploring it. Every time I worked on this introduction, I had trouble containing it. It kept evolving into a bigger project. Nevertheless, something compelled me to proceed first with this collection to see what I had said and what more needs saying.

I have a further incentive. When it comes to pastoral and practical theologies, people suffer scholarly amnesia with a variety of symptoms. We overlook ground already covered by previous scholarship in the field. We forget to cite each other's work, a common practice in other disciplines but less so in the practical fields. We read widely outside our own disciplines as much as within them. We invite scholars from other fields to speak at our conferences and respond to our papers at the American Academy of Religion (AAR) rather than pulling from our own ranks. I just caught myself falling prey to this amnesia while chairing a 2010 AAR session re-examining the "clerical paradigm." In my opening remarks I made no mention of my own essay on the fallacy of the paradigm (Chapter 7), even though the essay had helped spark the session. Nor did I mention the wider conversation and an important project and book edited by Dorothy

Bass and Craig Dykstra, *For Life Abundant,* that pushed me past complaint (about overuse of the clerical paradigm as *the* problem) to constructive response (Chapter 8).[14]

This is unnecessary modesty and even negligent. Our shared failure to retain and proclaim our history leads us and other scholars and ministers to overlook it. Scholars in other areas invent "new ideas" as if the study of religious practice, experience, and culture in pastoral and practical theologies never happened. So my audience for this book is not just pastoral and practical theologians but scholars in religious and theological studies more generally.

The Hurdles

Getting from the original idea to executing it has not been easy. Re-reading my work — an obvious first step in compiling an anthology — did not appeal to me. As I said to a couple of wonderful colleagues at the Collegeville Institute for Ecumenical and Cultural Research in Minnesota, where I finally went for three weeks to push forward after a few years of procrastination, I worried that the essays would be *boring* and *bad.* I am not feigning humility or showing a lapse in self-esteem here. This was a real concern. Just as I would prefer to teach a new class than re-teach an old one, I am impatient with work already done. This is a problem that impedes good teaching and research. (I have trouble teaching valuable ideas over and over or reading the same book twice.) Once I gain new insight, I have trouble seeing it anew. It no longer seems so remarkable. I assume it. I struggle to return to the position of the learner — the one who does not yet know this idea. I am also impatient with introductory and overview books (e.g., introductions to pastoral care). They seem dull. I like books on concrete topics. All this impeded my desire to return to or even recommend previous publications.

Of course, I had more disconcerting anxieties inherent in such a project, which anthropologist Sherry Ortner describes well in her own anthology as "a sense of packaging the self," and I had worries she does not name, such as aging and identity.[15] Am I old enough or established enough

14. See *For Life Abundant: Practical Theology, Theological Education, and Christian Ministry,* ed. Dorothy C. Bass and Craig Dykstra (Grand Rapids: Wm. B. Eerdmans, 2008).

15. Sherry Ortner, *Making Gender: The Politics and Erotics of Culture* (Boston: Beacon Press, 1996), p. ix.

to have amassed enough critical essays to make a statement about Christian theology? I have cast rough lines across paper as if in a sketchbook, offering varied descriptions of what is happening in pastoral and practical theology in individual essays, each influenced by its particular time and setting. Do these add up to a full-blown oil-on-canvas book?

The most unanticipated hurdle, however, arose in writing this introduction. Every time I began, under the guise and inspiration of writing a paper for this or that academic conference, I found myself writing another book. I wanted to write a simple historical overview to situate my work, and I wanted to offer clear definitions of the distinct but related enterprises of pastoral and practical theology. In both cases, my efforts to keep my remarks succinct and related to this book ballooned beyond it. As I tried to articulate definitions, developments, and debates around terms used to study religion and theology as these have shaped and been shaped by scholarship in pastoral and practical theology, my research outgrew its original intention as material for this introductory chapter. How could I contain my ideas and stay on task? Did this fresh material belong here or in a new book?

The Resolution and the Audience

I emerged from this impasse when I overcame resistance, re-read my essays, and realized that fifty-five years is plenty old enough. I found the essays neither bad nor boring. They seemed *relevant*, despite occasional datedness, and *well-argued*. As I wrote introductions for each essay to help the reader understand its origin, argument, and oversights, the process had the same effect of enlightenment on me. By the time I got to Chapter 12, I was not only clearer about the overarching argument; I saw the audience more clearly.

In contrast to other books I have written, *Christian Theology in Practice* is not directed at the adult-at-large or the practicing Christian or minister. In the past I have argued that pastoral and practical theologians often write for all three audiences of church, society, and academy, perhaps more than scholars in other fields. In books such as *Also a Mother* (1994), *In the Midst of Chaos* (2006), and even my published dissertation, *Death, Sin, and the Moral Life* (1988), I have had a cross-section of publics in mind. I have not had much interest in spending energy on a book for the academy alone. My writing on the discipline has happened more serendipitously in article and chapter form, often in response to specific requests. But when I finished the introduction for Chapter 12, I saw my audience more plainly than when I first wrote the essay and when I proposed this book four years ago. Here I write for colleagues and students in seminaries and undergraduate departments of religious studies. I also want to speak to doctoral students and future teachers in religion and psychological studies and in pastoral theology. I want religion and psychology scholars, whether in undergraduate departments as college faculty or in theological schools as pastoral theologians, to stay in conversation with each other, and I want colleagues in other areas of study to understand the importance of this historical relationship and future scholarship in theology/religion and the social sciences more broadly. Even though the task of sustaining these connections is challenging, my aim here is actually more limited than that of other books I have written for wider audiences. I just want to make a difference in the admittedly limited and elite culture of academics *for the sake of our wider publics.* Though more restricted, this academic audience is sufficient to my immediate aim of moving the discussion of the nature of Christian theology just a little bit forward.

One could argue, however, that my questions about Christian theology's inclusivity and social-political location are not intellectually elite debates, relevant to scholars alone. A critique and expansion of Christian theology in relation to practice have consequences that outrun the academy. Such redefinition has direct impact on institutions of higher education, challenging how graduate education prepares faculty for seminary teaching, how ministers study theology in seminary, and how people of faith perceive theology. In other words, how theology has been constructed in these institutions, largely under only one model of theology as "sure knowledge," or *scientia,* restricts its study and practice to certain select groups and limits its place in congregations and public life.[16] An important parallel actually exists between my earlier work on spirituality and children and this work on practical theology and all Christians. Just as I sought to return spirituality to children, mothers, and people in the midst of complicated, mundane lives in *In the Midst of Chaos,* so also am I working for a theology for all Christians in this book.

---

16. See Robert J. Schreiter, *Constructing Local Theologies* (Maryknoll, N.Y.: Orbis Books, 2002), pp. 87-91.

Other Decisions

On the way to writing the introduction, I wrote two essays that outgrew it. Both made their way into a grant proposal for another book, "Lived Theology: Understanding Its Politics, Rehabilitating Its Place." Deciding to reserve these essays for other projects took pressure off *Christian Theology in Practice*, making it a way station rather than a destination, my first rather than last words arguing for a wider range of ways to understand Christian theology. But this decision also deprived this introduction of important content that merits at least brief mention.

Also a Pastoral Theologian

One of these essays, "Also a Pastoral Theologian: In Pursuit of Dynamic Theology," has been published in the journal of *Pastoral Psychology*.[17] Even though I have chosen not to include it in this book, it partly belongs here. It emerged, after all, out of an attempt to situate the essays in this book in the context of historical and current developments in definitions of pastoral and practical theology. However, the essays I selected have a coherence that I was hesitant to upset. The journal article offers definitions and so belongs at the beginning of this book. But at the same time, it raises questions about how I use the terms in the rest of the book, and so it belongs conceptually and chronologically at the end. So, instead of trying to arbitrate where to put it, I have left it out and summarize its argument instead. This book will benefit from its critical distinctions between pastoral and practical theology that I have learned since writing the other essays without being encumbered by the entire argument. I encourage those still curious about the details to read the article itself.

In the article I trace divergent uses of the terms *pastoral theology* and *practical theology* in figures such as Schleiermacher, Hiltner, and Don Browning. As it turns out, Hiltner did not like the term *practical theology*. He worried that it would lead back to academic marginalization, even though he identified with Schleiermacher in making experience a subject of theology. I also clarify how the terms have been used in different loca-

---

17. Bonnie J. Miller-McLemore, "Also a Pastoral Theologian: In Pursuit of Dynamic Theology (Or: Meditations from a Recalcitrant Heart)," *Pastoral Psychology* 59, no. 6 (2010): 813-28.

tions and traditions. Most British authors, for example, see *pastoral theology* and *practical theology* as fairly interchangeable, with increasing preference for *practical theology* as it has acquired wider recognition as a discipline that points beyond the Christian pastorate. The Roman Catholic tradition often uses both terms to refer to various aspects of pastoral ministry rather than academic disciplines. There are, of course, twentieth-century Catholic advocates for the creation of practical theology as a discipline, such as Karl Rahner and, more recently, Kathleen Cahalan.[18] But, as Cahalan points out, the Catholic Church and its educational institutions currently lack the infrastructure to support it.[19]

I conclude my review of terms and their use in the article by arguing that since the mid-1950s and more so today, people use *practical theology* and *pastoral theology* in confusing and conflated ways, thereby losing sight of the unique contributions of each discipline. Failure to use the terms with sufficient clarity risks missing one of practical theology's distinctive contributions as that discipline most concerned with mediating and integrating knowledge within theological education and between seminary and congregation. We also lose sight of the distinctive resources of twentieth-century pastoral theology as developed in the United States in rigorous conversation with modern psychoanalytic theory and psychology. So, even though pastoral theology and practical theology share common interest in lived experience, they are not as interchangeable now as in other periods, places, and traditions. In fact, I see value in accentuating rather than glossing over the distinctions. Whereas practical theology is integrative, concerned about broader issues of ministry, discipleship, and formation, pastoral theology is person- and pathos-centered. I situate my work in pastoral theology within practical theology because of the latter's commitment to wider curricular and ministerial concerns. But I remain a pastoral theologian at heart, appreciative of its appropriation of psychology as a key means to comprehending what matters most to persons and their suffering and care.

18. Karl Rahner, "Practical Theology within the Totality of Theological Disciplines," in *Theological Investigations*, vol. 9, trans. Graham Harrison (New York: Herder & Herder, 1972).

19. Kathleen A. Cahalan, "Beyond Pastoral Theology: Why Catholics Should Embrace Practical Theology," in *Keeping the Faith in Practice: Aspects of Catholic Pastoral Theology*, ed. James Sweeney, Gemma Simmonds, and David Lonsdale (London: SCM Press, 2010), pp. 99-116.

Book Title

Thanks to Don Ottenhoff, the Executive Director of the Collegeville Institute, I had a subtitle for the book. After listening to me describe my audience and aim, he suggested that the book was about the search for and discovery of a discipline. But I wasn't sure about the main title. My dual alliance with both pastoral and practical theology created a dilemma. I didn't want to use either term alone. Neither encompasses the subject matter of the book, since it talks about both disciplines. But lumping them together conveys an easy agreement and creates a confusion I specifically wanted to avoid. I circumvented the dilemma when I became clearer about their distinctions while also realizing that both disciplines share an investment in practice and experience, the primary reason why I have found them attractive. *Christian Theology in Practice* names both disciplines and links them to a more encompassing, sustaining aim.

Discipline or Field

Scholars and students generally use two words to describe areas of study or expertise — *discipline* and *field*. Like *pastoral* and *practical*, these terms also get conflated when clearer definition might be helpful. In her work on the discipline of practical theology in Roman Catholic institutions, Cahalan borrows distinctions between *discourse, field,* and *discipline* suggested by Sandra Schneiders in an article about disciplinary developments in spirituality. Schneiders defines *discourse* as an "ongoing conversation about a common interest" among an eclectic range of people without much sense of common cause. *Field* has greater specificity and limits. It pertains to an "open space in which activities which have something in common take place."[20] People participate in a field when they have related interests but different specialties and levels of involvement, such as doctors, hospital administrators, lab technicians, and nursing home staff in the medical field. The term itself implies physical space, like a playing field where one crosses a boundary to leave or enter. A *discipline* is more fo-

---

20. Sandra M. Schneiders, I.H.M., "The Study of Christian Spirituality: Contours and Dynamics of a Discipline," in *Minding the Spirit: The Study of Christian Spirituality,* ed. Elizabeth A. Dreyer and Mark S. Burrows (Baltimore and London: Johns Hopkins University Press, 2004), pp. 6-7.

cused yet. It refers to "teaching and learning, including research and writ-ing" on a defined subject matter with distinct methods.[21]

Using this framework, we might describe practical and pastoral the-ology as *fields,* with the former broader than the latter, including it as one of its subsets. But they are also *disciplines* that have emerged over the past two centuries with distinct renewal movements in the mid-twentieth cen-tury for pastoral theology and in the 1980s for practical theology. Usually I vary my own usage of *discipline* and *field* merely for variety's sake and without conceptual gain. But both Schneiders and Cahalan point to the advantage of recognizing an important area of research and teaching as its own discipline. Disciplines "are not defined by natural law or by some Pla-tonic ideal toward which we are evolving," as Schneiders observes (citing a biblical scholar).[22] Rather, they emerge pragmatically when enough schol-ars circle around an area with similar questions, producing knowledge, classes, texts, conferences, and so forth.

Schneiders's 2004 essay itself reflects an important turning point for Christian spirituality, which deserves disciplinary recognition as a "fully developed partner in the academy," she argues, to prevent it from "prema-ture burial as a spurious academic enterprise."[23] Likewise, Cahalan argues that the same development is needed in practical theology. There is a prob-lem in Catholicism when pastoral theology is "at the same time everywhere and nowhere," used widely to refer to the pastoral ministry of the church but without any institutional structures to sustain it, such as graduate pro-grams, journals, and professional organizations. Catholic institutions should "join efforts [in Protestantism] in a renewed practical theology" as an academic discipline. This is needed not just for academic legitimacy, she underscores. Rather, "practical theology is a creative theological enterprise that is ambitiously exploring issues related to the lived Christian faith and the practice of ministry" that Catholics can "ill afford" to ignore.[24]

Discipline, of course, has other meanings related to raising children and cultivating faith which neither Schneiders nor Cahalan mention but which have implications for the creation and practice of academic disci-plines. When laypeople hear the term, they often assume that it refers to spiritual practices like fasting, praying, and keeping the Sabbath. When a

---

21. Schneiders, "The Study of Christian Spirituality," p. 7.

22. A. K. M. Adam, *What Is Postmodern Biblical Criticism?* (Minneapolis: Fortress Press, 1995), p. 62, cited by Schneiders in "The Study of Christian Spirituality," p. 5.

23. Schneiders, "The Study of Christian Spirituality," p. 21.

24. Cahalan, "Beyond Pastoral Theology," pp. 99-100.

casual acquaintance heard my book's subtitle, she said, "That's what I need — more discipline in my faith life." In parenting, discipline is partly about setting limits in light of the complexities of living well together. Discipline is not without its own ambiguities. It has sometimes referred to harsh methods that disturb and regulate the spirit in religious and family life. But when entered into with a spirit of grace and gratitude, discipline can become a place of encounter and learning. In my research on children, I discovered an article by psychologist Bruno Bettelheim, who reminded me of the theological meaning of *discipline*. *Disciple* is the root term for *discipline,* and Jesus embodied a unique approach to *discipleship,* compelling others to follow through compassion and example rather than through coercion or punishment.

Discovering a discipline in the academic sense, then, has a faint resemblance to these other important uses. *Discipline* means finding oneself drawn into a way of seeing, participating, behaving, and following. I hope that even in the midst of the most mundane chores of teaching, researching, advising, and serving on committees, my search for an academic discipline has had, at its best, as much to do with a quest for tutoring by and connection to the divine as it has with establishing an academic specialization to call my home.

To Revise or Not to Revise

I looked to a few master scholars, such as Ortner and Clifford Geertz, for moral support as I made other decisions. They both published collections in which they decided against revising and overhauling earlier essays to forge a more coherent argument. Ortner remarks, "There is something science fiction-like in trying to unwrite and re-write." Geertz deemed such revision inappropriate, misleading, and "not wholly cricket." (If the piece was that bad, it "ought not be printed at all.")[25] After all, the point of a collection is to show the development of ideas. Their only concession was correction of inaccuracies in factual details, typographical and grammatical errors, and inconsistent referencing style. I follow their example. I have also shortened the original title of each chapter to capture better its primary subject.

I found these anthropologists helpful in another way. Occasional the-

25. Ortner, *Making Gender,* p. ix; Clifford Geertz, *The Interpretation of Cultures: Selected Essays* (New York: Basic Books, 1973), p. viii.

ology is less ordered than systematic theology and much more like the "standard practice in cultural anthropology" described by Geertz in the introductory chapter of *The Interpretation of Cultures*. "We do not start out with well-formed ideas," he says, and then head off into the field. Rather, "we go off . . . with some general notions of what we would like to look into and how we might go about looking into them." The conclusions are "trailing constructions" rather than preconceived ideas "happily confirmed." So there is something of a magician's "sleight-of-hand" in books like *The Interpretation of Cultures,* where the author reconstructs the argument by looking back as if it were there all along.[26] Just as "one cannot write a 'general theory of cultural interpretation,'" as Geertz said, one cannot really write a general theory of faith practice and the discipline of studying it.[27]

Book Outline and Organization

I have read collections of previously published essays where authors hide the book's origins and readers only gradually realize that the chapters were not original to the book. I find this disconcerting and even a bit disingenuous. Moreover, since pastoral and practical theologians as well as many feminist and other liberation theologians see context as critical to insight, I include introductions that situate each chapter, provide connective tissue, and allow for reassessment and rebuttal. I also include the original source of each chapter on its first page. I do not want readers to have to search to find the publication information. I want readers to see the book as more than a random collection. But I also want them to know the particularities that gave rise to each piece. I think there is merit in a book that marks turning points in the evolution of a discipline as reflected through the lens of one particular scholarly trajectory. Identifying the context and oversights is essential to the argument itself. On its own, each chapter is a period piece that clarifies this or that confusion in the study of theology. Together, the chapters show the search for a discipline that fosters theology in a practical sense.

I arranged the chapters by theme into three sections and then chronologically within each section, except in Part I, where the two "living web" chapters belong side-by-side even though they are separated by over

---

26. Geertz, *The Interpretation of Cultures*, p. vi.
27. Geertz, *The Interpretation of Cultures*, p. 26.

ten years. A slow shift in interest is evident in my work from feminist psychology and pastoral theology in the 1990s (Part III) to practical theology and practice theory in the last ten years (Parts I and II). Accordingly, the earliest chapter in the book is on feminist maternal epistemology in 1992, and the most recent chapter is a definitional essay on practical theology in 2010. Chapter 1 begins with two challenges that awaited me when I crossed the street from University of Chicago's graduate program to teach at Chicago Theological Seminary: the diversity of gender, race, and religion, *and* the gap between theory and practice. Chapter 1 attends mostly to the former and its implications for pastoral care. But the book as a whole and my own research trajectory turn toward the latter.

What Is Not Here

Even though Geertz says that theory detached from "particular inquiries" is like "mere promissory notes,"[28] I chose not to include topical essays on concrete issues that have been an important subject for my research and teaching, such as mothering, parenting, children, spirituality, healing, illness, dying, and so forth.[29] My reflection on these topics demonstrates the kind of theological knowledge and method that this book attempts to validate. I recommend them to those who want living detail and illustration.

I also did not include two shorter essays — one on aesthetics in practical theology and another on wisdom in pastoral care and counseling — that would have made nice additions to Part II because they consider alternative ways of knowing. But they were written in response to other scholars' work, and understanding them in full requires knowing that work. A few insights from them are worth brief mention. I wrote the first essay in response to a paper delivered at an International Academy of Practical Theology session by German colleague Friedrich Schweitzer, and the second in response to a panel on *Shared Wisdom* by Pamela Cooper-White at the American Academy of Religion. In the former, I argue that the transformation sought in

28. Geertz, *The Interpretation of Cultures*, p. vi.

29. As a random selection, see, for example, "Doing Wrong, Getting Sick, and Dying," *Christian Century*, 24 February 1988, pp. 186-90; "Contemplation in the Midst of Chaos: Contesting the Maceration of the Theological Teacher," in *The Scope of Our Art: The Vocation of Theological Teachers*, ed. L. Gregory Jones and Stephanie Paulsell (Grand Rapids: Wm. B. Eerdmans, 2001), pp. 48-74; and "Children — Where Religion Hits the Road: Why Society Needs Religious Views of Children," *Conscience: Catholics for a Free Choice*, Autumn 2006, pp. 18-21.

practical theology through hermeneutics is ultimately insufficient without attention to "ritual, communal engagement, or . . . a social context for practicing skills, concrete models, and a living community." If practical theology's goals include transformation, then its home "lies as much with imagination as with interpretation, even though we have largely failed to articulate the relationship between practical theology as a hermeneutical discipline and practical theology as art."[30] I describe Cooper-White's *Shared Wisdom* as a book "filled with rich nuggets of proverbial religious 'truth,'" not unlike the book of Proverbs, but argue that she herself is largely unaware of this deeper theological knowing (*wisdom* in the book title came from the publisher). Her distillations of pithy truths scattered throughout the book function as a kind of theological wisdom or "pragmatic guidance to Christian compassion for the other." Her pastoral, therapeutic advice is actually an instance of "theological know-how of the best kind embedded in the practices, rituals, and routines of the deeply knowledgeable helper [minister and counselor]."[31]

I also came across a 1996 essay as I prepared this book that explains my "practical, feminist, Disciple view" and shows how the arguments I have pursued reflect an effort to integrate disparate elements of my own history.[32] Growing up in the Christian Church (Disciples of Christ) has had an influence, even if I have never particularly liked the traits that one prominent mid-twentieth-century Disciple named as most characteristic — "reasonable, empirical, pragmatic."[33] I identify nonetheless with a Dis-

30. Bonnie J. Miller-McLemore, "Aesthetics, Hermeneutics, and Practical Theology," in *Creativity, Imagination, and Criticism: The Expressive Dimension in Practical Theology*, ed. Paul Ballard and Pamela Couture (London: Cardiff Academic Press, 2001), p. 19.

31. Bonnie J. Miller-McLemore, "Wisdom in Pastoral Care and Counseling: What Does It Entail?" *Pastoral Psychology* 55 (2006): 219-20.

32. Bonnie J. Miller-McLemore, "Many Gifts, One Body: Towards a Practical, Feminist, Disciple View of Pastoral Care," in *Healing and the Healer*, ed. George F. Cairns, Lawrence A. Pottener, and Nancy U. Cairns (Chicago: Exploration Press, 1996), pp. 15-21. I also thank Jim Nieman for pointing out the value of a personal sociology of one's intellectual formation based on his reading of Neil Gross's *Richard Rorty: The Making of an American Intellectual* (Chicago: University of Chicago Press, 2008). Nieman sums up the thesis in a quote from p. 272: "Thinkers tell stories to themselves and others about who they are as intellectuals. They are then strongly motivated to do intellectual work that will, inter alia, help to express and bring together the disparate elements of these stories. Everything else being equal, they will gravitate toward ideas that make this kind of synthesis possible."

33. William B. Blakemore, "Reasonable, Empirical, Pragmatic: The Mind of Disciples of Christ," in *The Renewal of the Church*, vol. 1: *The Reformation of Tradition* (St. Louis: Bethany Press), pp. 161-83.

ciple history largely suspicious of theological speculation and creedal formulation. I have gone back time and again to Clark Williamson's more appealing portrait of Disciples as professing a belief in behavior and enactment rather than creeds, clergy, ritual, and theological doctrine. "In a behavioral practical system," I write, "how things are done, what one does, is a primary form of confession and a witness of faith. More oriented to the world than to the church, to ethics than to piety, Disciples seek to verify faith propositions by literally seeking to make them true."[34] Granted, there are problems with this outlook, including an overachieving Protestant work ethic and a righteousness about earning our salvation through works. But there is also positive affinity with the long-standing Jewish orientation of *tikkun olam* — repairing the world — where, as Judith Plaskow says, "no detail of life is too small to escape the possibility of consecration."[35]

Further Work

At least two decades before it became trendy in religious and theological studies, scholars in pastoral and practical theology were *engaging practice* in the dual sense of *engaging* as adjective and verb (practice is appealing, interesting, or engaging, and the act of studying or engaging practice is the work of Christian theology). Consequently, a broad and timely question stands behind the book and outruns it: As interest in religious practice has grown among scholars in all areas of religious and theological studies at large, what do pastoral and practical theologies have to contribute? The "lure of the practical," as one systematic theologian dubs it, has drawn a divergent array of scholars into its orbit.[36] Practice language is everywhere. The use of ethnography has become the rage. New research and doctoral programs have emerged in practical theology, theology and practice, religious practices, and lived religion with diverse aims, from educating people in the study of religious practices (e.g., Emory University), to prepar-

---

34. Miller-McLemore, "Many Gifts, One Body," p. 16, drawing on Clark Williamson, "Theology and Forms of Confession in the Disciples of Christ," *Encounter* 41, no. 1 (Winter 1980): 16.

35. Judith Plaskow, *Standing Again at Sinai: Judaism from a Feminist Perspective* (San Francisco: Harper & Row, 1990), p. 218.

36. Mary McClintock Fulkerson, "Theology and the Lure of the Practical: An Overview," *Religion Compass* 1, no. 2 (2007): 294-304.

ing people to educate future ministers (e.g., Vanderbilt University), to equipping people for work in the public sector (e.g., Chester University), to investigating lived or material religion (e.g., The Project on Lived Religion at the University of Virginia).

Many factors lie behind these developments, but scholarship in practical theology since the 1980s is surely among them. Practical theology should remain a primary intellectual resource. But to ensure this, continued reflection is needed on the nature of faith and ministry, the integration of scholarship and practice, the practice of teaching ministry, and the role of religion and theology in the public arena.

As these topics suggest, practical theology is about so much more than the bland shorthand descriptions or mantras often used to define it lately, such as the "correlation between the Christian tradition and contemporary experience" or the "study of the relationship between beliefs and practices." Practical theology redefines what constitutes theological knowledge and seeks a theology for the masses. It explores the dissonance between professed beliefs and lived realities through the study of practice and serves a "critical function" or testing of the practical veracity, as Karl Rahner says, of the claims of other theological disciplines as embodied in the life of faith.[37] It has a steadfast interest in matters that overstep any one discipline, such as integration in theological education and formation in Christian discipleship. And it has long sustained a desire and an intention to weave webs of connection between theological disciplines and institutions.[38]

This list of attributes is considerable. Each item represents a serious endeavor deserving the attention of a finely tuned academic discipline. And within practical theology as a field, various subdisciplines also have their own distinctive contributions. Pastoral theology, for instance, has a strong legacy of investigating human suffering and spiritual recovery, creating fresh theological loci such as pain, lament, and joy that are distinct from the conventional loci of Christology, ecclesiology, eschatology, and so forth. This suggests one of the better definitions that I offer elsewhere for both pastoral and practical theologians: "those preoccupied with everyday concerns that evade and disrupt traditional categories, doctrines, and loci in theological and religious study."[39]

---

37. Rahner, "Practical Theology within the Totality of Theological Disciplines," p. 104.

38. A recent example of this practical theological impulse is Richard Osmer's book titled *Practical Theology: An Introduction* (Grand Rapids: Wm. B. Eerdmans, 2008).

39. Miller-McLemore, "Also a Pastoral Theologian," p. 824.

The Tree, Theology, and God

If the tree was a common trope in Schleiermacher's time depicting educational structures as a science, why did he discard it? Was it in response to concern about which area has the most power? Was it worry over practical theology as the crown, the ruler of the whole? Or the reverse?

The tree is actually an ancient image of alternative modes of knowing. According to religion scholar Kelton Cobb, "Cosmic trees that allow traffic between the heavens and the earth are found in religious symbolism with some frequency — think of the Yggdrasil in Norse mythology, or the cross of Christ."[40] The tree appears across myth and religion as a symbol of life, wholeness, integrity, and wisdom that surpasses human understanding. Like all symbols, the tree also has its underside, its horrendous meaning. This is brought home powerfully in portraits of trees as places for crucifixion and lynching, such as "Strange Fruit," a song performed most famously by American jazz singer Billie Holiday. Over history, trees point to both moral degradation and triumph, eternal return, and resurrection. They produce fruit that poisons and rejuvenates. In other words, the image has greater reach than Schleiermacher imagined. In contrast to those who see rhizomes as a better model for theological knowledge, I think they offer a *different* rather than a *better* image. And they have their own downsides. Bermuda grass, for example, can self-repair a lawn, spreading to cover bare spots. But it is also extremely invasive and disruptive to other plants and habitats.

Trees have a grounding effect. Life among trees at church camps — backpacking, canoeing, and wilderness — has powerfully convicted me. I have been reconvicted at places like Holden Village at least partly because this Lutheran ecumenical retreat is nestled in the Cascade Mountains, where towering evergreen trees run from toe to tree line on each peak, disappearing into the horizon, dwarfing the village by their majesty and displaying a life span that far outreaches our own. More than official sacred sites, I aspire to go on a pilgrimage to the big trees, like the redwoods, only one forest among the world's largest trees (according to a son who has traveled to northern California to walk among them). Do not misread me here. I am not a druid or tree worshiper. Although no doubt there are some who would see my low sacrificial Christology, high incarnation, non-creedal, non-patriarchal view of God as unorthodox, I remain a Christian

---

40. Kelton Cobb, *The Blackwell Guide to Theology and Popular Culture* (Oxford: Blackwell, 2005), p. 114.

who believes God can be found anywhere God chooses. And I think God sometimes favors trees and children.

Years ago, while attending a Disciples General Assembly in Des Moines, Iowa, I realized the full place of the tree in my faith life when I worshiped in a sanctuary that was nearly identical to my home church. Almost everything was the same — the stone walls, the wood pews, the window at the back — *except* the stained glass at the front. The sanctuary had a cross where I was used to looking at a tree of life. As I sat in that strangely familiar yet unfamiliar space, I saw powerfully that my faith had been deeply shaped by a slightly different image. Sitting regularly in our sanctuary, I as an early believer gazed on God embodied in a fruitful tree of life, a tree that grows right out of the baptistery where Christians begin their life in Christ, sinks its roots deeply into the biblical traditions of the Hebrew people and early church, and sprouts an abundance of symbols of worship, nature, Jesus' ministry, and the church — bread, stalks of wheat, grapes, a chalice, lightning, rain, birds, towel and basin, nails and pincer, Epiphany star, three fish for the Trinity, and so on. Until that moment in the Iowa church, I did not realize the full impact of symbols and acts of regular worship on our religious thoughts and feelings.

I imagine that when people discussed the sanctuary's design, there was a debate. Some people argued for a cross, others for a tree. There is much to be said in the tree's favor even if something of the Christian gospel is lost. In Scripture, the tree of life is associated with creation (Gen. 2:9), wisdom (Prov. 3:13-18), calmness (Prov. 15:4), and healing (Rev. 22:2). Amid the ever more rapid destruction of the earth's inventory, the tree of life embodies a valuable idea voiced by the ecologically and theologically concerned: the world is God's body. It demands our deepest care for this generation and those to come. As Western and Northern Christians in Europe and the United States become a minority in the Christian world and in a world of diverse religions, the tree of life also suggests openness to the many ways in which the divine enters human life. It features prominently in Jewish traditions as well as in Christianity and other religions. The stained-glass tree in my home church includes Christ without excluding other ways to God.

The Trees and the Fall

For many Christians, *the Fall* refers to human bondage to sin and the anxiety, wounds, and pain that lead to harm, damage, wrongdoing, and failure.

That meaning has implications here. The following chapters have mistakes, misrepresentations, and oversights. Authors always stand to be corrected. Time will likely prove us at least partly wrong. And putting one's views into print makes them public, permanent, and vulnerable. A collection of previously published essays just makes the same mistakes over again.

Fortunately, writing is also full of promise, creating conversation with people you do not anticipate who pick up the book and find themselves in its world with new thoughts, possibly even provoked by the mistakes themselves. Authors use writing to solve our own problems. But it is about more than that. No matter how brief the reverberations of our words, writing has little value without readers, critics, and those who might live a little differently after having heard our words.

At the Collegeville Institute, another meaning of "the fall" arose in a powerful way. In my final effort to pull together this collection, I ended up at the Institute as a short-term scholar at the end of September and the beginning of October more by serendipity than planning. I had not chosen the height of the fall with any intent or purpose. It just fit well with my schedule. But the timing mattered. I had not anticipated seasonal support in writing. But I gratefully received it.

My desk faced a big window looking out on a lake ringed by trees, with St. John's University campus in the distance. Each day the sun moved from left to right, leaving sparkling patterns across the water and creating a mirage of double tree color, with the shore as a wavering dividing line. My surroundings pressed upon me my own aging and life's changes around me. I am moving into the fall of life. *Christian Theology in Practice* attests to that. I also went to morning and evening prayer with the Benedictine monks at St. John's Abby Church, further marking my day with reminders from the Psalms of the fleeting nature of life and the smallness of our being in God's world. When I arrived, the sugar maples were turning a brilliant red, and the northern birch outside my window was a golden yellow. Toward the end of my few weeks rereading essays and writing introductions, leaves rained down.

My words follow the same trajectory. Valuable but fleeting, they have done their work green on the tree; now they fall where they may, die, decay, and offer their life to the growth of other life. It is an odd project to republish previously published work. I was glad for theological reminders that calmed any pretensions I might have had about its place in the broader scheme of life.

PART I

LIVING WEB:
A SUBJECT MATTER

The Living Web and the State of Pastoral Theology

BACKGROUND AND INTRODUCTION

Small events can launch a career. I had taught no more than six or seven years and was recently tenured when *The Christian Century* invited me to contribute to a series of essays on various academic disciplines in 1993. Would I write on the state of pastoral care and counseling?

I had two immediate thoughts. Still wet behind the ears, I wondered if I really had the wherewithal for such a (grandiose) task. At the same time, a mentor (Martin Marty, I think) once told me to write down all my fresh impressions during the first few weeks in a new job or situation. You notice important aspects that soon disappear from sight. So, I reasoned, new scholars have one advantage. They see the whole in a fresh way.

I had a second problem, however. Would I identify the "field" in question as *pastoral care and counseling* or *pastoral theology?* The *Century* editors left that to my own discretion. So I focused on pastoral theology as the broader disciplinary category under which teaching and study of care and counseling are lodged (at least in most U.S. Protestant seminaries). Pastoral counseling no more defines the whole of the field than other aspects of pastoral theology, such as the dialogue between theology and psy-

---

This essay was originally published as "The Human Web and the State of Pastoral Theology" in *The Christian Century,* 7 April 1993, pp. 366-69. It was revised and reprinted by permission as "The Living Human Web: Pastoral Theology at the Turn of the Century," pp. 9-26 in *Through the Eyes of Women: Insights for Pastoral Care,* ed. Jeanne Stevenson-Moessner (Minneapolis: Fortress Press, 1996). Used by permission.

chology or the analysis of theology as embodied in practice (a task pastoral theology shares with practical theology). More important, the field was shifting from a rather singular fascination with individual counseling to a focus on aspects of care in broader communal and political contexts. Although pastoral counseling itself was shifting in the same direction, the state of the field encompassed more than expertise in care and counseling alone.

I now have the good fortune of receiving recognition for coining the "living human web" as the updated primary subject matter of the discipline, defined a half-century earlier by Congregational Church minister Anton Boisen as the "living human document." In reality, my essay describes more than prescribes, and my terminology simply captures what was in the air — a general argument for the critical role of the wider political context and the relocation of pastoral care within communities where the minister is not its only agent. Several colleagues used the metaphor of "web" almost simultaneously to describe this new focus.

The chapter below is a revised version of the original *Century* article, published three years later in *Through the Eyes of Women*, a second book in what became a four-book series on pastoral care with women edited by Jeanne Stevenson-Moessner. I used the occasion to develop the original essay in relationship to gender and sexism. One of the thornier questions I raise in this revision is whether pastoral theology's mid-twentieth-century academic marginalization is partly related to the field's long-standing interest in affectivity, emotion, relationships, and other matters equated with "women's work" and derided as not "valid" academic knowledge.

However, I would now qualify my characterization of the field's marginalization or instability. In this chapter as well as in Chapters 3, 6, and 9, I bemoan our identity crisis in ways I would avoid today. The discipline's long-term practical theological expertise in studying live subjects and religious practice, interests now shared with scholars across religious and theological studies, strengthens its importance and position in the academy. Neither the study of religion in universities nor faculty positions in pastoral theology have disappeared. Pastoral care and theology have had more job openings this year than ever. The closing of religion departments is less an issue now than it was then. If anything, religion is a hot topic, needing solid scholarship in a controversial historical time.

So, as I argue in the final chapter, scholars in pastoral and practical theology should refrain from proclaiming our confusion. Crisis and reconstruction characterize the work of all disciplines right now. Instead of meeting its demise, work in pastoral theology has morphed and reconstituted itself. Trends noted in this chapter have had institutional consequence. Recently, when several schools advertised openings in pastoral theology, they described positions in "congregational and communal care leadership" and "pastoral theology and congregational care." Practical theology is also in a period of revival and renewal. Interest in religious practice is now common across disciplinary areas. New doctoral programs and research projects in practical theology and religious practices have sprung up in major universities. The discipline of practical theology has supported curriculum revision and the creation of new integrative endeavors for contextual education and ministry programs. In a word, practical theology has thrived in this new context.

There is one meaning for *web* that goes completely unnoticed in my reflections: the World Wide Web (WWW). This omission reveals just how much has changed in the last fifteen years. In 1993 and 1996, faculty members who got on the Internet at all did so to retrieve e-mail; few surfed the Web because search engines for popular use were under construction almost simultaneously with the evolution of the human web as pastoral theology's subject matter. In fact, in 1993 the WWW became the preferred interface for interacting with the Internet. Shortly thereafter, Netscape Navigator appeared, then Internet Explorer, and the rest is history. If one believes in the interconnection and interdependence of all life, a premise behind the general idea of the web itself, then one knows that it is highly likely that our use of the term was shaped, at least indirectly, by the incredible technological developments hovering in the background, soon to become a dominant foreground.

After completing academic work in religion and psychology, I found myself teaching pastoral care at a seminary. In making that transition, I experienced two surprises. The first was the jolt of moving from the academic study of religion and social science to the peculiar discipline of pastoral theology. Although I had had clinical training and professional experience in chaplaincy, pastoral psychotherapy, and the church, I had never had an actual course in pastoral care or pastoral theology, nor had many of my courses emphasized pastoral or congregational practices. This gap between the study of religion and its practice was not just a personal quirk. Anyone who leaves the university religion department, degree in hand, and crosses the threshold of the seminary to teach will inevitably face professional dissonance. More specifically, pastoral theology is expected to be more oriented to ministerial practice than other theological disciplines; at the same time, it has struggled with the ambiguities of its identity midway between academy and the church. The routine use of the psychological sciences in the last few decades, while helpful, has also complicated the struggle.

The second jolt was encountering a student body that was approximately 50 percent women and 50 percent non-Caucasian. Despite my personal interest in listening to other voices, none of my graduate school courses in the early 1980s had required a text by a woman or by a person of color. In a society increasingly aware of the ways in which gender, race, class, and worldview shape our ways of knowing, my good intentions quickly proved to be insufficient in working with such diversity.

Both shocks represent significant issues in pastoral theology. It is a field that is still trying to clarify its identity in relation to the academy and the church and its methods in relation to the social sciences. And now it must do so while taking heed of many new voices that are contributing new perceptions of pastoral care. Both issues deserve further attention. In this chapter, I will look at each in turn. For those invested in pastoral care, counseling, and theology, this discussion is essential, I believe, to securing the place and the future of the field.

With both issues, this chapter is more an invitation to dialogue than an exhaustive attempt to define the field and to delineate solutions to current methodological, theoretical, and practical problems. Here I simply initiate a conversation that, fortunately, successive chapters in *Through the Eyes of Women: Insights for Pastoral Care* confirm, illustrate, expand, and qualify. While the first issue — the relationship between ministry, pastoral theology, and the academy — is not directly related to the book's focus on women and pastoral care, this issue is still important as it influences the future of the field and women as part of that. Furthermore, the devaluation of religion and religious institutions in the twentieth century is related to the devaluation of the feminine and the identification of the church with the feminine in its attention to emotion, care, nurture, and religious piety. The marginalization of the field of pastoral theology and theology more generally is intertwined with this characterization — certainly a problem about which women in pastoral care and theology ought to have concern.

Bridging the Gap between Academy and Church
or Falling into It? A Crisis of Identity

Whereas biblical studies experienced the impact of modernity in terms of historical-critical approaches to Scripture, the field of pastoral theology experienced it in terms of the emergence of psychology and sociology as disciplines. For the past four decades, pastoral theology's toehold in seminaries has depended to a considerable degree on its use of clinical psychology. Pastoral theologians may have felt uneasy about the ethos of pop psychology and self-analysis, but they flourished within it. Whereas in 1939 few theological schools offered counseling courses, by the 1950s almost all of them did. And 80 percent listed additional courses in psychology and had at least one psychologist on the staff. Similarly, in the clinical world in the 1940s, only a few Protestant hospitals employed full-time chaplains; by the 1950s almost 500 full-time chaplains were serving general hospitals, and 200 served in mental hospitals. As historian E. Brooks Holifield observes, "In a relatively brief period, . . . pastoral theologians had secured their place in academia."[1] Ministers interested in counseling had an expanding range of institutions in which to serve.

During this time, those in pastoral theology learned a great deal from psychology about understanding and respecting the inner experience of others. In the 1960s and 1970s, Carl Rogers's *Counseling and Psychotherapy* was a standard text in theological seminaries, and the fundamentals of empathic, reflective listening were a staple of introductory pastoral care courses.[2] In the 1970s and 1980s, Howard Clinebell's variation on this theme, *Basic Types of Pastoral Care and Counseling*, replaced Rogers's as the conventional textbook for introductory courses.[3] Although the first edition situates modern pastoral care within the longer history of pastoral ministry, the majority of the text devotes itself to individual counseling techniques for an array of problems. Students learn to understand, interpret, support, evaluate, probe, and advise — six "appropriate responses" in situations of crisis intervention, supportive counseling, marriage enrich-

1. E. Brooks Holifield, *A History of Pastoral Care in America: From Salvation to Self-Realization* (Nashville: Abingdon Press, 1983), pp. 270-71, 273.

2. Carl R. Rogers, *Counseling and Psychotherapy* (Boston: Houghton Mifflin Co., 1942).

3. Howard Clinebell, *Basic Types of Pastoral Care and Counseling: Resources for the Ministry of Healing and Growth* (Nashville: Abingdon Press, 1966). This text was revised and enlarged in 1984.

ment, grief care, and so on.[4] If there was any challenge to this approach, it was over the question of how directive to make the nondirective style, particularly when moral and religious judgments might qualify the psychological assessment.

At the same time, the widespread use of psychology fostered nagging questions about how pastoral theology could be both a genuinely theological and a scientifically psychological discipline. In 1973, in *The Living Human Document*, Charles Gerkin named this dilemma the "root question facing the pastoral care and counseling movement."[5] His answer, which proposes a dialogical, hermeneutical method of psychological and theological investigation of human experience as the primary text of pastoral theology, became one of the most well-liked and commonly endorsed characterizations of the field.

Gerkin and the distinguished pastoral theologian Seward Hiltner and others have found the "correlational" approach of Paul Tillich and "revised critical correlational" method of David Tracy helpful models for understanding the task of pastoral theology as an interdisciplinary endeavor. For Tillich, the questions raised by human existence, often helpfully named and analyzed by the human sciences, must be correlated with the answers of the Christian tradition. Tracy revises Tillich's one-directional juxtapositioning of "situation" and "message" by asserting that both the human sciences and theology suggest questions and answers; hence the dialogue is multidirectional. The human sciences not only provide answers; they may qualify those of religion. Persons who adopted this solution to Gerkin's "root question" have explored a variety of topics and clinical cases by matching texts in the sciences with Scripture and theological doctrine.

Nonetheless, neither Gerkin's text nor correlational methodology alone could dispel the persistent identity crisis. This confusion was readily apparent in the assorted job titles. Those in the field may teach pastoral care, pastoral counseling, pastoral psychology, pastoral theology, practical theology, religion and psychology, psychology of religion, religion and personality, religion and culture, and, most recently, ethics. As these titles reflect, the discipline has been roughly divided between those who emphasize practical care and counseling approaches, those engaged in the critical

---

4. Clinebell, *Basic Types of Pastoral Care and Counseling*, pp. 94-96.

5. Charles V. Gerkin, *The Living Human Document: Revisioning Pastoral Counseling in a Hermeneutical Mode* (Nashville: Abingdon Press, 1973; 1984), p. 11.

correlation of theology, religion, and the social sciences, and those involved in the empirical social-scientific study of religious experience. Meanwhile, the use of psychology has generated stereotypes of the field as oriented to skills and feelings and as therapeutically shrewd. Among clergy, this approach has generated an almost unhealthy reliance on psychological jargon and counseling techniques rather than on theological language, pastoral mediation, and congregational care. For this overemphasis, there is some reason for critique.

To look to the future, it is crucial not to forget the past. Early participants in the pastoral theological movement, finding propositional theology remote and barren, turned toward the vivid color and textures of clinical cases. In place of a transcendent doctrinal theology, traditionally imposed on believers in their religious crises with little or no sensitivity to their own experience or religious understandings, pastoral theologians found theological meaning in the lived moments of human suffering and joy. In contrast to religious generalities deduced from Scripture and church doctrine, religious truth was deeply inductive. It emerged out of reflection on personal struggles, with clergy working as mentors rather than as judges.

Part of the appeal of psychology has been its ability to bridge the distance between human suffering on the one hand and theology, philosophy, and ethics on the other. During my own graduate years, clinical training in both chaplaincy and pastoral psychotherapy was one way to link academy and church, although it received no official academic credit. When I began teaching, I tried — against the pressures of institutional structures — to maintain positions both in the seminary and in a pastoral counseling center. Without some kind of pastoral practice, I realized, my efforts in theological education were going to become a noisy gong, attempting to achieve a worthy goal but always lacking the one essential element of religious experience. I have also gradually recognized that my insistence on multiple roles had something to do with an approach to work typical of many women who resist the rigid, classificatory boundaries of most professions. It is not unusual for women to enter interdisciplinary fields, to attempt to integrate divergent foci such as psychology and spirituality, and to hold down more than one job at once.

I was intrigued, however, that few of my colleagues, mostly men, in other fields felt this same tug. Why shouldn't those being interviewed for seminary positions in biblical studies, ethics, or theology be asked about their pastoral practice? How did other seminary faculty resolve the question of the gap between academic theory and ministerial practice?

Pastoral theology discovered in the social sciences fresh models of how to relate theory and practice. In many respects, figures such as Freud, Heinz Kohut, Elisabeth Kübler-Ross, and M. Scott Peck write like sophisticated practical theologians. It is no small coincidence that when a friend in the midst of a marital crisis reached for a book, he bought one of Anne Wilson Schaef's popular titles. Kübler-Ross's *On Death and Dying* has been recommended more frequently by pastors and chaplains than any one religious or theological text. While these books may have what some might call "a religious flavor," they are written by psychologists from a distinctly psychological point of view, sometimes with rather unprofessional excursions into religious speculation. But therapeutically oriented books have reigned in part because they offer clarification: they translate theories of human nature, fulfillment, and anguish into understandable terms. Pastoral theology took up this helpmate both to its benefit and to its detriment. In a word, although it avoided theological abstraction and academic trivialization, it was lured toward technique, theological vacuousness, and an individualistic, subjectivist orientation.

In addressing the Society for Pastoral Theology in 1994, Liston Mills claimed that at last the pastoral theology that arose on the crest of modern psychology was no longer an up-and-coming movement. It was no longer caught in the exciting yet precarious moment of creating a new field. Pastoral theology was, he said, an established and respected discipline with both the stability and the increased responsibility that comes with this. Those in the field have to live with the ambiguities of its heritage.

A Shift toward Context, Collaboration, and Diversity

Most pastoral theologians and educators would still assert that empathic listening skills and sensitive individual counsel are prerequisites for ministry. But significant changes are afoot, symbolized both by the apparent decline in the popularity of Clinebell's text and the publication of a revised edition in 1984. Most pastoral educators and practitioners have added to their repertoire the theories of more recent schools of psychology such as family systems and object relations theories. More critical, however, are a number of other changes: the focus on individual counseling and educative listening has come under increasing criticism from a variety of angles; the prevalence of counseling courses has waned; "pastoral theology" has replaced "pastoral psychology" as the overarching theme; and the notion of care has returned to center stage, with counseling regarded as an important but not comprehensive specialty. Ultimately, almost everyone acknowledges the limits of the therapeutic paradigm and talks about sharpening our understanding not just of theological paradigms but of the social context as well, through the study of sociology, ethics, culture, and public policy. Specialized professions that rely on therapeutic paradigms, such as chaplaincy and pastoral psychotherapy, will be understood increasingly as only two of the manifestations of pastoral theology.

The focus on care narrowly defined as counseling has shifted to a focus on care understood as part of a wide cultural, social, and religious context. Initial examples of this change can be found in the new interest in congregational studies and in the ambiguous developments in pastoral psychotherapy. The world of parish ministry has offered an ill-sanctioned, little-recognized wealth of insight for learning. Recent congregational studies have also begun to confirm the congregational nature of pastoral care. Aware of the limits of relying primarily on one-to-one counseling and the expertise of the pastor, pastoral care curriculum has focused increasingly on how congregations provide care and on clergy as facilitators of networks of care rather than as the chief sources of care. For instance, Roy Steinhoff Smith, professor of pastoral care at Phillips Theological Seminary, requires students to work together in small groups in his introductory courses to evaluate their different congregations as "caring communities." Not only do students need the role play of individual counseling sessions; they need to study the ways in which clergy and members of religious institutions create and sustain networks of care. In a study of congregations and pastoral care, Don Browning concludes that while parishioners want and expect a minister to arrive when they face life-shaking crises and transitions, such as illness and death, this represents only a part of the broader care of the congregation. More often, a great deal of informal care takes place through diverse intercongregational activities, such as choir practice, women's circles, coffee hour, and Bible study. Although the minister must learn how to listen in individual counseling, equally essential to providing adequate pastoral care is the task of "facilitating the natural patterns of care that emerge in healthy congregations" and creating new avenues of care that build upon the special gifts and needs of individual members and the "psychosocial kinship groups" of the congregation as a whole.[6]

---

6. Don S. Browning, "Pastoral Care and the Study of the Congregation," in *Beyond Clericalism: The Congregation as a Focus for Theological Education,* ed. Joseph C. Hough Jr. and Barbara G. Wheeler (Atlanta: Scholars Press, 1988), pp. 107-8.

Similarly, illustrative shifts are occurring in pastoral counseling. On the one hand, pastoral psychotherapy has also ceased to be a movement. It has acquired the status of a recognized clinical profession. On the other hand, in part because of its relationship to religion and the congregation, it does not have the kind of recognition accorded secular therapeutic professions. From the perspective of those in secular circles, pastoral counseling lacks a clearly distinct identity in its affiliation with religion and the "pastoral." Yet, at the same time, confirming the place and importance of religion and theology in therapy continues to present challenges. Many chaplains and pastoral therapists have tenuous relationships with seminaries and congregations despite the notable contributions of clinical pastoral education and pastoral psychotherapy. As one avenue around this impasse, some pastoral counselors in the past two decades have turned, or returned perhaps, to age-old traditions of spiritual direction better understood within Catholic circles, now partially reconceived through the knowledge and practice of therapeutic modalities. On this score, recent books such as Elizabeth Liebert's *Changing Life Patterns: Adult Development in Spiritual Direction*[7] and the work of Henri Nouwen, Eugene Peterson, and others are important contributions.

Nonetheless, as pastoral theology curriculum in seminaries broadens, as the clinical identity of pastoral counseling solidifies, and as American health care reforms evolve, those in pastoral counseling training centers will have to address multiple questions about their appropriate ministerial, educational, and institutional place in relation to the congregation, the academy, and society. To be taken seriously by other mental health disciplines as well as by insurance companies and governmental structures, pastoral psychotherapy must develop its own evaluative criteria. To be taken seriously by churches and seminaries, it will have to affirm its connections and contributions to ministry and theological discourse. And to be taken seriously by people of color and by white women, it will have to include, even if only to a limited extent, social analysis of oppression, alienation, exploitation, diversity, and justice in its clinical assessment of individual pathology.

As I will develop further below, this final demand to attend to the wider cultural context, partially fostered by liberation perspectives, may be the most critical. At this point, let me delineate the ways in which a feminist perspective radically re-orients perception and understanding. Black feminist bell hooks

7. Elizabeth Liebert, *Changing Life Patterns: Adult Development in Spiritual Direction* (Mahwah, N.J.: Paulist Press, 1992).

argues, and I agree, that feminists have frequently been careless in failing to clarify agreed-upon definitions of feminism. Without them — with an "anything goes" attitude that feminism can mean anything anyone wants — we lack a solid foundation on which to construct theory and engage in meaningful praxis. Beneath its many current forms and definitions, some of which are too focused on rights, personal autonomy, and social equality, feminism is, in a word, a radical political movement. Hooks writes,

> Feminism is a struggle to end sexist oppression. Its aim is not to benefit solely any specific group of women, any particular race or class of women. It does not privilege women over men. It has the power to transform in a meaningful way all our lives.[8]

To call feminism simply a movement to make men and women equal reduces and even confuses its full intent, especially when sexual equality in the midst of difference remains an elusive ideal and discounts the weight of other inequities. Feminism reclaims the lost and denigrated voices of women and strives to eradicate the underlying cultural biases, including imperialism, economic expansion, and others biases that sustain sexism and other oppressions. A feminist perspective demands an analysis of structures and ideologies that rank people as inferior or superior according to various traits of human nature, whether gender, sexual orientation, color, age, physical ability, and so forth. Hence, to think about pastoral theology and care from this vantage point requires prophetic, transformative challenge to systems of power, authority, and domination that continue to violate, terrorize, and systematically destroy individuals and communities.

This emphasis on confronting systems of domination has been instrumental in creating the shift in pastoral theology from care narrowly defined as counseling to care understood as part of a wide cultural, social, and religious context. These two highly significant, related developments and commitments are perhaps most evident in a variety of recent publications in the field such as James Poling's *The Abuse of Power*, Pamela Couture's *Blessed Are the Poor?*, Larry Graham's *Care of Persons, Care of Worlds*, and my own *Also a Mother*.[9] These are the kinds of texts most likely to

8. bell hooks, *Feminist Theory: From Margin to Center* (Boston: South End Press, 1984), p. 26.

9. James Newton Poling, *The Abuse of Power: A Theological Problem* (Nashville: Abingdon Press, 1991); Pamela D. Couture, *Blessed Are the Poor? Women's Poverty, Family*

come under consideration in introductory pastoral care courses. All of these books, to varying degrees, challenge systemic structures and ideologies of patriarchy, individualism, self-sufficiency, rationalism, materialism, and so forth. They argue for alternative theological understandings of the social, cultural context as essential for adequate caregiving. Many in pastoral theology have traditionally harkened back to Anton Boisen's powerful foundational metaphor for the existential subject of pastoral theology — *"the study of living human documents rather than books."*[10] Today, the "living human *web*" suggests itself as a better term for the appropriate subject for investigation, interpretation, and transformation.

When I first pictured the "living human *web*" as a central theme of pastoral theology, I was thinking more of the three-dimensional net that a process-theology-oriented college professor etched on the flat classroom blackboard than the musty, sticky, annoying webs spun by insidious and numerous spiders in our old and not-so-clean house. Within the limits of chalk, blackboard, and his own imagination, John Spencer sought to illustrate the dense, multitudinous, contiguous nature of reality as he saw it over against the static interpretations of reality of much Western philosophy and religion. As I tried to understand why I believed what I believed and to formulate fresh theological constructions of my own, this raw depiction made a great deal of sense to me. It still does.

Although I did not consciously or intentionally make the connection, my use of the term *web* also results in part from feminist discourse. The most specific example that comes to mind is a book titled *From a Broken Web: Separatism, Sexism, and Self* by Catherine Keller, a systematic theologian also significantly influenced by process theology through the work of John Cobb. *From a Broken Web* refutes thousands of years of misogyny embedded in Western myths, philosophy, religion, and psychology. Keller's thesis is that sexism and separatism — the view of the self as essentially separate from others — are intricately interlinked in this history.[11] By sheer force of iconoclasm — juxtaposing hated images of women and

Policy, and Practical Theology (Nashville: Abingdon Press, 1991); Larry Kent Graham, *Care of Persons, Care of Worlds: A Psychosystems Approach to Pastoral Care and Counseling* (Nashville: Abingdon Press, 1992); and Bonnie J. Miller-McLemore, *Also a Mother: Work and Family as Theological Dilemma* (Nashville: Abingdon Press, 1994).

10. Anton Boisen, *The Exploration of the Inner World* (Chicago: Willet, Clark, 1936), cited in Gerkin, *The Living Human Document*, p. 37.

11. Catherine Keller, *From a Broken Web: Separatism, Sexism, and Self* (Boston: Beacon Press, 1986).

images of monsters, serpents, spiders, dragons, Medusa, Tiamat, Tehom, or the "deep" in Genesis (which Keller sees as the Hebrew equivalent to Tiamat), the "oceanic" in Freud — Keller reveals how repulsive and frightening the powers of interconnection and the wisdom of women have been made to appear. Distorted fears of enmeshment, entanglement, and loss surround the relationality represented by the female and the mother in Western history. The resulting animosity and fury toward women, monsters, serpents, spiders, dragons, Medusa, Tiamat, Tehom, and the "oceanic" has entailed the repression and banishment of connection itself.

By contrast, Keller asserts, the "self-structure of separation is a patriarchal artifice"; the "web is not originally a trap."[12] Using revised creation myths, object relations theory, process metaphysics, and feminist theology, she spins the new meanings of the connectivity of selfhood, religion, and all life. While aware of the limits of any one metaphor in a metaphysics of relationality, the image of the web "claims the status of an all-embracing image, a metaphor of metaphors, not out of any imperialism, but because, as a metaphor of interconnection itself, the web can link lightly in its nodes an open multiplicity of images."[13] What she calls "arachnean religion" involves the spider's genius of repairing the web that the separative self has broken, "spinning oneness out of many and weaving the one back into the many."[14]

Obviously, Keller's work is dense, highly technical, and not without its flaws. For my purposes, the important point is this: an alternative mythos resurrects the interconnectivity of selfhood. This mythos and the theology connected to it have funded a new approach in pastoral theology. More specifically, this means, for example, that public policy issues that determine the health of the human web are as important as issues of individual emotional well-being. Psychology serves a less exclusive, although still important, role, while other social sciences such as economics or political science become powerful tools of interpretation. In a word, never again will a clinical moment, whether of caring for a woman recovering from a hysterectomy or of attending to a woman's spiritual life, be understood on intrapsychic grounds alone. These moments are always and necessarily situated within the interlocking, continually evolving threads of which reality is woven, and they can be understood in no other way. Psychology alone cannot understand this web.

12. Keller, *From a Broken Web*, p. 137.
13. Keller, *From a Broken Web*, p. 218.
14. Keller, *From a Broken Web*, p. 228.

The move away from psychology is not without its drawbacks. Maxine Glaz has provocatively observed that the newly critical perception of psychology in pastoral theology may be part of an "impetus to avoid issues of gender." Just when women in pastoral theology begin to find feminist psychology an incisive tool for reconstructing pastoral care and theology, the "people of a dominant perspective emphasize a new theme or status symbol."[15] Glaz is right: we have some cause for concern about this change as a covert attempt to disempower the new participants in the pastoral theology discussion.

Women in pastoral theology would do well to retain the power of psychological analysis. First, to move beyond psychology too quickly is to underestimate the power of men like Freud and psychological definitions of human nature and fulfillment as culture- and consciousness-shaping forces. Moreover, new resources, such as Jessica Benjamin's *Bonds of Love* and Luise Eichenbaum and Susie Orbach's *Understanding Women* — to name just a few — challenge conventional understandings of female desire in Freud and others.[16] They provide fresh insight into intrapsychic need and interpersonal dynamics. Feminist psychology and therapy, joined by psychologies attuned to different ethnic groups, will continue to be vital tools. Indeed, women in pastoral theology need to correct the subtle biases of some theologians who dismiss too rashly all of modern psychology as individualistic and inept in social analysis. In truth, the use of recent psychology by pastoral theologians and by feminist theologians, as Keller herself reveals, will continue to reshape fundamentally the ways in which we think about selfhood, the needs of children, human development, religious behavior, and other phenomena. If those in theology understand mutuality better than they used to, feminist psychology is at least partially responsible.

Glaz's criticism points to the difficulty of bringing diverse voices into play. Criticism of the individualistic focus of pastoral care has come in part from feminist theology and black theology. Few books in pastoral theology have addressed cultural issues of gender, race, and class. Even the otherwise thorough, well-documented history of pastoral care by E. Brooks

15. Maxine Glaz, "A New Pastoral Understanding of Women," in *Women in Travail and Transition: A New Pastoral Care*, ed. Maxine Glaz and Jeanne Stevenson-Moessner (Minneapolis: Fortress Press, 1991), pp. 12, 29.

16. Jessica Benjamin, *The Bonds of Love: Psychoanalysis, Feminism, and the Problem of Domination* (New York: Pantheon, 1988); and Luise Eichenbaum and Susie Orbach, *Understanding Women: A Psychoanalytic Approach* (New York: Basic Books, 1983).

Holifield sees women, slaves, and "others" primarily as the objects of care, rarely as caregivers themselves, and never as the source of new ideas.[17] Some, like Clinebell, have tried to revise their basic texts to add new sections on "transcultural" perspectives.[18] David Augsburger's *Pastoral Counseling across Cultures* has received wide acclamation.[19]

However, such books represent — as the authors acknowledge — dominant perspectives. Augsburger's definition of an otherwise helpful idea, "interpathy," is a good illustration of the problem. He uses the term to encourage entering into a "second culture" with a respect for that culture "as equally as valid as one's own."[20] Many feminists and people of color have pointed out that the subordinates in a society already intimately know the foreign realities of at least two worlds, that of their own and that of the dominant group or groups. And they have often given the second culture undue credibility and deference. Augsburger's interpathy is absolutely necessary, but it is a trait more relevant for the dominant culture than for those in oppressed groups. They have been "embracing of what is truly other" for a long time.

By contrast, the first step of those in the "second culture" is to affirm their own realities as worthy of equal respect. For many women, well-trained in sensitivity to the needs of others and insensitive to their own suppressed desires, it is less a matter of bracketing and transcending one's own beliefs in order to feel as the other feels than of identifying for themselves what they feel and want at all. Significantly, even more than Caucasian women, African-American women, Asian women, and others must arbitrate between multiple, often hostile, cultures. For women, then, interpathy into the foreign beliefs of another culture necessarily implies envisioning distorted thoughts and feelings of repulsion, violence, fear, hatred — a problem Augsburger fails to note in his development of the concept (racism and sexism are conspicuous in their absence in the book's index).

With a few significant exceptions, women in pastoral theology have come up through the ranks of higher education approximately one generation behind women in religion and theology such as Rosemary Radford

17. E. Brooks Holifield, *A History of Pastoral Care in America: From Salvation to Self-Realization* (Nashville: Abingdon Press, 1983).

18. Clinebell, *Basic Types of Pastoral Care and Counseling.*

19. David W. Augsburger, *Pastoral Counseling across Cultures* (Philadelphia: Westminster Press, 1986).

20. Augsburger, *Pastoral Counseling across Cultures,* p. 14.

Ruether and Elisabeth Schüssler Fiorenza. A few women, such as Peggy Way and Sue Cardwell, have significantly impacted the field, although this occurred less through publications than through their compelling personal styles of teaching, speaking, and counseling. One possible reason for the lag in the more active participation by women in pastoral theology as a discipline is its proximity to the church and the conservative nature of congregational life. Despite the pastoral nature of much feminist theology and careful treatments of specific issues in pastoral care such as abuse and spirituality, there was no book by a single author on pastoral theology from a woman's or a feminist perspective until quite recently. With Valerie DeMarinis's *Critical Caring: A Feminist Model for Pastoral Psychology,* a new era has commenced. Pivotal articles by Christie Neuger and Carrie Doehring suggest that further developments are only a matter of time.[21]

These problems are partly less severe for black theology because of contributions from scholars with longer tenure in the academy such as Archie Smith and Edward Wimberly.[22] Still, wider recognition and reliance upon their work has been slow in coming. And until the recent publication of *WomanistCare,* the participation of African-American women has been almost entirely missing from the discussion.[23] Furthermore, *WomanistCare* is not explicitly presented as a book in pastoral theology. Meanwhile, more general books in theology such as Emilie Townes's *A Troubling in My Soul* are helpful resources and hopeful signs on the horizon for understanding care from a womanist perspective.[24]

What will it mean for the practice of pastoral care to bring new voices into play? *Women in Travail and Transition: A New Pastoral Care* offers an initial indication.[25] Edited by Maxine Glaz and Jeanne Stevenson-

---

21. Valerie M. DeMarinis, *Critical Caring: A Feminist Model for Pastoral Psychology* (Louisville: Westminster John Knox Press, 1993); Christie Cozad Neuger, "Feminist Pastoral Theology and Pastoral Counseling: A Work in Progress," *Journal of Pastoral Theology* 2 (Summer 1992): 35-57; and Carrie Doehring, "Developing Models of Feminist Pastoral Counseling," *Journal of Pastoral Care* 46, no. 1 (Spring 1992): 23-31.

22. Edward P. Wimberly, *Pastoral Care in the Black Church* (Nashville: Abingdon Press, 1979); and Archie Smith Jr., *The Relational Self: Ethics and Therapy from a Black Church Perspective* (Nashville: Abingdon Press, 1982).

23. *WomanistCare: How to Tend the Souls of Women,* ed. Linda H. Hollies (Joliet, Ill.: Woman to Woman Ministries, 1992).

24. Emilie M. Townes, *A Troubling in My Soul: Womanist Perspectives on Evil and Suffering* (Maryknoll, N.Y.: Orbis Books, 1993).

25. *Women in Travail and Transition,* ed. Glaz and Stevenson-Moessner.

Moessner, the book includes the work of five authors in ministerial settings and four in the academy. It aims to nurture intellectual acuity in the midst of pastoral practice. Chapters on new pastoral understandings of women and new pastoral paradigms bracket chapters on work, family, and alternative family forms, women's bodies, sexual abuse, battered women, and women's depression. Almost every man who has read this text in my courses testifies that it powerfully illumines women's lives. Women students want to send multiple copies to their ministerial colleagues, men and women alike. These students have heard a "cry," as one student expressed it, that they had never heard or understood before; they begin to hear in a different way.

Emma Justes states that if clergy "are unable to travel the route of hearing women's anger, of exploring with women the painful depths of experiences of incest and rape, or enabling women to break free from cultural stereotypes that define their existence," they should not be doing pastoral counseling with women.[26] This claim suggests limits to empathy that people in Carl Rogers's time never suspected. When those involved in pastoral care do not know how to recognize the realities of violence toward women, they foster further damage and violence. Particularly in situations of sexual abuse, for example, the problem in pastoral response is not too little empathy but too much indiscriminate empathy by an uninformed pastoral caregiver that surfaces long-repressed feelings that overwhelm rather than help the person in need.[27] All pastoral caregivers must sharpen their sensitivity to the stress that women experience as wage earners and homemakers,[28] the economic devaluation of women in the workplace and women's poverty,[29] health issues of concern to women, and the implications of female images of God for self-esteem.[30]

But these kinds of understandings are merely a beginning. The authors of *Women in Travail and Transition,* all white professional women in mainline faiths, invite "companion volumes written by nonwhite, ethnic, non-middle-class women within Western culture and by other women

26. Emma J. Justes, "Women," in *Clinical Handbook of Pastoral Counseling*, ed. Robert J. Wicks et al. (New York: Paulist Press, 1985), p. 298.

27. See, for example, Maxine Glaz, "Reconstructing the Pastoral Care of Women," *Second Opinion* 17, no. 2 (October 1991).

28. Miller-McLemore, *Also a Mother*.

29. Couture, *Blessed Are the Poor?*

30. Carroll Saussy, *God Images and Self-Esteem: Empowering Women in a Patriarchal Society* (Louisville: Westminster John Knox Press, 1991).

elsewhere throughout the world."[31] No Hispanic, Asian, African, or American Indian pastoral care and theology has been published, although Robert Wicks and Barry Estadt have recently edited a "brief volume" of the *"experience* and *impressions"* of pastoral counselors involved in ministry in ten different countries.[32] Few texts deal with the pastoral agenda for men that might include issues such as the fear, anger, and grief over role changes and vocational confusion or tensions between work and family. Protestant pastoral theology and related clinical associations have all but ignored rich traditions and histories of pastoral theology and spiritual direction in Roman Catholic, Jewish, evangelical, and other circles.

We cannot predict what difference other stories and traditions will make to general formulations of the field or in pastoral practice. When we admit that knowledge is seldom universal or uniform, and truth is contextual and tentative, we discover a host of methodological, pedagogical, and practical problems. If the field of pastoral theology can no longer claim unity in thought and mind, what commonalities of approach define the field as distinct and relevant? In many ways, teaching and ministry become harder, professors and clergy more vulnerable. We find that we do not yet have the right texts to assign in our classes or the right answers in the pastoral office. Pastoral theology's trademark of empathy for the living human document is confounded by the limitations of empathy in the midst of the living human web. Sometimes a person must admit an inability to understand fully the lived reality of the oppressions suffered by another. There may be boundaries beyond which empathy itself cannot go.

We do know that we can no longer ignore an author's or a parishioner's identity and cultural location. A "living human web" cannot simply be "read" and interpreted like a "document." Those within the web who have not yet spoken must speak for themselves. Gender, feminist, and black studies all verify the knowledge of the underprivileged, the outcast, the underclass, and the silenced. If knowledge depends upon power, then power must be given to the silenced. In part, the pastoral theology movement began with this claim: Anton Boisen, having suffered an emotional breakdown and finding himself inside a mental hospital, refused the marginalized, ostracized status of the mentally ill patient. He claimed the importance of what he learned about health, spirituality, and theology as

---

31. Glaz, "A New Pastoral Understanding of Women," p. vi.

32. *Pastoral Counseling in a Global Church: Voices from the Field,* ed. Robert J. Wicks and Barry K. Estadt (Maryknoll, N.Y.: Orbis Books, 1993).

learning that could occur from nowhere else than inside the experience of illness and suffering.[33] This lesson — that we must hear the voices of the marginalized from within their own contexts — is one that pastoral theologians have known all along, even when Boisen claimed the validity of his own mental breakdown, but perhaps never articulated in quite the way that it is now being addressed in this book and more widely.

Where Two or Three Are Gathered

Seven years after teaching my first introductory course, I finally created a course this spring with which I am fairly satisfied. Among its central objectives, it retains an emphasis on good listening skills, empathy, and moral and religious guidance; it adds an investigation of the networks of care in religious institutions; and it includes a study of diverse perspectives and of the interconnections between intrapsychic understandings, social analysis, and theological reflection. My satisfaction, I realize, is likely to be short-lived. The pressures on religion and higher education are immense. Entire religion departments in some universities have been shut down, and departments of religion and psychology and pastoral theology have sometimes been the first area cut. Likewise, the steady decline in numbers and monetary well-being of mainline denominations is already having an effect on seminary funding and constituencies. The reallocation of health care monies has affected and will continue to affect clinical pastoral care in hospitals and pastoral counseling institutions. Pastoral theology, however, has weathered rather well the challenges of the two fundamental crises described in this chapter. It has survived turmoil over its identity crisis and has actually done better than many other disciplines in theology in respecting a pluralism of voices.

Women in pastoral theology have much to contribute. Distinct from the claim in the preface of *Women in Travail and Transition* that "no individual woman in our field could undertake the complete project,"[34] now several women in the field are qualified to draft a book on pastoral care and women. Yet it is less clear that any individual woman would want to do so. In *Through the Eyes of Women,* then, the choice to co-author in the broadest sense becomes ever more deliberate and intentional. Most of us

33. Boisen, *The Exploration of the Inner World.*
34. Glaz, "A New Pastoral Understanding of Women," p. vi.

realize that this collaborative endeavor is more than — perhaps better than — what anyone might have written alone.

Pragmatically, our time and energies are already quickly consumed by the extra responsibilities of representation, mentoring, and such that are typical of women in previously male-dominated professions. More important, feminism has learned the dangers of attempting to speak for all women in some generic sense. Our united effort defies mathematical and empirical logic that contends that "$1 + 1 = 2$." One plus one becomes something entirely new, different, and more than the mere summation of its parts. Our shared meals, correspondence, phone calls, and late-night hotel-room conversations affirm a religious truth that "where two or three are gathered in my name, I am there among them" (Matt. 18:20).

The benefits of cooperation are evident both in terms of content and in terms of method. The collective text taps into areas of expertise that each author has developed out of particular passions and experiences. Few of us could address adequately, with the kind of depth and insight demonstrated here, the wide range of critical issues that this book covers. Into the web the authors weave issues thus far overlooked in the care of and care by women, many of them clandestine matters about which women, particularly women in churches, have not spoken freely, openly, and honestly — anger, aggression, eating disorders, hysterectomies, rape, lesbianism, aging. Most of the authors are different from the women who participated in the first collaborative effort. There has been a more intentional inclusion of non–European-American perspectives.

True, the main voices remain European-American, and other yet unexplored topics will come to the minds of our readers. Nonetheless, this volume in pastoral care is moving in the right direction. Like *Women in Travail and Transition,* it sustains the conversation between women in the academy and those involved in practicing pastoral care. Every chapter holds the tension between psychological analysis of the internal processing of personal experience and social analysis that situates individual issues within a more complex web of human interaction that includes divine intervention and grace.

Methodologically, participating in this volume did not mean dispatching twenty-five pages, written in the solitary confinement of one's office, to the editor and the publisher. Unlike many edited books, this book is written with the purpose of the entire book and the work of each other in mind. Individual chapters have been circulated among us for shared commentary. Even as I write, the conversations of my sisters at our meeting during the Society for Pastoral Theology ring in my ears. Just as feminist therapeutic theory defines differentiation as individuation in connection to others, the authors, while separately focused on individual areas of expertise, write in close connection to and knowledge of each other.

This approach is not one most of us learned in our respective institutions of higher education; academic rewards and dictates of professional survival often forbid it. Nonetheless, the choice to collaborate affirms the priority and value of relationality and working together to create a reality greater than any of its parts.

More broadly speaking, pastoral theology in general has much to contribute. The methods of pastoral theology have demonstrated the value of "thick description" as a powerful beginning point for all the fields of theological study.[35] "Thick description" means seeking a multilayered analysis of human strife, including detailed, intricately woven, "experience-near" rather than "experience-distant" readings of the "living human document." Standing explicitly between academy, church, and society, those in pastoral theology know intimately the limits of academic exercises and the necessity of religious experience in the creation of theology. We have found in the psychological sciences a lesson in practical theorizing. Better than most others in religious studies, we understand some of the problems and the possibilities involved in using the social sciences as a tool of analysis. We know the difficulties of marginalization. And we have grasped with greater ease than many in theology the importance of claiming one's own, often silenced, subjectivity.

Second, pastoral theologians, women and men alike, know the limits of knowledge apart from sensitive listening to the context, finding in the voices of women and people of color new ways of knowing and being. Those involved in forming the Society for Pastoral Theology itself struggled to make white women and women and men of color central to the construction of the field, perhaps more than is typical in most academic societies. We know the tensions and difficulties of actually respecting and mending the living human web. On both scores, pastoral theology is challenging theology and theological education to reconsider its foundations.

35. Clifford Geertz, *The Interpretation of Cultures* (New York: Basic Books, 1973), pp. 3-30.

CHAPTER 2

Revisiting the Living Document and Web

BACKGROUND AND INTRODUCTION

The "web" metaphor continues to be useful as a term defining new parameters for the discipline of pastoral theology. But it has its downsides. One major problem is its widely varied meanings. Some use it to talk about the important role of the congregation as a community in ministry. Others use it to talk about new ways of understanding selfhood as defined in relationship or interdependence with others. Recently, some have seen it as interchangeable with the term *integration* and the need to build bridges (or webs of connection) in theological education between disciplines and between academy and church. I intended it largely as a political and theological idea about the responsibilities of the discipline in relationship to new understandings of culture, power, and the nature of selfhood and the divine. This essay reflects my growing conviction that it was time for someone to name these different uses as well as their contributions and pitfalls.

A second problem with the metaphor is the vast expanse of the web as a definition for the boundaries of a single discipline. How can any one area bear the responsibility for such a wide range of issues and do the job well? These are a few of the questions that I take up here, fifteen years after my first run. For me, these questions arose largely in teaching pastoral care.

This essay was originally published as "Revisiting the Living Human Web: Theological Education and the Role of Clinical Pastoral Education," *The Journal of Pastoral Care and Counseling* 62, no. 1-2 (Spring-Summer 2008): 3-18. Used by permission.

Students found it hard enough to learn how to listen well to a person in need, much less incorporate theology into practice. How would I then teach how to facilitate care in wider communities, for example, or how to effect change in public policy, delivery of governmental services, or long-standing patterns of poverty? For hospital chaplains Kitty Garlid and John Bucchino, who invited me to speak at the 2007 East by Northeast Association of Clinical Pastoral Educators Spring Conference in Stony Point, New York, such questions about where to focus one's energy were live. They arose right in the middle of care delivery and in the midst of teaching increasingly diverse students from differing religious and cultural backgrounds. What had been a back-burner issue for me (and might have remained so) came to the forefront as a result of the inspiration of several savvy hospital chaplains and educators on the East Coast who saw that the metaphor of web both enriched *and* complicated their ministry and teaching.

In working on my keynote address, I gained fresh appreciation for Clinical Pastoral Education (CPE) and its contributions. It had defied powerful trends in classical twentieth-century theological education that made theology an increasingly remote enterprise for elite academic experts. One of my favorite lines in the chapter is my claim that CPE (and pastoral theology) acted as a thorn in the flesh of theological schools in the mid-1960s on three counts: "It insisted on the merits of close study of real-life situations, it turned to the sciences to enrich such study, and it demanded that close study of the person keep its eye on the social context." These advances may sound old hat now, but they were highly significant at the time and should be celebrated among the field's accomplishments.

A key thesis of the chapter that gets lost in the forest for all the trees is my argument that we need to reclaim the field's expertise on the human document. Our turn to the web as a primary disciplinary metaphor has led us to forget the value and power of such knowledge. To put it simply, CPE and pastoral theology help people understand themselves better. Both seek to understand personal experience and subjectivity. In the past fifty years, they have discovered pedagogical and theological strategies for uncovering the biases that complicate and cloud a person's ability to read a situation and respond faithfully. They know how to form, reform, and expand self-knowledge and compassion in ministry. A pitfall of our use of the web and the new focus in seminaries on "congregational care" is a loss of what Sigmund Freud called "closely hovering attention" to intrapsychic and interpersonal health. Colleagues such as Robert Dykstra and Rodney Hunter have expressed similar concerns. The health and vitality of congregations and institutions depend on the maturity and virtue of its leaders. If statistics on increasing clergy burnout, depression, hypertension, sexual misconduct, use of drugs, and so forth are any indication, ministers and those in the helping professions continue to need resources to understand and moderate their own needs, desires, and emotional and spiritual well-being. No other area of the theological curriculum is poised to address this. This is a gift and capacity that should not be lost. The best way to describe the primary subject of the discipline, as I argue in the chapter, should actually be the "human document within the web."

Sometimes seminary professors do not consider the repercussions of what they say and write in the academy. So when several people flagged a shift in pastoral theology several years ago from "living human document" to "living human web," none of us really considered directly what this would mean for Clinical Pastoral Education (CPE) programs themselves.[1] Born in the clinic, the phrase *living document* gravitated over time to the academy. It came to serve as a placeholder for the subject matter of pastoral theology, exemplified in books like Charles Gerkin's *The Living Human Document*,[2] and for the importance of such "documents" in theological education alongside more commonly recognized texts of Scripture and tradition. When academics like myself recently argued that the web had replaced or superseded the document as our primary text, in other words, we

1. See Larry K. Graham, *Care of Persons, Care of Worlds: A Psychosystems Approach to Pastoral Care and Counseling* (Nashville: Abingdon Press, 1992); Bonnie J. Miller-McLemore, "The Human Web and the State of Pastoral Theology," *The Christian Century,* 7 April 1993, pp. 366-69, and "The Living Human Web: Pastoral Theology at the Turn of the Century," in *Through the Eyes of Women: Insights for Pastoral Care,* ed. Jeanne Stevenson-Moessner (Minneapolis: Fortress Press, 1996), pp. 9-26; John Patton, *Pastoral Care in Context: An Introduction to Pastoral Care* (Louisville: Westminster John Knox Press, 1993); Brita Gill-Austern, "Rediscovering Hidden Treasure for Pastoral Care," *Pastoral Psychology* 43, no. 4 (1995): 233-53; Pamela D. Couture, "Weaving the Web: Pastoral Care in an Individualistic Society," in *Through the Eyes of Women: Insights for Pastoral Care,* ed. Stevenson-Moessner, pp. 94-104; and Daniel J. Louw, "Pastoral Hermeneutics and the Challenge of a Global Economy: Care to the Living Human Web," *The Journal of Pastoral Care and Counseling* 56, no. 4 (2002): 339-50.

2. Charles V. Gerkin, *The Living Human Document: Revisioning Pastoral Counseling in a Hermeneutical Mode* (Nashville: Abingdon Press, 1984).

were not thinking explicitly of CPE. We were focusing primarily on the academic use of metaphors to characterize a field of study.

Yet this shift in metaphors does matter for CPE. The living document has been its cornerstone. Anton Boisen coined the phrase almost seventy-five years ago,[3] and until at least the 1990 *Dictionary of Pastoral Care and Counseling,* CPE was still essentially defined *as* "supervised encounter with living human documents."[4] Pastoral theology itself emerged as a discipline in the Protestant United States in part, if not directly, from this clinical context. What are the repercussions, then, of this move away from clinic to web for CPE and theological education?[5]

At least four kinds of issues, with accompanying questions, have surfaced as a result of this shift,[6] and all four suggest a need to revisit our metaphors for pastoral work:[7]

3. Anton Boisen, *The Exploration of the Inner World: A Study of Mental Disorder and Religious Experience* (New York: Willet, Clark & Co., 1936).

4. Edward E. Thornton, "Clinical Pastoral Education (CPE)," in *Dictionary of Pastoral Care and Counseling,* ed. Rodney J. Hunter (Nashville: Abingdon Press, 1990), p. 177; see also Thornton, *Professional Education for Ministry: A History of Clinical Pastoral Education* (Nashville: Abingdon Press, 1970).

5. In addition to these theoretical and rhetorical shifts, there have also been institutional shifts. Most early professors of pastoral care, such as Liston Mills and James Lapsley, emerged out of clinical settings closely connected with CPE and/or AAPC. Over the last generation, this connection has weakened. In fact, Mills and Lapsley themselves saw the need for a separate organization or academic society for professors in pastoral theology capable of supporting the newly established discipline. One consequence of the creation of the Society for Pastoral Theology in 1985, anticipated even at the start, was the educational distance this advanced between clinic or practitioner and scholar or professor, especially as the latter found it increasingly difficult to serve as a responsible professional citizen of both clinical and scholarly societies (attending all the annual meetings, paying the dues, and so forth) and more generally to *sustain* both vocations. For an institutional overview of developments in clinical training in the last decade, see Loren L. Townsend, "Ferment and Imagination in Training in Clinical Ministry," in *Pastoral Care and Counseling: Redefining the Paradigms,* ed. Nancy Ramsay (Nashville: Abingdon Press, 2004).

6. These questions and the content of this address evolved out of e-mails and conversation with Kitty Garlid and John Bucchino prior to the East by Northeast ACPE Bi-Regional Spring Conference, April 23-25, 2007, in Stony Point, New York. I welcomed the opportunity to present the keynote address and to learn from colleagues on a panel that followed (B. Blodgett, L. Hummel, B. Hoffman, and M. Springer), as well as from those who attended. I thank Kitty, John, panelists, and participants for their fruitful contributions.

7. For a sampling of the many metaphors for the pastoral caregiver rather than for the subject matter of the field, see Robert C. Dykstra, *Images of Pastoral Care: Classic Readings* (St. Louis: Chalice Press, 2006).

- *Teaching:* People are weighing the positive contributions of the living web for teaching students and seminaries, such as a greater emphasis on systems and communities and the value of group work, over against its limitations, such as confusion over the place of the person and personal identity. How does the metaphor of web both enrich and problematize the teaching and experience of CPE?
- *Religious diversity:* Given CPE's religiously liberal history, chaplaincy programs are challenged today by a kind of diversity that original claims about the need to consider marginalized voices in the web did not consider: the increase in religious diversity among students and religious conservatism in particular. How does the commonly liberal chaplain work with today's more conservative students and trends?
- *Seminary relations:* People also wonder about the working relationship between CPE and seminary education. What is the role of each institution in the education of ministry students? What do we mean by theological reflection, and what does each institution contribute to this?
- *Historical understanding:* These considerations ultimately lead to historical questions about the development of the educational challenges that CPE and seminary education face today. What are some of the problems in both arenas, and how did they develop?

As I sometimes say to students working on papers or dissertations, we have lots of questions here, maybe too many for one article. An entire article could be devoted to the question of *religious diversity*. Here I want to focus primarily on *history* and secondarily on *seminary relations* and *teaching,* with the hope that doing so creates fresh ways to rethink student diversity in ensuing conversation. My questions are the following: What are some of the problems in theological education, and how did they develop? What is the place of CPE in the curriculum? How does the living web as a metaphor for the subject of pastoral care enrich and confuse our work?

In exploring these questions, I see my task as primarily descriptive, helping recall CPE's place in the history of education. However, I do have a quiet agenda. Least controversial, I simply argue that the metaphor of the living web has undeveloped potential and overlooked problems. Although I do not list places where we are stuck in the web (so to speak) until the end, going over our history sheds light on them. More radically, however, as I came to realize the more I explored these questions, CPE's original metaphor has merits worth underscoring and retrieving. The focus on human documents responded to theological education's distance from practice, providing fresh means for an enriched engagement between practice and theory, even if it did not resolve the problem and even if it neglected religious texts, congregational settings, and social and political realities in the process. Ultimately, I suggest that "the living document within the web" is the metaphor that best captures the subject matter of both CPE and pastoral theology.

My Own History with CPE

"What about participating in a program in hospital chaplaincy?" suggested my favorite religion professor at a small liberal arts college in the Midwest. "That would allow you to consider the interplay between psychology and religion." This certainly caught my attention. A psychology major, I knew he understood me better than anyone in my own department. Looking back, I see how much he shaped my vocation, more than I realized, through conversations that I really do not recall in any detail.

Lost also from memory is exactly how I found myself in a CPE program in Indianapolis for the winter-quarter senior year. But forever stamped onto my personal history is how getting to know a handful of Catholic sisters and mid-life Protestant pastors disenchanted with parish ministry, through group and individual supervision and conversation, changed the course of my life. When I returned to campus, I presented a senior project on chaplaincy and on religion and psychology in the early movement of pastoral theology that completely befuddled my psychology professors. But I knew I would pursue more education in religion eventually, and a year later I applied to divinity programs with the distant dream (still not realized) of becoming a CPE supervisor.

A couple of summers later, I took another unit of CPE (for credit this time), and a few years after that I persuaded Jim Gibbons and Mary Wilkerson at Billings Hospital (now University of Chicago Hospital and Clinics) to let me participate in a year-long internship on a part-time basis while working on a Ph.D., the academic degree to which I had gravitated. Not only love of reading and writing led me out of a professional ministry degree and into a doctoral program in religion and psychology. I was pragmatic: As a woman, I wanted the highest degree I could get, even though I equivocated throughout this time over exactly what I wanted to do with it.

Vocational insight came in unexpected *kairos*-like epiphanies. I had one such moment with chaplaincy. One day, walking out of the hospital, I suddenly realized I did not want to spend every day of my working life there. My reasons were tangibly elusive — the medicinal smell, the clean tile, the bright light, and, more subtly, the short-term nature of relationships, the marginalization of religion in all that went on there, and the looming cloud of struggle and mortality. But for all practical purposes, my chaplaincy career ended then.

However, my commitment to and appreciation for the practice of patient care and the wider enterprise of CPE have not diminished. Knowing how people in the gastrointestinal clinic dealt with cancer changed how I understood and eventually wrote about Christian views of sin, guilt, illness, and healing. More important, hearing my own foibles and oversights refracted back to me through verbatims and supervisory and peer feedback *changed me.* At the heart of my own formation, therefore, lies a natural inclination for the kind of learning focused on living documents that I first experienced exactly thirty years ago among a circle of Catholic sisters and Protestant men in the one old building that the medical complex did not want. I am invested in the continued place of such learning in theological education.

History of Protestant Theological Education

How does my own story of the value of alternative approaches to learning connect with the bigger story of seminary education and CPE? What were the limitations of classical Protestant education, as Boisen and others saw them, and how did CPE try to resolve them? Why did Boisen see the need to give actual *human* documents the same weight as biblical, historical, and doctrinal texts?

While I recognize CPE's current religious diversity, an initial focus on Protestantism is appropriate here. Although Boisen did not discuss it explicitly, he challenged a major split between theory and practice in education that has deep roots in Protestant intellectual history. Of course, Catholic, Jewish, and other religions have their own versions of this gap between religious study and everyday practice.[8] But CPE began as a liberal

8. One can find parallel problems in other traditions, such as medieval scholasticism and the application of rationally conceived manuals of moral theology to pastoral

Protestant movement, and Protestantism has shaped the curricular organization of theological schools in other religious traditions in the United States more generally, including the adoption of CPE in a variety of non-Protestant contexts.

Two problems have plagued Protestant theological education since the nineteenth century — what has been commonly called the "clerical paradigm" in the 1980s literature in practical theology[9] and what I have recently labeled the "academic paradigm." The former is well-known. The latter has been obscured by our very captivation with the diagnosis of the clerical paradigm.[10]

What is the problem of the clerical paradigm? Essentially it is the reduction of the aim of theological education over the last two centuries from the pursuit of *theologia* or wisdom of the divine to a narrow preoccupation with teaching ministerial skills to individual pastors. In an effort to secure a place for the study of theology in the modern university in the face of the Enlightenment's unsettling questions about religious authority, nineteenth-century Protestant theologian Friedrich Schleiermacher defined theology as a science, comparable to its companion sciences of medicine and law, with religion as its object, clerical education as its aim, and several specialized areas as its components.[11] A new "theological encyclopedia" emerged that gradually divided education into the so-called classical areas of Bible, history, and doctrine, which were said to possess the theory or truths of the tradition, and the practical arts that apply these truths to ministry, centered almost entirely on the technical functions of clergy. In the 1980s, the hope was to get "beyond" such "clericalism" in theological

---

ministry in Catholicism, for example, or the emphasis on instruction in Bible, commentaries, and rabbinic literature rather than the arts of ministry as the center of education in Judaism.

9. See, for example, Edward Farley, "Theology and Practice outside the Clerical Paradigm," in *Practical Theology: The Emerging Field in Theology, Church, and World*, ed. Don S. Browning (San Francisco: Harper & Row, 1983), pp. 21-41, and *Theologia* (Philadelphia: Fortress Press, 1983). For a bibliography of the 1980s literature on practical theology and theological education more generally, see *Theological Education* 30, no. 2 (1994): 89-98.

10. Bonnie J. Miller-McLemore, "The 'Clerical Paradigm': A Fallacy of Misplaced Concreteness?" *International Journal of Practical Theology* 11, no. 2 (2007): 19-38, and "Practical Theology and Pedagogy: Embodying Theological Know-How," in *For Life Abundant: Practical Theology in the Education and Formation of Ministers*, ed. Dorothy C. Bass and Craig Dykstra (Grand Rapids: Wm. B. Eerdmans, 2008).

11. Friedrich Schleiermacher, *Brief Outline of the Study of Theology*, trans. Terrence N. Tice (Richmond, Va.: John Knox Press, 1966).

education, as the title of one book put it, and back to contextual, congregational, and theological approaches.[12]

Several years ago I began to feel troubled by the increasingly careless usage of this initially useful phrase of the "clerical paradigm" by those in practical theology as a shorthand code for everything that has gone wrong with theological education. This has overlooked a second major problem, the rise of what I would call the "academic paradigm" or the view of theology as something reserved for learned "experts" removed from everyday life.[13] Over the last century, many scholars tried to solve the problem of theology's increasing marginalization in the academy and modern society by becoming ever more sophisticated. They began to write for a public removed from Christian life and ministry. Few parishioners saw such technical theological activity as something in which they engaged. When they wanted to understand their religious lives, they turned instead to those better able to provide lively language — psychologists, economists, political scientists, and even authors of spiritual memoirs. The problem, in other words, is not just "clericalization" or an education aimed only at technical clerical skills but an equally troubling "academization" or an education aimed primarily at producing scholars.

Despite considerable change in practical and systematic theology in recent years, theological education is still partly entrapped by both problems. One principle that shaped the organization of the "theological encyclopedia" — the distinction between theory and practice — simply exacerbated the division between practical theology and all the other areas. A major study of theological education in the 1950s deplored the implication behind these curricular divisions that the classical areas are somehow "impractical" and the practical arts lack a "body of knowledge."[14] But the study did not dispel them. Such perceptions are still common today. It may help to remember the kind of understandings that have shaped ministerial education not that long ago. A 1980s dictionary defines Christian "theology" as the "rational account" of Christian faith performed by a "minority

---

12. Joseph C. Hough and Barbara G. Wheeler, *Beyond Clericalism: The Congregation as a Focus for Education* (Atlanta: Scholars Press, 1988).

13. Miller-McLemore, "The 'Clerical Paradigm'" and "Practical Theology and Pedagogy."

14. H. Richard Niebuhr, Daniel Day Williams, and James M. Gustafson, *The Advancement of Theological Education: The Summary Report of a Mid-Century Study* (New York: Harper & Brothers, 1957); also see William B. Oglesby, "Theological Education and the Pastoral Care Movement, Protestant," in *Dictionary of Pastoral Care and Counseling,* ed. Hunter, p. 1261.

of Christians" or the "intellectual elite" in institutions of higher education.[15] "Systematic theology" receives almost the same definition. It is "that form of specialism which seeks . . . a rational and orderly account of the content of Christian belief."[16] "Pastoral theology" is theology for the "work of ministry."[17] This is the legacy and context in which CPE's effort to move theology closer to the realities of living human documents stands.

History of CPE: Recollecting the Movement's Story

Historically, CPE arose out of disenchantment with the academic model of theology and education. In one of the founding developments, Episcopalian physician William Keller established a social service summer school in 1923 in Cincinnati to bring theological students into direct contact with persons in need. A few years later, physician Richard Cabot published a "Plea for a Clinical Year in the Course of Theological Study," convinced that such exposure would enhance future ministry. Under Cabot's auspices, Anton Boisen began a training program, urging students to see the "living human document" of patients struggling with illness as essential to learning theology, as essential as close study of textual documents of Scripture and tradition.[18]

A prominent interpreter of pastoral theology's history, church historian E. Brooks Holifield, pays insufficient attention to the centrality of this disenchantment with classical education in the rise of CPE in his dictionary entry on the movement. Instead, he emphasizes, perhaps inordinately, another dimension of its rapid growth and appeal — its turn to the behavioral sciences. The pastoral care movement gained prominence in the United States after 1945, he says, as an attempt to "refine ministry by drawing upon the findings of modern medicine, psychotherapy, and the behavioral sciences."[19] Pastoral care capitulates, he believes, to secular sci-

15. S. W. Sykes, "Theology," in *Westminster Dictionary of Christian Theology,* ed. Alan Richardson and John Bowden (Philadelphia: Westminster, 1983), p. 566.

16. Sykes, "Systematic Theology," in *Westminster Dictionary of Christian Theology,* ed. Richardson and Bowden, p. 560.

17. Rodney J. Hunter, "Pastoral Theology," in *Westminster Dictionary of Christian Theology,* ed. Richardson and Bowden, p. 428.

18. E. Brooks Holifield, "Pastoral Care Movement," in *Dictionary of Pastoral Care and Counseling,* ed. Hunter, p. 847.

19. Holifield, "Pastoral Care Movement," p. 845.

ence and its values, especially individualism, a concern most evident in how he tells the longer history of the field in his book on pastoral care, which looks primarily at the impact of secular developments rather than at what was happening internally to seminary education.[20] This concern reflects a wider enduring suspicion apparent at the start of the movement about the social sciences and a fear (sometimes justified) that the focus in CPE moves away from divine to human action and from pastoral and theological to medical and psychological models of care.[21]

CPE leaders themselves may have lost a full memory of the movement's longer theological history, especially as CPE has grown, diversified, and moved into new contexts. Just as individuals need to understand their own history, so also does such understanding benefit larger organizations. Two points of recollection are important here: We need to remember the movement's view of and response to the problems of seminary education and the important role this played, and we need to remember the important emphasis on the wider social sphere from the beginning of the movement.

First, it is important to recognize that the early pastoral care movement had, in William Oglesby's words, "a varied and at times tense relationship" with theological education.[22] CPE was inspired, as Edward Thornton argues, both by the appeal of the "methods of medical education, psychology, and social work" *and* as a reaction "against the limitations of classical theological education."[23] The sciences appealed to early founders precisely because they presented a viable means to address this disenchantment. People turned to psychology not so much because they were caving in to secular culture, as Holifield implies, nor because they sought "academic or scholarly respectability," as Edward Farley asserts,[24] but because they found in the sciences a powerful way to understand religious experience and healing (perhaps better at the time than that found in theology).

20. E. Brooks Holifield, *A History of Pastoral Care in America: From Salvation to Self-Realization* (Nashville: Abingdon Press, 1983).

21. See Oglesby, "Theological Education and the Pastoral Care Movement, Protestant," p. 1261.

22. Oglesby, "Theological Education and the Pastoral Care Movement, Protestant," p. 1260.

23. Thornton, "Clinical Pastoral Education (CPE)," p. 178.

24. Edward Farley, "Practical Theology, Protestant," in *Dictionary of Pastoral Care and Counseling*, ed. Hunter, p. 935.

The sciences — psychology and medicine in particular — possessed at least four attributes that offered a means to bridge the split between theory and practice or between human suffering and abstract theology. They *translated sophisticated theories* of human nature, fulfillment, and anguish into concrete and understandable terms. They *demonstrated the value of close observation* of people's lives and the intelligence that evolves directly out of this. They *underscored the centrality of personal formation* as critical to faithful ministerial leadership. Finally, they *suggested a method of case study* as a means to bring these insights and values together. Early participants in the movement found propositional theology barren, especially when imposed on believers in religious crises without sensitivity to their experience or religious understandings. By contrast, the sciences fostered a deep respect for the subject. So, in Thornton's words, "parishioners, patients, clients, inmates" became the "primary instructors in CPE,"[25] and "participation" gained "equal standing with proclamation" as a means to grasp Christian faith.[26] Meaning of all kinds, including theological meaning, emerges out of personal struggles, with clergy working as mentors and participants rather than as judges or scholars.

The method of case notes, then case study, and eventually verbatims, or word-for-word transcriptions of pastoral interactions, emerged as a pedagogical hallmark. The case, presented and discussed in the bounded context of a small group of peers with close oversight of a supervisor, provides a self-contained unit of practice available for analysis and reflection. Although based largely on the medical case conference, the verbatim focuses as much on the subjective recollection as the objective event. Long before those in philosophical and social theory developed the argument that interpretation is colored by the pre-understandings which people bring to the text,[27] those who implemented the case study method recognized that verbatims said as much or more about the person reconstructing the incident than about the actual case itself. Many people used verbatims specifically for this purpose, relying heavily on the communal knowledge that emerged spontaneously among trusted colleagues and supervisors trained to see and name such personal and vocational oversights and omissions.

So verbatims, shared and worked through in the small group, be-

25. Thornton, "Clinical Pastoral Education (CPE)," p. 179.
26. Thornton, "Clinical Pastoral Education (CPE)," p. 180.
27. See Hans-Georg Gadamer, *Truth and Method* (New York: Crossroad, 1982).

came a way to understand hidden or unrecognized dynamics internal to a person's worldview that deeply shaped how she or he responded. "Miscolorations and gaps are as revealing" of a student's self-experience as "accurate descriptions." They are, says Thornton, echoing Freud's view of dreams, the "royal road into a student's personal learning issues."[28] In fact, practical theologian Don Browning turns to CPE in his articulation of practical theological methods precisely because of its focus on the person of the ministerial student and the centrality of the person and personal experience in all interpretation. Most efforts in theology to interpret situations seldom consider the "personal histories that people bring" as a key factor. "This is a significant loss," Browning contends, "to practical theology and theological education."[29] As CPE suggests, personal needs distort as much as inspire interpretation. Recognizing and working through this puts research on more honest grounds.

CPE's emphasis on personal formation should not obscure a second point of necessary recollection — the important role of the wider social sphere in the CPE movement from its beginning. The value of social work and social service is not new, arising only with the metaphor of the living web. Keller's efforts in Cincinnati, for example, focused on social service agencies. His new graduate program in applied religion encouraged students to "correlate the social with the spiritual" and to "'tie-up' the practical social approach with the pastoral office."[30]

The pastoral care movement was originally an expression of the social mission of liberal churches to those outside their doors. Pastoral care in hospitals and prisons touched people "who might otherwise not venture near a church or pastor," according to Rodney Hunter, and most counseling centers began as ecumenical ventures of public outreach and witness.[31] Social concern about the destructive nature of a highly industrialized society and the modern specialization of health care motivated the pastoral movement, partly through the influence of the Frankfurt School of social the-

---

28. Thornton, "Clinical Pastoral Education (CPE)," p. 180.

29. Don S. Browning, *A Fundamental Practical Theology: Descriptive and Strategic Proposals* (Minneapolis: Fortress Press, 1991), p. 59.

30. Thornton, "Clinical Pastoral Education (CPE)," p. 178.

31. Rodney J. Hunter, "The Therapeutic Tradition of Pastoral Care and Counseling," in *Pastoral Care and Social Conflict*, ed. Pamela D. Couture and Rodney J. Hunter (Nashville: Abingdon Press, 1995), p. 23; see also Couture, "Pastoral Care and the Social Gospel," in *The Social Gospel Today*, ed. Christopher H. Evans (Louisville: Westminster John Knox Press, 2001), p. 161, and Couture, "Introduction," in *Pastoral Care and Social Conflict*, p. 13.

ory.[32] Chaplains were uniquely positioned, in fact, to offer a prophetic critique of modern medical establishments "from within."[33] In direct contrast with pre-twentieth-century pastoral care that focused on individual moral behavior, early advocates for CPE proposed a more holistic model of healing, recognizing many factors — medical, social, psychological, and spiritual — and seeking cooperation with other health professionals. Wayne Oates, a prominent leader in pastoral theology in the mid-twentieth century, argued that the medical or clinical model of intervention places undue blame on the individual rather than seeing symptoms as a "magnifying glass for the sickness of a community as a whole."[34] Troubled parishioners offer "'a microscopic lab report' on the massive social injustices that need changing," he contended.[35] Churches have the corporate means and position to initiate public transformation. Ordination by definition, Oates maintained, "rules out the luxury of a *purely* private ministry that ignores society."[36] Both Oates and Seward Hiltner actually refused to join the American Association of Pastoral Counselors (AAPC) when it was formed in 1963 because they feared its specialization, its move away from the church, and its proclivity toward private practice. Individual healing cannot take place, as Edward Wimberly said fifteen years later, until it "takes place in the structure of the total society."[37]

In short, through its focus on living documents, the pastoral care movement bequeathed to theological education at least three elements, nicely itemized by Marie McCarthy in a short essay on the movement among Catholics: "increased awareness of the sociocultural factors impacting theology and ministry, increased sensitivity to human needs and concerns, and an increased appreciation of the role of the humanistic sciences in theological education."[38] Another way to say this: CPE played a prophetic or thorn-in-the-side role in theological education on at least three counts. It insisted on the merits of close study of real-life situations,

---

32. Hunter, "The Therapeutic Tradition of Pastoral Care and Counseling," p. 20.

33. Hunter, "The Therapeutic Tradition of Pastoral Care and Counseling," p. 22.

34. Wayne E. Oates, *Pastoral Counseling* (Philadelphia: Westminster Press, 1974), p. 163.

35. Oates, *Pastoral Counseling*, p. 160.

36. Oates, *Pastoral Counseling*, p. 21; emphasis in text.

37. Edward P. Wimberly, *Pastoral Care in the Black Church* (Nashville: Abingdon Press, 1979), p. 21.

38. Marie McCarthy, "Theological Education and the Pastoral Care Movement, Roman Catholic," in *Dictionary of Pastoral Care and Counseling*, ed. Hunter, p. 1262.

it turned to the sciences to enrich such study, and it demanded that close study of the person keep its eye on the social context. Perhaps more needs to be done to recover, celebrate, and revive these initial inclinations.

A Short History of the Living Human Web

Claims about the living web operated as one such corrective reminder of this legacy, whether people realized it or not. Several years ago, in response to a request to describe the "state of the field" for a magazine reporting on several areas of the seminary curriculum, I described one of the notable changes in pastoral theology as a move from "care narrowly defined as counseling to care understood as part of a wide cultural, social, and religious context."[39] I observed that Boisen's 1930s metaphor of the "living human document" as a prime text had mutated into the "living human web." Other scholars also called attention to this development.[40]

One insight gleaned from the web's short history: "web" is less contained and more expansive as a metaphor than "document." Its possible connotations are many, perhaps even too abundant and indescribable to prove concise enough to guide a field or direct clinical and pastoral care. When people use this phrase, its meaning shifts. Consequently, they are not always talking about the same phenomenon. In fact, the metaphor has received at least four different, even if closely related, emphases worth noting and understanding — political/liberationist, ecological/contextual, congregational, and educational.

My own work emphasizes as "most critical" the political or liberationist use of the metaphor and the need to attend to social inequities and injustices that perpetuate suffering.[41] Basically this means identifying the political prejudices or discrimination based on difference that shape health, illness, and care. My own particular social location — as a white

39. Miller-McLemore, "The Human Web and the State of Pastoral Theology," p. 367, and "The Living Human Web: Pastoral Theology at the Turn of the Century," in *Through the Eyes of Women: Insights for Pastoral Care*, ed. Stevenson-Moessner, p. 14; Bonnie J. Miller-McLemore and Brita Gill-Austern, "Introduction," in *Feminist and Womanist Pastoral Theology*, ed. Bonnie J. Miller-McLemore and Brita Gill-Austern (Nashville: Abingdon Press, 1999), p. 13.

40. Graham, *Care of Persons, Care of Worlds*; Patton, *Pastoral Care in Context*; Gill-Austern, "Rediscovering Hidden Treasures for Pastoral Care"; Couture, "Weaving the Web"; Louw, "Pastoral Hermeneutics and the Challenge of a Global Economy."

41. Miller-McLemore, "The Living Human Web," p. 15.

Protestant woman educated in the 1980s at the University of Chicago, where none of the required texts on my doctoral exams included the voices or perspective of women or non-Caucasians — especially provoked this. At that time, few pastoral theological books addressed gender, race, class, or sexual orientation. When I crossed the street and began teaching in a neighboring seminary, I encountered a student body of 50 percent women and people of many colors. So the original version of my essay on the web concludes: "A 'living human web' cannot simply be 'read' and interpreted like a 'document.' Those within the web who haven't yet spoken must speak for themselves." This means attending to the knowledge of the "underprivileged, the outcast, the underclass, and the silenced."[42]

When other people such as Pamela Couture and Larry Graham use the metaphor, they highlight the embedded or contextual nature of all individual problems and the need to challenge the social order. In the same volume where a revised version of my essay on the living web appears, Couture has a chapter titled "Weaving the Web: Pastoral Care in an Individualist Society" that argues for addressing the "social ecological" framework of "public and ecclesial policies" that influence suffering and healing. This requires greater knowledge of public policy and even major overhaul of the "basic commitments" or "theoretical base" of our discipline.[43] As Graham asserts, it is simply "unthinkable" to offer pastoral response to individuals "without a grasp of the horrible ubiquity and devastating consequences" of wider patterns of domination and violence.[44]

Others focus more explicitly on a congregational interpretation. When John Patton described the "paradigm shift" in pastoral theology as a change from the "clinical pastoral" to the "communal-contextual" paradigm, he meant to signal a fresh commitment to the congregation and community as the heart of pastoral care rather than the pastor or pastoral counselor.[45] Brita Gill-Austern uses the metaphor similarly to describe the importance of nurturing the "ecology of care" within congregations.[46] Pastoral theologians in non-Western contexts have long recognized the significance of the community in caregiving.[47]

---

42. Miller-McLemore, "The Living Human Web" and "The Human Web and the State of Pastoral Theology," p. 369.

43. Couture, "Weaving the Web," pp. 95, 103.

44. Graham, *Care of Persons, Care of Worlds*, p. 17.

45. Patton, *Pastoral Care in Context*, pp. 4-5.

46. Gill-Austern, "Rediscovering Hidden Treasures for Pastoral Care," p. 234.

47. See *Pastoral Counseling in a Global Church: Voices from the Field*, ed. Robert J.

Finally, and most recently, religious education professor Rick Osmer has used the metaphor to flag two distinct educational and theological web-like connections, the first between the practical subdisciplines (e.g., care, education, preaching, leadership, and so forth), and the second between practical theology, congregation, and society.[48] As one student said in CPE, "Seminary provides the dots [courses and requirements]; CPE helps connect them." This use of the term *web* to talk about integration reflects the dire need to find better ways to help students connect what they learn in seminary as they move into ministry. It also reflects the immense scholarly and institutional developments that have occurred in the subdisciplines and in practical theology itself since Boisen's time.[49] The web suggests pastoral theology's "response-ability" within the web of church and society, as one chaplain supervisor describes it, for strengthening our ability to respond as God might to those in need, wherever they find themselves.[50] For all these persons, then, the web is useful as a way to highlight the function of CPE and practical theology as a "bridge" between disciplines and between academy, church, and society.

Wicks and Barry K. Estadt (Maryknoll, N.Y.: Orbis Books, 1993); Henry S. Wilson, Judo Poerwowidagdo, and Takatso Mofokeng, *Pastoral Theology from a Global Perspective: A Case Study Approach* (Maryknoll, N.Y.: Orbis Books, 1996); Emmanuel Lartey, *Pastoral Counseling in Intercultural Perspective* (London: Cassell, 1997); Howard W. Stone, "Sojourn in South Africa: Pastoral Care as a Community Endeavor," *The Journal of Pastoral Care* 50, no. 2 (1996): 207-13; Larry K. Graham, "Pastoral Theology as Public Theology in Relation to the Clinic," *The Journal of Pastoral Theology* 10 (2000): 1-17; Louw, "Pastoral Hermeneutics and the Challenge of a Global Economy."

48. Richard R. Osmer, *Practical Theology: An Introduction* (Grand Rapids: Wm. B. Eerdmans, 2007).

49. For example, the following subdisciplines have established societies to promote scholarship and teaching in individual fields: Association of Theological Field Education (1956); North American Academy of Liturgy (1960s); Academy of Homiletics (1965); Association of Professors and Researchers in Religious Education (1970); and Society for Pastoral Theology (1985). Paralleling the effort in the 1980s to move beyond traditional definitions of practical theology as restricted to these subdisciplines and ministerial technique, the national-level Association of Practical Theology (APT) was formed in 1984, building on efforts of prior societies for the practical fields whose history stretches back a half-century. These academic societies, combined with the formation of the International Academy of Practical Theology (IAPT) in 1993, demonstrate an increased level of national and international scholarly interest and production.

50. Both this observation and the one above were made by participants at the East by Northeast ACPE Bi-Regional Spring 2007 Conference.

Stuck in the Web: Problems and Potential

How does the living web as a metaphor enrich and problematize our work? Where are we stuck? As we have seen, we get stuck when we do not remember our own history and when we use one word to mean many things. We are also stuck because we are not sure how to incorporate this idea into our teaching and because we face a new kind of diversity. The metaphor extends the range of our pedagogical accountability to the wider social context and urges political sensitivity to marginalization, power, and voice.

"So which is more important — the person or the web?" Liston Mills, my predecessor at Vanderbilt, asked me after I presented my essay on the living human web during a job interview over a decade ago. On what or whom does the caregiver focus — the person or the web? In other words, how does one push for more adequate health care for indigent families, for example, or reproductive rights for women *and* offer good care and counseling?

Scholars and practitioners in the field have not wholly resolved such questions. I think I partly evaded Mills's question at the time by insisting on the interconnection between person and web and the need to focus on both. But perhaps these two goals are not mutually exclusive. Perhaps we now need to find a fresh way to characterize the field and its focus and say this more clearly: our subject matter is the "living document within the web."

This does change the nature of our teaching and training. For several decades, pastoral theologians have learned well how to teach students about personal interventions in the midst of pastoral crises. Learning how to intervene pastorally on a congregational, social, or cultural level now needs a similar kind of extended attention, discussion, and programmatic strategizing. It will require other means besides individual counsel that pastoral theologians have begun to enumerate, such as active confrontation of unjust situations, public education, public networking, community action in congregations, support groups, preaching on hard biblical passages, and creative use of ritual and liturgy.[51] It will require closer alle-

---

51. See, for example, Don S. Browning, "Mapping the Terrain of Pastoral Theology: Toward a Practical Theology of Care," *Pastoral Psychology* 36, no. 1 (1987): 10-28, and "Pastoral Care and the Study of the Congregation," in *Beyond Clericalism*, ed. Hough and Wheeler; Stephen Pattison, *Pastoral Care and Liberation Theology* (Cambridge: Cambridge University Press, 1994); Francis C. McWilliams, "Pushing Against the Boundaries of Pastoral Care: Clinical Pastoral Education in Urban Ministry Settings," *The Journal of Pastoral Care* 50, no.

giance with other areas of study both internal to theological education, such as religious ethics and religious leadership, and beyond the study of religion, such as social ethics[52] and sociology.[53] It will require change both at the ideological level of new, theologically grounded, radically social constructs of the self and at the institutional level of social organization of training centers and schools.[54]

This broadens the scope of pastoral responsibility and action beyond its conventional boundaries of individual counseling and personal care to the public arena. This also changes the primary pastoral functions of healing, sustaining, guiding, and reconciling and suggests the importance of resisting, empowering, and liberating.[55] This presents new challenges in

---

2 (1996): 151-60; Lartey, *Pastoral Counseling in Intercultural Perspective;* S. St. John Redwood, *Pastoral Care in a Market Economy: A Caribbean Perspective* (Barbados, Jamaica, Trinidad, and Tobago: University of the West Indies Press, 2000); Nancy J. Ramsay, "Navigating Racial Difference as a White Pastoral Theologian," *The Journal of Pastoral Theology* 12, no. 2 (2002): 11-27; Daniel R. Streck and Valburga Schmiedt Streck, "From Social Exclusion to Solidarity: A Latin-American Perspective of Pastoral Practices," *International Journal of Practical Theology* 6, no. 1 (2002): 138-49; Bonnie J. Miller-McLemore, "Pastoral Theology as Public Theology: Revolutions in the 'Fourth Area,'" in *Pastoral Care and Counseling,* ed. Ramsay, and "Pastoral Theology and Public Theology: Developments in the U.S.," in *Pathways to the Public Square: Practical Theology as Public Theology,* ed. Elaine Graham and Anna Rowland (Bloomington, Ind.: Xlibris, 2004).

52. See Archie Smith Jr., *The Relational Self: Ethics and Therapy from a Black Church Perspective* (Nashville: Abingdon Press, 1982).

53. See George M. Furniss, "The Forest and the Trees: The Value of Sociology for Pastoral Care," *The Journal of Pastoral Care* 46, no. 4 (1992): 349-59, and *The Social Context of Pastoral Care: Defining the Life Situation* (Louisville: Westminster John Knox Press, 1994).

54. Barbara McClure, "Toward Pastoral Counseling in a Post-Individualistic Mode: Assessing the Current Model and Making Proposals for Change," Ph.D. dissertation, Emory University, 2003. McClure argues that efforts to change pastoral theology's individualistic focus have stalled out because criticism has remained largely ideational or ideological and has not considered adequately institutionalized teaching and counseling practices. Training in pastoral care and counseling would not eliminate the very important one-on-one work. Instead, it would foster an "action-oriented, participatory model" of care and counseling aimed at challenging narrow, individualistic solutions and encouraging social action. [This dissertation has since been published as *Moving Beyond Individualism in Pastoral Care and Counseling: Reflections on Theory, Theology, and Practice* (Eugene, Ore.: Cascade Books, 2010).]

55. William A. Clebsch and Charles K. Jaekle, *Pastoral Care in Historical Perspective,* 2d ed. (New York: Aronson Press, 1983); Carroll A. Watkins Ali, "A Womanist Search for Sources," in *Feminist and Womanist Pastoral Theology,* ed. Miller-McLemore and Gill-Austern, pp. 51-64.

pastoral formation that stretch beyond understanding intrapsychic and interpersonal dynamics to understanding social and cultural formation. Clinical supervision and training programs will have to consider new means by which to encourage self-awareness of social location and public responsibility. Close work with the individual continues; the individual is simply understood in more complex ways.

Finally, what about the challenge of honoring diverse religious views? Initially the need to recognize diversity within the living human web arose because of the presence of women, people of color, and those of diverse sexual orientation in the graduate classroom and clinic and new awareness of social problems of sexism, racism, and heterosexism. Today we face a growing religious diversity among students and related prejudices, fears, and differences of belief and practice. Religious groups today are divided not just over biblical interpretation and beliefs but also over major social issues, such as gay and lesbian rights, women's roles in family and society, war, gun control, and so forth.

Two observations might help frame reflection on an issue that deserves further attention beyond this article. First, the prior sensitivity to diversity with respect to racism, sexism, and heterosexism in CPE and pastoral theology in general rests on basic political premises of tolerance for difference and justice for the oppressed, premises characteristic of liberal religions and not always shared by more fundamentalist religions. There is in CPE, in other words, a justified commitment to pluralism and justice. So CPE programs can welcome all religious perspectives. But they can do so only if those who confess particular beliefs and practices remain open to hearing and welcoming other views, particularly the views of the downtrodden (e.g., minorities, women, people of color, people of diverse sexual orientations). Inclusion of religious difference should not come at the cost of exclusion of other differences and progress made here.

Second, the self-critical self-awareness that has served as a trademark of CPE's approach has a significant role to play here. This approach is actually a legacy of CPE's reforming Christian heritage, what Paul Tillich called the "critical principle" of Protestantism that protests identifying anything finite with the infinite God.[56] This Protestant principle also has roots in the Jewish tradition (and, for example, its view of the divine as unnamable, the one before whom one shall have no other gods) and resonance in the self-critical aspects of other religious traditions.

56. Paul Tillich, *The Protestant Era* (Chicago: University of Chicago Press, 1948).

This does not mean that everyone must be religiously liberal. It does mean that participants must possess a critical or prophetic or reforming or apophatic element in their religious belief. One must be able to stand back from one's own religious claims, explore where they came from, what moral and religious idolatries they foster, what emotional and political needs they serve, and how they have evolved as one has developed from child to adult, laity to clergy, and insider to one willing to engage one's tradition with outsiders.

Growing Edges for CPE

This investigation of the intersecting aspirations of the living document, web, and theological education suggests some growing edges for CPE in relationship to seminary education.

Connection to Congregations

Situated within non-congregational and non-educational medical institutions, CPE has faced questions about its primary loyalty and purpose throughout its history. This position outside both church and academy inherently creates tensions. Like the Protestant men and Catholic sisters I met in my college foray into CPE, many early leaders were disenchanted with parish ministry and seminary education and happy to be outside both, experimenting with innovative ways of practicing faith and learning. However, according to Edward Thornton, CPE ultimately sees itself as "a function of the sponsoring church or synagogue" and "a part of theological education"[57] despite the tension between the values and needs of its constituencies.

If this is so, CPE needs to continue to give attention to church and synagogue. Money has been a factor. Due largely to lack of funding from congregations, CPE has few programs in the "minister's own clinic, i.e., local congregations,"[58] apart from pilot projects and programs supported by well-to-do communities. Programs struggle to prepare students for congregational ministry standing at a distance. Tension between training peo-

57. Thornton, "Clinical Pastoral Education (CPE)," p. 178.
58. Thornton, "Clinical Pastoral Education (CPE)," p. 181.

ple for the specialized ministry of chaplaincy and training for all ministry settings is "inherent in the setting in which CPE is offered," in Thornton's words.[59] The living document in the parish is not "the person in 'crisis and/or pathology' but rather the person in normal, ordinary, routine pilgrimage of life."[60] Are there ways to strengthen knowledge about and connections to congregational ministry?

Theological Content

CPE has never tried to provide theological content or dogmatic answers based on the texts of specific religious traditions. "ACPE offers a method of interpreting human experience, not a theological construction," Thornton reports.[61]

This is great as far as it goes. It just does not go far enough. The focus on method over content has given CPE immense versatility in attracting people from many religious traditions besides Protestant Christianity. Consequently, however, it has not helped students from all traditions connect back up with such content, much of which is encountered in the seminary classroom and religious communities. So CPE's theological analysis in case analysis often seems arid and empty. It does not reflect the study that most students have had to engage in prior to, during, and after CPE, whether in preparation for priesthood, rabbinate, or other religious office. The failure to bring together the *formal theology* of classroom texts and religious communities and traditions with the *inductive theology* of clinical cases is a huge loss of possible connection and enrichment.

Of course, this is a two-way street. Seminary professors, especially those outside practical theological disciplines, seldom ask students to use case material from their CPE as a basis for engaging the religious texts of a tradition in coursework. Nor do they try to glean from the theological learning that emerged in CPE experiences. In a recent curricular review at our school, we took a baby step in this direction that was actually considered a major innovation: Students in a second semester of constructive theology reflect on an actual *case* from field education using one of the

59. Thornton, "Clinical Pastoral Education (CPE)," p. 179.

60. R. Nace, "Parish Clinical Pastoral Education: Redefining the Human Document," *The Journal of Pastoral Care* 35, no. 1 (1981): 58-68, cited by Thornton in "Clinical Pastoral Education (CPE)," p. 181.

61. Thornton, "Clinical Pastoral Education (CPE)," p. 175.

texts of the course, and students in field education use a specific text from another course in their theological reflection in their verbatims. What are some other fresh ways to bring together the different kinds of theological reflection in these two settings of school and clinic?

Social-Political Context

Little more needs to be said here. Simply to reiterate, the mid-twentieth-century pastoral care and counseling movement focused extensively on the personal. Pastoral theologians and counselors were distinguished by their close attention to an individual's "full uniqueness," made known through intimate, emotional self-disclosure. This emphasis sometimes diverted important attention away from the "public self" and its social responsibilities.[62] Pastoral theology remains accountable to particular persons in need. But now it involves analyzing power and social constructions of selfhood, giving public voice to the socially marginalized, and arguing for alternative theological understandings of the social context as essential for adequate care. Are there imaginative ways to make these new goals manageable while also recognizing the real limitations of time, energy, and expertise by CPE supervisors and professors of pastoral care and the advantages of focusing on the person or the individual in both teaching and pastoral care? This is a huge and challenging question that will not be easily resolved.

Reclamation of Previous Strengths

Recognizing the advantage of focusing on the person brings me back to affirming CPE's unique gifts. What are CPE's gifts to theological education, and how might they be deepened? Never again can persons in pastoral care regard a symptom as unrelated to the social context. But students continue to ask what is unique about pastoral theology as an area of study, and I ask myself that question as well. My answer usually includes recognition of the value of *psychology* in understanding persons and religious practices, the importance of considering the *individual* within a social context, and the focus on *suffering and healing*. Reviewing the history

---

62. Rodney Hunter, "The Personal, Concept of, in Pastoral Care," in *Dictionary of Pastoral Care and Counseling*, ed. Hunter, p. 893.

of the living human document suggests that there is a real place for a continued emphasis on the person as document and on how a person's own background and experience shape interpretation of the context and of those individuals in crisis and in need of care. Such careful, intense, well-supervised self-reflective practice in ministry simply does not happen in theological schools or in other kinds of field placements. I encourage CPE to enrich but not to lose this critical aspect of what it does to enhance theological education.

CHAPTER 3

Pastoral Theology as Public Theology

BACKGROUND AND INTRODUCTION

In 2002, the International Academy of Practical Theology announced its biannual 2003 conference theme. Under the leadership of Elaine Graham as host, the meeting in Manchester, England, was titled "Theology and Public Life: Practical Theology in an Age of Pluralism." As home to the Industrial Revolution and as a city undergoing post-industrial revitalization with religious communities playing a role, Manchester was a good site for this topic. Around the same time, U.S. colleague Nancy Ramsay invited me to join a small group of scholars updating the 1990 *Dictionary of Pastoral Care and Counseling*. Kathy Armistead, the editor at Abingdon Press, did not envision a brand-new dictionary, a job that would require the same massive expenditure of energy as its first run. Instead, the press sought a book on key developments in the fifteen years since the first edition, a book which would double as an appendix to the second edition of the *Dictionary*.

At first, I was surprised by the topic the editors asked me to address: pastoral theology's turn to public theology. Even though the idea did not immediately excite me as a topic for a dictionary supplement — or for a conference, for that matter — it deserved attention in both spheres. The

---

This essay was originally published as "Pastoral Theology as Public Theology: Revolutions in the 'Fourth Area,'" in *Pastoral Care and Counseling: Redefining the Paradigms*, ed. Nancy Ramsay (Nashville: Abingdon Press, 2004), pp. 44-64. Used by permission.

turn to the public did mark a major change in pastoral theology, care, and counseling since the *Dictionary*'s publication. As I discovered when I went to look it up, the entry "public" only appears in the *Dictionary* under the heading "Public/Private Interface," and there it simply redirects readers: "*See* Personal, Sense of."

That pretty much says it all. Mid-twentieth-century pastoral theology focused, sometimes excessively and exclusively, on the personal. My initial indifference to the theme of public theology actually had more to do with familiarity or issue fatigue. Like a fish in water, ten years after describing the shift from document to web, I didn't see anything remarkable in 2002 about the turn to the public. Readers will notice an inevitable repetition of claims across the first three chapters (e.g., pastoral theology as socially oriented from the beginning). Scholars are lucky to have *one* good idea in a career. Naturally we keep circling around it, and people keep asking us to write about it.

My familiarity with the topic of public theology goes further back. During doctoral study at the University of Chicago in the 1980s, use of the term was common. My advisor, Don Browning, called for greater attention to the moral and public context of care as early as his 1976 book, *The Moral Context of Pastoral Care*. The turn to the public suggested by Browning and others was actually one of the key developments supporting the international renovation of practical theology as a discipline in the 1980s by people across theological areas. Scholars took up a mandate issued by Catholic systematic theologian David Tracy in the mid-1980s, naming society, rather than academy or church, as practical theology's primary audience. So I presumed a public focus as an already generally accepted reality in pastoral theology rather than something new.

The following chapter performs three tasks as part of a common assignment shared with other authors who contributed to *Pastoral Care and Counseling: Redefining the Paradigms*. It tells my story (very briefly) and the story of public theology as a general term and as it emerged specifically within pastoral theology. It gives several examples of topics that pastoral theologians have approached with this lens (e.g., sexual violence, family values, and health care). And it considers implications for pastoral care, counseling, and ministerial formation.

Despite the intent of the final section on ministerial implications, I do not think the account of pastoral theology as public theology directly serves seminary students, ministers, chaplains, or counselors — the primary audience of the original *Dictionary*. It is more relevant to scholars who need to understand the history and contemporary forms of this disciplinary change as it shapes teaching and research than it is to pastors and counselors who face the public challenges I name. There are merits of academics writing for other academics, of course. But one casualty is the neglect of other constituencies. Pastoral theologians probably recognize this more acutely than any group in *academe*. Our field has little meaning if it means nothing to those in ministry and congregations. Perhaps the step back in the *Dictionary* supplement from these wider publics is a natural problem in the development of a discipline. But I would love to see a second supplement to the *Dictionary* written with helping professionals and everyday believers more explicitly in mind.

Just as my 1993 article on the living web does not notice the World Wide Web growing in the background, so this chapter has a social context that is visible only in retrospect. The theme of the International Academy conference arose in the aftermath of 9/11. Papers were written with international conflict looming. The conference itself occurred in Britain on the heels of the decision of the United States and Britain to go to war in Iraq. For me, the war hung like a dark cloud over the conference. I was not proud to be an American participant whose first language was English, the *lingua franca* of the conference. I now see my comments in the chapter on the need for a public theology capable of respecting diverse religious traditions and dispelling hatred and fear as all too brief. The need for a public theology that addresses "how people with many differences and serious religious convictions can live together well in an increasingly perilous world" now presses upon us ever more urgently.

I did go ahead and present a paper at the Manchester conference, helped along by my work on the *Dictionary* supplement. A similar chapter appears in the conference volume titled *Pathways to the Public Square: Practical Theology in an Age of Pluralism* (Lit-Verlag). Because the conference volumes have limited circulation, I was grateful for the wider exposure of *Pastoral Care and Counseling* and the *Dictionary*'s second edition. Although the basic content and argument of both essays are similar, the conference chapter has a different subtitle ("Developments in the U.S.") and emphasis. It frames the question about public theology around advances in *practical theology* more than around *pastoral care, counseling, and theology*. As this itself suggests, practical and pastoral theology alike have participated in this turn to the public even though they have focused on distinct subject matter.

———∞∞∞———

Significant shifts in the subject matter of pastoral theology, care, and coun-seling have occurred in the United States in the last decade. Several years ago I described one of the notable changes as a move from "care narrowly defined as counseling to care understood as part of a wide cultural, social, and religious context."[1] Anton Boisen's wonderful 1950s metaphor of "the living human document" as a prime text has mutated into "the living hu-man web." Pastoral theologians and counselors today are more accountable in study and practice to the political and social factors that impinge on peo-ple's lives on local and global levels than previous definitions of the field have acknowledged or allowed. Other scholars have also called attention to this development.[2] My own particular social location as a White main-stream Protestant educated at the University of Chicago in the 1980s espe-cially provoked and reflects this change. Chicago has had a significant im-pact on the move of pastoral theology toward public theology, as has the liberation theology to which I turned when I began teaching in 1986 and found conventional pastoral resources ill-equipped to understand women's plight in sexist societies.

The *Dictionary of Pastoral Care and Counseling* appeared on library shelves in 1990 after many years of organization, just as pastoral theologians rounded the corner on this re-orientation. The only entry in the *Dictionary* under "public" is "Public/Private Interface." And it simply tells readers to "*See* Personal, Sense of. *See also* Prophetic/Pastoral Tension in Ministry; Shame." The former describes the mid-twentieth-century pastoral care and counseling movement as focused on the personal. Pastoral theologians and counselors were distinguished by their close attention to an individual's "full

1. Bonnie J. Miller-McLemore, "The Human Web and the State of Pastoral Theology," *The Christian Century,* 7 April 1993, p. 367, and "The Living Human Web: Pastoral Theology at the Turn of the Century," in *Through the Eyes of Women: Insights for Pastoral Care,* ed. Jeanne Stevenson-Moessner (Minneapolis: Fortress Press, 1996), pp. 9-26.

2. Larry Kent Graham, *Care of Persons, Care of Worlds: A Psychosystems Approach to Pastoral Care and Counseling* (Nashville: Abingdon Press, 1992); John Patton, *Pastoral Care in Context: An Introduction to Pastoral Care* (Louisville: Westminster John Knox Press, 1993); Brita Gill-Austern, "Rediscovering Hidden Treasures for Pastoral Care," *Pastoral Psychology* 43, no. 4 (1995): 233-53; Pamela D. Couture, "Weaving the Web: Pastoral Care in an Individu-alistic Society," in *Through the Eyes of Women,* ed. Stevenson-Moessner; and a decade later, Daniel J. Louw, "Pastoral Hermeneutics and the Challenge of a Global Economy: Care to the Living Human Web," *The Journal of Pastoral Care and Counseling* 56, no. 4 (2002): 339-50.

uniqueness," made known through intimate, emotional self-disclosure. This emphasis diverts important attention away from the "public self" and its social responsibilities.[3] The entry "Prophetic/Pastoral Tension in Ministry" attempts to correct this powerful leaning toward individual subjective experience.[4] The pastoral should not be equated without remainder with the personal. But even here the focus is on the interdependence of "personal health and social improvement," and not yet upon pastoral counseling's public responsibilities or upon the ways in which the very core of the personal is socially constructed.

Rodney Hunter's editorial preface briefly notes that the *Dictionary* appears at a time of historical ferment. Major representatives of the field "have begun to advance new understandings" that challenge its "subjective individualism" as well as its "sexism, racism, psychologism, . . . clericalism, ahistoricism, and lack of moral and religious criticism."[5] Indeed, the attention given to each of these concerns has stretched the field's horizons from a discipline centered primarily on individual well-being to one centered on the close connections between private and public. It is important to document the factors that have contributed to this transformation.

How has pastoral theology gradually shifted in the past two decades toward new subject matter and methods related to public theology? What distinctive contributions do pastoral theologians have to offer? And what does pastoral theology as public theology mean for the discipline's future and for theological education and the church more broadly speaking? This essay will begin the task of answering these questions, exploring factors that have ignited concern about public theology and examples of pastoral theology's reconceptualization as public theology. I will conclude by suggesting ramifications for pastoral care and formation.

"Public theology" is itself a phrase needing more explanation. In broad terms, "public theology" attempts to analyze and influence the wider social order. It has received considerable attention in the past two decades by a variety of theologians wanting to challenge religion's modern privatization and affirm its wider public relevance. Different from civil religion's generic universal appeal, public theology attempts to make a recognizably valid and self-critical claim for the relevance of specific re-

3. Rodney J. Hunter, "The Personal, Concept of, in Pastoral Care," in *Dictionary of Pastoral Counseling and Care,* ed. Rodney J. Hunter (Nashville: Abingdon Press, 1990), p. 893.

4. Harvey Seifert, "Prophetic/Pastoral Tension in Ministry," in *Dictionary of Pastoral Counseling and Care,* ed. Hunter, pp. 962-66.

5. *Dictionary of Pastoral Counseling and Care,* ed. Hunter, p. xii.

ligious beliefs and practices. This entire essay, especially the first section on the trends behind its pastoral emergence, traces ways in which those outside and within pastoral theology have redefined both public theology and the field itself. Many scholars to whom I refer, such as Paul Tillich, use the term "practical theology" more than "pastoral theology" to talk about the broad area in theological study that encompasses pastoral care, counseling, preaching, educating, and so forth, and their academic disciplines, such as pastoral theology, homiletics, and religious education. This conventional definition of practical theology, however, has itself undergone revision in light of developments in public theology. Its mission now extends well beyond ministerial practices to theological engagement of public issues of significant practical and pastoral consequence, such as child welfare and economic justice.

My focus throughout is primarily on the United States. This does not mean that a similar movement of pastoral theology toward public theology is not occurring in other places around the world. Although space does not allow close examination of the latter, I will attempt to indicate critical places of intersection and parallel developments outside the United States. There are also important intercultural differences in conceptualizing public theology that require more attention than I can give them. The U.S. context is especially shaped by divergent interpretations of the First Amendment's constitutional separation of church and state. Public theology looks different in other countries where religion is either established by the state (e.g., Britain) or disenfranchised (e.g., China). Moreover, whereas European practical theologians are troubled about Christianity's decline, many mainstream pastoral theologians in the United States worry more about the growth of conservative evangelical forms of Christianity. Even mainstream Christianity still does fairly well in some parts of the country, such as the South. An extensive religious pluralism, accentuated by the liberalization of immigration laws in the 1960s, also characterizes U.S. society. Although the dominant religion of the past — Christianity — professes to do and have a "theology," many dominant religions in other societies do not make such claims or seek a public theology.

Trends behind the Push for Public Theology

Several economic, political, and cultural developments external to religious and theological studies have encouraged the development of public theology in the United States. On the economic front, major funding organizations, such as the Lilly Endowment, Pew Charitable Trusts, and the Henry R. Luce Foundation, have made Christianity's public role a major initiative, supporting programs that have engaged significant public dilemmas, such as the family. These organizations have funded innumerable conferences, projects, publications, and university centers aimed at bringing together academy, church, and the wider public around a number of pressing issues.[6] In part, these foundations are concerned about the post–civil rights decline in Protestantism's social activism and, as troubling, the new Christian Right's increased prominence and ability to influence society through large conglomerate operations. The desire is not for a return to mainline hegemony but for greater understanding of Christianity's proper role in public policy formation in an increasingly diverse and religiously plural society.

On a more political front, politicians and public intellectuals have renegotiated the delicate lines of state and church separation by proposing an enhanced role for "faith-based organizations" and "faith-based initiatives" supported by taxes to deliver social services. Moreover, some public spokespersons talk about the need to bring faith perspectives to bear on national moral issues, such as overcoming racism or strengthening the family, where government efforts have essentially failed. The expectation that religious communities might provide both service and values has increased pressure on theologians to reconsider religion's public role.

Finally, religion's de-privatization is also related to cultural shifts. Public intellectuals no longer have faith in the power of value-free science or even the state and the market to solve all social dilemmas. Problems, such as the growing poverty of the Two-Thirds World and international interreligious conflict, call for serious deliberation. Instead of labeling particular religious beliefs as arbitrary, unimportant, or irrational, many people suggest that they now have a legitimate, even if necessarily delimited, place in public discourse and decisions.[7] New talk about "civil society" is not a return to a generic civil religion but a reclaiming of the importance of beliefs and practices in all their particularities. Public theology offers

6. See, for example, Bonnie J. Miller-McLemore, "The Public Character of the University-Related Divinity School," *Theological Education* 37, no. 1 (2000): 49-61, written as a result of participation in a consultation sponsored by the Association of Theological Schools.

7. Stephen L. Carter, *The Culture of Disbelief: How American Law and Politics Trivialize Religious Devotion* (New York: Anchor Books, 1994).

critical and constructive reflection upon the civil relevance of particular religions.[8]

While not usually acknowledged, dire pastoral needs stand behind the aspiration for public theology. As sociologist Robert Wuthnow remarks, the debate about religion and civil society is not so much about "preachers in politics or even about First Amendment freedoms; it is about the quality of social life itself."[9] The lure of public theology arises from deeper questions about how people with many differences and serious religious convictions can live together well in an increasingly perilous world. Christians, among other religious groups, face complex dilemmas as they attempt to live lives shaped by religious values. Dilemmas previously considered private and sometimes trivial, such as whether to get married and have children or how to dispose of one's trash, are now seen as having unavoidable national and even international implications. Religious leaders can no longer bracket pastoral needs from public consideration.

Theological trends internal to religion have also influenced pastoral theology toward public theology. In particular, debates between Chicago's David Tracy and Yale's George Lindbeck about Christianity's place in society have had a considerable role. Ronald Thiemann, for example, pursued such questions to distinguish his position from the more sectarian approaches of Lindbeck and Stanley Hauerwas.[10] He describes more than defines public theology as a theology "based in the particularities of the Christian faith while genuinely addressing issues of public significance."[11] Victor Anderson condenses descriptions of Thiemann, William Joseph Buckley, and Roger Shinn to characterize public theology as the "deliberate use of distinctively theological commitments to influence substantive public debate and policy."[12]

These wide-ranging definitions, however, could potentially refer to almost any socially conscious theological position, as the rest of Ander-

---

8. Linell Elizabeth Cady, *Religion, Theology, and American Public Life* (Albany: State University of New York Press, 1993), pp. 21-25.

9. Robert Wuthnow, *Christianity and Civil Society: The Contemporary Debate* (Valley Forge, Pa.: Trinity Press International, 1996), p. 2.

10. Ronald F. Thiemann, *Constructing a Public Theology: The Church in a Pluralistic Culture* (Louisville: Westminster John Knox Press, 1991), p. 12.

11. Thiemann, *Constructing a Public Theology*, p. 19.

12. Victor Anderson, "The Search for Public Theology in the United States," in *Preaching as a Theological Task: World, Gospel, Scripture*, ed. Thomas G. Long and Edward Farley (Louisville: Westminster John Knox Press, 1996), p. 20.

son's essay illustrates. My interest here is to focus on one place where the term got codified in the Chicago-Yale debate. In the debate, the Chicago school gets accused of compromising Christianity's distinctiveness in its revisionist efforts to participate in public deliberations. The Yale school, on the other hand, is charged with lacking a genuine public theology in its postliberal attempts to preserve the unique language and rules of the Christian narrative and community. Thiemann and others, such as William Placher and David Kelsey, have responded to such allegations with their own versions of how a confessing Christian who takes Christianity as authoritative can effectively address political and social issues.[13]

Several prominent scholars in the "Chicago school," such as Tillich, Tracy, James Gustafson, and Don Browning, influenced pastoral care and counseling toward public theology through their sway over doctoral students. They joined a gestalt of interest in the public church, public ministry, and public intellectuals among other early twentieth-century Chicago scholars such as Shailer Mathews, and more recent figures such as Martin Marty, Robin Lovin, and Clark Gilpin.[14] Tillich's correlational method and his theology of culture[15] had a fundamental impact through his influence on his Chicago colleague, Seward Hiltner, and on Hiltner's students, such as Browning, and even on Browning's students, such as Pamela Couture and myself. More recently, Tracy's efforts to refine the correlational method and to assert the essential public responsibility of fundamental, systematic, and practical theology in an increasingly pluralistic world provided powerful impetus for pastoral theology to develop its public contributions.[16] Most pastoral theologians and counselors today employ some

13. William Placher, "Revisionist and Postliberal Theology and the Public Character of Theology," *The Thomist* 49, no. 3 (July 1985): 392-416; and David Kelsey, "Church Discourse and Public Realm," in *Theology and Dialogue: Essays in Conversation with George Lindbeck*, ed. Bruce D. Marshall (Notre Dame: University of Notre Dame Press, 1990).

14. See, for example, Martin E. Marty, *The Public Church: Mainline, Evangelical, Catholic* (New York: Crossroad, 1981); *Religion and American Public Life*, ed. Robin Lovin (New York: Paulist Press, 1986); and Clark Gilpin, *Public Faith: Reflections on the Political Role of American Churches* (St. Louis: CBP Press), and *A Preface to Theology* (Chicago: University of Chicago Press, 1996).

15. Paul Tillich, *Systematic Theology*, vol. 1 (Chicago: University of Chicago Press, 1951), and *Theology of Culture* (London: Oxford University Press, 1959).

16. David Tracy, *The Analogical Imagination: Christian Theology and the Culture of Pluralism* (New York: Crossroad, 1981), and "The Foundations of Practical Theology," in *Practical Theology: The Emerging Field in Theology, Church, and World*, ed. Don S. Browning, pp. 61-82 (San Francisco: Harper & Row, 1983).

version of this liberal model, however modified by revisionist, liberation, or postmodern theology.

Liberal views of the public, however, came under attack by liberation theology. In Rebecca Chopp's words, "While liberal-revisionist theologians respond to the theoretical challenge of the nonbelievers among the small minority of the world's population who control the wealth and resources in history, liberation theologians respond to the practical challenge of the large majority of global residents who control neither their victimization nor their survival."[17] The public is no longer the modern scientific audience that worried Tillich or the scientifically disenchanted postmodern audience that plagues Tracy. Instead, liberation theologians address those previously marginalized, silenced, and erased from social history, political voice, and theological mediation.

Liberation theology began in the early twentieth century in Latin America as a Roman Catholic movement focused on liberating the poor from systematic economic exploitation and securing justice for the oppressed.[18] Since its inception, liberation theory has been taken up by Protestants, the women's movement, black power consciousness-raising, German critical theory, and others around the world and applied to many kinds of social oppression besides poverty, such as racism, sexism, heterosexism, and colonialism. It seeks to free or liberate those who suffer from social inequities and oppression not merely through discourse but through practical grassroots strategies for social structural change. Problems previously defined along private lines as signs of personal weakness and moral turpitude — for example, drug use, alcoholism, depression, poor academic performance, and even failed marriages or delinquent children — are redefined in broader public and political terms as a result of unjust patriarchal social structures and racist ideologies. Recent feminist, post-structuralist, and postmodernist theory takes the premise that "the personal is political" to a new level: The personal is not only political; it is socially constructed. That is, power relationships in history and society

17. Rebecca S. Chopp, "Practical Theology and Liberation," in *Formation and Reflection: The Promise of Practical Theology,* ed. Lewis S. Mudge and James N. Poling (Philadelphia: Fortress Press, 1987), pp. 121, 128.

18. Gustavo Gutiérrez, *A Theology of Liberation: History, Politics, and Salvation,* trans. and ed. Sister Carida Inda and John Eagleson (Maryknoll, N.Y.: Orbis Books, 1973); Juan L. Segundo, *The Liberation of Theology,* trans. John Drury (Maryknoll, N.Y.: Orbis Books, 1976); and Leonardo Boff and Clodovis Boff, *Introducing Liberation Theology* (Maryknoll, N.Y.: Orbis Books, 1987).

construct the self. Theologians must take seriously the social location of the self, the ways language constructs reality, and the impact of power on language and subjectivity.

While the Chicago school affected central pastoral theologians who came within its orbit, liberation theology's transformation of pastoral theology was more widespread. Few, if any, contemporary pastoral theologians or counselors have escaped its impact. Although the influences on pastoral theology are many, liberation theology helped transform pastoral theology toward public theology by identifying the ways in which society indelibly constructs selfhood in oppressive ways, by redefining the nature of the public, and by demanding a prophetic reorientation toward it.

Developments in Pastoral Theology

Different Representations of the Changes

Pastoral theologians have described the development of pastoral theology as public theology in different ways. In 1993, in an introductory overview, John Patton announced a "paradigm shift."[19] Prior to the mid-twentieth century, pastoral theology adhered to a "classical paradigm" that, as Rodney Hunter puts it, "concentrated primarily and often exclusively on the gospel message."[20] Clergy diagnosed problems in religious terms and responded with Christian solutions, often relying on rituals, such as prayers, the laying on of hands, or confession and absolution of sins.

Both the "clinical pastoral" and the "communal-contextual" paradigms have appeared in the last half-century, each one representing what Patton sees as a major redefinition of focus and method. The clinical paradigm that arose mid-century and shaped the *Dictionary* drank deeply from the wells of modern psychology, using its insights into emotional dynamics and its therapeutic techniques to shape a new kind of spiritual care attentive to the inner needs of individuals in crisis. Diagnosis relied heavily upon psychological categories, amended with theological reflection, and

19. John Patton, *Pastoral Care in Context: An Introduction to Pastoral Care* (Louisville: Westminster John Knox Press, 1993), pp. 4-5.

20. Rodney J. Hunter, "Spiritual Counsel: An Art in Transition," *The Christian Century*, October 2001, p. 20.

solutions almost always included some kind of empathic listening, however modified by more directive techniques.

The most critical aspect of the new communal-contextual paradigm, according to Patton, is its fresh commitment to the community rather than the pastor or pastoral counselor as the heart of pastoral care. The audience is "no longer . . . the male clergyperson of European ancestry." Both clergy and laity — "all sorts and conditions of God's people" — offer care in a variety of contexts and Christian communities.[21] Pastoral care has yet to tap the community's rich resources, according to Brita Gill-Austern. She uses the metaphor of web to describe the importance of nurturing the interconnections or the "ecology of care" within congregations.[22] Pastoral theologians in non-Western contexts have long recognized the significance of the community in caregiving.[23] Conferences overseas in the last decade have actually convinced scholars in the U.S. about this.

In contrast to Patton and Gill-Austern, I use the image of the web to depict a major change in the field as a whole, and I describe that change in terms of a modification in primary subject matter from "the living human document" to "the living human web."[24] My focus is less on who offers care (clergy or laity) or how care is offered (hierarchically or collaboratively) and more on what care involves today. Genuine care now requires understanding the human document as necessarily embedded within an interlocking public web of constructed meaning. Clinical problems, such as a woman recovering from a hysterectomy or a man addicted to drugs, are always situated within the structures and ideologies of a wider public context and never purely interpersonal or intrapsychic. Where Patton credits Vatican II and ecumenism as major factors broadening pastoral care's context, I see liberationist perspectives as more instrumental. Criticism of pastoral care's individualism and the necessity of confronting systems of domination have come largely from feminist, black, and — more recently — Asian, Latino/a, and African theologies. To think about pastoral care from this perspective requires prophetic,

---

21. Patton, *Pastoral Care in Context*, p. 3.

22. Gill-Austern, "Rediscovering Hidden Treasures for Pastoral Care," p. 234.

23. Emmanuel Lartey, *Pastoral Counseling in Inter-cultural Perspective* (Frankfurt: Peter Lang, 1987); *Pastoral Counseling in a Global Church: Voices from the Field*, ed. Robert J. Wicks and Barry K. Estadt (Maryknoll, N.Y.: Orbis Books, 1993); Henry S. Wilson et al., *Pastoral Theology from a Global Perspective* (Maryknoll, N.Y.: Orbis Books, 1996).

24. Miller-McLemore, "The Human Web and the State of Pastoral Theology," and Miller-McLemore, "The Living Human Web."

transformative challenge to systems of power, authority, and domination that continue to violate and oppress individuals and communities nationally and internationally.[25]

Pastoral theology brought to theory-bound doctrinal theology a wealth of vivid, concrete human experiences through a new tool. The case study or verbatim, developed in clinical programs in the mid-twentieth century and shaped by the medical and social sciences, focused closely on particular interchanges and emotional, theological dynamics between and internal to an individual and a caregiver. Even today one rarely finds pastoral theological reflection that does not include some kind of "case" material. What has changed, however, is the way in which the case is understood, analyzed, and positioned. Pastoral theologians now work hard to locate material publicly, as part of a wider social and cultural web.

In 1992, Larry Graham called for a new "psychosystems approach" to replace what he named the previous "existential-anthropological mode." He saw in the latter a progressively "widening split between care of persons and care of the larger environments in which persons live."[26] In addition to liberation theology, he finds family systems theory and process theology suggestive. Just as liberation theology contends that troubled persons, families, and groups reflect serious problems in the cultural context, so also family systems therapy argues that individual symptoms are simply signs of serious dysfunction in the larger family social system.

A few years later, Pamela Couture also described a new "social ecological foundation" for pastoral care and counseling which positions personal suffering within its wider "web." She worries in particular about the individualistic premises that almost completely determine economic and political policy. She finds expertise in public policy, history, and particular religious traditions requisite for an adequate publicly oriented pastoral theology. In her words, "to offer adequate care beyond the 1990s we will want to become as expert about public policies affecting the family and health as we are about the workings of various personality types." Nothing

25. See, for example, Stephen Pattison, *Pastoral Care and Liberation Theology* (Cambridge: Cambridge University Press, 1994); *The Arts of Ministry: Feminist-Womanist Approaches*, ed. Christie C. Neuger (Louisville: Westminster John Knox Press, 1996); *Liberating Faith Practices: Feminist Practical Theology in Context*, ed. Denise Ackermann and Riet Bons-Storm (Leuven, the Netherlands: Peeters, 1998); and *Feminist and Womanist Pastoral Theology*, ed. Bonnie J. Miller-McLemore and Brita L. Gill-Austern (Nashville: Abingdon Press, 1999).

26. Graham, *Care of Persons, Care of Worlds*, p. 12.

less than a reformulation of the "basic commitments of our discipline" is needed.[27] When pastoral theology attempts to engage the "social context, economics, cultural meanings and practices" in its understandings of pastoral care, it has affinity with other kinds of public theology.[28]

Historical Complications

Every historical typology has the danger of oversimplification. Pastoral theology and care has never been quite as individualistically or personally focused as often portrayed. Historian E. Brooks Holifield's frequently cited history of pastoral care, for example, depicts the discipline's development primarily along one declining trajectory — the widely lamented growth in American individualism.[29] Anxieties about the church's love affair with psychology and counseling led him to characterize the field as evolving from an emphasis on salvation in the premodern world to a modern obsession with self-realization. Yet even the early twentieth-century pastoral care movement held other social and religious commitments in tension with psychology. Moreover, a great deal has transpired since Holifield completed the book. His otherwise well-documented history positions women, slaves, and "others" primarily as the objects of care, rarely as caregivers, and seldom as the source of new ideas. Many pastoral theologians and counselors have been attracted to new psychologies that are not inevitably individualistic even if focused on the individual, as evident, for example, in family systems theory, feminist psychology, and theories of selfhood in object relations.

One could even argue that the original turn to psychology by pastoral theologians included a public dimension. As Hunter notes, "pastoral counseling represents a profoundly important expression of the liberal churches' social mission." By this, he means that pastoral counselors opened their doors as inclusively as possible. Pastoral counseling "reaches persons who might otherwise not venture near a church or pastor," and who might benefit from religious wisdom without the fear of "proselytizing or moralistic judgment."[30] Most counseling centers began as ecumeni-

27. Couture, "Weaving the Web," p. 103.

28. Larry Kent Graham, "Pastoral Theology as Public Theology in Relation to the Clinic," *Journal of Pastoral Theology* 10 (2000): 6, 9.

29. E. Brooks Holifield, *A History of Pastoral Care in America: From Salvation to Self-realization* (Nashville: Abingdon Press, 1983).

30. Hunter, "Spiritual Counsel," p. 23.

cal ventures and still pride themselves on their receptivity of believers and nonbelievers. While indiscriminate tolerance loses sight of specific Christian beliefs, this does not negate the ideal of public service and witness with which many centers began.

Hunter's positive assessment of the therapeutic tradition's public inclination is quite different from Holifield's. Hunter argues that a social concern about the destructive nature of a highly industrialized society motivated the pastoral movement from the beginning, partly through the influence of the Frankfurt School of social theory. The movement changed the previously narrow pastoral focus on individual moral behavior into a holistic view of healing that involves persons' needs in their totality. Chaplains were actually uniquely positioned to offer a prophetic critique of modern medical establishments "from within."[31] And they realized a level of public cooperation with other health professionals that challenged the modern specialization of health care long before medicine's recent fascination with spirituality. The movement also made a prophetic social demand on churches to engage more authentically as a community. Indeed, "when done artfully," therapeutic intervention enhances a person's public moral capacities and self-examination. Therapeutic confrontation itself can be "a powerful and significant moral practice."[32]

By the early 1980s, Edward Wimberly and Archie Smith had already made a clear case for the communal and public nature of pastoral care and the inextricable connection of social ethics and psychological therapy in the black church.[33] Perhaps ahead of his time, Smith testifies powerfully to the ways in which the social oppressions of racism create personal suffering and call for care that involves social activism. And Wimberly's *Dictionary* essay on black American pastoral care reminds readers that black pastoral theology has had a long commitment to attending to "social structures and conditions" and to the "corporate" dimensions of both church and wider society.[34]

---

31. Rodney Hunter, "The Therapeutic Tradition of Pastoral Care and Counseling," in *Pastoral Care and Social Conflict,* ed. Pamela D. Couture and Rodney J. Hunter (Nashville: Abingdon Press, 1995), p. 22.

32. Hunter, "The Therapeutic Tradition of Pastoral Care and Counseling," p. 25.

33. Edward P. Wimberly, *Pastoral Care in the Black Church* (Nashville: Abingdon Press, 1979); and Archie Smith Jr., *The Relational Self: Ethics and Therapy from a Black Church Perspective* (Nashville: Abingdon Press, 1982).

34. Edward P. Wimberly, "Black American Pastoral Care," in *Dictionary of Pastoral Counseling and Care,* ed. Hunter, pp. 93-94.

As these observations indicate, the history of pastoral theology as public theology is more complex than one might guess initially. One might even argue, as does Couture, that "twentieth-century education in pastoral care had its roots in the social gospel, and after intense work on various forms of personal relationships in the decades after World War II, has made natural strides toward returning to that heritage."[35] An edited volume, *Pastoral Care and Social Conflict*, makes precisely this point. The "core identity" of the field lies in the ways in which "its twin emphases on persons and society . . . inform theology."[36] Current problems with sustaining a public voice for pastoral theology go right back to the bifurcation of an effort that, with Walter Rauschenbusch's immersion in New York soup-kitchen ministry, once joined social ethics and pastoral care as two sides of the same coin.

Whether this return to the social gospel is as "natural" or as steady as Couture hopes waits to be seen. Some of the difficulty has to do with a tension notable from the beginning between those who supported the development of pastoral counseling as a specialized ministry, such as Carroll Wise and Howard Clinebell, and those who thought this was fraught with problems. Both Seward Hiltner and Wayne Oates disagreed strongly with pastoral counseling as a "private" practice. Instead, they insisted it remain located within the church and refused to join in the formation of the American Association of Pastoral Counselors (AAPC) in 1963.[37]

Oates and others protested the medical or clinical model of intervention precisely on the grounds that it distorted the intricate relationship between private and public. It placed undue blame on the individual rather than seeing symptoms as a "magnifying glass for the sickness of a community as a whole."[38] Personal needs arose precisely out of some kind of public failure. In fact, pastors who do counseling stand in a unique position. They have "'a microscopic lab report' on the massive social injustices that need changing."[39] Moreover, church structures provide the corporate means and position to initiate public transformation. The very nature of

---

35. Pamela D. Couture, "Pastoral Care and the Social Gospel," in *The Social Gospel Today,* ed. Christopher H. Evans (Louisville: Westminster John Knox Press, 2001), p. 161.

36. *Pastoral Care and Social Conflict,* ed. Couture and Hunter, p. 13.

37. E. Brooks Holifield, "Pastoral Care Movement," in *Dictionary of Pastoral Counseling and Care,* ed. Hunter, p. 848.

38. Wayne E. Oates, *Pastoral Counseling* (Philadelphia: Westminster Press, 1974), p. 163.

39. Oates, *Pastoral Counseling,* p. 160.

ordination "rules out the luxury of a *purely* private ministry that ignores society [and] removes the distinctly prophetic element from the counseling."[40] Perhaps more needs to be done to recover some of these initial inclinations in the field toward public theology.

Pastoral Theology Turns Public

This interest in retrieval of public dimensions itself, however, is what makes the contemporary situation distinctive. Figures like Oates still regarded clinical training as one of their mainstays. Broadly speaking, two primary factors distinguish the most recent move toward public theology: concern about the public silence of mainstream Christianity on key social issues, and awareness of the serious limitations of the pastoral focus on the individual alone. Recent pastoral theologians and counselors have attempted to shape public discourse on a wide range of dilemmas that have critical social and political implications, such as health care, the family debate, welfare policy, Western economic imperialism, and domestic violence. This shift in focus goes against the grain of the stereotypical understanding of pastoral care and counseling as merely focused on personal, spiritual care of parishioners and of practical theology as only knowledgeable about clerical skills.

Explicit ideas about pastoral theology as public theology made their way into the field initially through Browning. Both his earlier work and a later publication position pastoral care as a ministry of the church within the world.[41] In the former, Browning actually says pastoral care has become "impaled" upon the division between "private and public" in its focus on personal problems without "sensitivity to . . . larger social-ethical questions."[42] Restricting pastoral care to assistance to individuals in crisis fails to socialize believers to particular understandings of the church, and, most important for this essay, ignores the critical task of interpreting modern culture and articulating a social ethic relevant to public problems.[43]

Perhaps more influential than James Gustafson's advocacy of secular sciences in understanding the church was his portrayal of the church as a

40. Oates, *Pastoral Counseling*, p. 21; emphasis in the text.
41. Don S. Browning, *The Moral Context of Pastoral Care* (Philadelphia: Westminster Press, 1976), and *Religious Ethics and Pastoral Care* (Philadelphia: Fortress Press, 1983).
42. Browning, *The Moral Context of Pastoral Care*, p. 17.
43. Browning, *The Moral Context of Pastoral Care*, p. 21.

"community of moral discourse,"[44] a phrase Browning adopts as his own in his claim that pastoral theology is responsible for public moral understandings. For Browning, pastoral care occurs as part of the church's dialogical mission related to both faith and society. It is not simply care of persons but also must involve care of systems as well as attention to the dominating public or cultural constructions of care.

This stance evolved in response to two problems — pastoral restriction to what Edward Farley called the "clerical paradigm" (or pastoral care defined around the skills of individual clergy)[45] and pastoral substitution of psychology for theology. A pastoral theology whose subject matter includes "more encompassing social systemic and policy issues in care" broadens the range of pastoral care to the "care of the congregation and the care of the laity, both for one another within the congregation and for the world around the congregation." It requires skills not just in facilitating care within the local church but also in creating strategies to shape society and culture.[46]

The pastoral task with regard to the world is twofold. First, in the manner of a good theology of culture, it involves discerning the quasi-religious norms and assumptions behind all acts of care, pastoral and secular alike. Second, it requires articulating alternative public norms derived from the Christian tradition. The task here is not just "to state the norms . . . for the faithful (although certainly for them), but also to determine whether these norms have general public meaning, that is, whether they have general significance even for those who are not explicitly Christian."[47]

Although this shows the influence of the Chicago school, Browning largely fails to credit liberation theology. In Romney Moseley's *Dictionary* entry on liberation theology and pastoral care, he succinctly captures the change it inspires:

44. James M. Gustafson, *The Church as Moral Decision Maker* (Philadelphia: Pilgrim Press, 1970), pp. 83-97.

45. Edward Farley, "Theology and Practice outside the Clerical Paradigm," in *Practical Theology,* ed. Browning, p. 26, and *Theologia* (Philadelphia: Fortress Press, 1983), p. 85.

46. Don S. Browning, "Mapping the Terrain of Pastoral Theology: Toward a Practical Theology of Care," *Pastoral Psychology* 36, no. 1 (Fall 1987): 14-15. See also Browning's *Religious Ethics and Pastoral Care,* p. 19, and "Pastoral Care and the Study of the Congregation," in *Beyond Clericalism: The Congregation as a Focus for Theological Education,* ed. Joseph C. Hough Jr. and Barbara G. Wheeler (Atlanta: Scholars Press, 1988), pp. 103-18.

47. Don S. Browning, "Pastoral Theology in a Pluralistic Age," in *Practical Theology,* ed. Browning, pp. 194-95.

From a liberationist's perspective one should conceive of pastoral care fundamentally as the care of society itself. That is, one should understand the needs and hurts of individuals in their primary relationships — the primary focus of pastoral care and counseling — in terms of the macrosocial power relationships of domination and exploitation. For these larger relationships structure selfhood, personal experience, and individual behavior in fundamental, if usually unrecognized, ways. Thus pastoral care must always engage in a mutually critical conversation with theological and social scientific methods informed by an emancipatory praxis.[48]

Even though Moseley's article and a few others on feminist and black theology appear in the *Dictionary*, the volume reflects an assimilation mentality characteristic of early stages of consciousness-raising in general. It insightfully includes new voices, inviting a number of African-American men and European American women to contribute articles on race and gender with the hope of fostering greater interest in and attention to these issues. But by and large, pastoral theologians could not foresee the major conceptual redefinition of pastoral theory that has occurred since the *Dictionary*'s publication, particularly in regard to its public responsibilities posed by particular marginalized groups. The allure of the clinical pastoral method tended to obscure the emerging significance of these other movements and newer literatures.

A great deal has happened under liberation theology's influence that goes beyond the public theology of most pre-1985 texts, as the next section will demonstrate. Today most pastoral theologians recognize problems of sexism and racism as central considerations in conceptualizations of pastoral care. In an impressive survey of women's contributions over the past four decades, Kathleen Greider, Gloria Johnson, and Kristen Leslie, in fact, contend that women "contributed precisely and significantly" to the evolution of the new contextual communal paradigm. Under this fresh rubric, pastoral theologians give more attention to "caring communities and the impact of context on human experience and care" than in the typical clinical pastoral psychology of the 1970s and 1980s.[49] But more important for

48. R. M. Moseley, "Liberation Theology and Pastoral Care," in *Dictionary of Pastoral Counseling and Care*, ed. Hunter, p. 646.

49. Kathleen Greider, Gloria Johnson, and Kristen Leslie, "Three Decades of Women Writing for Our Lives," in *Feminist and Womanist Pastoral Theology*, ed. Miller-McLemore and Gill-Austern, p. 22.

public theology, women address the ekklesia, the human community in God writ large, as distinct from the institutional church. That is, women are more prone to address "more culturally diverse 'congregations'. . . beyond the walls of church buildings," such as hospices, hospitals, prisons, and universities. They attempt to bring Christian ideas into public deliberation over such issues as service, covenant, ritual, and the common good.[50]

Beyond the United States, others argue for similar changes in language, pastoral identity, and action. Danilo and Valburga Streck assert that within the incredibly diverse mosaic that shapes the heritage of those in Latin America, pastoral theologians have a mandate to create social solidarity among those excluded from political, economic, and religious power.[51] Similarly, British practical theologian Stephen Pattison claims that only a "socio-politically aware and committed pastoral care" can liberate the field from its "therapeutic captivity."[52] Dutch practical theologian Riet Bons-Storm and South African practical theologian Denise Ackermann presume that social analysis of the construction of gender is absolutely necessary for adequate pastoral care. In many of the chapters in their edited book, this leads almost inevitably to concerns about corporate justice and communal action.[53] And John Redwood contends that pastoral care in the Caribbean must attend to economic pressures and take an active stand against insidious capitalistic greed and hopelessness in the face of poverty.[54]

New Subject Matters of Public Relevance

Pastoral theology as public theology has appeared most distinctively around prominent public issues that have irrevocable pastoral dimensions. Although the issues are many, I mention briefly three prominent concerns as examples: violence, families, and public health. Pastoral theologians have played a public role in reshaping understandings of sexual violence as

50. Greider et al., "Three Decades of Women Writing for Our Lives," pp. 27-28.

51. Danilo R. and Valburga Schmiedt Streck, "From Social Exclusion to Solidarity: A Latin American Perspective of Pastoral Practices," *International Journal of Practical Theology* 6 (2002).

52. Pattison, *Pastoral Care and Liberation Theology*, p. 221.

53. Ackermann and Bons-Storm, *Liberating Faith Practices*, p. 5.

54. S. St. John Redwood, *Pastoral Care in a Market Economy: A Caribbean Perspective* (Barbados, Jamaica, Trinidad, and Tobago: University of the West Indies Press, 2000).

not simply a personal or familial issue but also a social and religious matter.[55] It has little to do with sexual desire and everything to do with destructive perversion of social power as a consequence of sexist and racist ideologies and institutions. James Poling's work on abuse nicely illustrates the transformation.[56] Repeatedly, he uses the phrase "personal, social, and religious" to describe the necessary scope of pastoral work. He, along with Marie Fortune and others, has helped institute regular programs of education and policy formation that have raised the consciousness of the wider public.

Poling names this pastoral issue a specifically public and theological problem closely related to Christian views of sacrifice, God's omnipotence, human impotence, and women's necessary submission. Moreover, pastoral theology must give public voice to those least heard. Indeed, "those with the least power can reveal the most"[57] — a major premise from which Poling has not wavered as he has ventured into explorations of the evils of racism and market capitalism.[58] Pastoral care thus requires responding on each of these public levels. It must challenge public ideals and structures, listen to those publicly silenced, and reconstruct religious beliefs and practices that perpetuate major social problems such as racism, sexism, and economic exploitation.

The ideology of the family as a private, patriarchal institution has contributed significantly to the problem, hiding abuse from public view. Other pastoral theologians have answered the call of Poling for a "reformulated family mythos" that establishes the equality between the sexes and the rights of children.[59] Couture's work and my own work on mothers and

55. See, for example, Nancy J. Ramsay, "Sexual Abuse and Shame: The Travail of Recovery," in *Women in Travail and Transition: A New Pastoral Care,* ed. Maxine Glaz and Jeanne Stevenson-Moessner (Minneapolis: Fortress Press, 1991); Karen Lebacqz and Ronald G. Barton, *Sex in the Parish* (Louisville: Westminster John Knox Press, 1991); Marie M. Fortune and James N. Poling, *Sexual Abuse by Clergy: A Crisis for the Church* (Decatur, Ga.: Journal of Pastoral Care Publications, 1994); and *Violence against Women and Children: A Christian Theological Sourcebook,* ed. Carol J. Adams and Marie M. Fortune (New York: Continuum, 1995).

56. James N. Poling, *The Abuse of Power: A Theological Problem* (Nashville: Abingdon Press, 1991).

57. Poling, *The Abuse of Power,* p. 14.

58. James N. Poling, *Deliver Us from Evil: Resisting Racial and Gender Oppression* (Minneapolis: Fortress Press, 1996), and *Render unto God: Economic Vulnerability, Family Violence, and Pastoral Theology* (St. Louis: Chalice Press, 2002).

59. Poling, *The Abuse of Power,* p. 133.

children and our joint research on the family along with Browning, project director of a major Lilly Grant on Religion, Culture, and Family, offer another important instance of pastoral theology going public.[60] On each account — with mothers, fathers, children, and families — the case is made that Christianity has a formative role to play in shaping public discourse and policy.

The family project involved cross-disciplinary conversations between those in pastoral theology and scholars from historical, ethical, systematic, and biblical disciplines and the publication of a series of books geared to a wider public audience. The capstone volume of the initial grant, *From Culture Wars to Common Ground,* authored by five pastoral theologians all schooled at Chicago, draws on the other books to develop a publicly and pastorally sensitive evaluation of and response to contemporary family dilemmas.[61] As with violence, families are understood in "psychocultural-economic" terms. They are not just psychological realities based on human needs or private interests grounded in individual freedoms. They are cultural, religious, and economic institutions with wide-ranging public ramifications. Consequently, the book considers a diversity of public voices that have dominated the family debate. And the concluding chapter articulates not only what churches can do internally to strengthen families but what they must do in the realm of public policy, such as advocating for family-friendly workplace policy and critiquing distorted media images.

To make a public difference, one can distance but not remove particular Christian claims from their specific Christian location, such as claims about equal regard as part of God's covenant love for creation. The goal at its broadest level is to "define the role of religion" in "America's struggle to strengthen its families."[62] More specifically, the book attempts to fashion a new public family ethic of equal regard or mutuality that has relevance not

60. Pamela D. Couture, *Blessed Are the Poor? Women's Poverty, Family Policy, and Practical Theology* (Nashville: Abingdon Press, 1991), and *Seeing Children, Seeing God: A Practical Theology of Children and Poverty* (Nashville: Abingdon Press, 2000); Bonnie J. Miller-McLemore, *Also a Mother: Work and Family as Theological Dilemma* (Nashville: Abingdon Press, 1994), and *Let the Children Come: Revisioning Childhood from a Christian Perspective* (San Francisco: Jossey-Bass, 2003); and Don S. Browning et al., *From Culture Wars to Common Ground: Religion and the American Family Debate* (Louisville: Westminster John Knox Press, 1997).

61. Browning et al., *From Culture Wars to Common Ground.*

62. Browning et al., *From Culture Wars to Common Ground,* p. viii.

only for confessing Christians but also for wider society at a time of great cultural need. It is not triumphalist about Christianity's virtues — at best "'a treasure in earthen vessels.'" But Christianity, carefully re-interpreted, does have distinctive contributions to make to public ideals of democracy within families.[63] Lifting up its gifts to believers and nonbelievers alike does not require finding generally agreeable truths that just happen to correspond with the Bible or whittling down religious convictions to a generic love or justice. Rather, one mines the richness of particular Christian attempts to understand love to determine what, if anything, they might add in all their specificity to the greater good. In fact, the hope is to contribute to a religious and cultural revolution on par with past social revolutions with which Christianity had a major role.[64] As reiterated boldly in an appendix to the second edition (in 2000), ultimately the book tries to "overcome the marginalization of Christian theology in public discourse" and establish the value of Christian norms.[65]

Finally, as a last and significant example, a great deal has happened in health care to propel pastoral care and counseling into public theology. Pastoral counseling's presence has changed dramatically in the last ten years in terms of both its public prominence and its health policy activities. As Roy Woodruff, fifteen-year executive director of the AAPC, remarked in personal conversation, "Five or six years ago, I had to explain pastoral counseling and the AAPC. I virtually never have to do so anymore."[66]

Rather than distinguishing pastoral and secular counseling, Woodruff now spends more time clarifying the difference between the interfaith efforts of pastoral counseling and the more conservative, biblically literalist, evangelistic perspective of the newly formed American Association of Christian Counselors. At this point, pastoral counseling's looser organizational church connections — something about which Seward Hiltner and others originally worried — have proved an advantage. The wider public appreciates pastoral counseling and the AAPC precisely because of its recognition of diversity and its efforts to inform rather than convert the public to any particular Christian position.

63. Browning et al., *From Culture Wars to Common Ground*, p. 3.

64. See Browning et al., *From Culture Wars to Common Ground*, p. 25; Kyle A. Pasewark and Garrett E. Paul, *The Emphatic Christian Center: Reforming Christian Political Practice* (Nashville: Abingdon Press, 1999), p. 306n.97.

65. Browning et al., *From Culture Wars to Common Ground*, p. 341.

66. Personal communication, 18 July 2002.

A major turning point came with the Clinton administration's efforts to reform the U.S. health care system in the early 1990s. It drew pastoral counselors and their representatives onto public roads previously less traveled. The AAPC and pastoral counseling are now regularly recognized simply because representatives showed up for meetings and kept showing up. Recently, the AAPC has also begun responding differently when national tragedies and issues arise, such as September 11 and the sexual abuse scandal in the Catholic Church. The AAPC makes public pronouncements and receives phone calls from news organizations for comment and reflection.

A prime motivation for showing up on Capitol Hill was to establish pastoral counselors as recognized health care providers. To garner additional support for its proposal that pastoral counselors be included in Medicare's roster of approved caregivers, the AAPC commissioned a national political survey of one thousand likely voters. Following up on a 1992 Gallup Poll, Greenberg Quinlan Research asked respondents about the connections between their religious beliefs and counseling. Results revealed not only clear affirmation of the links but also confirmed that a high percentage of respondents "would prefer to seek assistance from a mental health professional who recognizes and can integrate spiritual values into the course of treatment."[67] More people choose pastoral counselors and others with religious training than any other type of counselor.

Whereas the AAPC had no representatives on the Hill when the *Dictionary* appeared, today lobbying efforts have become a prime responsibility. Regular legislative consultation occurs between pastoral counseling representatives, legal advocates, and members of Congress. Pastoral counselors attempt to influence health care spending in faith-based initiatives, working, for example, to obtain a counseling training grant for minority persons. Other efforts in public theology have arisen at the state level with the growth of managed care. Pastoral counselors have sought licensure and third-party payments as professionals with comparable credentials to other recognized clinicians. Perhaps most symbolic of the overall change, pastoral counseling appeared for the first time in the government publication of *Mental Health, the United States, 2002* alongside other mental health professions.[68]

Changes in chaplaincy are a bit less dramatic, perhaps because chaplains have had a longer-standing investment in public issues related to health

67. Greenberg Quinlan Research (2000). See http://www.aapc.org/survey.htm.
68. See http://www.mentalhealth.org/cmhs/Mental HealthStatistics/default.asp.

care than pastoral counselors. There are, however, still markers of advances in public theology and recognition. For the first time in the late-1980s and early 1990s, the Joint Commission on the Accreditation of Healthcare Organizations (JCAHO) required institutions to establish that they care for patients' spiritual needs. Current lobbying efforts on the part of the Association of Clinical Pastoral Educators (ACPE), in fact, concern exactly how this requirement can be met. According to Teresa Snorton, executive director of the ACPE, the organization hopes to get JCAHO to specify clinically trained individuals as providers.[69] Similarly, in recent years the ACPE has worked with Medicare to establish clinical pastoral education as equivalent to medical residency in providing care and with the federal Health Care Financing Administration (HCFA) to specify pastoral care as a reimbursable expense. In a final ruling in 2001, after a nearly two-decades-long governmental process, including debate about the separation of church and state, the HCFA named clinical pastoral education and pastoral counselors as allied health care professionals and included them in allowable Medicare costs.[70]

Recently, the five largest chaplaincy organizations worked together on a document that establishes chaplaincy's role and importance in public health care.[71] The paper draws on empirical studies to demonstrate the health-related benefits of religious practices and the positive difference of professionally trained chaplains. There are also changes in the ways that chaplains interact with the public. With the relatively new recognition of palliative care's significance, physicians and others have become more receptive to the religious care offered by chaplains. The *Journal of Pastoral Care* regularly features essays deliberating on the legal, political, and moral implications of such dilemmas as assisted suicide, withholding nutrition and hydration, AIDS, and hospice care.

Growing public interest in spirituality opens up doors to chaplains. Some have begun to use the terminology of spiritual, religious care rather than pastoral care to describe their work, not as a cheap imitation of popular trends but to make it more accessible to the wider public. Pastoral care is often equated with particular traditions, whereas spiritual care is more inclusive of diverse perspectives.[72] Of course, this change in terminology is

---

69. Personal communication, 1 August 2002.

70. L. White, "Medicare Passthrough Update," *ACPE News* (March/April 2001): 2-3.

71. "Professional Chaplaincy: Its Role and Importance in Health Care," ed. Larry Vandecreek and Laurel Burton, *The Journal of Pastoral Care* 55, no. 1 (2001): 81-97. (See http://www.professionalchaplains.org/index.aspx?id=229.)

72. See Herbert Anderson, "Spiritual Care: The Power of an Adjective," *The Journal of*

not without its hazards and problems. Sensitivity to other religious cultures, for example, requires knowledge and training. Eclectic spirituality often ignores to its detriment the value of specific institutional commitments, religious communities, and particular traditions and rituals. Nonetheless, the use of the term "spiritual care" signals a move toward a more inclusive, publicly accessible activity than "pastoral care," which has traditionally been associated primarily with ordained Christian ministry.

Implications for Pastoral Care, Counseling, and Formation

What are some of the specific implications of these moves toward public theology for the practice of pastoral care and counseling and the formation of its practitioners? With "the living human web," on what or whom does the caregiver focus — the person or the web? Scholars in the field have not wholly resolved this question. For several decades, pastoral theologians have learned well how to teach students about pastoral interventions in the midst of personal crises. Pastoral theology has spawned congregational programs focused almost entirely on individual care, such as Stephen Ministries and Parish Nursing. Such programs consume significant resources to reach a relatively small population in need. They do not do much at a public level, such as challenging God imagery that perpetuates abuse or addressing harmful health and welfare policies.

Learning how to intervene pastorally on a congregational, social, and cultural level now needs the same kind of extended attention, discussion, and programmatic strategizing. It will require closer allegiance with other areas of study, such as social ethics, and investment in other forms of practice, such as public networking and community action. Ministers will now have to know how to analyze communal resources, enter and organize communities for action, and balance ministry to individuals in crisis and social advocacy.[73]

This presents new challenges in pastoral formation, adding to the already demanding need to understand intrapsychic and interpersonal dy-

---

Pastoral Care 55, no. 3 (2001): 233-37; and Peter L. VanKatwyk, "Pastoral Counseling as a Spiritual Practice: An Exercise in a Theology of Spirituality," *The Journal of Pastoral Care and Counseling* 56, no. 2 (2002): 109-19.

73. See, as a good example, Frances C. McWilliams, "Pushing against the Boundaries of Pastoral Care: Clinical Pastoral Education in Urban Ministry Settings," *The Journal of Pastoral Care* 50, no. 2 (1996): 151-60.

namics the need to understand social location and identity, political policies, and public responsibilities. Emmanuel Lartey's "intercultural approach" nicely illustrates this new attempt to bridge the wisdom in both
"private care" or individual counseling and "public struggle" or social liberation praxis as the two crucial bookends to adequate pastoral care.[74] Distinct from pre-1990 texts that focused almost solely on the former, Lartey's
work spends time exploring alternative methods that require pastoral engagement in concrete experiences with the poor, situational analysis, and
social transformation. Nancy Ramsay's work on systemic white complicity
in endemic racism also reflects this shift in focus and method. Identifying
and resisting collusion on individual, institutional, and cultural levels is a
moral mandate within the classroom, requiring a second look at curricula
and syllabi, a rigorous investigation of one's own racial and cultural history, and a good grasp of social analysis and models of anti-racist action.[75]

Clinical supervision and training programs certified by the AAPC,
the ACPE, and other bodies will now have to consider such methods as
part of clinical training and determine new means by which to encourage
and assess self-awareness of social location and social identity. Pastoral
identity now involves more than intrapsychic awareness, psychological insight, and religious interpretation. It demands cultural and political sensitivity, social activism, understanding of the congregation as a social institution, and faithful, sometimes prophetic, convictions.

Close work with the individual continues; the individual is simply
understood in new, possibly more complex ways. Psychology and counseling remain significant, but their singular status has changed. Most pastoral
theologians today believe that pastoral caregivers must add to their repertoire other disciplines, such as political science, economics, sociology, and
feminist theory.[76] These other bodies of knowledge help disclose not just
how individuals function but how congregations and the wider public
shape individuals. Affecting public rhetoric and policy issues that determine the health of the human web is as important as addressing impedi-

74. Lartey, *Pastoral Counseling in Inter-cultural Perspective*, pp. 103-4.
75. Nancy J. Ramsay, "Navigating Racial Difference as a White Pastoral Theologian,"
Journal of Pastoral Theology 12, no. 2 (2002): 24-25.
76. See, for example, Couture, *Blessed Are the Poor?*; George M. Furniss, "The Forest
and the Trees: The Value of Sociology for Pastoral Care," *The Journal of Pastoral Care* 46, no.
4 (1992): 349-59, and *The Social Context of Pastoral Care: Defining the Life Situation* (Louisville: Westminster John Knox Press, 1994); and *Feminist and Womanist Pastoral Theology*, ed.
Miller-McLemore and Gill-Austern.

ments to individual emotional well-being. This broadens the scope of pastoral responsibility and action beyond its conventional boundaries of individual counseling and personal care to the public arena.

Redefinition of pastoral theology as public theology also means new delineation of pastoral care's central functions of healing, sustaining, and guiding as defined by Hiltner and then refined by William Clebsch and Charles Jaekle to include reconciling.[77] Certainly emphasis on individual healing, sustaining, guiding, and reconciling still stands as critical to good pastoral care. But again and again in publications over the last decade one hears new phrases that point toward a different set of priorities with greater public ramifications: resisting, empowering, and liberating.

Resistance, empowerment, and liberation all entail a deconstruction of limited definitions of reality and a reconstruction of new views of the world and one's valued place within it. Although these new functions do not replace the prior ones or exhaust the implications of pastoral theology as public theology, they provide a good sense of the direction toward which pastoral theology as public theology points caregivers. These functions provide alternative means to achieving healing, guidance, sustenance, and reconciliation that require fresh public understanding and response.

Carroll Watkins Ali was among the first to argue explicitly that previous metaphors are inadequate when considered within the African-American context. It is almost ridiculous to talk about sustenance when many poor black women face more serious questions of sheer survival. And reconciliation as previously understood ignores core questions of public compensation for and correction of racism's injustices. Pastoral care aimed at reconciling individuals is "premature and futile until the inequities between Blacks and Whites have been removed" and the dominant culture finds a way to acknowledge and atone for the "dehumanizing injustices" of the "last four hundred years."[78] Individual healing cannot take place until, as Wimberly said more than two decades ago, it "takes place in the structure of the total society."[79]

Other pastoral theologians have made similar claims more recently in pastoral situations of sexual abuse, domestic violence, and depression.

77. Seward Hiltner, *Preface to Pastoral Theology* (New York: Abingdon Press, 1958); and William Clebsch and Charles Jaekle, *Pastoral Care in Historical Perspective*, 2d ed. (New York: Aronson, 1983).

78. Carroll A. Watkins Ali, "A Womanist Search for Sources," in *Feminist and Womanist Pastoral Theology*, ed. Miller-McLemore and Gill-Austern, p. 55.

79. Wimberly, *Pastoral Care in the Black Church*, p. 21.

With abuse, rushed forgiveness short-circuits recovery and avoids the inevitable rage that deserves recognition. Effective pastoral care must "be broader than care for those immediately affected."[80] In depression, "cultural and theological messages of worthlessness and weakness need to be dispelled."[81] And for the battered woman, the "basic need is empowerment."[82] While these are only examples, they represent the public language that has grown common in pastoral scholarship of the last decade. It is rare to find an article today that does not refer to social advocacy or to a common range of interventions that involve greater reach than individual counsel, such as "breaking the silence" within congregations and beyond, active confrontation of abusive behavior, false stereotypes, and unjust situations, public education, support groups, preaching on hard biblical passages that deal with these issues (e.g., the rape of Tamar), and more conscientious pastoral use of ritual and liturgy in public situations as far-ranging as those of abuse, divorce, and child-rearing.

Pastoral work on new public fronts alters its position in what has been narrowly conceived as the theological school's "fourth area." As defined by nineteenth-century theologian Friedrich Schleiermacher in his attempt to make a place for Christian theology in the modern university, the first area is the Bible. Many schools in the United States, including the one in which I teach, began as Bible schools. The typical curriculum adds Christian history and systematic theology as areas two and three. In some university settings where it is difficult to legitimize doctoral studies in religion, the "fourth area," with its greater proximity to the church, is the first to drop out. Even in self-standing seminaries, all three areas are commonly considered prior to and more fundamental than the fourth area, which is, despite a couple of decades of protest, still often characterized as the application of what is learned in the other three arenas to ministerial practice. As a rule, pastoral theologians have not been happy with this designation, especially when it implies marginalization, devaluation, and trivialization and ignores the theological construction that occurs within pastoral theology. Asserting the public value of pastoral insights — pastoral theology as public theology — participates most immediately in the protest against such misunderstandings.

80. Ramsay, "Sexual Abuse and Shame," p. 121.

81. Christie C. Neuger, "Women's Depression: Lives at Risk," in *Women in Travail and Transition,* ed. Glaz and Stevenson-Moessner, p. 158.

82. Joann M. Garma, "A Cry of Anguish: The Battered Woman," in *Women in Travail and Transition,* ed. Glaz and Stevenson-Moessner, p. 136.

Many implications of this shift remain to be seen over the course of the next decade. While some of the *Dictionary*'s articles reflect initial hints of the changes described in this chapter, significant developments have occurred since its publication that reflect broader trends in society at large. Today, changes in the cultural climate, as illustrated by the increased receptivity to spirituality as a part of health, have opened up new public space for pastoral care and counseling. Pastoral theology remains accountable to particular persons in need. But now it involves analyzing power and social constructions of selfhood, giving public voice to the socially marginalized, and arguing for alternative theological understandings of the social context as essential for adequate care not only in congregations but also in society at large. Its unique contribution to public theology will lie precisely in its ability to use what it knows best — intimate understanding of individual religious experience and its religious significance — to shape wider public policies and ideals.

CHAPTER 4

Practical Theology: A Definition

BACKGROUND AND INTRODUCTION

So far the chapters in Part I have focused primarily on pastoral theology, understood within U.S. Protestantism as that branch of practical theology focused on pastoral care and counseling. Even though my job title has varied and the area in which I have worked has gone by different names, I have basically served since 1986 as a faculty member in pastoral theology.

Why change the subject to practical theology, then, and include this chapter? The short answer is that in the last five years, editors of two dictionary projects, *The New Westminster Dictionary of Christian Theology* and *The Encyclopedia of Religion in America,* invited me to contribute entries on the term. A more complete answer, however, requires mention of two key developments that have shaped my recent work.

In 2003-2004, on behalf of the Graduate Department of Religion at Vanderbilt University, I co-chaired a planning grant, "Teaching for Ministry," funded by the Lilly Endowment, Inc., aimed at creating a new doctoral program to prepare students for seminary teaching. An interdisciplinary group of faculty met bi-weekly for the academic year, reading literature in practical theology and theological education, listening to invited experts, and talking about components of a new program.

This essay was originally published as "Practical Theology" in *Encyclopedia of Religion in America,* ed. Charles Lippy and Peter Williams (Washington, D.C.: Congressional Quarterly Press, A Division of SAGE Publications, 2010), pp. 1739-43. Used by permission.

There were times that year and in years since that our department received a grant for a ground-breaking curriculum in theology and practice when I tired of hearing colleagues and newly admitted students ask, "What *is* practical theology anyway?" I explained, but not always easily or successfully. This is not a simple question, and practical theology is not an easily defined category.

Eventually I came up with a more thorough answer, as the chapter below illustrates. I was greatly helped by a second foundational experience — participation in a consultation on Practical Theology and Christian Ministry that began in 2003, also funded by Lilly. It gathered a group of about twenty scholars and ministers from a variety of disciplines and traditions a couple of times a year for several years. Its most obvious outcome was an edited book, *For Life Abundant: Practical Theology, Theological Education, and Christian Ministry* (Wm. B. Eerdmans, 2008).

Of more significance for me, our work together changed my understanding of practical theology in two fundamental ways. First, discussing each other's research, syllabi, and accounts of ministry re-oriented my view of practical theology's aim. Disciplinary expertise is always highly valued. But its ultimate aim lies beyond disciplinary concerns in the pursuit of an embodied Christian faith. Second and related to this, I gained a clearer picture of the multivalent nature of practical theology. Practical theology as a term refers to at least four distinct enterprises with different audiences and objectives, the two just named (a *discipline* among scholars and an *activity of faith* among believers) and two common uses elaborated below (a *method* for studying theology in practice for theological educators and ministers and a *curricular area* of subdisciplines in the seminary).

In other words, the invitation to write this chapter came at an incredibly propitious time. It was only because of the Lilly consultation that I found myself in a position to write a definitional entry on practical theology and accept an offer in 2008 to edit *The Blackwell Companion to Practical Theology*, which uses the four-part definition as its organizational infrastructure. As with the idea of the living web, the essay below owes a heavy debt to colleagues. Indeed, each time I read it, I hear the words of others, in particular Dorothy Bass, Kathleen Cahalan, Craig Dykstra, Serene Jones, James Nieman, and Ted Smith.

There were, of course, other earlier influences worth mention. Before I graduated from Chicago in 1986, I benefited indirectly from the birth of a new doctoral program in practical theology and the efforts of Don Browning, one of its leaders, to redefine the term as he worked toward what became one of his pivotal books in 1991, *Fundamental Practical Theology*. Since the early 1990s I have served in leadership positions in two practical theology societies (the Association of Practical Theology and the International Academy of Practical Theology).

More generally, the first decade of the twenty-first century brought changes that made scholarship in practical theology especially valuable. Vanderbilt's program in theology and practice is not a doctoral program in practical theology *per se*, even though students may minor in the discipline. It includes a range of innovative components designed to engage students from all areas of doctoral study in formation for seminary teaching. However, the discipline of practical theology — its ideas and methods — was absolutely crucial in the program's creation and remains important to its future and the future of graduate study elsewhere. New programs in practical theology and religious practices have sprouted up in the last decade at influential institutions such as Emory, Duke, and Boston University in the United States and the University of Manchester in Britain. Interest in practice has attracted a divergent array of religion and theology scholars. Many people across disciplines are now talking about matters central to practical theology, such as the use of the social sciences to study religious experience, the use of ethnography to study theology, the investigation of material practices, the study of culture as a central category for analysis, and the location of scholarship in its personal and social context. In 2005, for the first time in its history, the largest academic society for the study of religion in North America, the American Academy of Religion, accepted a proposal for a program unit in practical theology, a genuine mark of progress for the field. In short, the time was ripe for disciplinary redefinition.

The benefit of the following definition is its descriptive rather than prescriptive intent. Although I sketch the history of the term, the real contribution of the essay, in my view, is its fourfold definition. I try to describe the varying contexts and ways in which people commonly use the term. Identifying the different uses helps straighten out the confusion when people use the same term for different purposes. I also try to distinguish its use in the United States, other countries, and religious traditions as well as its connection to other disciplinary areas, such as religious studies and systematic theology.

Those who find definition helpful may wonder about the difference between the chapter below and my entry in *The New Westminster Dictionary*, which was written first (and has yet to go to press). Its threefold definition of practical theology as a *field, method,* and *activity* of faith does not distinguish practical theology as a *curricular area* (with a variety of subdisciplines) from practical theology as a *discipline* (with a minority of scholars who self-identify primarily as practical theologians). I now find this oversight odd because practical theology as a collection of subdisciplines is one of the most common ways the term is used, especially in Protestant seminaries. But the earlier entry does a better job of exploring what the assorted uses of the term share in common (e.g., a focus on local, concrete religious experience and its transformation). And it says explicitly what I discovered in collegial conversation: Contrary to popular opinion, the plurality of purpose and definition is not a problem. It is a "strength and attribute inherent in the very nature of the term 'practical' itself."

Practical theology is a term commonly used in Christian theology for a general way of doing theology concerned with the embodiment of religious belief in the day-to-day lives of individuals and communities. Its subject matter is often described through generic words that suggest movement in time and space, such as *action, practice, praxis, experience, situation, event,* and *performance.* Its subject is also associated with action-oriented religious words, such as *formation, transformation, discipleship, witness, ministry,* and *public mission.* In its focus on concrete instances of religious life, its objective is both to understand and to influence religious wisdom or faith in action. Ultimately, practical theology is normatively and eschatologically oriented. That is, it not only describes how people live as people of faith in communities and society. It also considers how they might do so more fully both in and beyond this life and world.

In its focus on the tangible and local, practical theology joins efforts in the United States to recover the sensate, material side of religion obscured by modern interest in the scientific and philosophical study of beliefs. Where historians and sociologists of religion have begun to examine *lived religion,* those who engage in practical theology investigate *lived theology,* extending interest in rituals and practices to questions about how theology or knowing and loving the divine takes shape in everyday life and how everyday life influences theology. Some practical theologians, particularly in Europe, limit practical theology to a discipline involving the empirical study of religion. But most people value its wider normative aims to enrich the life of faith for the sake of the world.

Catholics in general and many Protestants outside the United States use the terms *pastoral theology* and *practical theology* interchangeably. This is less true for Protestants in the United States, where *pastoral theology* primarily refers to reflection on pastoral care and counseling. Pastoral and practical theology share historical roots but have diverged considerably. Figures such as Seward Hiltner (1909-1984) and Anton Boisen (1876-1965), often cited by Europeans as forerunners of modern practical theology, are seen by most scholars in the United States as dedicated to care and counseling. Although *pastoral* also refers to ministry in general, it is associated largely with the special activity of care and shepherding. The Protestant use of *practical theology* has more affinity with what some Catholics have called *contextual* or *local theology.*

Practical theology has also been contrasted with systematic or doctrinal theology, which traditionally centered on proclaimed beliefs. Although this contrast reinforces a problematic split between theory and practice, it does highlight a difference in emphasis. Practical theology as a discipline has a longer history of attention to faith in the midst of daily life. This difference has come under increasing pressure as practical theologians attend to theory, systematic theologians attend to practice, and people in other disciplines and settings also seek to understand faith in action. Although such nuances in definition have evolved largely within Christianity, analogous interest in lived faith or practiced theology exists in other religions.

History and Context

Practical theology shares with biblical, historical, and doctrinal theology a common academic trajectory in the German Protestant university of the 1800s that fostered the development of theology as a *Wissenschaft* (science) and field of study increasingly removed from ecclesial and creedal interests. Christian theology in general has never been solely a matter of abstract truths. It has always included guidance for faithful living and attention to obtaining salvation. But with the dawning of the modern era, people such as Friedrich Schleiermacher (1768-1834), the father of liberal theology, sought to justify theology as a scientific discipline deserving of a place within the modern university. In an effort to keep pace with the spirit of the age, theology in Europe and North America became increasingly focused on a descriptive history and philosophy of ideas, distancing itself from religious practice and seeking a systematic coherence and rigor on par with the sciences.

On U.S. soil, this view of theology as objective, critical, and academic rather than evangelistic, experiential, confessional, ecclesial, and practical became institutionalized in the late nineteenth- and early twentieth-century structures of graduate seminary education. Other traditions besides Protestantism and some religions, such as Reform Judaism, have felt the impact of this development and have adopted similar educational divisions between practical and classical disciplines. Eastern Orthodoxy, Catholicism, and Anglicanism sustained greater appreciation for practice through rich liturgical traditions, development of mystical and spiritual theology, and convictions about worship as the heart of theology. Nonetheless, these traditions have struggled to find a place for practical theology. Ambivalence about practice has deeper roots in twelfth-century scholasticism, the Aristotelian model of theology as a theoretical science that attempted to reconcile Christianity with secular philosophy, and the development of cathedral universities. As the center of theological study shifted from households and small religious communities to large monasteries and then universities, debates over whether theology was a practical orientation to lived faith or a speculative contemplation of divinity aimed at knowledge for its own sake were decided largely in favor of the latter. In Catholicism, practical theology has sometimes been limited to a pastoral and moral theology devoted to ministerial oversight and training priests for the office of confessor.

Since the middle of the twentieth century, however, several developments fostered a climate of unrest and a rebirth of national and international interest in enriched understandings. Key among the influences was the rapid growth in the social sciences, psychology in particular, and their usefulness in understanding experience. With the insights of psychology and case study methods, early pastoral theologians Boisen and Hiltner argued for "the living human document" as a subject of study comparable to written texts and for "operation-centered" theology as deserving a place alongside "logic-centered" theology. Theology emerges out of experience, and practical theology has content not derived solely from historical and philosophical theology. Correlation, understood as a fluid dialectic between human situation and religious message, emerged as an influential method in support of this claim and became a staple in the growth of practical theology. Critical social theory in Europe in the 1930s and, three decades later, Latin American liberation theology and related developments, such as black and feminist theology, demanded that theology begin with grassroot encounter, address the needs of the oppressed, and work for social change. During the last decades of the twentieth century, philosophy itself took a turn toward the practical among divergent intellectuals, such as Jürgen Habermas, Alasdair MacIntyre, Pierre Bourdieu, and Michel de Certeau, giving scholars dependent on European continental philosophy the language and methods to validate practice as a worthy object of study.

Practical theology has attracted wide attention in recent years through fresh publications, renewed academic societies, new graduate programs, and interest in lived theology among those outside the academy. Its boundaries and horizons are being stretched further by developments in the study of practice, empirical methods, the analysis of power and social location, religious pluralism, and globalization. Practical theology is recognized, like cultural anthropology, "for the delicacy of its distinctions, not the sweep of its abstractions," to borrow Clifford Geertz's words.[1] But its definition quickly moves beyond thick description. Practical theology is ultimately a normative project guided by the desire to make a difference in the world.

Practical Theology in the Twenty-First Century

As a result of its history, the term *practical theology* gets used today in at least four different ways. It refers to (1) an activity of believers seeking to sustain a life of reflective faith in the everyday, (2) a curricular area in theological education focused on ministerial practice, (3) an approach to theology used by religious leaders and by teachers and students across the curriculum, and (4) an academic discipline pursued by a smaller subset of scholars to sustain these three enterprises.

An Activity of Believers

At its most basic level, practical theology is performed by those who thoughtfully seek to embody deep convictions about life and its ultimate

1. Clifford Geertz, *The Interpretation of Cultures* (New York: Basic Books, 1973), p. 25.

meaning in the midst of ordinary and extraordinary circumstances. Few laypersons actually use the word *theology* to describe this activity. Professing Christians, for example, might talk about this more belief-based or "confessional" practical theology as following Jesus or living out the gospel of love and justice. Professing Jews might say that faith requires *tikkun olam,* repair of the world. Practical theologians in more secular contexts, such as Britain, have argued that this dialogical and largely Christian understanding of practical theology as reflective enactment of faith is useful to all people, Christian or not, who wish to connect beliefs and values to practice and life. It is particularly relevant in public service and educational institutions where religious practices and convictions play a significant role.

A Curricular Area

Seminary deans, students, and graduates of programs in theological study usually have a more specific meaning in mind when they speak of practical theology. They use the term to refer to a distinct area of the curriculum aimed at enhancing religious life through congregational and public ministry. Practical theology is concerned with religious leadership broadly construed to include not only local congregations but also other forms of social service and public influence. Several subspecialties are conventionally grouped under the rubric of "ministerial" practical theology, such as pastoral care, homiletics, worship, mission, evangelism, leadership, and education. Common commitments to teaching a practice for the sake of ministry unite these specialties. But in many cases, the claims and methods of practical theology as an academic discipline operate implicitly, and faculty may not recognize the broader practical theological assumptions that organize their teaching and research. Even when practical theology does constitute the larger domain within which faculty understand their work, academics are more likely to identify themselves by their specialty as scholars in homiletics or pastoral care, for example, than as practical theologians.

An Approach to Theology and Religious Faith

Since its re-emergence in the 1980s, practical theology designates more than the theology of the pastorate or the methods and objectives that unite the ministerial subdisciplines. Building on its three-century history in university and seminary education, scholars have expanded its meaning and mission. Practical theology seeks religious knowledge in the service of a larger *telos* (end or aim) of enriching the life of faith in the world. It is not only a branch of study, but a way of doing theology attentive to lived faith. This definition, aimed at re-orienting theological education toward its ultimate end, challenges conventional divisions between classical and practical disciplines, academy and congregation, and theory and practice. Despite the organizational and structural usefulness of such divisions, they have led to a misperception of theological education as either merely about acquiring technical pastoral skills (the clerical paradigm) or merely about acquiring cognitive knowledge of history and doctrine (the academic paradigm). In reality, all theology is practical at heart, and practical theology, redefined more expansively, has the good of the larger whole in mind. It involves the study of faith toward the end of divine flourishing in human life and the world.

Questions about the usefulness of Scripture, history, and doctrine arise here not in a narrow utilitarian sense but with this larger purpose in mind. This goal-oriented or teleological practical theology is an endeavor intentionally oriented toward particular goods and ends in which many different people — believers, clergy, and faculty across the curriculum — have some investment. In fact, all theological disciplines have or should have, as the influential twentieth-century Catholic theologian Karl Rahner argued, an element of practical theology contained within them. Some recent systematic and historical theologians with convictions about liberation or interest in studying theology through new means, such as ethnography, have understood the boundaries of their work as falling within this wider realm, if not the discipline, of practical theology. In turn, believers and religious leaders are also significant partners in a theology whose aim in the study of Scripture, doctrine, and life is faithful practice. Their efforts to embody faith are not lower-level versions of a more sophisticated academic theology, simplified for the masses. Rather, they possess a theological intelligence and imagination unique to the concrete demands of practice, and they thereby contribute to the general construction of religious tradition and community. This definition obviously extends the boundaries of the term to include faculty, religious leaders, and believers who may not consider themselves practical theologians and are not practical theologians in the strict sense of the term as a curricular area or discipline.

Practical Theology: A Definition

An Academic Discipline

Although relatively few people identify themselves foremost as practical theologians, a subset of people undertake the critical task of clarifying the divergent aims of practical theology. Scholars who call themselves practical theologians, often in addition to another primary disciplinary identity, are invested in sustaining the three other modes of practical theology. They see themselves as responsible for the maintenance and enrichment of practical theology as a multifaceted confessional, ministerial, teleological, and academic enterprise. Supported by new national and international guilds, such as the Association of Practical Theology and the International Academy of Practical Theology, they understand the value of research and teaching in practical theology as a discipline and a field that contain these four aspects, even if they also recognize that the ultimate aim is not disciplinary knowledge for its own sake but the equipping of religious leaders and believers in fostering life abundant.

Toward this end, practical theologians assume a number of tasks. They explore the activity of believers through descriptive study and normative assessment of local theologies. They seek to discern common objectives among the ministerial subdisciplines and in the study of theology more generally. They study patterns of integration, formation, and transformation in theological education and vocational development. They seek methods by which students, faculty, and ministers might bridge practice and belief, such as ethnography, narrative theory, case study, and the hermeneutical circle of description, interpretation, and response. They develop theologies of discipleship, ministry, and faith, using secular sources, such as the social sciences and literature, in addition to Scripture, history, and doctrine. In each instance, the development of theory aims to enhance the connective web of theological formation, bridging specific disciplines and ecclesial and educational institutions toward the aim of ministry and the life of faith.

Scholars in practical theology come from a number of areas, predominantly pastoral theology and religious education in the United States, for example, and social and political theology and ethics in Britain. They often devote more attention to concrete topics (important to teleological practical theology), such as mental illness, children, poverty, and social policy, than to disciplinary issues in practical theology. However, their approach to these topics is guided by methods and objectives of the discipline.

DISTINGUISHING THESE four separate but related uses is an important advance. Practical theology has expansive boundaries. The term gets used in many academic and plain-sense ways as an activity in religious contexts, an overarching rubric for a collection of subdisciplines, a type of theology, and a discipline within the study of religion in North America. Its subject matter intentionally extends beyond a disciplinary department in the university and seminary to the broader *telos* of faith that guides religious communities. Its participants are equally wide-ranging. Nearly everyone in theological education and religious life has a role to play.

PART II

PRACTICAL WISDOM:
A WAY OF KNOWING

CHAPTER 5

A Maternal Feminist Epistemology

BACKGROUND AND INTRODUCTION

After teaching for three years at Chicago Theological Seminary, I received an invitation in 1989 to address the equally novice Society for Pastoral Theology, formed in 1985. I had just begun to attend its annual June meetings with regularity. But I was part of a ground swell of women who began to teach and write in the field.

Women academics in pastoral theology lagged a generation behind those in other disciplines who had published classic works by the mid-1970s and early 1980s (e.g., Rosemary Radford Ruether in historical theology, Beverly Wildung Harrison in theological ethics, and Elisabeth Schüssler Fiorenza in New Testament). There was no comparable book in pastoral theology until the early 1990s. In fact, the first such book in 1990 by Gail Unterberger, *Through the Lens of Feminist Psychology and Feminist Theology: A Theoretical Model for Pastoral Counseling*, did not receive much attention despite its novelty and importance as a sign of change.

I have speculated on reasons behind this lag, such as the discipline's proximity to ministerial practice and formation. The church remains a conserving and even conservative institution that continues to resist women's leadership in many denominations even as women make progress in other spheres. In the United States, women such as Peggy Way and

---

This essay was originally published as "Epistemology or Bust: A Maternal Feminist Knowledge of Knowing," *Journal of Religion* 72, no. 2 (April 1992): 229–47. Used by permission.

Sue Cardwell made their way into the discipline in the 1970s, earning doctorates and teaching despite the inhospitality of its male leaders, such as Seward Hiltner. Way and Cardwell were amazing teachers and mentors who changed women's lives. But they did not produce much literature. Cardwell never wrote a pastoral theology book, and Way's first book appeared in 2005. The discipline as a whole was young, as the recent creation of the Society itself reflects, evolving from a "movement" into a stable academic position only in the latter half-century. The lag in women's scholarly production was likely related to this as well.

So, when I received a request to speak at the 1990 Society conference, there were no books on women, gender, and sexism in pastoral theology. Feminist theory, however, had had a major impact. And women in pastoral theology had made their presence known. A year or two before my plenary, senior colleague Carol Saussy, with the support of her academic sisters, asked the men to take a back seat outside the inner circle of women and hold their tongues when she presented her work-in-progress on self-esteem, women, and god imagery. The aim was not to make men feel isolated or alienated, although it was a novel experience for some to lack public voice in an academic setting. The real purpose was to create space for women to speak.

Other outcomes were inevitable. The experience provoked anger and anxiety and invited new questions. If context and gender shape knowledge, then how does one recognize any general pastoral theological truths? How do we know what we know about God, faith, and care? Not surprisingly, the Steering Committee named *epistemology* the 1990 conference theme. Herbert Anderson, a colleague close by in the consortium of seminaries in Chicago, extended a helping hand, a role he has served with many colleagues (often accompanied by Swedish dishes laid out in mealtime splendor). In informal phone conversation, he raised the question that I pursue in this chapter: Do you know any differently as a biological mother?

I offer a cautious yes, claiming a distinct kind of maternal knowing that works at the intersection of culture and body, affected powerfully but not ultimately by hormones and physiology. I had two sons, four years old and one year old, and was pregnant with my third. It was a daring argument at the time because it is questionable whether one can argue from bodies to knowing without overestimating biology and nature. Moreover, women still suffered the negative consequences of centuries of fatalistic natalism that equates motherhood and adulthood and defines a woman's fulfillment as dependent on giving birth. I wanted to dispel the myth of biology as destiny at the same time that I wanted to understand the contours of a particular kind of embodied knowing.

I had already started thinking about these questions before the invitation. One of the first courses I created, "Readings in Feminist Psychology," was really an excuse to read books I had longed to pick up in my final doctoral years. We read recently published texts in psychology and women, now considered classics, by Jean Baker Miller, Nancy Chodorow, Carol Gilligan, Anne Wilson Schaef, and Mary Field Belenky and colleagues.

According to my faculty advisor, Don Browning, journal articles often lay groundwork for books, as his own publications demonstrate. This was true for "Epistemology or Bust," which paved the way for a 1994 book, *Also a Mother: Work and Family as Theological Dilemma.* I wrote several essays during this time on women's "generativity" that fed into the book. I chose to include "Epistemology or Bust" here over the other essays because it focuses specifically on knowledge and the development of a discipline.

Today I find some of the chapter's claims dated, obvious, or overstated (e.g., feminist theory challenges universalist claims to truth; the academy rejects women; only a rehabilitation of maternal care will save society). I would soften superlatives and delete adjectives (e.g., "serious and sustained social action"). I would take more seriously differences in mothering across cultures and races, as I start to do in *Also a Mother.* However, the basic argument about the value of maternal knowing continues to have as much relevance in theology as it had two decades ago. There were theologians at the time, such as Sallie McFague, who suggested imagery of God as mother. But they almost always spoke of mother in ideal terms and gave minimal attention to actual mothering and its realities and conflicts. Only a handful of books broached questions of women's embodiment and Christian theology. Since then, I am glad to say, a few others have taken them up. But, compared to feminist scholarship in fields outside theology and religion, scholars in theology mostly ignore motherhood. Childhood studies in theology have grown. I still do not see much attention paid to parents and mothers.

Of fresh interest to me today is the close correspondence in this chapter between maternal knowing and how I have come to understand knowledge in practical theology. Maternal knowing "involves a particular, relational, and at times 'transdisciplinary' investment" and recognizes the role of the communal alongside the personal. Both maternal and practical knowing look beyond cognitive or conceptual knowing and find a home in story and incidental truths. Knowledge is limited, tentative, and idiosyncratic because knowers pursue connection rather than exactitude. Nursing and caring for young children requires a nonlinear or "circular bodily reasoning that interweaves physical sensation, momentary cognition, behavioral reaction, and a physical sensing and intellectual reading of the results." So does practical knowing. I claim that maternal thinking suggests a better way to understand the relationship between theory and practice than "almost anything I have seen in the current literature of practical theology." It demonstrates graphically that theory does not preclude nonverbal insight and that practice is never unreflective or unmediated action.

Maternal knowing has the potential to imitate God's body in action, displaying through its ministrations and knowledge the power "to create personhood and community, to create or thwart life itself." The discipline of paying attention "over and over" also forms the caregiver. This practical and maternal knowing is worthy of reclamation in theological education and the church. For those who engage in practical and maternal knowing, thinking about how we know what we know often stands in a very secondary position to responding to the other in need, a phenomenon the chapter describes.

In a much-discussed book, *Women's Ways of Knowing,* Mary Field Belenky, Blythe McVicker Clinchy, Nancy Rule Goldberger, and Jill Mattuck Tarule document women's struggles to find voice in educational contexts dominated by men.[1] Women must traverse serious social hurdles in the development of their minds. Confident at age eleven, confused by sixteen, girls "go underground." In Carol Gilligan's words, "they start saying, 'I don't know. I don't know. I don't know'"; they begin not knowing what they had known in response to a culture that sends the message "Keep quiet and notice the absence of women."[2] Even more critically, women learn to doubt not only what and how they know but even *how they go about knowing.*

1. *Women's Ways of Knowing: The Development of Self, Voice, and Mind,* ed. Mary Field Belenky, Blythe McVicker Clinchy, Nancy Rule Goldberger, and Jill Mattuck Tarule (New York: Basic Books, 1986).

2. Francine Prose, "Confident at 11, Confused at 16," *New York Times Magazine,* 7 January 1990, p. 23, based on a review of *Making Connections: The Relational Worlds of Adolescent Girls at Emma Willard School,* ed. Carol Gilligan, Nona P. Lyons, and Trudy J. Hanmer (Cambridge, Mass.: Harvard University Press, 1990).

At the same time, several women in the Belenky et al. study point to a particular life experience that dramatically transformed their ways of knowing: the process of becoming a mother.[3] Does this suggest that there are some qualities particular to a mother's way of knowing? What might it mean to acclaim "maternal thinking," to use Sara Ruddick's term, as a significant source of knowledge?[4] Do women as mothers have some kind of singular standpoint on matters of knowledge and truth?[5]

While we feminist theologians have a great deal at stake in this discussion, we have kept a safe distance from these questions. We advocate maternal god imagery and language but say little about actual mothers and mothering. Many of us are mothers, but few of us explore in any depth what we learn about theology from this pivotal life experience. Yet how can we endorse a method that begins with experience and then skip over the hours that many of us spend birthing, tending, and mentoring? How can we talk about God as mother when so much controversy and misunderstanding about the institution and experience of motherhood abound? Out of maternal experiencing and thinking, I would argue, emerges a yet-only-minimally articulated way of being and knowing. Select aspects of such knowing have the potential to inform and radically alter our theologizing. Elsewhere I have discussed the latter possibility in terms of revisioning dominant ideals of generativity from the perspective of a feminist theologian and mother.[6] Here, I will first look briefly at the ramifications of a feminist epistemology within the academy and then demon-

---

3. *Women's Ways of Knowing*, ed. Belenky et al., pp. 35-36, 142-43.

4. Sara Ruddick, *Maternal Thinking: Toward a Politics of Peace* (Boston: Beacon Press, 1989), and "Maternal Thinking," *Feminist Studies* 6 (Summer 1980), reprinted in *Mothering: Essays in Feminist Theory*, ed. Joyce Treblicot (Totowa, N.J.: Rowman & Allanheld, 1983), pp. 213-30 (citations below refer to the latter).

5. See Nancy C. M. Hartsock, "The Feminist Standpoint: Developing the Ground for a Specifically Feminist Historical Materialism," in *Feminism and Methodology*, ed. Sandra Harding (Bloomington: Indiana University Press, 1987), pp. 157-80.

6. See the following by Bonnie J. Miller-McLemore: "Produce or Perish: A Feminist Critique of Generativity," *Union Seminary Quarterly Review* 43, nos. 1-4 (1989): 201-21; "Women Who Work and Love: Caught between Cultures," in *Women in Travail and Transition: A New Pastoral Care*, ed. Maxine Glaz and Jeanne Stevenson-Moessner (Philadelphia: Fortress Press, 1991), pp. 63-85; "Returning to the Mother's House: A Feminist Look at Orpah," *Christian Century*, 17 April 1991, pp. 128-30; "Produce or Perish: Generativity and New Reproductive Technologies," *Journal of the American Academy of Religion* 59 (Spring 1991): 39-69; and "Let the Children Come: A Feminist Maternal Perspective," *Second Opinion* 17 (July 1991): 10-25.

strate the viability of the metaphor of mothering as an appropriate epistemological mode for the discipline of theology.

We can hail a ground-breaking exception to the dearth of material on motherhood in theology: a recently published *Concilium* issue edited by Anne Carr and Elisabeth Schüssler Fiorenza titled *Motherhood: Experience, Institution, Theology.*[7] The text reflects a certain novice state of affairs: many of the essays remain at the level of critique of the institution and its ideologies; fewer consistently draw on or expound comprehensive constructions derived from the intimate, immediate experiences of a mother. Perhaps one of the more remarkable contributions of this volume is its suggestion that the paradigm of motherhood has "the capacity not only for overcoming the split between the worlds of women and men but also splits among different cultures, nations, races, classes, and religions."[8] Even though I write very much as a white, middle-class mother, the last category, if carefully and critically considered, may offer a common language or at least a starting point for dialogue across differences of sex, age, class, sexual orientation, ethnicity, and worldview.

By emphasizing gender and the implications of bearing and suckling children, I do not mean to discount these other equally valid factors. At this point I simply want to assign a certain priority to experiences of gender and motherhood. Both mark major categorical distinctions. Whether genes or environment, the phenomenological fact remains that as early as eighteen months and at least by three years of age, a child sees herself or himself as a gendered person and not as a generic human. Despite current debate over the biological or social construction of sexuality and parenthood and the wide fluctuation in practice, a person still usually claims a sexual identity as either male or female and, at some point in this process of differentiation, envisions on some level the potential of either motherhood or fatherhood.

In a preliminary way, let me address two questions that forbid simple

---

7. *Motherhood: Experience, Institution, Theology,* ed. Anne Carr and Elisabeth Schüssler Fiorenza, Concilium Series, vol. 206 (Edinburgh: T&T Clark, 1989). Another important exception is Christine E. Gudorf's insightful article titled "Parenting, Mutual Love, and Sacrifice" in *Women's Consciousness, Women's Conscience: A Reader in Feminist Ethics,* ed. Barbara Hilkert Andolsen, Christine E. Gudorf, and Mary D. Pellauer (San Francisco: Harper & Row, 1985), pp. 175-91. In her chapter on God as mother in *Models of God: Theology for an Ecological, Nuclear Age* (Philadelphia: Fortress Press, 1987), pp. 97-123, Sallie McFague has approached some of these questions, but much more indirectly and, significantly, without considering the problems of modern models of parenthood.

8. "Editorial," in *Motherhood,* ed. Carr and Schüssler Fiorenza, p. 4.

answers. Do mothers qua mothers encounter a singular knowing unique to their mothering? Can men experience it? Women's embodiment, specifically the experience of pregnancy and birth, represents a distinct perspective and may evoke particular ways of perceiving and thinking. I say "may evoke" because I do not intend to depict a universal or essential category; not all birthing, nursing women inherently share one distinct mode of knowing. Nor should this common womanly experience dictate limited social roles that, by contrast, remain extremely malleable. And I say "evoke" because, although men do not have the physical equipment per se to experience maternal knowing per se, embodied moments of non-mothers have comparable evocative power to shape and inform our "'knowledge' of knowing."[9] Becoming a parent, biologically and through adoption, elicits changes — sometimes strikingly unexpected changes. What is learned from biological motherhood has parallels in other persons in form, not in exact content. It is with the desire that reflection on such analogues be triggered that I say we have something to learn from birthing, lactating women. In this way, the richness of knowing is deepened.

Following Donna Haraway's suggestion, then, I present a "view from a body" that is "always a complex, contradictory, structuring, and structured body."[10] I use the term *gender* primarily to refer to socially constructed sexual identity. Yet gender always has biological linkage, just as sexuality never exists in some pure and untainted physical essence apart from social interpretation.[11] The capacity for maternal knowing begins as a biological potential, but it never stands alone as an innate, unadulterated fact.[12] While drawing on the particularities of my own biologically shaped

9. Paul Tillich, *Systematic Theology*, vol. 1: *Reason and Revelation: Being and God* (Chicago: University of Chicago Press, 1951), p. 71.

10. Donna Haraway, "Situated Knowledges: The Science Question in Feminism and the Privilege of Partial Perspective," *Feminist Studies* 14, no. 3 (Fall 1988): 589. This essay originated as a commentary on Sandra Harding's *The Science Question in Feminism* (Ithaca, N.Y.: Cornell University Press, 1987).

11. I caution against laying the dualistic grid of nature/nurture, biology/environment, and sexuality/gender over maternal knowing. While such categories are strategically useful, they are not helpful when reified in the tradition of Western binary oppositions. See Joan L. Griscom, "On Healing the Nature/History Split in Feminist Thought," in *Women's Consciousness, Women's Conscience*, ed. Andolsen, Gudorf, and Pellauer, pp. 85-98; and Susan Griffin, *Woman and Nature* (New York: Harper & Row, 1978).

12. See Martha McClintock's comments on the complex meanings of *innate* in "Considering a Biosocial Perspective on Parenting," *Signs: Journal of Women in Culture and Society* 4, no. 4 (Summer 1979): 703-10, written in response to Alice S. Rossi, "A Biosocial Per-

encounters with giving birth and nursing, I propose maternal knowing not as an intrinsic norm or ideal but as an unexplored avenue that will, I hope, suggest the limits of current understandings and the possibilities of alternative modes to be explored.

Epistemology or Bust: Where Are We Really Headed?

Many rightfully question the viability of conversations about epistemology as Western European philosophy has traditionally construed them. In pursuit of universalizable truths, knowledge has been defined so as to exclude certain select groups of persons "as subjects in its production" and "as critics of its products."[13] For the most part, women and minorities have remained consumers only. Among women, mothers — regardless of race, class, and worldview — have had less opportunity to participate and have seldom been recognized for their critical, albeit hidden, part in the production of knowledge.

The vital role of gender in knowing has come to the fore explicitly only with the advancement of feminist reflection[14] and the achievement of a "critical mass"[15] of women in academe. Initially more attention went to

spective on Parenting," *Daedalus: Journal of the American Academy of Arts and Sciences* 106 (Spring 1977): 1-31.

13. Morris Taggart, "Epistemological Equality as the Fulfillment of Family Therapy," in *Women in Families: A Framework for Family Therapy,* ed. Monica McGoldrick, Carol M. Anderson, and Froma Walsh (New York: W. W. Norton, 1989), p. 100.

14. See, e.g., such works as *Men's Studies Modified: The Impact of Feminism on the Academic Disciplines,* ed. Dale Spender (Oxford: Pergamon Press, 1981), and Spender, *For the Record: The Meaning and Making of Feminist Knowledge* (London: Women's Press, 1985); *Women's Ways of Knowing,* ed. Belenky et al.; *Discovering Reality: Feminist Perspectives on Epistemology, Metaphysics, Methodology, and Philosophy of Science,* ed. Sandra Harding and Merrill Hintikka (London: D. Reidel, 1983); Jean Grimshaw, *Philosophy and Feminist Thought* (Minneapolis: University of Minnesota Press, 1986); *Gender/Body/Knowledge: Feminist Reconstructions of Being and Knowing,* ed. Alison M. Jaggar and Susan R. Bordo (New Brunswick, N.J.: Rutgers University Press, 1989); Mary E. Hawkesworth, "Knowers, Knowing, Known: Feminist Theory and Claims of Truth," *Signs: Journal of Women in Culture and Society* 14, no. 3 (Spring 1989): 533-57; comment and reply on Hawkesworth, "Knowers, Knowing, Known," *Signs: Journal of Women in Culture and Society* 15, no. 2 (Winter 1990): 17-28; and Jane Flax, *Thinking Fragments: Psychoanalysis, Feminism, and Postmodernism in the Contemporary West* (Berkeley and Los Angeles: University of California Press, 1990).

15. This is a term used by John Naisbitt and Patricia Aburdene in their demographical study of women in the professions, *Megatrends 2000* (New York: William Morrow, 1990).

closely related questions of methodology. As feminist conversations moved from critique to constructive proposal, attention to methodological distinctions revealed fundamental epistemological differences. Recent conversations, such as those of the Mud Flower Collective's *God's Fierce Whimsy*[16] and Patricia Schechter and respondents' "A Vision of Feminist Religious Scholarship" in the *Journal of Feminist Studies in Religion*,[17] make it clear that feminist theology raises not only issues of method and content. At heart, feminist methodologies present an epistemological challenge to academic and Enlightenment ideologies of reason, science, and knowledge. The question is not simply what and how we think about religion, but who is doing the thinking, and what counts as theological and religious knowing.

What happens when women do the thinking? Feminist scholarship challenges core assumptions of Western claims to objective, universalizable truth. It proclaims the contextual, including gendered, quality of all knowing. Women's knowing also suggests the epistemological priority of the communal alongside the personal and affirms the significance of multiplicity and diversity, gender and otherwise. Knowing involves a particular, relational, and at times "transdisciplinary" investment.[18] It builds on personal and communal experience, intuition, nonlinear thought, spontaneity, and disclosure. Often a feminist epistemology is not simply or even primarily a body of concepts or a philosophy; women know by telling stories,[19] by sharing "small truths,"[20] by recovering the incidental.

Among themselves, women often participate in what might be described as "womanly discourse." On the surface, this discourse may seem indirect, while subtly ideas develop and communication occurs. For knowledge depends on care; truth demands intimacy, equality, and a refusal to impose on others. Even in public forums, a frequently operating but often implicit norm for women is that persons ought to engage in the

16. The Mud Flower Collective, *God's Fierce Whimsy: Christian Feminism and Theological Education* (New York: Pilgrim Press, 1985).

17. Patricia Schechter and respondents, "A Vision of Feminist Religious Scholarship," *Journal of Feminist Studies in Religion* 31 (Spring 1987): 91-111.

18. Stephen Toulmin, "Theology in the Context of the University," *Theological Education* 26 (Spring 1990): 62.

19. See Eleanor Humes Haney, "What Is Feminist Ethics? A Proposal for Continuing Discussion," *Journal of Religious Ethics* 8 (1980): 117.

20. Patricia Spacks, "In Praise of Gossip," *Hudson Review* 35 (1982): 24, quoted in *Women's Ways of Knowing*, ed. Belenky et al., p. 116.

passionate, equilateral buildup of a topic. When a female speaker enters in, she will more likely enlarge on a previous point, suggest related ideas, add a personal anecdote, or make encouraging interjections rather than abruptly change the subject. Neither conversation nor knowledge is plied as an attempt to hold the floor. They are reciprocal exchanges often intended to draw in others. Knowledge is seldom singular, "separative,"[21] universal, or uniform; truth is multiple, complex, connected, sometimes idiosyncratic and unique, concrete, and specific. Knowledge is seldom final; truth is limited and tentative in the best sense of the word — that is, tentativeness and partiality not for their own sake but for the prospect of connections.[22]

I mention only a few qualities of a feminist epistemology, many of which have the danger of stereotype and misuse. Of equal importance, I believe, is a slightly different concern: How have or will such qualities of perceiving and verifying truth influence epistemological theory, practice, and experience in the study of theology? In other words, what happens to women and men when, as a woman in a recent editorial on abortion in *The Christian Century* requested of the National Conference of Catholic Bishops, we ask men "to retreat from public debate for a while"?[23] What happens when we argue that "only women can *know*"?[24] What happens when we claim that certain ideas arise primarily from women's struggle and that others ought to use them with wariness?

If nothing else, for many men women's knowing remains an intrusion and a hassle. But more, the "sheer audacity," writes family theorist Morris Taggart, "of introducing a WOMAN as . . . commentator and fellow yearner" calls "everything . . . into question." "How can I deal with the anxiety," he reveals, "that comes from feeling like a guest in (what I had assumed was) my own house?"[25] Women and men alike continue to underestimate the immense apprehension that relinquishing power and prestige produces.

Little awareness of these powerful dynamics can lead to abstract criticism or outright attack of the female speaker by men who claim priv-

21. See the definition and use of this term by Catherine Keller, *From a Broken Web: Separation, Sexism, and Self* (Boston: Beacon Press, 1986), p. 9.

22. Haraway, "Situated Knowledges," p. 584.

23. Susan Maloney, S.N.J.M., "Catholic Bishops and the Art of Public Moral Discourse," *The Christian Century,* 9 May 1990, p. 486.

24. Taggart, "Epistemological Equality as the Fulfillment of Family Therapy," p. 110.

25. Taggart, "Epistemological Equality as the Fulfillment of Family Therapy," p. 110.

ileged knowledge — she has failed, it is said, to include women of color, the aging, or some other group or factor. The hidden injury is that she has not included "him" or not honored the familiar rules of academic discourse. Given the deep-seated nature of these reactions, pure rational discussion about the impact of gender is inadequate to the task of intellectual change.

Women's modes of knowing *are* unsettling; they fly in the face of qualities valued and judged superior within the academy. Perhaps some of the wariness about incorporating feminist knowing in theology is related to the devaluation that the discipline already knows within the university at large in its attention to other kinds of knowledge than knowledge that corresponds to external data. But, as Jane Flax suggests, "If [we feminists] do our work well, 'reality' will appear even more unstable, complex, and disorderly than it does now."[26] Commitment to partial perspectives and power-sensitive conversation suggests "a confusion of voice and sight, rather than clear and distinct ideas" as the most adequate model for rational, objective inquiry.[27]

Words Pregnant with Meaning

At times, motherhood is the epitome of disorder and messiness. Retrieving anything related to motherhood has inherent dangers. Feminists have worked hard to counter the damaging consequences of equating women with the biological roles that they fill. For too long, men have defined women almost exclusively in terms of their sexual function as wives and mothers, seeing sociological structures as biological and psychological givens. We certainly do not want to perpetuate self-restricting definitions of gender complementarity and oppressive circumstances of injustice.

Nor do I want to equate a biological process — the capacity to bear children — with full normative humanity.[28] Rather, I wish to point toward a broader vision that has an important connection with the biological process of birth but draws on it metaphorically to move toward more general meanings. My remarks are not inclusive in an immediate sense, drawing as

26. Jane Flax, quoted by Wendy Luttrell, book review, *Signs: Journal of Women in Culture and Society* 15 (Spring 1990): 636.

27. Haraway, "Situated Knowledges," p. 590.

28. Beverly W. Harrison, "Theology of Pro-Choice: A Feminist Perspective," in *Abortion: The Moral Issues,* ed. Edward Batchelor Jr. (New York: Pilgrim Press, 1982), p. 220.

they do on singular experience, but they are intended as illustrative of epistemological possibilities. They are not a judgment on the childless.

A third related problem is that under the sway of patriarchy, persons have romanticized motherhood and created the "fantasy of the perfect mother."[29] Joint idealization of disinterested love and self-sacrificing motherhood creates virtues impossible to achieve; worse, it completely distorts relationships between parent and child, mother and father. We would do well to remain wary of the potential misappropriation even of the recent work of some feminists such as Carol Gilligan to reinforce stereotyped views of women as more giving and nurturant.

It is important to counter these misunderstandings by offering a fuller view of the demands of mothering and a more complex definition of care. Can we not uncover an experience of motherhood that lies somewhere between the extremes of oppressive traditional discourse and avant-garde feminist protest that totally rejects this but offers nothing in its place? Although perhaps impossible, as a white woman who experiences motherhood in a Western, capitalistic, patriarchal society, I want to stand in the "no-man's-land" between this either/or and grapple with the potential power of woman's experience of reproduction and relationality. For I agree with Julia Kristeva that, while a certain brooding feminism protests the fact of motherhood itself, "genuine feminine innovation . . . will not be possible until we have elucidated motherhood, feminine creation, and the relationship between them."[30]

So what, as Kristeva asks, "do we know about the inner discourse of a mother?"[31] Not much. Silence reigns in most public realms. If we have known little about women's ways of knowing, we know even less about a mother's. From literature to liturgy, the many Marys keep "all these things, pondering them" in their hearts.[32] Hymns sing the thoughts of Father, the

---

29. Nancy J. Chodorow and Susan Contralto, "The Fantasy of the Perfect Mother," *Social Problems* 23 (1976), reprinted in *Rethinking the Family*, ed. Barrie Thorne with Marilyn Yalom (New York: Longman, 1982), pp. 54-75, and also in Nancy J. Chodorow, *Feminism and Psychoanalytic Theory* (New Haven: Yale University Press, 1989), pp. 79-96.

30. Julia Kristeva, "Un nouveau type d'intellectuel: Le dissident," *Tel quel* 74 (Winter 1977): 6-7, quoted by Susan Rubin Suleiman, "Writing and Motherhood," in *The (M)other Tongue: Essays in Feminist Psychoanalytic Interpretation*, ed. Shirley Nelson Garner, Claire Kahane, and Madelon Sprengnether (Ithaca, N.Y.: Cornell University Press, 1985), p. 360.

31. Kristeva, "Un nouveau type d'intellectuel," quoted by Suleiman, "Writing and Motherhood," pp. 352, 368.

32. Luke 2:19 (RSV).

Master and Lord. But where do we hear about the ruminations of the Mother-God? Have you ever considered the circumstances of the anxious, withdrawn, and hostile mother said to breed a schizophrenic son in the family systems theories of Gregory Bateson,[33] or the inner thoughts of the depressed mothers credited with depriving the child of adequate mirroring by psychoanalyst Heinz Kohut?[34] Psychoanalytic epistemology gives maternal censorship a certain scientific validity. The rational-cognitive or mathematical law and principal language of most Western moral theory has been that of the father. "The mother's voice," says Nel Noddings, "has been silent."[35] Or, have you ever wondered about "Portnoy's *mother's* complaint," in the words of Pauline Bart?[36] Few mothers have created enduring literature; those who have seldom look to their mothering as a central source of their work.[37] Mother as speaking subject is missing from literary, psychoanalytic, ethical, and religious dramas.

What more might we understand if we could know from the inside out, through the eyes of the mother intricately engaged in the process? As literary scholar Susan Rubin Suleiman asserts, as long as we continue to concentrate on "the-mother-as-she-is-written rather than on the-mother-as-she-writes, we shall continue in our ignorance." It is high time "to let mothers have their word."[38] Mothers know something important about epistemology in a negative sense from the constrictions that *prevent* knowledge of knowing or, at least, its careful, critical articulation. Mothers also have accessibility to certain invaluable ways of knowing, particularly

33. Gregory Bateson sees the mother as key cause in an early paper with Jackson, Haley, and Weakland (1956), pp. 212-13, quoted by Debra Anna Luepnitz in *The Family Interpreted: Feminist Theory in Clinical Practice* (New York: Basic Books, 1988), p. 153.

34. See selected cases in Heinz Kohut, *How Does Analysis Cure?* (Chicago: University of Chicago Press, 1984), pp. 16-17, 29-30, 126-51, and in "The Two Analyses of Mr. Z," *International Journal of Psychoanalysis* 60, no. 3 (1979): 3-27, in which Kohut blames the "faultily responsive *maternal* self object" for various emotional pathologies. The mother is sole source of psychic harmony and yet called an "object" at one and the same time. Only the child's point of view finds representation.

35. Nel Noddings, *Caring: A Feminine Approach to Ethics and Moral Education* (Berkeley and Los Angeles: University of California Press, 1984), pp. 1-2.

36. Pauline Bart, quoted by Luepnitz, *The Family Interpreted*, p. 167.

37. Tillie Olsen, *Silences* (New York: Delta, 1965), pp. 19, 32. For notable exceptions, see Tillie Olsen, *Tell Me a Riddle* (New York: Dell, 1956); Alicia Suskin Ostriker, *The Mother/Child Papers* (Boston: Beacon Press, 1980); Robin Morgan, *Lady of the Beasts* (New York: Random House, 1976); and Jane Lazarre, *The Mother Knot* (New York: Dell, 1977).

38. Suleiman, "Writing and Motherhood," pp. 358, 360.

bodily knowing. Indeed, a certain superiority of knowledge of human nature and nurture rests on a maternal labor historically defined as inferior to the more "valuable" or "productive" labor of men.

What Is Really More Important? What Is More Valuable?

Thinking about knowing from a maternal perspective renders clear the secondary nature of the whole question. I wonder if, in actual fact, a more authentic *knowing* is not that which responds on demand to the immediacy of the cry of the moment. We are most knowing when passionately engaged in life's struggle, not when detached. Conflicts between the desire to live fully now and the need to distance oneself in order to create enduring ideas have banished much of the world's greatest wisdom. The academy does not usually understand this tension; a mother might.

This whole exercise of mine ultimately rests on the back of my sitter and in part, as it should, on my husband, who both practice the knowing that I preach. I am still unsure about the trade-offs. I cannot begin to describe the multiple costs of putting these words on paper. I lost many precious moments playing with my two sons. The waste of a mother's creative energies in this daily conflict between work and love, Suleiman argues, "cannot be overestimated."[39] Nothing has ever subverted my peace of mind as much as my small sons, and yet nothing has ever taught me as much about myself, my place in the world, culture, patience, people, life. Would many a man weigh these tensions? I doubt it. Or at least not overtly, or not until recently.

While motherhood heightens these relational tensions, by no means are they restricted to mothers. To theorize about knowing maternally comes at the expense of moments with babies. To theorize about knowing in theology in general has its price and rests on the backs of those others who practice the insights and carry on the tasks of living. It rests on those on the front line. Which comes first and, when out of time, what gives? One's gender just may tip the scale.

All this points to a second constriction especially understood by mothers: to consider how we know and our grounds for knowing comes only with freedom and with time for reflection. To consider epistemology, then, is a kind of luxury, previously granted only to those with power.

39. Suleiman, "Writing and Motherhood," p. 362.

Bodily, monthly, women know life's limits. Two times pregnant and pregnant again, I face the conflicts of "conceiving" in scholarly and familial ways at the same time; constant, so-called morning sickness, indescribable fatigue, and what one study called the "diminished cognitive acuity" in the first and third trimester[40] take their toll.

But these are trivial beside the heavier physical, emotional, and spiritual demands of maintaining daily life. Women know the strain of "holding up half the sky" or, often, more than their share. Virginia Woolf, fictitiously reprimanding women for their lesser accomplishments, demands their excuse: Her women reply, "We have borne and bred and washed and taught perhaps to the age of six or seven years, the one thousand six hundred and twenty-three million human beings who are, according to statistics, at present in existence, and that, allowing that some had help, takes time."[41] To articulate how we know what we know requires provisions that many women and most mothers lack: space, time, energy, money, permission, circumstances, choice, education, travel, varied experience, and two other critical ingredients indispensable to full creativity — what Tillie Olsen calls "unconfined solitude" and "the *essential angel*" — the woman whose name appears on dedication pages — who assures a "daily life made easy and noiseless . . . by a silent, watchful, tireless affection."[42]

Beyond these restrictions, serious connection to another being involves a constraint — what Kristeva calls a pain that "comes from the inside" and "never remains apart": "You may close your eyes, . . . teach courses, run errands, . . . think about objects, subjects." But a mother is "branded by pain" that begins at conception and never goes away.[43] Right at this pregnant moment, I am one but two — a publicly, academically subversive state, "a continuous separation, a division of the very flesh," says Kristeva. My self is multiple, divided between a part of me — "what was mine" — for which I care but which my two sons, little knowing, carry forth into the world "hence-

---

40. N. Murai, "A Study of Moods in Pregnant Women," *Tohoku Psychological Folk* 34 (1975): 10-16; and A. Jarrahi-Jadeh et al., "Emotional and Cognitive Changes in Pregnancy and Early Puerperium," *British Journal of Psychiatry* 115 (1969): 797-805, cited by Sheri Fenster, Suzanne B. Phillips, and Estelle R. G. Rapoport, *The Therapist's Pregnancy: Intrusion in the Analytic Space* (Hillsdale, N.J.: Analytic Press, 1986), p. 1.

41. Virginia Woolf, *A Room of One's Own* (New York: Harcourt, Brace & Co., 1957), p. 116.

42. Joseph Conrad, quoted by Olsen in *Silences*, pp. 12, 34.

43. Julia Kristeva, "Stabat Mater," in *The Kristeva Reader*, ed. Toril Moi (New York: Columbia University Press, 1986), p. 166.

forth . . . irreparably alien." As long as the woman has the womb that carries "this internal graft and fold"[44] — the seed that divides, grows, and then is severed at the umbilical cord — we should only talk cautiously about an emotional and cognitive equity between mothers and fathers as "easily attainable." At this point, we cannot ignore, asserts Alice Rossi, a "biologically based potential for heightened maternal investment."[45] Biology or not, we cannot deny what Sara Ruddick calls the "passions of maternity" that are "so sudden, intense, and confusing that we often remain ignorant of the . . . *thought* that has developed from mothering."[46]

Epistemology *and* Bust: What Does It Mean to Lactate?

Despite or partly because of these passions, a particular discipline of knowing does develop. Having children forever changes a woman's knowledge of knowing. Parting the passions to articulate in what ways comes less easily. From quickening to birth to giving suck to today's daily throes, I have come to appreciate the integrity of bodily knowing. Holding infant and child at the intersection of nature and symbolic order, I as woman and mother have what Suleiman calls "privileged" access to the order of culture and language and to the power of nurture.[47]

How might we systematically conceptualize this maternal knowing that, in novelist Mary Gordon's words, is more physical and certainly more erotic "than anybody admits"?[48] By no sheer coincidence, the scriptural use of the verb "to know" refers to the intimate act of sexual intercourse. Yet even in our supposedly sexually liberated era, Western theology and philosophy still speak "like a Greek man,"[49] inserting a wedge between sex

44. Julia Kristeva, "Stabat Mater," pp. 178-79. See also Iris M. Young, "Pregnant Subjectivity and the Limits of Existential Phenomenology," in *Descriptions*, ed. Don Ihde and Hugh J. Silverman (Albany: State University of New York Press, 1985), pp. 25-26, 27-31, and "Pregnant Embodiment: Subjectivity and Alienation," *Journal of Medicine and Philosophy* 9, no. 1 (1984): 47-54; and Adrienne Rich, *Of Woman Born: Motherhood as Experience and Institution* (New York: Bantam Books, 1977), pp. 47-48, 161.

45. Rossi, "A Biosocial Perspective on Parenting," p. 24.

46. Ruddick, *Maternal Thinking*, p. 213.

47. Suleiman, "Writing and Motherhood," p. 367.

48. Interview with fiction author Mary Gordon, *Chicago Tribune*, 3 December 1989, sec. 6, p. 3. See also Rossi, "A Biosocial Perspective on Parenting," pp. 16-17.

49. J. Giles Milhaven, "A Medieval Lesson on Bodily Knowing: Women's Experience and Men's Thought," *Journal of the American Academy of Religion* 57, no. 2 (Summer 1989): 355.

and maternity and ignoring differences in epistemology that arise from different kinds of sexual experiences and bodies, the most obvious of which are male and female. Disembodied, dispassionate reason still seems more trustworthy and valid.

But as a mother, I find that this is simply not true at some very crucial points. To echo Beverly Harrison's remark about Christian ethics, a maternal feminist epistemology is "profoundly worldly, a spirituality of sensuality." It reminds us that all knowledge is body-mediated.[50] As point of proof, what does it mean to lactate — to have a body that, sensing another's thirst, "lets-down,"[51] drenching me with sweet-smelling milk?[52] Does it alter knowing? I know physically through a muscular ache; apart from the ache, I can scarcely know. In this knowing, few abstractions come between me and the other, mouth to nipple — no bottle, no instrument to measure birth size or fetal movement. As with pregnancy, lactation subverts artificial boundaries between self and other, inside and outside. Both undermine the integrity of my body and root me fluidly, solidly to the earth. I know by knowing the feelings of the other physically because they are paradoxically both mine and not mine, a continuity in difference rather than a polar opposition *or* an enmeshed symbiosis. I know by an affective connection that moves toward differentiation, not by comparison, contrast, and critique *or* by some idealized oneness or union with the child. I know immediately, tactilely, erotically — the "lowest and least worthy of all human senses," according to Aquinas.[53] To a great degree, how-

50. See Beverly Wildung Harrison, "The Power of Anger in the Work of Love: Christian Ethics for Women and Other Strangers," *Union Seminary Quarterly Review* 36 (1981): 45, 48.

51. The hormone "oxytocin acts upon the basket cells around the alveoli, causing them to constrict, and . . . to squeeze out the milk in the phenomenon known as 'milk let-down'" (Rossi, "A Biosocial Perspective on Parenting," p. 17; see also B. Berde, *Recent Progress in Oxytocin Research* [Springfield, Ill.: Charles C. Thomas, 1959]).

52. I chose pregnancy and lactation because of the powerful physical and metaphorical implications and because of their primary meaning at this time in my life. Other phenomena could serve as sources of reflection here. See the attention to menstruation, menarche, and/or menopause in Genia Pauli Haddon, *Body Metaphors: Releasing God-feminine in Us All* (New York: Crossroad, 1988); Penelope Washbourn, *Becoming Woman: The Quest for Wholeness in Female Experience* (New York: Harper & Row, 1977), and "Becoming Woman: Menstruation as Spiritual," in *Womanspirit Rising* (New York: Harper & Row, 1979), p. 247; and Christine Downing, *Journey through Menopause: A Personal Rite of Passage* (New York: Crossroad, 1987).

53. Milhaven, "A Medieval Lesson on Bodily Knowing," p. 358. For his documentation on this, see J. Giles Milhaven, "Thomas Aquinas on Sexual Pleasure," *Journal of Religious Ethics* 5 (1977): 157-81.

ever untrustworthy or dangerous, at least in the Western history of sexuality, I must rely on a bodily passion, a knowing driven by a welcomed lust or need that seeks satisfaction. In this state of awareness, I have actually left a train car in which a child cried because of the stir it created in me; in general, just the sight of a baby can evoke a milk let-down response in lactating mothers. In this state I learn, change, and develop; if I do not, the child will not. Yet most theories see the process toward individuation as only the child's.

Maternal thinking begins to suggest a way to understand the problem of integrating praxis and theory better than almost anything I have seen in the current literature of practical theology. It challenges false dichotomies: theory does not involve, as much as many have wished, "verbalizable knowledge" and insight;[54] practice does not mean unmediated action. Both involve qualities more nebulous, fleeting, relative, and momentary. Authentic reflective praxis requires a knowing in which "what one learns cannot be applied exactly, often not even by analogy, to a new situation."[55] In the movement between knowing and acting, I use a mode of circular bodily reasoning that interweaves physical sensation, momentary cognition, behavioral reaction, and a physical sensing and intellectual reading of the results — a trial-and-error, hit-and-miss strategy that in its bodily ethos surpasses that described under the rubric of Catholic moral casuistry.[56] When it works, I relax; when it fails, I repeat it ceaselessly because I must; when it fails one too many times, I must master a physical desire to retaliate in stormy, mindless abuse.

Fleshly knowing, then, has inherent value as well as immense power for misuse. But, I believe, it is better to try to understand it than to repress it and suffer the negative consequences of abuse that our society has begun to recognize. Partially justified fears of the dangers of bodily sensuality have turned us away from distinguishing its possible resources. In contrast to the hierarchy of knowledge that ranks rational above other forms, we know much in and through our bodies that is intrinsically valuable and precious.

Let me dare to go one step further: female anatomy in general provides its own ground for metaphor that theories of knowledge have pre-

54. This is a term used by Kohut in his critique of Freud's "moralistic obsession" with "objective truth" (Kohut, *How Does Analysis Cure?*, pp. 54-56; see also pp. 59-60).

55. Ruddick, *Maternal Thinking*, p. 219.

56. For a similar example of the relational casuistry between a mother and an infant, see Noddings, *Caring*, pp. 31-35.

ferred to ignore. All knowing is not phallic. That is, if men think phallicly, to borrow Freud's compelling and sometimes ill-used analogy, women think and know vaginally. Or, in actuality it is not a matter of naming a replacement organ, as I discover when I explain female genitalia to my four-year-old son. Women's organs have an intrinsic multiplicity that cannot be easily explained. What might this greater multiplicity in sexual form and function mean for women's knowing in general? The hymen and the "two-lipped vulva," as noted by Jacques Derrida and Luce Irigaray, suggest fluid, diffuse, multiple, embracing language in place of the linear, unified, and visible language of the phallus.[57] Not surprisingly, we find Nel Noddings and the women interviewed by Belenky and her colleagues describing a knowing that involves not projection but a receiving into oneself.[58] Note, however, this is *not* necessarily a passive receptive knowing but an active engagement on a different basis than we have thus far understood. For the receptive vagina is also the "birth-pushing womb,"[59] the nurturing breast an industrious milk-making organ. Nor, might I add, is the penis always assertively erect, and behind it lies the much ignored, more vulnerable scrotum.

Biology is not destiny, but it does shape how we know. With child at breast, women have particular knowledge rooted in their bodies. Ultimately, to lactate when another thirsts teaches a certain empathic, connected knowing. Beverly Wildung Harrison claims that this womanly knowledge of nurture and the arts of human survival, grounded in the biological constant of childbearing and nursing, far surpasses any technological power in its ability not only to create solid bonds between people but also to create personhood and community, to create or thwart life itself.[60]

The activity of birthing, giving suck, and rearing hones this distinctly human power. Through long hours of arduous practice, mothers acquire an entire moral and metaphysical discipline of thought to assure the preservation, growth, and acceptability of their children.[61] As identified by Ruddick, genuine care of a small being demands finely tuned attitudes and virtues of holding, humility, resilient cheerfulness, good humor, and ultimately the capacity for what she calls "attentive love." The exercise of

57. *The (M)other Tongue*, ed. Nelson Garner et al., pp. 23-24.
58. Noddings, *Caring*, p. 30; *Women's Ways of Knowing*, ed. Belenky et al., p. 122.
59. Haddon, *Body Metaphors*, pp. 11-12.
60. Harrison, "The Power of Anger in the Work of Love," pp. 44, 47-48.
61. Ruddick, *Maternal Thinking*, pp. 214-16.

"keeping over acquiring, of conserving the fragile, of maintaining whatever is at hand and necessary to the child's life," of loving without seizing or using — all this requires deep reserves of energy, extended periods of patient waiting, and a heightened intellectual activity.[62] This "caring labor" leads to a "rationality of care" that exemplifies many of the alternative ideals of reason and morality recently formulated by feminists.[63]

An Agenda for Theology: A Maternal Feminist Perspective

The concept of maternal knowing, rooted in the physical realities of mothering, offers important criteria for an alternative epistemology. Difference in embodiment necessarily implies difference in thinking. Heretofore this difference has meant dramatic disadvantages for women. The time has come to allow difference to empower rather than divide and oppress. Maternal knowing has immense possibilities for informing social, ethical, economic, and political stances.[64] A normative and political imperative for theology resides in this epistemological stance. Indeed, the test of one's philosophical epistemology becomes "clear at the level of action," in Harrison's words.[65]

Maternal knowing refers to thinking particular to women who have known another inhabiting themselves and have maintained this very interior link by suckling, carrying, sharing bed, body, and soul, and, finally, letting loose to live. At the same time, motherhood and its corresponding knowing has ramifications for those besides biological mothers, even in a culture such as ours that has increasingly moved away from communal responsibility for children and that, in its fascination with new technologies, is obsessed with reproducing biological progeny.[66] Other traditions cor-

---

62. Ruddick, *Maternal Thinking*, pp. 217, 223-24.

63. Ruddick, *Maternal Thinking*, p. 46. She cites Hilary Rose, "Hand, Brain, and Heart: A Feminist Epistemology for the Natural Sciences," *Signs: Journal of Women in Culture and Society* 9 (1983): 73-90; Carolyn Whitbeck, "A Different Reality: Feminist Ontology," in *Beyond Domination,* ed. Carol Gould (Totowa, N.J.: Rowman & Allanheld, 1983); Noddings, *Caring;* and Carol Gilligan, *In a Different Voice* (Cambridge, Mass.: Harvard University Press, 1982).

64. Others make a similar case. See Ruddick, *Maternal Thinking*, pp. 224-27, and *Maternal Thinking,* part 3; Emily Martin, *The Woman in the Body: A Cultural Analysis of Reproduction* (Boston: Beacon Press, 1987), part 4; and Kristeva, "Stabat Mater," p. 185.

65. Harrison, "The Power of Anger in the Work of Love," p. 54.

66. See Miller-McLemore, "Produce or Perish: Generativity and New Reproductive Technologies."

rect ours here. Ghanaian theologian Mercy Amba Oduyoye remarks, "I have no biological children . . . but I have children." In a definition derived from Akan culture, mothering is "a religious duty" that all persons in a healthy society should embody if persons "are to be fully human, nurtured to care for, and take care of themselves, one another, and of their environments."[67]

Thus, those who have bodies capable of bearing fruit and who have imaged, if not in actuality experienced, the idea of bodily sustenance of another have a working familiarity with maternal knowing. And men, who do not have such knowledge, need to begin to listen and imagine. In the end, men cannot fathom what is rooted in very definitive bodily experiences. But even if men cannot fathom maternal knowing in its physicality, those who have "slept like spoons"[68] around pregnant women through long nights of childbearing and then, ultimately, spooned on through the throes of birthing and the trials of rearing know something of its depth and potential. Not only do I not exclude men; I would ask more of men and fathers. For to excuse them from the regime of tending life or to deprive them of their own versions of maternal or parental practice is to lose a precious resource and to negate a viable avenue of full humanhood. This is not to say that men (or, for that matter, women) must replicate the bodily knowing involved in an act like lactating. Nor can men participate in many of the primary cognitive and emotional activities of maternity. Rather, this is to urge that persons begin to listen to and consider the existential and even physiological analogues in their own lives that carry a kindred power of perception, connection, and insight into themselves and into the processes of sustaining another.

Let me clarify further: it is not possible for non-mothers to accomplish by empathy or analogy *exactly the same* intellectual and moral feats that for mothers are rooted in select bodily experiences. But a mother's public expression of epistemological insights should be given authority to evoke *parallel but distinct* insights for non-mothers that pertain to the intimate care of another being. The physicality of childbearing and rearing is critical. But it is not exhaustive of the possibilities. There are other avenues to some of the important insights that maternal knowing suggests. And

67. Mercy Amba Oduyoye, "Poverty and Motherhood," in *Motherhood: Experience, Institution, Theology,* ed. Carr and Schüssler Fiorenza, pp. 23-24.

68. See John Giles Milhaven, "Sleeping Like Spoons: A Question of Embodiment," *Commonweal,* 7 April 1989, pp. 205-7.

there are other significant bodily knowings to which we should begin to attend. Maternity is not the norm from which all other kinds of knowing and loving are judged. Rather, maternity is a singular and seldom-explored voice to which others, particularly men, should harken as a new source of critique and renewal of current models of relationality, love, care, and work and of current approaches to ethics, theology, and epistemology.

The physical acts of giving birth and nursing are transformative modes that point to the many other ways of being parental. Not only do human beings have a potential or even a natural "parental instinct" for giving and securing life, according to Sallie McFague; persons also have a normative imperative to extend this instinct of life preservation beyond their lives to the lives of others and to the life of the world.[69] This means actual hands-on involvement in parental exercises and in its teachings. As Nancy Chodorow, Dorothy Dinnerstein, and others have argued, until men become more involved in child rearing, psychic dynamics that subtly support the narrow parameters of current models of preservation and care will go unchallenged, and human possibilities for fuller development will remain limited.[70]

But, for all their attention to the mother, Chodorow and Dinnerstein neglect biological phenomena involved in childbearing and remain mostly negative about the mother's role. They demand an equality that ignores fundamental physiological differences between men and women and the related epistemological distinctions that I have suggested. I want to avoid their covert disdain of the privileged perspective that women have known as mothers. Deep cultural ambivalence about connection and care tempts us to discount a mother's works of love as "mundane, and undramatic, too distracting from the business of world-rule."[71] When persons remark that the "*only* difference between males and females is simply that females bear young and nurse," that "only" stands as a major reproductive and endocrine difference that we have yet to grasp fully for fear of returning to unfair categorizations and stereotypes.[72] The power to reproduce the species that is biologically unique to women and historically the chief source of our oppression must be reclaimed for the power it holds.

69. McFague, *Models of God*, pp. 105, 119-20.

70. Nancy J. Chodorow, *The Reproduction of Mothering: Psychoanalysis and the Sociology of Gender* (Berkeley and Los Angeles: University of California Press, 1978); Dorothy Dinnerstein, *The Mermaid and the Minotaur: Sexual Arrangements and Human Malaise* (New York: Harper & Row, 1976).

71. Harrison, "The Power of Anger in the Work of Love," p. 47.

72. See Rossi, "A Biosocial Perspective on Parenting," p. 9.

Mothers know much about generativity that we ought not to disregard. Recovering maternal knowing leads us to consider a more adequate public ideal of generativity. Just as childbearing was never intended by nature as a trade-off for neglecting all other forms of satisfaction and achievement,[73] neither were men in the public work world intended to neglect the lessons of human relationality. Women's ways of understanding generativity and guiding the next generation have applicability to many other kinds of working and caring. Ideally, maternal knowing involves a careful reading of the other, oneself, and human nature; it can teach a mode of ethical reasoning that heightens empathy and reflexivity; it can foster a deeper grasp of self and yet push one to transcend oneself in a renewed consideration for children at large and those in need of care.

Children give a new view of people in general, leading to an identification with plights and causes previously unknown and bringing a fresh commitment to the broader community.[74] Somehow, through the mutual understanding learned and practiced over and over in the intense moments of attachment with a little, developing person, one who has truly cared for a child gains new modes of relating and new empathy for others — parents, other children, one's spouse, the oppressed. The capacities and values of maternal knowing are tasks and qualities worthy of recapitulation beyond the narrow confines of the mother-child dyad. Only recognition and recovery by both women and men of qualities and ways of knowing heretofore devalued and privatized will suffice.

Ultimately, fresh ways of interpreting the bodily processes of reproduction, child care, and parenting have transformative social and political implications. A maternal feminist epistemology, if adopted, warrants serious and sustained societal action that would challenge and alter structures and ideologies of care and generativity both within the religious academy and beyond. Internally, it requires a theology that challenges its early twentieth-century heritage — an objectivist pursuit of universalizable truths and a "masculine definition of care" that promotes "a vocabulary of toughness, realism, masculinity, efficiency," and envisions the minister as "a man of imposing physique . . . six feet tall and exuding strength."[75] Externally, maternal feminist epistemology requires a public critique of ac-

73. Germaine Greer, *The Female Eunuch* (St. Albans: Granada Publishing Ltd., 1971), p. 248, cited by Washbourn, *Becoming Woman*, p. 104.

74. Gudorf, "Parenting, Mutual Love, and Sacrifice," pp. 177-78.

75. E. Brooks Holifield, *A History of Pastoral Care in America: From Salvation to Self-Realization* (Nashville: Abingdon Press, 1983), pp. 167-68, 178.

ademic ideals of knowledge and social and economic norms of care that artificially separate public material productivity from private pro-creativity, nurturance, and tending, rewarding the former and disregarding and devaluing the latter.

My suggestion, then, for the epistemological reflections of theology is both limited and challenging: to recognize gender differences and to re-cover suppressed but invaluable dimensions of "our bodies, ourselves" that inform theories and practices is task enough. A liberated consciousness of the potential power of women's sexuality and mothering and a renewed awareness of the latent powers and vulnerabilities of men, heretofore suppressed under the reign of patriarchy, would transpose our ways of knowing both in theology and in society. Attention to the role of gender and to the experience of mothering provides an avenue toward greater recognition and comprehension of other contextual factors that critically impinge on and influence our epistemologies. Although we have a long way to go before accomplishing these reconstructive tasks and deepening our conversation, we are on our way — or, at least, a pregnant pastoral theologian has had her word.

CHAPTER 6

The Subversive Practice of Pastoral Theology

BACKGROUND AND INTRODUCTION

I tell students to avoid bloated titles. Then, I go and write one myself. But there was a lot riding on this essay. So I must have thought I had to say it all in the original title (see below).

This is a chapter whose contents I have neglected in the years since its publication. I prepared the essay in the mid-1990s, shortly after I joined Vanderbilt's faculty, for a doctoral colloquium introducing the study of religion to entering students in the Graduate Department of Religion. Faculty members took turns presenting their disciplines. I wrote out my remarks in more detail than the occasion called for, perhaps as much for my own sake as that of students. But as a result I had a manuscript ready when two senior scholars, Dutch theologian Riet Bons-Storm and South African theologian Denise Ackermann, asked me to contribute an essay to the first international book of feminist practical theology, *Liberating Faith Practices: Feminist Practical Theologies in Context,* in the late 1990s. I thought my essay fit their aims. Their edited volume as a whole is worth greater notice.

Some of the chapter's ideas about pastoral knowledge are now commonplace, such as the need to recognize the influence of context or the

This essay was originally published as "The Subject and Practice of Pastoral Theology as a Practical Theological Discipline: Pushing Past the Nagging Identity Crisis to the Poetics of Resistance," in *Liberating Faith Practices: Feminist Practical Theologies in Context,* ed. Denise Ackermann and Riet Bons-Storm (Leuven, the Netherlands: Peeters, 1998), pp. 175-98. Used by permission.

place of power analysis and a hermeneutic of suspicion in interpreting traditions and situations. At the same time, the chapter is full of surprises and foreshadowing. What emerges is a portrait of a discipline that disrupts Western epistemological assumptions. In my attempt to identify pastoral theology's best attributes, I end up questioning the linear, systematic, abstract, and highly cognitive nature of Western twentieth-century theology.

First, the chapter describes how contemporary pastoral theology fits into the evolution of Western knowledge, born at the intersection of modernity and postmodernity. Pastoral theology is as old as any other kind of theology, with roots in the early Christian movement and church fathers. But as a recognized academic enterprise, located largely in Protestant university divinity schools and seminaries, pastoral theology is a quintessentially modern discipline. It was shaped from the beginning by twentieth-century psychology and yet thrown almost immediately into the confusion of postmodern deconstruction. I also trace the evolution of its academic guilds. Although Edward Farley and others characterized guild proliferation as a perfect instance of the growing specialization and fragmentation, this chapter suggests that something else was going on. Something was not quite working in theology proper that left pastoral and practical theologians scrambling for new definitions and styles. In fact, the chapter's portrait of a disciplinary identity crisis is overstated, as I argue in my introduction to Chapter 1. Now I would describe the pluralism in job and area titles as a sign of vitality rather than confusion or disintegration. And I would argue that the real crisis lies not in pastoral theology but in theological education, its academic captivity, and loss of relevance.

Second, the chapter suggests that disembodied knowing is ultimately insufficient for understanding the subject matter of faith and its practice. Pastoral theology and practical theology pursue a participatory, performative, and proactive kind of knowing that stays close to the ground, attends to human agony and ecstasy, and attempts to relieve suffering. They do not just resist modern objectivity; they declare human subjectivity complex and unfathomable. They aim at *connection* as much as *truth* (an insight also described in Chapter 5) and recognize an inherent not-knowing and misunderstanding that pervade the knowing that comes through human empathy. I compare pastoral theology to poetry, prayer, and psychoanalysis in its desire to fathom what resides below or outside consciousness and to express the inexpressible.

Third and finally, the chapter foreshadows work to come. When I blur the distinction between practical theology and pastoral theology, I perpetuate a problem I have since criticized. I say "perhaps" I lumped the two disciplines together "too carelessly." Now I would excise *perhaps* and confess that in fact I jumble the terms. In my original presentation, I doubt I used the phrase "practical theology" much, if at all. But when I revised the essay for a practical theology book, I just changed some of my references, knowing all the while that the terms were not interchangeable. I just did not want to go to the trouble to explain the differences. I also assumed that the distinctions I had learned in a U.S. Protestant context were universal and obvious. Now I know that Protestants and Catholics as well as U.S. scholars and scholars elsewhere do not use the terms uniformly.

To make matters more complicated, when it comes to epistemology and method, there *is* an important overlap between the two disciplines. The chapter is on what U.S. Protestants regard as *pastoral theology* more than *practical theology.* This is evident in my attention to the self, personal narrative, and individual healing. Yet, even here, in pastoral theology's interest in lived experience, response to suffering, and disruption of Western patterns of knowing, the discipline shares attributes with the wider field of practical theology. And I am wary here and in Chapter 9 when practical theology tempers these unsettling epistemological claims through greater abstraction in order to obtain academic recognition.

This chapter and Chapter 9 also contain a promissory hint of an argument I developed several years later (in an article that is now Chapter 7) about the overuse of the *clerical paradigm,* or the orientation of theological education to teaching skills, as *the* diagnosis of theological education's problems. Its prominence has misled us into undervaluing practice and overlooking the blight of the *academic paradigm.* I argue that problems reside not only in practical theology or in a narrow focus on skills but also in the move of other theological disciplines away from messy human suffering, complicated religious and ministerial practices, and ambiguous faith claims. The modern establishment of theology as a university discipline subjected it to "external scientific, rationalistic standards of knowledge" that make it difficult to appreciate other kinds of truths, a concern developed further in Chapter 7.

To identify the existential subject of pastoral theology, many scholars in the United States hearken back to Anton Boisen's foundational metaphor.

Distinct from other areas of religious study, the object is "the study of living human documents rather than books."[1] Elsewhere I have critiqued the individualistic leanings of this metaphor and its focus on the "separative" self as a singular document rather than the "connective" self as participatory and the weave of the wider context.[2] And I suggest an alternative, related image: to study religion in pastoral theology is to study the living web. I do not think it too exaggerated to say that further reflection on the subject and practice of pastoral theology as a practical theological discipline is needed now more than ever before.

The Persistent Identity Crisis

Compared to many areas in the study of religion, religion and personality — a name used by some academic programs in the United States to encompass the many facets of the field that includes pastoral theology — is strikingly young. So, for example, Vanderbilt University Divinity School added its first full-time faculty member in the area of pastoral counseling in 1959. The position was defined in relation to psychology and the medical school around counseling as a special ministerial skill alongside administration, preaching, and communications. Whereas biblical studies in the United States formed its earliest academic society in the late 1800s, pastoral theology did not begin to gather its members into a distinct organization until after the middle of this century. In 1984 The Association of Practical Theology (APT) was formed, partially under the influence of Don Browning. And in 1985 The Society for Pastoral Theology (SPT) was initially convened by Liston Mills and James Lapsley. Both organizations attempted to address concerns not adequately met through a slightly older organization, The Association of Seminary Professors in the Practical Fields (ASPPF). The ASPPF had been established by Ross Snyder and Seward Hiltner in the

1. Anton Boisen, (1950), cited by Charles Gerkin, *The Living Human Document: Revisioning Pastoral Counseling in a Hermeneutical Mode* (Nashville: Abingdon Press, 1973, 1984), p. 37.

2. Bonnie J. Miller-McLemore, "The Human Web and the State of Pastoral Theology," *The Christian Century*, 7 April 1993, pp. 366-69, and "The Living Human Web: Pastoral Theology at the Turn of the Century," in *Through the Eyes of Women: Insights for Pastoral Care*, ed. Jeanne Stevenson-Moessner (Minneapolis: Fortress Press, 1996), pp. 9-26. See also Catherine Keller, *From a Broken Web: Separation, Sexism, and Self* (Boston: Beacon Press, 1986).

1950s and became the Association of Professional Education for Ministry in the 1970s in an attempt to widen its membership beyond seminary education and the "practical" fields before disbanding in 1982.[3]

To push these examples a bit further, initially the American Association of Pastoral Counselors, an organization for the certification of therapists and an important part of the pastoral theology movement in the 1960s and 1970s, felt threatened by the revival of the SPT because it would inevitably draw academics away. And in the last few years the APT has had a revival of its own, which will in turn, I believe, challenge the numbers and strength of the SPT. Certainly the creation of the International Academy of Practical Theology in 1992 promises both to increase the visibility of certain facets of the discipline and to siphon off energies formerly devoted more narrowly to pastoral theology.

Meanwhile, many U.S. scholars in the general area of religion and personality, particularly those in universities and colleges, do not see either of these organizations as primary. They work more explicitly in the area of religious studies and are likely to attend the American Academy of Religion or the Social Scientific Study of Religion. Some pastoral theologians attempt to maintain an allegiance to these organizations as well.

During the past century, professional guilds have come to wield a power over religion — how it is studied and taught in the United States — that is seldom recognized, studied, or understood. However, the point of these extended examples at the moment is rather simple: Although in one sense predecessors in the field date back to Kierkegaard, Luther, Catholic moral theology, Augustine, even Jewish rabbinical counsel and early house-church movements, in another sense the current area of religion and personality does not know any pre-scientific, pre-Enlightenment, pre-modern period, before which its study of religion was not influenced by rational, scientific methods. In a sense, pastoral theology is a modern study of religion par excellence, coming to fruition precisely as a result of new so-called objective, measurable, empirical means of knowing the "truths" of human experience. In other words, the field did not consolidate its academic position until after the social sciences, psychology in particular, had given new life to the study of the person, religious experience, pastoral care, and ministry. In some settings the field was organized around a narrow model of professional training. Moreover, just as the field might

---

3. Some of this history of the organizations has been recounted to me by colleagues Herbert Anderson and Liston Mills.

have begun to consolidate its parameters and assumptions about the study of religion, modern models of knowing and truth began to fall apart. Hence, unity, values, and facts in the study of religion are challenged anew by postmodern understandings of truth as contextual, culture-bound, value-loaded, subjective, allusive, and so on. How could a movement become established in a context where established disciplines of religious and theological studies themselves were under fire?

So, on the one hand, the modern psychologies of Freud, James, Jung, and others gave lifeblood to the study of religion in theological schools and clinical settings and led to a powerful new movement of religion and personality and the renewal of pastoral theology, care, counseling, psychotherapy, and, most recently, spiritual direction. On the other hand, the movement was split right from the beginning.

This split is perhaps best exemplified in the diverse names by which those who work in the general area of religion and personality identify what they do: those in the area may teach psychology of religion, sociology of religion, religion and personality, religion and culture, pastoral care, pastoral counseling, pastoral psychology, pastoral theology, practical theology, religion and psychology, and, most recently, ethics or moral theology. As these titles reflect, the practice of the discipline in the United States can be roughly divided into three groups: those involved in the empirical or hermeneutical social-scientific study of religious experience; those interested in practical and pastoral theology, care, and counseling; and those engaged in the critical personal and cultural correlation of theology and the social sciences.

Where one stands within this threefold classification partially corresponds to the location of one's primary work in seminary or university-related divinity school or college and university. It also partially corresponds to the location of one's work in relation to the recent and complex distinction between and debate about theological studies and religious studies. On this score, it is interesting to note that teaching in the field within a university-situated divinity school, as distinct from a free-standing seminary or a department of religion in a university or college, presents unique challenges by forcing careful attention to the dual commitments of the academic study of religion *and* the professional training of ministers who profess faith. It is in such a context that I seek further insight into the nature of the discipline of pastoral theology.

My own research on the subjects of families, mothers, work, love, and death and dying has tended to fall into the two categories of practical, pastoral theology and critical correlation of religion and culture, reflecting both where I have come to teach and my own scholarly interests.[4] However, as a feminist pastoral theologian I identify the critical correlation of religion and culture as an essential component of an adequate practical, pastoral theology. The important point for the moment, however, is less my own particular approach. Rather, the point is this: Anyone who wants to write a comprehensive text in the general area of religion and personality must first address and in some fashion dispel the persistent identity crisis of the field or at least situate one's work in relation to this crisis. This also means addressing the conflicts in the study of religion more broadly speaking. And given the nature of the academic debate over matters of religious beliefs and the pursuit of knowledge, neither of these tasks promises an easy entrance into the discussion.

Bellying through the Darkness: Rudimentary Definitions

My beginning proposition about how one studies religion in the general area of religion and personality studies, and pastoral theology within that area, is simple, even if its practice issues in terribly complex questions, forms, and problems: One studies religion at the point where human suffering evokes or calls for a religious response and sometimes at the point where a religious response is given and/or experienced. As black feminist bell hooks puts it, one dares "to create theory from the location of pain and struggle." Indeed, she expresses her gratitude to those who so risk, for "it is not easy to name our pain, to theorize from that location"; it takes courage to "expose wounds" and to lend one's experience as a "means to chart new theoretical journeys."[5] In a poem that picks up the metaphor of weave and web, "Needle/Plow," Barbara Seaman captures some of what happens among scholars in religion and personality and pastoral theology.[6] "Knowing how to pull a straight line will help, but it's depth," she says, "that matters — being willing to push through the obvious weave of the world to the underview . . . that and not being afraid to belly through darkness. . . ."

4. Bonnie J. Miller-McLemore, *Death, Sin, and the Moral Life: Contemporary Cultural Interpretations of Death and Dying* (Atlanta: Scholars Press, 1988); *Also a Mother: Work and Family as Theological Dilemma* (Nashville: Abingdon Press, 1994).

5. bell hooks (Gloria Watkins), *Teaching to Transgress: Education as the Practice of Freedom* (New York: Routledge & Kegan Paul, 1994), p. 74.

6. Barbara Seaman, "Needle/Plow," *The Christian Century*, 6 November 1996, p. 1062.

Measured against this definition, sometimes the best pastoral theology does not evolve from those who call themselves pastoral theologians. Church historian Roberta Bondi's work is a wonderful case in point. Protesting against the ways both the repressive images of an authoritarian God in her confessional Baptist background and the objective abstractions of her higher academic education distort the Christian theological enterprise, she redefines "the primary stuff of theology." Theology is about the "messy particularity of everyday lives examined with excruciating care and brought into conversation with the great doctrines of the Christian tradition."[7] And while bell hooks would not identify herself as a pastoral theologian, when her efforts to address the sufferings and healing of African-American women lead her to emphasize the wisdom of the elders, the movement of the spirit, and the resources of religious traditions and communities despite their occasional hypocrisy, then she qualifies as such.[8]

If a comprehensive orientation distinguishes the area of religion and personality and pastoral theology within it, it is the focus on living, rather than dead persons and cultures, the focus on the psyche, whether understood as ego, soul, or self, and the focus on the clinical or therapeutic or healing dimension of psyche and living persons.[9]

In the last decade or so, under the influence of many kinds of liberation theology, especially feminist theologies, these three foci have engendered a fourth related interest in the political dimension of healing that sees a prophetic, social, proactive stance as imperative for pastoral theology. Beyond the conventional modes of healing, sustaining, guiding, and reconciling of William Clebsch and Charles Jaekle with which pastoral care has been routinely equated, the intent becomes resisting, empowering, nurturing, and liberating.[10]

Although significantly influenced by other contemporary theological movements, this political imperative in pastoral theology is not simply

7. Paul Slentz, student book report on *Memories of God: Theological Reflections on a Life* by Roberta C. Bondi (Nashville: Abingdon Press, 1995).

8. See bell hooks, *Sisters of the Yam: Black Women and Self-Recovery* (Boston: South End Press, 1993).

9. I acknowledge my colleague in Hebrew Bible, Douglas Knight, for this characterization during a colloquium in which I presented parts of this chapter.

10. This is partially based on Carroll Weaver's informal remarks during a panel at the American Academy of Religion, November 1996, drawing on her dissertation work on womanist pastoral theology. See William Clebsch and Charles Jaekle, *Pastoral Care in Historical Perspective*, 2d. ed. (New York: Aronson, 1983).

a borrowing from other areas of study in religion, but is foreshadowed within the field itself. An emphasis on political and social freedom has roots among the early founders of the movement such as Boisen and Hiltner, who were themselves influenced by Erich Fromm and the Frankfurt School of social theory.[11] One could feasibly argue that even the common title of religion and personality signals broader interests than a focus on the individual psyche, since it borrows from anthropology the term of *personality* as always culturally reflexive and constructed. Furthermore, this suggests that a better comprehensive title for the area might be religion, personality, *and culture.*

Notably, this fourth focus signals a rapprochement between the work in pastoral theology and the work in other fields besides Bondi in church history, such as the work in systematic theology by Catherine Keller, Rita Nakashima Brock, Marjorie Suchocki, and others. As postmodernism and liberation movements challenge basic definitions of truth and reality, others in the field of religion have themselves become more interdisciplinary and anthropological in their approaches. Understanding lived subjective experience becomes an important means of mapping the making and unmaking of culture in a variety of religious disciplines.[12] If God is seen as located within the other and within the outcast and dispossessed, then students in a variety of previously distinct disciplines of religious studies must develop fresh ways to relate and focus on the other. If "postmodernism signals not an absolute breaking-up of the hegemony of modern Western culture"[13] but a receptivity to other perspectives and values as part of the complex constellation that comprises human life, then scholars in pastoral theology join others in adopting a notably postmodern, deconstructivist tone and method while harboring residual modern faiths and hopes.

It is also important to note briefly the convergence and divergence of pastoral and practical theology, which the threefold classification above lumps perhaps too carelessly into one group. Recognition of the importance of pastoral theology as distinctly focused on particular hu-

---

11. Rodney J. Hunter, "The Therapeutic Tradition of Pastoral Care and Counseling," in *Pastoral Care and Social Conflict*, ed. Pamela D. Couture and Rodney J. Hunter (Nashville: Abingdon Press, 1995), p. 20.

12. These remarks are by Paula Cooey, "Theological Anthropology after Modernism," The American Academy of Religion, New Orleans, November 1996.

13. Maureen Dallison Kemeza, "Dante as Guide and Provocation," *The Christian Century*, 20-27 November 1996, p. 1148.

man anguish and responses makes me wary of too quick a move from pastoral theology into the broader or more comprehensive realm of practical theology as one means to retain a foothold in the academy. And in some cases, academic survival is precisely what deliberations about practical theology seem to have as their agenda. Practical theology, perhaps because it sometimes can operate at a greater level of abstraction and theoretical generalization than pastoral theology, seems to obtain thereby some kind of scholarly validity. But this validity, just as the organizations in the example above, remains precarious due to practical theology's unavoidable interests in and even confessional commitments to the church and faith itself. In addition, abstraction and objectivity have been used to obscure and silence other perceptions and truths. In a postmodern context, one must wonder about the adequacy of a discipline predicated on modernist scientific values.

Nonetheless, a practical theological methodology remains critical and useful, less in and of itself, and more in approaching and constructing particular submovements, including those of pastoral care, religious education, liturgical studies, and so forth. So, to attend and respond to human distress in pastoral theology, I use practical theological steps — commonly identified by scholars such as Don Browning, Thomas Groome, James and Evelyn Whitehead, and others — of descriptive understanding, comparative analysis in dialogical conversation with religious and secular resources, evaluation, and decision.

Illustrative Readings in the Weave of the World

To develop the idea that one studies religion in pastoral theology at the point where human suffering evokes or calls for a religious response and sometimes at the point where a religious response is given and/or experienced, I turn to three selected readings from Augustine, Boisen, and my own book, *Also a Mother.* I offer these readings as purely illustrative and without explicit analysis, prior to making some suggestive generalizations. I want to move readers into direct engagement with the difficult and complex task at hand when studying religion in pastoral theology, by locating concretely the study of religion in diverse moments of suffering from which religious reflection, and perhaps theology, emerges or has emerged. Having done that, rather than analyze any one of these readings, I will make three general observations about the study of religion in pastoral theology and conclude with a brief identification of some of the problems and possibilities. The illustrative selections from texts are mostly random; any number of readings — C. S. Lewis's *A Grief Observed;* womanist essays on suffering and evil in *A Troubling in My Soul;* recent stories of the struggles of gay men and lesbians in *Wrestling with the Angel* — could serve this purpose.[14] However, the readings from Augustine and Boisen represent pivotal voices that have shaped the field. I include an excerpt from *Also a Mother* to demonstrate some of the changing parameters of the field and my work within it. Any number of selections from the texts could be used; I merely chose one reading from many that embody acute moments of struggle.

A corollary intent behind inserting these voices, unanalyzed, into this chapter is to evoke through them echoes of each person's own moments of encounter with what David Tracy calls "limit situations," from which almost all interest in the study of religion flows regardless of the eventual form that religious study takes.[15] To a greater extent than other areas of religious studies, religion and personality studies in general, and pastoral theology more specifically, make limit situations a central focus. My hope in this chapter is not just to come to an understanding of how scholars, myself included, work in the sometimes boundary-less field of religion and personality studies, but to spark each reader's own reflection on her own work within the study of religion. Rather than analyze each reading as a limit situation from which further religious and theological reflection emerges, I will make several observations about the nature of religious study in pastoral theology with these illustrative moments in the background.

Reading 1

And I, as I looked back over my life, was quite amazed to think of how long a time had passed since my nineteenth year, when I had first become inflamed with a passion for wisdom and had resolved that, when once I found it, I would leave behind me all the empty hopes and deceitful frenzies of vain desires. And now I was in my thirtieth year, still

14. C. S. Lewis, *A Grief Observed* (New York: Bantam Books, 1961); *A Troubling in My Soul: Womanist Perspectives on Evil and Suffering,* ed. Emilie Townes (Maryknoll, N.Y.: Orbis Books, 1993); and Brian Bouldrey, *Wrestling with the Angel: Faith and Religion in the Lives of Gay Men* (New York: Riverhead Books, 1995).

15. David Tracy, *Blessed Rage for Order: The New Pluralism in Theology* (New York: Seabury Press, 1975), pp. 93, 104-8.

sticking in the same mud, still greedy for the enjoyment of things present, which fled from me and wasted me away, and all the time saying: I shall find it tomorrow. See, it will become quite clear and I shall grasp it. . . . But where shall I look for it? And when shall I look for it? . . . And where can I find the books? From where can I get them and when can I get them? Can I borrow them from anybody? . . .

But these are not the thoughts I should have. . . . Life is a misery, death an uncertainty. Suppose it steals suddenly upon me, in what state shall I leave this world? . . . Shall I be punished for my negligence? Or is it true that death will cut off and put an end to all care and all feeling? . . . So I used to speak and so the winds blew and shifted and drove my heart this way and that, and time went by and I was slow in turning. . . .[16]

Reading 2

While working one day on the Statement of Belief — I think it was Wednesday, October 6 — some strange ideas came surging into my mind, ideas of doom, ideas of my own unsuspected importance. With them began the frank psychosis. . . . It began without evidence of undue exaltation . . . [but then] everything began to whirl. It seemed that the world was coming to an end.

. . . As I look back upon the strange ideas which came flooding into my mind during the disturbed periods . . . [I see that] the sufferer is striving desperately to face what for him is ultimate Reality. Thus interpreted, an acute schizophrenic episode assumes the character of religious experience. It becomes an attempt at thoroughgoing reorganization, beginning at the very center of one's being, an attempt which tends either to make or break the personality.[17]

Reading 3

Resolution of the daily conflicts [of family and paid work] leads inevitably to contradictions, frustrations, ambiguous solutions, and hard choices. One day, while trying to revise a manuscript during the naptime of one of my sons, I recall feeling torn between my desire for

16. *The Confessions of St. Augustine*, trans. Rex Warner (New York: Mentor, 1963), pp. 127-29.

17. Anton Boisen, *Out of the Depths: An Autobiographical Study of Mental Disorder and Religious Experience* (New York: Harper & Brothers, 1960), pp. 79-83, 205.

total uninterrupted silence and horror at my fantasy that a capricious god might grant me my impulsive wish and I would lose my children forever.... A hundred times — and not for the last time by any means — I have wondered, Am I attempting a self-defeating feat, trying to "conceive" in professional and familial ways at the same time? . . .

. . . Having children forever changed my way of knowing and thinking about generativity. Parting the passions to articulate those ways comes less easily.... How might we systematically conceptualize this maternal knowing that in [Mary] Gordon's words is more physical and certainly more erotic "than anybody admits"? . . . As point of proof, what does it mean to lactate, to have a body that, sensing another's thirst, "lets-down", drenching me with sweet-smelling milk? Does it alter knowing?

. . . In the movement between the knowing and acting of nursing and tending an infant, I use a mode of circular bodily reasoning, interweaving physical sensation, momentary cognition, behavioral reaction, and a physical sensing and intellectual reading of the results — a trial-and-error, hit-and-miss strategy, which, in its bodily ethos, surpasses that described under the rubric of Catholic moral casuistry.... In contrast to the hierarchy of knowledge that ranks rational knowledge above other forms, we know much in and through our bodies that is intrinsically valuable and precious. . . .

. . . Maternal generativity begins to suggest a way to understand the problem of integrating praxis and theory better than almost anything I have seen in the current literature of practical theology. It challenges false dichotomies: Theory does not involve simply verbalizable knowledge and insight, as much as many have wished. Practice does not mean unmediated action. Both involve qualities more nebulous, fleeting, relative, and momentary. Theory involves the passing recognition of empathic attunement; practice, movement within the realm of attuned theory.[18]

Refusing the Pretense of Objectivity

The following observations are not meant to be comprehensive. They are, in fact, hard to organize. As one way to do so, I rely on a quote from

18. Miller-McLemore, *Also a Mother*, pp. 30-32, 146-49.

Mary K. DeShazer's book, *A Poetics of Resistance: Women Writing in El Salvador, South Africa, and the United States*, cited by Christine Smith in an essay on preaching. According to DeShazer, poetry participates in resistance in at least three ways: (1) poems "refuse the pretense of objectivity"; (2) they "violate poetic decorum in order to invite conflict and confrontation"; and finally, (3) they "call forth from their audience an alternative complicity, a willingness to participate in a re-visionary project — ethical, political, literary — that could actually make a difference in the lives of the marginalized."[19] The study of religion in pastoral theology has many qualities, but these three capture assumptions in its modern history that have become more pronounced in our time of postmodernity.

DeShazer argues that poems of resistance "refuse the pretense of objectivity, instead asserting polemically the terms of their engagement with the topic at hand. In so doing, they claim as their own the task of historiographic reconstruction."[20] Recognizing the pretense of objectivity and identifying one's particular context and perspective characterize the work of many current scholars in pastoral theology more than those in religion and personality engaged in the social-scientific study of religious experience. But it presents challenges to both parties. With the hermeneutic of suspicion as defined by Elisabeth Schüssler Fiorenza, conscious partiality is sought rather than objectivity, participation replaces spectator knowledge, the starting point is to change the status quo, and research is a process of consciousness-raising that assists women.[21]

To study religion from this vantage point, then, means to engage in a power analysis of the biases behind the construction of theories about human nature, not unlike that now engaged in by some biblical scholars studying scriptural texts. Power analysis entails an investigation into and deconstruction of the framework that defines the context and nature of suffering and a reconstruction of the nature of suffering from alternative standpoints. Human suffering, then, is not defined simply along individ-

19. Mary K. DeShazer, *A Poetics of Resistance: Women Writing in El Salvador, South Africa, and the United States* (Ann Arbor: University of Michigan Press, 1994), p. 271, cited by Christine M. Smith, "Preaching as an Art of Resistance," in *The Arts of Ministry: Feminist-Womanist Approaches*, ed. Christie Cozad Neuger (Louisville: Westminster John Knox Press, 1996), p. 47.

20. DeShazer, *A Poetics of Resistance*, p. 271, cited by Smith, "Preaching as an Art of Resistance," p. 47.

21. Cited by Judith Orr, "Administration as an Art of Shared Vision," in *The Arts of Ministry*, ed. Neuger, p. 138.

ual psychological lines. It calls for new psychological and religious understandings that take into account the social, political, and religious contexts of suffering. Echoing an early women's movement slogan that the personal is political, personal *suffering* is political.

When "truths" about religious ideas such as sin or servanthood or love are relocated within alternative subjectivities, suddenly other understandings become apparent. For example, as many feminist theologians have elaborated since Valerie Saiving's classic 1960s essay, "sin" is not always or necessarily pridefulness or will to power or assertion or misuse of one's freedom. When the temptation to sin is experienced in other contexts, certainly that of some women and those with fewer choices and less freedom, the temptation comes as the lure of self-dispersion, relentless self-castigation, fragmentation, loss of voice, and loss of self in life's endless details. Or, as another example, the idea of "servanthood" as Christian ideal takes on new meanings when womanist Jacquelyn Grant claims a particular subjectivity and context. It matters historically, in the U.S. context of slavery and its aftermath, she asserts, that some folk have been "more servant than others." The theme of servanthood can be retained *only* if it means to join "in the struggle of the redeemer against oppression, wherever it is found" as servants of the liberator Jesus.[22] Or, to take one last instance, Protestant definitions of the ideal of human love as self-sacrificial *agape* tend to distort and abort the struggles among those previously silenced and marginalized. Sociologist of religion Cheryl Townsend Gilkes concludes an essay about the ways in which dominant cultural norms of beauty undercut the self-esteem of African-American women with a dialectical understanding of self-love and love of others. At this moment in history, "Self-love . . . is probably the most critical task we complete in establishing our commitment 'to survival and wholeness of entire people, male and female.'"[23] New, candidly subjective contexts mean new definitions in religion and personality. These are voices to be taken seriously precisely in their concrete particularities and contextual subjectivity.

This creates a bit of turmoil around a key thematic term in the field: empathy. Sparked by Carl Rogers' idea of unconditional positive regard, fur-

---

22. Jacquelyn Grant, "The Sin of Servanthood," in *A Troubling in My Soul,* ed. Townes, pp. 204, 213.

23. Cheryl Townsend Gilkes, "The 'Loves' and 'Troubles' of African-American Women's Bodies," in *A Troubling in My Soul,* ed. Townes, p. 247.

ther refined within object-relations theory and Kohutian self-psychology, and used within a variety of venues in religion and personality, empathy has operated as both a prominent method of knowing and a critical aspect of human responsiveness. Yet the extent and capacity of empathy are now under some question. Scholars and practitioners can no longer assume that with proper psychological technique — analysis, mirroring, interpretation — or with proper religious studies technique — cultural anthropology, interdisciplinary investigation, phenomenology, hermeneutics — one can finally know the "other" in the study of religion. As I argue in "The Living Human Web," empathy is confounded by its limitations. "Sometimes a person must admit an inability to fully understand the lived reality of the oppressions suffered by another. There may be boundaries beyond which empathy itself cannot go."[24]

The goal shifts, then, from understanding *qua* understanding to connectivity in difference. Relationality as simply connectedness no longer suffices; relationality now means particularity and differentness as well as connectedness.[25] David Tracy lends theoretical support for this shift in his work on religion in a postmodern age of plurality and ambiguity: "Empathy is much too romantic a category to comprehend this necessary movement in interpretation from otherness, to possibility, to similarity-in-difference."[26] The intent in practical theology in listening to voices distinctly different from our own, according to Christine Smith, is "to move more fully and faithfully into what those differences can mean for all of us." These "holy places of difference . . . challenge and terrify" rather than enlighten the listener.[27] To discern the true and the good in religion requires not just dialogue, but something a bit more elusive, which practical theologian Carol Hess calls "hard dialogue" — difficult, painful questions, awareness of one's personal and cultural biases, and interaction with difference.

---

24. Miller-McLemore, "The Living Human Web," p. 21.

25. Carol Hess, "Education as an Art of Getting Dirty with Dignity," in *The Arts of Ministry,* ed. Neuger, p. 65.

26. David Tracy, *Pluralism and Ambiguity: Hermeneutics, Religion, and Hope* (San Francisco: Harper & Row, 1987), pp. 20-21.

27. Smith, "Preaching as an Art of Resistance," in *The Arts of Ministry,* ed. Neuger, pp. 52, 56.

Violating Religious and Theological Decorum

Mary DeShazer asserts that poems of resistance "violate poetic decorum in order to invite conflict and confrontation. They express anger . . . they hammer readers with . . . fierce rhetoric questions designed to evoke discomfort."[28] Contrary to the supposition that religion can be defined, systematized, or made coherent, to study religion in pastoral theology is to confront the limitations of imposed frameworks. The intent of the study is to get at the inexpressible without losing a genuine sense of it — much like prayer or poetry. Pastoral theology violates religious and theological decorum by claiming theology as messy and by assuming a face-to-face starting point.

The attempt to give order and coherence is not wrong in and of itself, but only as it stifles questions, hides human fallibility, or limits the range of questions and answers to its own order. In the art of education, Carol Hess argues,

> There is nothing wrong with the systematic presentation of tradition and belief, especially in a time when there is so little knowledge of the tradition. There is something drastically wrong, however, with approaches to teaching that do not foster the type of question and depth conversation that is necessary for growth in theological maturity.[29]

Adequate theological method in practical theology must attend to the "messy, dirty, earthy side of life": "life lived in engagement with this world is messy, conflicted, rough, dynamic, and weatherbeaten."[30] Presentational teaching or lectures have a place only if they invite "backtalk." This metaphor from bell hooks in *Talking Back: Thinking Feminist, Thinking Black,* calls to mind a style of preaching and teaching that depends on participatory response, encouragement, engagement, and correction.[31] Academic scholarship in pastoral theology is clearly less interactive and more static than this, but nonetheless works better with an evocative, open-ended, less

28. DeShazer, *A Poetics of Resistance,* p. 271, cited by Smith, "Preaching as an Art of Resistance."

29. Hess, "Education as an Art of Getting Dirty with Dignity," in *The Arts of Ministry,* ed. Neuger, pp. 75-76.

30. Hess, "Education as an Art of Getting Dirty with Dignity," in *The Arts of Ministry,* ed. Neuger, pp. 75-76.

31. bell hooks, *Talking Back: Thinking Feminist, Thinking Black* (Boston: South End Press, 1989).

than conclusive, back-talk style that invites the listener into conversation. In this vein, writings that employ taped conversations, such as the final chapter on communion in *Setting the Table* or *God's Fierce Whimsy,* can have a more powerful or more memorable impact on the reader than a systematic presentation of the same ideas.

In *Lift Every Voice,* an edited collection of liberation "theologies from the underside," Susan Thistlethwaite has a taped and transcribed dialogue with Mary Pellauer about grace and healing in the midst of violence against women — a topic about which Pellauer cannot bring herself to sit down and write. Pellauer observes,

> We're giving people messages about the meaning of theology — for instance, that it is primarily written and not oral. But our experience over the last twenty years has been that it has been in face-to-face conversations that we have learned to do theology in a new way. . . . Theology is not nearly so static as we may have thought when we read the final products in books or essays.

Later in the conversation, she notes, "Theology is not like mathematics — it's not a discipline for young persons at the end of adolescence. It's a discipline in which you need *time* to experience and to live with some insights, so you know what they mean over the long run."[32]

Current work in pastoral theology draws on liberation theology partly because there are distinct affinities in particular methods that violate academic decorum. Liberation theologian Otto Maduro identifies three premises in liberation studies: (1) ordinary human life has precedence over "doing theology"; (2) all theology is theology of specific life experience and attempts to respond to particular, not universal, experience; and (3) theology is a result of "life in community, shared faith, multiple efforts."[33] The hoped-for intent, I would add, is to find "classic" expressions, as Tracy describes them, of the particular that point beyond themselves to hints of more broadly shared experiences.

Practical theologian Don S. Browning makes a related argument for

32. Mary D. Pellauer with Susan Brooks Thistlethwaite, "Conversation on Grace and Healing: Perspectives from the Movement to End Violence against Women," in *Lift Every Voice: Constructing Theologies from the Underside,* ed. Susan Brooks Thistlethwaite and Mary Potter Engel (New York: Harper & Row, 1990), pp. 170, 175.

33. Otto Maduro, *Religion and Social Conflict* (1992), cited by Lallene Rector, unpublished manuscript.

a new starting point for theological studies. The starting point is not biblical studies, historical studies, theological studies, and then practical studies, as in the nineteenth-century ordering of theological study that characterizes the discipline. Our contemporary turmoil within these categories seems to reflect a paradigm shift waiting to happen. The starting point is what Browning calls "fundamental practical theology" with historical theology, systematic theology, and "strategic practical theology" as moments within this more inclusive framework.

This framework stresses the priority of practical interests in the formation of our cognitive and moral world. Hans-Georg Gadamer and others argue that practical application shapes from the beginning theoretical questions. Rather than concern with practice as an act that follows understanding or the application of theory to the specifics of praxis, "concern with practice, in subtle ways we often overlook," guides the hermeneutic process from the beginning.[34] In a sense, one moves from theory-laden practice to practice-laden theory back to theory-laden practice.

The problem of the "clerical paradigm" — that is, the focus on techniques of professional ministry as the main subject of modern practical theology — is partially due to the limited horizons of the practical theological fields and the obsession with technical training in counseling skills. But the problem is not only a problem within the field; it is also a larger systemic issue. The problem of the "clerical paradigm" is also a result of the movement of systematic and construction theology away from the messiness of human suffering, the complications of religious and ministerial practices, and the ambiguities of faith claims and spiritual experiences. Schleiermacher's efforts succeeded in securing a place for theology in the university, but they came at a cost. Not only did he tend to see theology as reflection on ministerial expertise. The establishment of theology as a university discipline also subjected theology to singular external scientific, rationalistic standards of knowledge that ignore other "habits of attention," "provinces of meaning," and "modes of experience" and sometimes remove it from vital sources in religious faith and practice.[35]

Browning's approach, as the method in liberation theology, has other historical precedents in Roman Catholic theology, in pragmatic philoso-

34. Don S. Browning, *A Fundamental Practical Theology: Descriptive and Strategic Proposals* (Minneapolis: Fortress Press, 1991), pp. 7-8.

35. See Martin E. Marty, "The Modes of Being, Doing, and Teaching, and Discovering," *Criterion* 35, no. 2 (Spring/Summer 1996): 25-36.

phy, and in empirical theology. In her book titled *Body, Sex, and Pleasure,*
Catholic ethicist Christine Gudorf, for example, asserts that the first step
in reconstructing Christian sexual ethics is not to begin with particular
traditions, scriptures, or doctrinal faith statements, but "to understand as
best we can human sexuality itself, and in this day and age this means consulting both biological science as well as the experience of human individuals and communities." We need to "begin doing ethics with a description
of the reality of our situation." Once done, we can turn to reflections on
the religious dimensions or theological reflection on the meaning and significance of what has been described.[36]

In an emphasis on the messiness of face-to-face encounter, poetry,
prayer, psychoanalytic understanding of religion, and pastoral theology
are at least united in this one premise about expressing the inexpressible:
"under each speech is an underlying text written on the threshold of the
unconscious."[37] Each practitioner — poet, mystic, analyst, pastor/scholar
— is willing, in the words of my introductory poem, "to push through the
obvious weave of the world to the underview, always turning the surface
over like looking at both sides of an argument."

Calling Forth Participation

Finally, DeShazer contends that poems of resistance "call forth from their
audience an alternative complicity, a willingness to participate in a re-
visionary project — ethical, political, literary — that could actually make a
difference in the lives of the marginalized."[38] One studies religion by
standing at the point where human suffering evokes or calls for a religious
response and sometimes at the point where religious response is given or
experienced. For many scholars in religion and personality, working from
the vantage point of suffering necessarily entails a proactive starting point.
The intent is to break silences, to challenge the status quo, to participate in
what womanist theologian Emilie Townes calls the "radical truth-telling"
required by an ethic of justice and love.

36. Christine E. Gudorf, *Body, Sex, and Pleasure: Reconstructing Christian Sexual Ethics* (Cleveland: Pilgrim Press, 1994), pp. 3-5.

37. Ralph L. Underwood, *Pastoral Care and the Means of Grace* (Minneapolis: Fortress
Press, 1993), p. 30.

38. DeShazer, *A Poetics of Resistance,* p. 271, cited by Smith, "Preaching as an Art of
Resistance."

The focus on truth-telling was partially responsible for the original appeal of the psychological sciences among those in religion. Freud appeared as the psychological inheritor of Copernicus and Darwin, telling people the truths, not of earth's revolution around the sun or humanity's evolution from animal, but of the unconscious motivation of their overt behavior, social norms, and rationalizations. More recently, the regard for truth-telling among those in pastoral theology is partially responsible for the attraction to liberation theories and theologies. Boisen and others asked the question of the meaning of religious struggles from within the midst of these struggles, focusing on the clinic and, in Boisen's case, even his own flight into schizophrenia. In so doing, Boisen gave fresh visibility to the voice of the institutionalized patient. Liberation theologies ask a similar question, but further refined by demands for justice of a dramatic political nature (gender, ethnic, racial, class, and so forth). As Audre Lorde puts it: "In my social location, where is justice struggling to be born and how can I help?"[39]

In the midst of the rich diversity of voices in theologies of liberation in *Lift Every Voice,* Mary Potter Engel and Susan Thistlethwaite note a prominent commonalty in the first paragraph of their introduction: "What these different theologies do share is their commitment to social justice," in essence their "solidarity with those suffering and in need" in particular contexts. This entails the attempt to speak "with and on behalf of" rather than "to or for" certain communities. It entails a "crucial shift in the role of theologian from individual scholarly authority to reflective community advocate." This shift is evident in the collaborative work that hopes to evolve a more "communally based and authorized theology," despite the general academic disdain for collectively authored publications.[40]

Advocacy is not new to religious and theological studies: Bonhoeffer defines the study of religion as a twofold exploration of the knowledge and experience that human evil will have its day alongside the insistence that it is the responsibility of each human being, especially if Christian or in some other way religiously committed, to prevent evil from having its day. Perhaps the focus has sharpened slightly in current practical theological circles: the focus, as Christine Smith identifies it, is struggle and survival in

---

39. Audre Lorde, "The Master's Tools Will Never Dismantle the Master's House," in *This Bridge Called My Back: Writings by Radical Women of Color,* ed. Cherrie Moraga and Gloria Anzaldua (Watertown, Mass.: Persephone Press, 1981), p. 100, cited by Engel and Thistlethwaite in *Lift Every Voice,* p. 14.

40. Thistlethwaite and Engel, "Introduction," in *Lift Every Voice,* pp. 1-2.

the midst of suffering rather than enlightenment and transformation in the midst of privilege and power.

Problems and Possibilities

The evolving definitions of the study of pastoral theology as a practical theological discipline portend problems and possibilities. I will name only a few questions that arise from the precarious position of pastoral theology as a discipline peculiarly poised between practice, person, psychology, liberation theology, confessional religious congregations, and the academy. Tracy identifies three publics for which those in religion write: academy, society, and church.[41] More than in any other area in the study of religion, those in pastoral and practical theology often attempt to speak and write for all three. Is this impossible or simply wrongheaded? Or does this bring critical relevance to the exercise?

This cross-public audience is not a new phenomenon; perhaps historically those in religion who have worked in ways analogous to the field of pastoral theology today also addressed multiple publics. However, a chief difference today is the striking divisions between these three publics in terms of language, standards of truth, practices and rituals, and norms. To write for all three publics has become more difficult than before. The tensions are heightened by U.S. universities whose standards emphasize "efficiency" and "effectiveness" measured by quantitative standards. Not surprisingly, problems of identity, definition, and clarity about the parameters plague the field. Moreover, pastoral theology is a discipline within the academy of religion that necessarily draws on a variety of other areas of study, from early Jewish and Christian studies to recent history of religion in America, ethics, and systematic theology. Often this means that it tends to do many tasks poorly rather than one task well. What are the foundational texts internal to the field, if significant resources are either suffering moments, science, or other religious texts? And who reads our texts? If only those in the church public buy and read them, how will scholars further theoretical reflection? Finally, the field joins other fields in arbitrating the tension between the particularity of religious and philosophical traditions and the claims to universality of theological and ethical discourse. If

---

41. David Tracy, *The Analogical Imagination: Christian Theology and the Culture of Pluralism* (New York: Crossroad, 1981), p. 5.

particularity determines truth, what of wider, possibly universal religious and moral claims?[42]

At the same time, could the field's struggles with marginalization and confusion also be the field's gift to the study of religion? From a disadvantageous position on the brink of academic discourse, the field offers a few strengths to current religious and theological studies. The field of pastoral theology has a long, complicated history adjudicating questions of interdisciplinary work — the use of the human sciences — within the study of religion. Such interdisciplinary study has begun to characterize almost all areas. Second, the field has an important history of attention to thick description of religious phenomenon, praxis, and experience, including attention to the complexities of marginalized experience. Finally, over against ideals, which climaxed in the mid-twentieth century, that religion could be, and perhaps should be, studied by non-participants, the field cannot avoid difficult questions about the place of faith and religious conviction in the study of religion as an element of the context in which the scholar-teacher herself is often located.

These three general contributions by no means prove that pastoral theology has answers to current research questions on these matters. Rather, simply stated, pastoral theology is "looking at both sides," "always turning the surface over . . . not being afraid to belly through darkness or cut through any weedy tangle of thread-roots." Pastoral theologians have the dubious honor, as Larry Graham remarks, of being "among the first to show up" and among the last to "give answers."[43]

---

42. See Lisa Sowle Cahill and James F. Childress, *Christian Ethics: Problems and Prospects* (Cleveland: Pilgrim Press, 1996).

43. Larry Kent Graham, "Pastoral Theology and Gay and Lesbian Experience" (unpublished ms., p. 1) [now published as *Discovering Images of God: Narratives of Care among Lesbians and Gays* by Westminster John Knox Press, 1997]. On the one hand, pastoral theologians attempt to "be present to" the suffering, while on the other they press what is heard into "constructive religious interpretation." He reflects Hiltner's own position that "unaddressed theological issues often arise from the particularity of human experience" and, if pressed, interpretation of what happens in concrete experience has the potential for constructing new theological understandings or clarifying unresolved matters in the tradition (citing Seward Hiltner, *Preface to Pastoral Theology* [Nashville: Abingdon Press, 1958]).

CHAPTER 7

The Clerical and the Academic Paradigm

BACKGROUND AND INTRODUCTION

Chapters 7 and 8 are companion pieces. I wrote them around the same time I wrote the definition of practical theology in Chapter 4, and they reflect influences described in greater detail in its introduction. Beginning in 2003, I helped oversee a one-year planning grant and then a full-fledged grant for a doctoral program in Theology and Practice in Vanderbilt's Graduate Department of Religion, joining faculty peers in investigating the problems in theological education and developing a curriculum in response. During this same period and of greater conceptual influence, I also met regularly with faculty and ministers in a Lilly Endowment seminar on practical theology and Christian ministry. We used a variety of practices to uncover fresh meanings for theology and ministry — sharing syllabi, trying out definitions, writing papers and reading each other's papers, reading testimonies of ministerial formation and examples of practical theology, and, of course, talking — lots of talking.

One of the challenges we faced in both contexts was to understand the history of theological education and the study of theology more generally. Those interested in such matters can hardly avoid systematic theologian Edward Farley's treatise, *Theologia: The Fragmentation and Unity of Theological Education,* published during the 1980s renaissance in practical

---

This essay was originally published as "The 'Clerical Paradigm': A Fallacy of Misplaced Concreteness?" *International Journal of Practical Theology* 11, no. 2 (2007): 19-38. Used by permission.

theology. Since its publication, you can see its influence on many practical theological works that try to situate the problem historically before turning to their primary concern. Even historians such as Randy Maddox rely on Farley's categories to describe modern developments.

So how accurate and helpful are Farley's terms if they still carry so much weight? This was actually a question I wanted to explore long before either the planning grant or the Lilly seminar. As is evident in Chapters 6 and 9, I had felt annoyed with the term "clerical paradigm" for years. The seminar afforded me an excuse to figure out why. My annoyance came as much from practical experience as conceptual concern, as the chapter's opening explains. I knew from watching my husband that all the cognitive learning he had done at the University of Chicago Divinity School did not finally add up to excellent ministerial practice. Its teachings did not exhaust the kind of knowledge he needed to pastor a small working-class congregation in a struggling industrial community south of the city. This was also true for me in my work in institutions around the city as chaplain, youth minister, pastoral counselor, and finally teacher of ministers. Both my husband and I believed rhetoric that circulated among students about the superiority of our education. Chicago teaches students how to think as the most important foundation for doing ministry; only the surrounding seminaries stooped to teaching ministry itself. I am not saying Chicago faculty said anything like this. This was graduate-student lore; it seemed to be in the rarified air we breathed. Maybe it made us feel better about ourselves. I began to see its fallacy when I moved closer to ministry.

There is some truth about the value of a classical education. I have benefited immensely from the rigor of comprehensive master's exams on Western history and contemporary study of religion, lectures and courses on classical theologians, philosophical and theological ethics, psychological and sociological theory, and rigorous processes of qualifying examination, dissertation proposal, and so on. I remain grateful for the privilege of such an education. Without it I am not sure where I would be or what I would be doing. But I doubt it would fit as well as my current situation, and I could not do my current job well without it. I expect similar intellectual work from my own students. So how to articulate what is missing without devaluing its contributions?

The Lilly seminar not only provided space to raise this question. It also offered plenty of colleagues to catch and correct me when I got carried away. I can see places in the chapter where I temper my argument, praising Farley's contributions and clarifying that my debate was less with him than his legacy. In fact, I end up arguing that you can see in Farley himself a concern similar to the one I raise about the *academic paradigm* or the *cognitive captivity of theology* that readers have ignored or de-emphasized. I think both Farley and I agree that systematic theology is in crisis at least as much as, if not more than, practical theology.

My annoyance comes through in the chapter anyway. Overuse of the clerical paradigm to describe *the* problem in theological education has led us to devalue all things *clerical* or *practical* as lesser than all things *academic,* despite Farley's and anyone else's intention. Maybe this is a temptation of the academy at large that precedes Farley, and he just falls prey to it. This pattern pertains in diverse areas of the university, from literature and foreign languages to the physical and social sciences. Faculty who work on practical dimensions of their discipline somehow have less status, even if their research and teaching require more time, ingenuity, and complexity. The problem reflects an epistemological bias that we think our way into acting rather than the other way around (or some more genuinely dialogical approach). Theology shares this problem with the wider academy and yet has its own unique challenge. Its subject matter, variously defined as God, love of God, faith, religious practice, and so on, requires a multiplicity of ways of knowing, many of which go unrecognized in academic contexts. When theology tries to remain true to both the church and the academy, it finds itself in a tenacious and insidious double bind: "Too pious for the academy, it [becomes] too academic for the church."

This chapter has a second grievance. It calls for a rehabilitation of the idea of *application* and *know-how,* and even of *hints and helps.* The word *apply* itself has fallen on hard times in many practical theological circles. We insist our discipline does not apply truths from more theoretical areas. But then the whole question of use and application gets dropped, despite the reality that ministers and others have to do something with what they learn. Unthinking dismissals of *"mere* know-how," as if know-how is easy knowledge to master, overlook the complicated relationship between *techne* and *phronesis* and the role of know-how in the greater pursuit of ministerial wisdom. Famous musicians do not cease doing scales. Learning to play an instrument requires a finely tuned dialectic between daily exercise and artistry.

Finally, I complain about Farley's longing for theology as "one thing." Recognizing theology's plurality of contexts and purposes, as I do in the definition in Chapter 4 or as others such as Robert Schreiter and

Kathryn Tanner have done, is a better approach. In essence, practical theology, as one sort of plurality, has been trying to come to the rescue of Christian theology for the past several decades, even if often unrecognized, uncelebrated, and unwelcome. For practical theologians, theology entails not just thinking critically about faith but embodying it wisely in practice.

Whereas some of the other chapters in this book can stand alone, this chapter cannot. To get from complaint to constructive proposal, you need to read Chapter 8 on practical theology and pedagogy. And to grasp Chapter 8, I recommend the edited book of which Chapter 8 is only a part and from which it received its life-breath, *For Life Abundant*.

The seminary where I first taught pastoral care sits across the street from the university where I did my graduate work in religion and psychology. When I crossed the street from academic study to ministerial teaching two decades ago, however, I entered a new world. Many of my students were second-career adults ready to move into ministerial vocations. Eager to learn theology, they also wanted to know how to use it.

Around the same time, my husband left doctoral study to pastor a small, working-class congregation in the suburban outskirts of the city. To keep a dwindling membership afloat in a marginal neighborhood, he needed resources neither of us had imagined in graduate school. He eventually acquired the skills and wisdom that helped sustain a vibrant ministry. I had a similar experience developing expertise in training as a pastoral counselor. Oddly, though, the literature in practical theology of the 1980s defined this kind of attention to "hints and helps" as a problem. For the most part, it still does.

Negative comments about the problem of "tips and hints" and "applied theology" are common among those who teach in practical theology in the United States and beyond. Such comments are voiced regularly at meetings and appear in our publications. In one fell swoop, practical theologians dismiss "application" and "rules of thumb" as distasteful leftovers from the days of the "clerical paradigm," when theological education focused solely on equipping clergy. Criticism is seldom turned back on systematic theology or any other area of the curriculum. For example, a recent book on theological method bemoans the recent history of "'applied' or pastoral theologies, with the latter as the 'hints and helps' of pastoralia" or "merely applications of truth found within systematic theology."[1] The story of the clerical paradigm encapsulates our history, and the history is seldom told in any other way.

Is there a subtle disdain hidden in the analysis of this 1980s literature, I began to wonder, for the wisdom specific to clergy and congregational ministry? I have continued to consider this question as I work with students going into ministry. Why did the phrase "clerical paradigm" arise as a primary way to characterize the problem of theological education? Why did it gain such staying power? Does it adequately comprehend the problems faced by practical theology and pastoral practitioners? Does it contain hidden prejudice against practice and doubts about the church itself?

Proclamations about the clerical paradigm, first suggested by systematic theologian Edward Farley, established a major precedent for the ensuing discussion. It is time to look more carefully at the original source of this term and ask what was helpful about the portrait and what dilemmas it left unresolved. Such an investigation will allow us to assess where previous attempts to reinvigorate practical theology succeeded and where they went astray.

The concept of the clerical paradigm has so dominated the discourse, I will argue, that it has distorted our perception, misdirected blame, and hence left other problems unattended, particularly the rise of what I will call the "academic paradigm." In relying heavily upon the construct of clerical paradigm, theologians eager to revitalize practical theology inadvertently denigrated congregational and pastoral "know-how." This was not their intent, but it was a consequence of the increasingly careless usage of an initially useful term. Although I begin with an analysis of Farley's proposal, I do not take issue so much with its original formulation as with its subsequent use. Nor do I focus on the institutional or empirical question of whether or not seminaries are teaching ministerial skills and practices. Instead, I am interested in the shared rhetoric about the problem and solution in theological education that has subtle and not-so-subtle consequences for institutional life. Perceptions of the clerical paradigm as the main problem have perpetuated a "fallacy of misplaced concreteness," as Alfred North Whitehead might say, or the mistaking of a helpful generalization for concrete reality.[2]

---

1. *Theological Reflections: Methods,* ed. Elaine Graham, Heather Walton, and Frances Ward (London: SCM Press, 2005), p. 3.

2. Alfred North Whitehead, *Process and Reality: An Essay in Cosmology* (New York:

Behind my analysis stand two aims that go beyond the boundaries of this essay but merit brief mention. I have a wider interest in assessing the practical theological literature of the 1980s in general and a desire to explore and reclaim the value of pastoral know-how. The important efforts of the 1980s both advanced the discussion and left some serious problems unresolved. On the one hand, scholarship in practical theology contributed to a major re-orientation in theological education in the United States. It identified religious practices as a valid subject matter, contested conventional curricular divisions between theory and practice in the classical and practical fields, and embodied a dialectical engagement between situations, religious traditions, and Christian convictions in teaching and research. On the other hand, some commentators, such as David Kelsey and Barbara Wheeler, argue that the discussion of theological education and practical theology has made little real difference in the actual practices of faith and ministry and in the overall organization of theological study in seminaries, divinity schools, and graduate programs.[3] There are many reasons for the limited impact of practical theology. But a key question has been overlooked. How do those who practice ministry embody theological knowledge? How do they learn how to practice? As I will ultimately conclude, the field of practical theology needs to learn a lot more about practical theological know-how: how to teach it, how to learn it, and how to demonstrate it.

The Clerical Paradigm as the Problem in Practical Theology

Encouraged by professional interest and institutional support, several scholars contributed significantly to the repositioning of practical theol-

---

Harper, 1929). Whitehead defined the fallacy as "neglecting the degree of abstraction involved when an actual entity is considered merely so far as it exemplifies certain categories of thought" (p. 11). This is the "fallacy involved whenever thinkers forget the degree of abstraction involved in thought and draw unwarranted conclusions about concrete actuality." See Herman E. Daly, John B. Cobb, and Clifford W. Cobb, *For the Common Good: Redirecting the Economy towards Community, the Environment, and a Sustainable Future* (Boston: Beacon Press, 1989), p. 36.

3. David H. Kelsey and Barbara G. Wheeler, "New Ground: The Foundations and Future of the Theological Education Debate," in *Theology and the Interhuman: Essays in Honor of Edward Farley*, ed. Robert R. Williams (Valley Forge, Pa.: Trinity Press International, 1995), p. 189.

ogy as a respectable academic enterprise in the 1980s.[4] They agreed almost universally that previous eras, dating back to Schleiermacher in the nineteenth century, had defined the field too narrowly. "Clerical paradigm" became the code term for this problem. Farley first proposed the phrase as a way to characterize the troubling preoccupation of theological education and practical theology with ministerial skills of individual pastors.[5] He was not alone in raising this concern. Others before Farley, such as Alastair Campbell, had already identified the problem.[6] With this phrase, however, and a powerful historical portrait to match, Farley codified it.

The clerical paradigm soon became a widely used shorthand for everything that was wrong with previous understandings of theological education and practical theology. In the reigning model, the so-called classical areas of Bible, history, and doctrine convey the theory or truths of the tradition, while the practical arts then apply them to ministry, centered almost entirely on the technical functions of clergy. In the 1980s, the hope was to get "beyond clericalism" in theological education, as the title of one book put it, and back to contextual, congregational, and theological approaches.[7] Rightfully redefined, practical theology, like theological education in general, entails more than the know-how of parish ministers and ought to involve theological engagement with contemporary issues and the Christian gospel both in congregations and in society at large.

Few people have stopped to assess the adequacy of this portrayal. Most simply assume the clerical paradigm sufficiently defines the predicament, partly because it has done such a good job of capturing an important aspect of theological education's entrapment in scope and method. As an introduction to one major edited volume observes, the idea is "so widely held that it is often taken to be self-evident."[8] Some

---

4. For an excellent bibliography, see *Theological Education* 30, no. 2 (1994): 89-98.

5. Edward Farley, "Theology and Practice outside the Clerical Paradigm," in *Practical Theology: The Emerging Field in Theology, Church, and World,* ed. Don S. Browning (San Francisco: Harper & Row, 1983), pp. 21-41; and Edward Farley, *Theologia: The Fragmentation and Unity of Theological Education* (Philadelphia: Fortress Press, 1983), p. 87. Although Farley continues this argument in later work, this essay focuses primarily on its initial appearance in these earlier publications. See Edward Farley, *The Fragility of Knowledge: Theological Education in the Church and the University* (Philadelphia: Fortress Press, 1988).

6. Alastair V. Campbell, "Is Practical Theology Possible?" in *Scottish Journal of Theology* 25, no. 2 (May 1972): 217-27.

7. Joseph C. Hough and Barbara G. Wheeler, *Beyond Clericalism: The Congregation as a Focus for Theological Education* (Atlanta: Scholars Press, 1988).

8. Barbara G. Wheeler, "Introduction," in *Shifting Boundaries: Contextual Approaches*

scholars take issue with Farley, but the debate has rarely questioned this basic category.[9]

Farley's *Theologia* is indeed a pivotal and informative text. It gives a detailed interpretation of developments in theological education from early Christianity through the twentieth century and formulates a response. Farley begins with what he admits is a "tendentious genetics" of the assumptions behind the current organization of theology, making a largely lost history available for re-analysis before offering his prescriptive response. For those wanting to understand practical theology's plight and the gulf between academy and church, it is a good place to start. Even though Farley focuses primarily on mainstream Protestant theological education, he believes that parallel developments occurred in Roman Catholic and evangelical circles. As he notes, the "theological encyclopedic movement is as much a Catholic as a Protestant work."[10]

Theologia basically tells the story of theology's displacement as the "unity, subject matter, and end of clergy education" and its replacement by the clerical paradigm.[11] Here Farley is not talking about theology as conventionally understood today in terms of systematic or constructive doctrinal work as one of many areas of study. Indeed, this understanding is an unfortunate fallout of the encyclopedic movement of eighteenth-century Germany and its instantiation in educational institutions and academic societies up through today. Instead, he refers repeatedly throughout the book to a time when theology was "one thing" rather than many, a "single science" pertaining to the salvific wisdom of God. Culminating with Schleiermacher's *Brief Outline of the Study of Theology* but continuing well into twentieth-century curricular structures, the attempt to establish the validity of studying Christianity within the modern university led to the

---

to the Structure of Theological Education, ed. Barbara G. Wheeler and Edward Farley (Louisville: Westminster John Knox Press, 1991), p. 9.

9. According to Kelsey and Wheeler, "Nothing published so far has challenged either Farley's explanation of the almost universal experience of fragmentation or the terms he uses to analyze theological education's malaise" ("New Ground," in *Theology and the Interhuman*, ed. Williams, p. 183). An exception to this claim might be found in Joseph C. Hough Jr. and John B. Cobb Jr., *Christian Identity and Theological Education* (Chico, Calif.: Scholars Press, 1985), pp. 3-5. They briefly deny that confinement by the clerical paradigm is the crux of the problem and assert that the key dilemma is confusion in the church about ministerial leadership. See also other chapters in *Shifting Boundaries*, ed. Wheeler and Farley.

10. Farley, *Theologia*, p. x.

11. Farley, *Theologia*, p. ix.

elaboration of a "theological encyclopedia" dividing theology into sub-disciplines of Bible, dogmatics, history, and practical theology. Theology was portrayed as a science, comparable to its companion sciences of medicine and law, with religion as its object, clerical education as its aim, and several specialized areas as its components.

In a summary of his thesis, Farley says, "the problem of the study of theology, the *one thing,* eventually gives way to the problem of theological encyclopedia, *the interrelating of the many things.*"[12] When the "one thing" split into four branches and each branch divided into more subspecialties, each specialty established its own fiefdom with its "sociological accoutrements" of guilds, journals, methods, and scholars.[13] These areas evolved more out of circumstance than through any clear rationale about their necessity or their relationship to the whole. One principle that did shape this re-organization — the distinction between theory and practice — simply exacerbated a growing division between practical theology and all the other areas.

Although Schleiermacher had a slightly different tripartite schema in mind, it was he who proposed what Farley calls the "clerical paradigm" as theology's aim.[14] Schleiermacher equated theology with law and medicine as practical sciences designed for the promotion of social goods. For theology this good was the church's need for an educated leadership. Although Schleiermacher also saw the Christian experience of redemption by Christ as a material purpose for theological education, this understanding gradually vanished over the next century, and the clerical paradigm "became virtually universal" as the key formal rationale.[15] Practical theology became a culminating cluster of courses directed toward the tasks and functions of ordained ministry. In a footnote, Farley clarifies,

> Hereafter, this expression, *clerical paradigm,* will be used to refer to the prevailing (post-Schleiermacher) Protestant way of understanding the unity of theological education. . . . Although this paradigm will be questioned as an adequate approach to theological education's unity, the author wishes to avoid the impression that this is a questioning of either the validity of clergy education itself or of the validity of education for specific activities and skills.[16]

12. Farley, *Theologia,* p. 54; emphasis supplied.
13. Farley, *Theologia,* pp. 4, 105.
14. Farley, *Theologia,* pp. 85, 87.
15. Farley, *Theologia,* p. 94.
16. Farley, *Theologia,* p. 98; emphasis in original.

Is the Clerical Paradigm the Main Culprit?

Did Farley succeed in avoiding these pitfalls observed in passing in a footnote? Even if he did, have those who followed him maintained the importance of educating clergy for "specific activities and skills"? In a later chapter in *Theologia,* Farley makes mono-causal statements about the problem of the clerical paradigm that seem to betray his good intentions. The reason that Protestant churches do not see theology as meaningful, he insists, "is simply the triumph and narrowing of the clerical paradigm."[17] The clerical paradigm is also "responsible for" a truncated view of practice and even for the alienation of ministry students from "praxis, that is, from issues of personal existence and social justice." Not only that, but the clerical paradigm "appears to be one of the historical forces at work in the American exclusion of 'theology' from the university."[18]

One upshot of such claims is that the clerical paradigm, and in time practical theology and the church in general, begin to take heat that rightfully belongs with systematic theology and the other disciplines. The "clerical paradigm" becomes a scapegoat for larger problems faced by systematic theologians, especially theology's own marginalization in both the academy and the wider public. In actuality, I believe, the singular focus on professional pastoral skills is more a symptom than a cause of theology's demise.

What has been overlooked in Farley's aftermath is his critique of the whole of theology. He argues that two premodern understandings of theology underwent unfortunate transformation in modernity. From early on, *theology* referred to both the personal salvific knowledge of God and the discipline or organized study of such knowledge. A great change, which he frequently dubs "cataclysmic" because of its "radical departure" from previous patterns, came with developments leading up through the Enlightenment to today.[19] With the rise of rationalism, historical-critical method, and separation of different theological sciences, theology's fundamental focus on "sapiential and personal knowledge" of divine being and the promotion of "a Christian *paideia*" or cultivation of this divine wisdom was lost. Theology as *habitus* or as an act of practical wisdom about the divine became instead a "generic term for a cluster of disciplines."[20]

---

17. Farley, *Theologia,* p. 131; emphasis supplied.
18. Farley, *Theologia,* p. 133.
19. Farley, *Theologia,* pp. 39, 49, 62.
20. Farley, *Theologia,* p. 81.

Education was rendered simply an "aggregate" or "mélange of introductions" to all the divergent specializations. Theological understanding was displaced as the overall purpose and dispersed "into a multiplicity of sciences."[21] The two types of theology continue, but now in deranged form. In his words,

> Theology as a personal quality continues . . . not as a salvation-disposed wisdom, but as the practical know-how necessary to ministerial work. Theology as discipline continues, not as the unitary enterprise of theological study, but as one technical and specialized scholarly undertaking among others; in other words, as systematic theology.[22]

In short, practical theology was not the only area blighted. All areas lost touch with their rightful theological meaning, systematic theology included.

Farley himself loses sight of this dimension of his analysis. Later in *Theologia*, he simplifies his picture of the problem and describes it as the "'clericalization' of theology." He says, "In the clerical paradigm, theology . . . is something for the clergy alone."[23] Yet one could easily argue, or perhaps should more accurately argue, that in the *academic paradigm* theology became something for the academy alone. Congregations avoid theology not because they see it as clerical, as he argues, but because they see it as intimidating and reserved for learned academic experts who have influenced clergy. The problem is not just "clericalization," in other words, but an equally troubling "academization" of theology. At the same time, theology is excluded from the university not just because it is equated with preparation for ordained ministry, as Farley emphasizes, but because of its revelatory, confessional nature.[24] That *theologia* or knowledge of the divine gained through revelation no longer has standing in the academy poses a greater problem than Farley acknowledges.[25]

Theologian Van Harvey suggests that systematic theology's own peers have also squeezed it out (even though he himself largely agrees with

21. Farley, *Theologia*, pp. 14, 15, 49.
22. Farley, *Theologia*, p. 39.
23. Farley, *Theologia*, pp. 130, 169.
24. Farley, *Theologia*, pp. 114, 134.
25. Farley's positive argument that theology can have a post-confessional form in the university is brief. See *Theologia*, pp. 161, 198. The question of how *theologia* can be sustained within the secular university is revisited in Farley, *The Fragility of Knowledge*, pp. 56-82.

Farley's diagnosis that clerical professionalism has led to theology's marginalization). Biblical and historical studies have retained a purpose and place despite historical criticism and the demise of speculative metaphysics. They did so, however, by displacing systematic theology. "The development of specialized Old and New Testament had the effect of taking away two of the traditional fields of competence claimed by the systematic theologian," Harvey says. "What was once the subject matter of theology was, as it were, subcontracted out to New Testament studies, church history, philosophy of religion, and ethics."[26] Not surprisingly, systematic theologians became increasingly confused about the nature of their own particular expertise. I see a further example of this confusion as systematic theologians attempt to reclaim the study of Christian practices as central, territory already traversed and studied by practical theologians.

One way that systematic theology has tried to retain a place in the university in the last several decades is by becoming ever more sophisticated. Theology is not just "*perceived* as technical," as Farley says. It has *become* technical, and not just because of the clerical paradigm. In the last several decades, systematic theologians began to write for a public removed from Christian life and ministry. Few parishioners saw such abstruse theological activity as something in which they engaged. When they wanted to understand their religious lives, they turned instead to scholars better able to provide lively, meaningful language: psychologists, economists, political scientists, and even authors of spiritual memoirs. Thus, in the "academic paradigm," systematic theology faced a no-win situation. Too pious for the academy, it became too academic for the church.

In other words, Farley actually exposes an academic paradigm as virulent and problematic as the clerical paradigm. Perhaps if he had so labeled systematic theology's plight, preoccupation with the clerical paradigm might have been tempered and some of the unhelpful consequences avoided, including a phraseology that bestowed a subtle negative connotation on "clergy" and largely ignored the "academic" dilemma. One ironic result is that in some cases the practical areas became even less relevant to ministry and more removed from practice, lest faculty be accused of merely promoting clerical skills.[27] Theologians in both systematic and

26. Van A. Harvey, "On the Intellectual Marginality of American Theology," in *Religion and Twentieth-Century American Intellectual Life*, ed. Michael J. Lacey (New York: Cambridge University Press, 1989), pp. 188, 190.

27. This can be illustrated by curricular conclusions like the following: "Seminaries need to resist the pressure to do a quick curricular fix to 'prepare' pastors to be better leaders

practical theology underestimated the intelligence involved in practice and overlooked the limitations of merely academic knowledge.

What Happens to Application in the Academic Paradigm?

Fixation on the clerical paradigm as the key problem in theological education and practical theology has had the odd consequence of further devaluing the already questionable status of congregational life, ministerial practice, and clergy competence. This is unfortunate and probably not the end Farley or others had in mind. As Farley himself acknowledges, Schleiermacher valued such practice. Schleiermacher saw theology, along with medicine and law, as different from the pure conceptual science of philosophy precisely because they all embrace practices. All three "originate in the need to give cognitive and theoretical foundations to an *indispensable practice*" that responds to "fundamental human needs," whether spiritual, social, or physical.[28]

What then was the end Farley desired, if not an enhancement of clerical practice? He recommends the recovery of *theologia* or an "education which centers on a *paideia* of theological understanding."[29] "*Paideia*" implies the holistic involvement of the learner and includes all Christian believers. However, the context and actual exercise of *paideia* go largely unexamined. Little is said about how to cultivate and enact it. In the sequel to *Theologia* that extends Farley's reflection on education, *The Fragility of Knowledge*, this term receives surprisingly little attention despite its potential.

Instead, the emphasis falls heavily on the cognitive. The general goal of theological education is facilitating theological "thinking." There is nothing wrong with emphasizing critical rational intellect in ministry. Indeed, a ministry informed by scholarship, book learning, and reflection is highly desirable. A problem arises, however, as practical theologian Craig

---

of Christian education programming in local churches. Such a response ignores the validity of the critique of the 'clerical paradigm.' Rather, seminaries need to become . . . communities of reflective activity seeking wisdom about 'the believer's existence and action in the world' (Farley)." See Barbara Brown Zikmund, "Theological Seminaries and Effective Christian Education," in *Rethinking Christian Education: Explorations in Theory and Practice*, ed. David S. Schuller (St. Louis: Chalice Press, 1993), pp. 121-22.

28. Farley, *Theologia*, p. 86; emphasis in original.

29. Farley, *Theologia*, p. 181.

Dykstra points out, when intelligence receives a narrow definition as primarily linguistic, logical competence. This ignores a range of intelligences and qualifications related to somatic, spatial, kinesthetic, aesthetic, and personal knowing, as identified by Howard Gardner and others.[30]

The problem is not just a matter of a limited definition of intelligence, however. A larger theoretical and methodological issue is at stake. Ultimately, few people attempt to challenge or dismantle the valuation of theory over practice or the one-directional relationship between theory and practice evident in Schleiermacher and the gradual devaluation of practice that resulted.[31] Theory drives practice, acting is ultimately subordinate to thinking, and critical reflection occupies a more important place than practical competence, a conviction that continues to shape theological curriculum.

In descriptions of practical theology, interpretation has been key. Action and implementation are often afterthoughts, even though both of these are understood as important elements in the science of hermeneutics. Practical theologian Don Browning, paraphrasing Richard Bernstein and Hans-Georg Gadamer, says that in the practical wisdom necessary for ministry, "understanding, interpretation, *and application* are not distinct but intimately related."[32] Major spokespersons in practical theology such as Browning and Farley, however, have had immense interest in the first two: understanding and interpretation. They have had less to say about "application."

All agree that practical theology involves more than application of theory to practice. Concern about application shapes understanding from the beginning. Yet they seldom ask how understanding actually informs action. When Farley takes up "action" later in *The Fragility of Knowledge*, he does so briefly and only as one of several "interpretative" modes of education. He does not describe its concrete actualization in faith, ministry,

---

30. Craig Dykstra, "Reconceiving Practice in Theological Inquiry and Education," in *Virtues and Practices in the Christian Tradition: Christian Ethics after MacIntyre*, ed. Nancey C. Murphy, Brad J. Kallenberg, and Mark Thiessen Nation (Notre Dame: University of Notre Dame Press, 1997), p. 177n.29. This article first appeared in Wheeler and Farley, *Shifting Boundaries*, pp. 35-66. Most recently, Dykstra has talked about this intelligence in terms of "pastoral imagination" and "pastoral excellence."

31. John E. Burkhart, "Schleiermacher's Vision for Theology," in *Practical Theology*, ed. Browning, pp. 52-53.

32. Don S. Browning, *A Fundamental Practical Theology: Descriptive and Strategic Proposals* (Minneapolis: Fortress Press, 1991), p. 39; emphasis supplied.

and congregation.[33] Unfortunately, no one really wants to talk about application or use of knowledge. It is still basically left to the various subdisciplines of practical theology to figure out how knowledge will shape and be shaped by practice. Application is something that happens in some ill-defined fashion there. In the end, "clerical tasks" are, sadly, no more than just that: technical chores that distract from theology's more fundamental aim of reflection and interpretation. Since the educational focus on such tasks has been defined as the problem, little attempt is made to fit them back into the picture at all.

Is There Anything Commendable about Practical Know-How?

In the last few years, several people have begun to question cognitive or cerebral definitions of practical theology's task. This is most apparent in the far-reaching discussions about "practice." Farley's work itself helped propel others to "reconceive practice," as Craig Dykstra titles an important 1991 article. This article is one of the first attempts in practical theology to develop the concept of practice. Informed by a close reading of Farley, Dykstra also criticizes theological education's focus on individual clergy skills. It is philosopher Alasdair MacIntyre, however, who provides the infrastructure that allows Dykstra to depart from Farley's agenda, and precisely around the reconstruction of practice.[34] An impoverished understanding of practice is a serious part of the problem in theological education, Dykstra argues, including the failure to include practice in the areas of Bible, history, systematic theology, and ethics, and to see that such disciplines are themselves a form of practice.

Dykstra likes but essentially redefines Farley's heady *habitus*. For Dykstra, *habitus* refers to the "profound, life-orienting, identity-shaping

33. Farley, *The Fragility of Knowledge*, pp. 153-55. Even though Farley titles his most recent book *Practicing Gospel*, his primary practice is still thinking. He defines theology as "interpretative or thinking activity" rather than faith active in the world. See Edward Farley, *Practicing Gospel: Unconventional Thoughts on the Church's Ministry* (Louisville: Westminster John Knox Press, 2003), p. 7.

34. Dykstra, "Reconceiving Practice in Theological Inquiry," in *Virtues and Practices in the Christian Tradition*, ed. Murphy et al. Although he identifies several influential scholars such as Robert Bellah, Hans-Georg Gadamer, Stanley Hauerwas, and Jeffrey Stout, Dykstra says that the "most important single text" is Alasdair C. MacIntyre, *After Virtue: A Study in Moral Theory* (Notre Dame: University of Notre Dame Press, 1981).

participation in the constitutive practices of Christian life." In a footnote, he observes that such wisdom requires "not only insight and understanding but also the kind of judgment, skill, commitment, and character that full participation in practices both requires and nurtures."[35] Practices such as interpreting Scripture, worship, prayer, confession, service, and so forth shape wisdom. Education, therefore, must take place in close proximity to them. Dykstra observes in another footnote, "Significant connections between actual engagements in the practices and inquiry carried out in a context formed through them [are] vastly underemphasized by Farley." Farley restricts learning to "analysis and interpretation of the cognitive products of practice."[36] For Dykstra, *habitus* moves away from technological and abstract knowledge toward knowledge gained in community, through history, as a result of concrete, complex, holistic engagement in Christian faith as a way of life.

Farley only partially anticipates the enhanced validation of practice that has occurred since Dykstra's article (even though the title of Farley's recently published collection, *Practicing Gospel,* shows its impact). Don Browning, for example, also draws on MacIntyre but positions him beside other practical philosophers interested in hermeneutics and pragmatism. Browning affirms theology "as a practical discipline through and through," the "theory-laden" nature of all practice, and the fluid movement from practice to theory back to practice required of all good theology.[37] Elaine Graham titles her book on pastoral theology *Transforming Practice,* apparently unaware of Dykstra's similarly titled essay. Graham uses MacIntyre, Pierre Bourdieu, and other philosophers to redefine practice as the proper focus of pastoral theology. Pastoral theology "properly conceived" is a "performative discipline" where the focus is right practice or "authentic transformatory action" rather than right belief.[38] In a recent essay, Dorothy Bass highlights four contributions of this attention to practice. It connects thinking and doing (practice requires and gives rise to knowledge), confirms the social character of thought and action (practice requires community), highlights the historical character of social life (practice exists over

35. Dykstra, "Reconceiving Practice in Theological Inquiry," in *Virtues and Practices in the Christian Tradition,* ed. Murphy et al., p. 176n.28.

36. Dykstra, "Reconceiving Practice in Theological Inquiry," in *Virtues and Practices in the Christian Tradition,* ed. Murphy et al., p. 176n.29.

37. Browning, *A Fundamental Practical Theology,* pp. ix, 6, 7.

38. Elaine L. Graham, *Transforming Practice: Pastoral Theology in an Age of Uncertainty* (London: Mowbray, 1996), p. 7.

time), and attends to that wisdom which is yet inarticulate (practice involves people of all sorts).[39]

All this is well and good. Such scholarship, however, still leaves unaddressed the standing of practices that are particular to clergy. As one reviewer of *Transforming Practice* comments, Graham is simply following a trend (which I believe is evident in the discussion in general) that perceives the focus on pastoral skills as just "too narrow." The reviewer summarizes that Graham desires a "less clerical and more communal understanding of pastoral theology."[40]

I see a problem with the ready dismissal of clergy practice. Are such skills too narrow, or has their value been fundamentally misunderstood? I do not want to re-inscribe practical theology as concerned only with ministerial technique, but are there any particular tasks for which pastors ought to be prepared and with which theological education ought to grapple? Is there any know-how that is not, as Dykstra and others so readily repeat, "*mere* know-how"?[41]

In a response to a colloquy in the late 1970s honoring pastoral theologian Seward Hiltner, Rodney Hunter is among the first to identify pastoral theology as a "form of practical knowledge." He lifts up a problem that remains unresolved despite all the attention others have given it in the intervening years. Pastoral theology stands in a quandary because the "distinctive character of practical knowledge in relation to other kinds of knowledge has not been clearly enough understood." Such "practicality rightly understood can be as profound and significant as descriptive insight into reality or visions of the good."[42]

Hunter attempts a brief but helpful phenomenology of what this kind of knowledge actually looks like. "Whereas descriptive knowledge tells about what is," he observes, "and normative knowledge tells what

39. Dorothy Bass, unpublished paper, "Notes for Remarks to the Planning Committee on Teaching for Ministry," Vanderbilt Divinity School, 6 November 2003. See her earlier edited works for a fuller examination of these four aspects: *Practicing Our Faith: A Way of Life for a Searching People*, ed. Dorothy C. Bass (San Francisco: Jossey-Bass, 1997); and *Practicing Theology: Beliefs and Practices in Christian Life*, ed. Miroslav Volf and Dorothy C. Bass (Grand Rapids: Wm. B. Eerdmans, 2002).

40. Robin Gill, review of Elaine Griffin's *Transforming Practice: Pastoral Theology in an Age of Uncertainty*, in *Theology* 100 (May-June 1997): 228.

41. Dykstra, "Reconceiving Practice in Theological Inquiry," in *Virtues and Practices in the Christian Tradition*, ed. Murphy et al., p. 180.

42. Rodney J. Hunter, "The Future of Pastoral Theology," in *Pastoral Psychology* 29, no. 1 (Fall 1980): 65, 69.

ought to be, practical knowledge gives information about how to do things." This knowledge is not just about skill; it "must be gained pragmatically" through repeated exercise of skill and testing of rules of thumb.[43] Although it involves more than memorizing a set of simple sequential instructions, it does require initial step-by-step "trial and error" activity by the learner and "show and tell" between virtuoso and amateur. Through such pastoral apprenticeship, one acquires a kind of "wisdom of experience." Here Hunter is not talking about "experience" conventionally understood as personal growth in self-awareness but as a "form of knowledge that has accrued and matured through a history of practical, contingent events."[44]

Of final significance, Hunter notes that there is the distinctive paradoxical challenge and even impossibility of learning a practical knowledge that sees its source and goal as "religious." Religious knowledge entails wisdom about living at the very boundaries of human existence (e.g., sin, death, and meaninglessness) and about living in the grace that transcends these limits (e.g., redemption, salvation, and liberation). This raises an extremely difficult question about whether or to what extent one can really teach and learn such practical theological knowledge.

This exegesis of practical theology, practical knowledge, and practice suggests that learning practical theology has as much affinity with learning an art or a sport as learning law or medicine. As liturgical scholar John Witvliet argues, art and music offer intriguing alternative ways to think about the Christian life as an "ongoing, communal improvisatory performance."[45] Most notably for my purposes here, he observes that "music and art education give more sustained, habitual attention to the basic 'skills' than does theological education." He continues, "In piano and violin, you never graduate from playing scales. These exercises are fundamental in shaping and maintaining muscle memory." What, then, he asks, "are the scales we need to practice in theological education?"[46] This is an excellent question and is precisely the question that has been dismissed in the concern about the clerical paradigm. What are the scales needed for faithful practice of ministry? How do practical theologians understand and teach scales as an integral part of the larger enterprise of theological education?

43. Hunter, "The Future of Pastoral Theology," p. 65.
44. Hunter, "The Future of Pastoral Theology," p. 67.
45. John Witvliet, "Music/Practical Theology Comparison," unpublished manuscript, Seminar on Practical Theology and Christian Ministry, 8-9 October 2004, p. 1.
46. Witvliet, "Music/Practical Theology Comparison," p. 16.

Witvliet begins to answer Hunter's concern about how to learn something that borders on the transcendent or the unattainable. Music, like theology, "uses concrete cultural artifacts but also deals with the ineffable." Simply because music seeks to express the inexpressible does not mean, however, that acquiring the ability to make music is something mythical, esoteric, or extraordinary. Indeed, learning music is a form of education worth "demythologizing." It is honed by "ordinary activities such as practice, experiencing good examples, and taking small steps toward the kind of expression we long to offer."[47] Music is an embodied art that one learns at least initially through repeated practice of particular gestures and body movements, including how to stand, where to position one's hands, mouth, arms, and so forth.[48]

Just as technique and musicianship in art education are interdependent "right from the start," so also are skills and *theologia* interdependent from the beginning in theological education. Doing scales is an inherent facet of the imaginative synthesis of the art itself. Drawing on V. A. Howard, Witvliet emphasizes that one must live in the tension between drudgery or "means without dreams" and fantasy or "dreams without means." Indeed, the best mentor embraces "scales" *and* "artistry," "hard work *and* soaring vision."[49] One must rehearse concrete skills without losing desire for and pursuit of the occasional enactment of a surprising, satisfying aesthetic event.

My youngest son has been trying to learn guitar. For good and then for ill, he hears his oldest brother playing fluently, and he quits practicing. He seems to assume that guitar-playing entails instant good music and that consequently he is, as he concludes, "no good at it." He displays an all-

47. Witvliet, "Music/Practical Theology Comparison," p. 7.

48. Dorothy Bass, "Response to Witvliet," unpublished manuscript, Seminar on Practical Theology and Christian Ministry, 8-9 October 2004.

49. Witvliet, "Music/Practical Theology Comparison," pp. 7-8; Dorothy Bass, "Notes on the Meeting," unpublished manuscript, Seminar on Practical Theology and Christian Ministry, 8-9 October 2004, p. 3. Witvliet quotes V. A. Howard: "My overall purpose is to show how means and dreams get connected." See V. A. Howard, *Learning by All Means: Lessons from the Arts* (New York: Peter Lang Publishing, 1992), p. xiv. Witvliet also quotes Bennett Reimer: ". . . technique now, musicianship later [is a misconception that] has plagued performance teaching in music education throughout its history. [This] accounts for much of the convergent, rule-learning-and-following, technique-dominated, rote nature of the enterprise. . . . The solution is to recognize and cultivate their interdependence right from the start." See Bennett Reimer, *A Philosophy of Music Education: Advancing the Vision* (Saddle River, N.J.: Prentice Hall, 1989), p. 130.

too-human desire: he wants to skip the tedious intervening steps — chord repetition, chord progression, finger-strengthening exercises, missed notes, poor performance — and just play guitar. The discussion in theology seems stuck right here also. Scholars and students want to skip over practice, scales, and skills, and just play *theologia* in the church and society.

What about Learning *Theologia,* Skills and All?

This analysis leads to a final problem in the literature on theological education and practical theology in the 1980s: No one attends to the social realities of seminaries and divinity schools. The theologians writing this literature were mostly talking among themselves and not about theological education as a social enterprise. The literature does not study, as Barbara Wheeler and David Kelsey observe, concrete practices of schools themselves.[50]

Farley's and Kelsey's comments on curricular change and its limited place in their books on theological education are illustrative. Farley reiterates that his book is "not a curriculum proposal." It offers "no blueprint of theological study, no detailed plan for curricular reform" and brackets such institutional and pedagogical dimensions.[51] In almost identical fashion, Kelsey insists that to understand God truly "is not a pedagogical proposal. It does not imply any particular recommendations . . . and carries no necessary pedagogical consequences."[52] Both restrict their work to generic theoretical frameworks.

In the preface to *Theologia,* Farley admits that he underwent a "serious change of mind" about this. He meant to focus on curriculum (even if still not on pedagogy), but his initial intent to consider a "new theological encyclopedia" or a new course of study eventually gave way to a focus on theology's centrality.[53] Such curricular and pedagogical efforts are needed, and his recovery of theological education's proper aim will support them,

50. Kelsey and Wheeler, "New Ground," in *Theology and the Interhuman,* ed. Williams, pp. 192-93.

51. Farley, *Theologia,* pp. 12, 13.

52. David H. Kelsey, *To Understand God Truly: What's Theological about a Theological School* (Louisville: Westminster John Knox Press, 1991), p. 111.

53. Farley, *Theologia,* p. x. In his later work, Farley picks up the concern about the structure of curriculum but still protests that he is not trying to suggest an "ideal curriculum" or specific proposals. Farley, *The Fragility of Knowledge,* pp. xi, 103.

but he keeps his focus on the "conceptual" problem of ideas and attitudes despite his recognition of the need for more "thoroughgoing reform."[54]

Throughout *Theologia,* Farley notes several times the especially significant influence of graduate programs. They "may be the fourfold pattern's real home and its strongest institutionalization."[55] They embody and perpetuate the divisions between fields in the most acute sense through each new generation of scholars. Yet minimal suggestion is made about how a revitalization of *theologia* might impact them and their education. There is acknowledged need for curricular re-organization in both seminary and graduate education that gives greater attention to practice and its pedagogical engagement, but there are no guidelines on what this might look like.[56]

I teach at the institution where Farley contributed significantly to curricular revisions that proposed the "minister as theologian" as a key motif guiding the formation of ministry students. The degree includes a senior project that involves, potentially at least, serious integration of course work and ministerial experience around a problem in the practice of ministry. Whether faculty are able to model such complex integrative work themselves or guide students toward it is another question. Too often, "minister as theologian" has meant "minister as scholar" rather than "minister as practitioner."

Not until Farley retired did he realize how his teaching had often missed the mark. He shaped generations of students in powerful ways, but he "missed a rather plain pedagogical truth," he admits. Rather than focusing on his "students' eventual use" of systematic theology in concrete struggles over questions of faith, he taught it as an academic field largely isolated from situations of relevance, a pedagogy destined to be "shed like a heavy coat in hot weather" upon graduation. "The truth is that most of my students will not imitate, repeat, or even be very interested in the contents and issues" of his own scholarly specialty as they pursue ministry.[57]

54. Farley, *Theologia,* p. 6.

55. Farley, *Theologia,* pp. 199, 112.

56. Farley, "Theology and Practice outside the Clerical Paradigm," in *Practical Theology,* ed. Browning, p. 38. Recent activity in doctoral programs, such as the new program in Theology and Practice at Vanderbilt University, are beginning to address this.

57. Edward Farley, "Four Pedagogical Mistakes: A *Mea Culpa*," *Teaching Theology and Religion* 8, no. 4 (2005): 200-203. This article reflects Farley's growing awareness of the entrapments of the "academic paradigm," even though he does not use this term or recognize the need for more extensive critique of the intellectualist tradition of theological interpretation.

Despite a "lifetime of teaching theology," he "never asked" whether "theology can be taught," a question few practical theologians can avoid in their teaching.[58]

What then does it take to shape the theologically wise pastor? People in practical theological areas confront this question long before retirement, when they first cross the classroom threshold in the role of professor. The pursuit of this question and the question of how to teach a practice unites those who teach in practical theological areas, whether pastoral care, homiletics, leadership, education, spirituality, social action, or mission.[59] This pedagogical difference also sometimes presumes and generates a more fundamental epistemological difference over whether one thinks one's way into acting or acts one's way into thinking. The 1980s literature often implicitly assumes that one thinks one's way into acting. It leaves the question of how action transforms thinking largely unexplored. It did, however, plant the seed for a moderating position in which theory and practice "dialectically" influence and transform each other that paved the way for more innovative pedagogical practices in practical theological pedagogy.[60] In how they teach (for example, in assignments or class sessions organized around enactment, practice, and play of various kinds), many practical theologians today seem to presume, often without articulating it, that practice engenders thinking as much as thinking enriches practice.

Even with such able dialectics, however, a genuine validation of practice still eludes us. Until recently, scholars of religion as a whole overlooked the material character of religion, privileging word and idea over practice and the material world. Learning centers on books and libraries and not on "non-written expressions," as religion scholar Colleen McDannell argues in her research on "material Christianity." We have associated material, unwritten expression and practice with the mundane, the bodily, the unsophisticated, and the profane, and therefore have dismissed them.[61]

---

58. Edward Farley, "Can Preaching Be Taught?" *Theology Today* 62, no. 2 (July 2005): 171-80.

59. I take up this subject matter more extensively in another essay, "Practical Theology and Pedagogy: Reappraising Theological Know-How," in *For Life Abundant: Practical Theology and the Education and Formation of Ministers,* ed. Craig Dykstra and Dorothy C. Bass (Grand Rapids: Wm. B. Eerdmans, 2008). See Chapter 8.

60. For example, David Tracy, *Blessed Rage for Order: The New Pluralism in Theology* (New York: Seabury Press, 1975), p. 243.

61. Colleen McDannell, *Material Christianity: Religion and Popular Culture in America* (New Haven: Yale University Press, 1995), p. 14.

Reclaiming Know-How

In *Theologia* and work that built on it, Farley and others do a service for the theological academy. They call attention to the reduction of theological education and practical theology to the training of clergy. They question its institutional compartmentalization. They reclaim theology as a responsibility of the entire curriculum and the church. Subjugation by the clerical paradigm is not, however, the problem that we once thought.

My argument is not so much with Farley himself as with the continued and unquestioned overuse of "clerical paradigm" as code language for everything that is wrong with theological education and practical theology. Many people latched on to the critique of clericalism but missed the important depiction of systematic theology's demise. Had Farley named the reduction of theology to the rational, orderly study of doctrine the "academic paradigm" or the "cognitive captivity" of theology, perhaps some of the problem might have been alleviated. Instead, the clerical paradigm and its message — that theological education is *not* about teaching pastoral skills — became our narrative. Despite good intentions, the monolithic concern about the clerical orientation has tended to cast a negative shadow over practice, particularly clergy practice, and has hidden intricate interconnections between wisdom and know-how, interpretation and performance.

Recognizing this leads to new questions.[62] What is theological know-how? What forms does it take for clergy? How do different areas of study contribute to its enhancement? How does one teach know-how? There are also relational questions. What is the relationship between "scales" and "artistry" in ministry? What is the connection between know-how and other kinds of knowledge, between knowledge and action, and between practical knowing and the kind of knowing necessary for knowing God? We need to learn more about how people embody knowledge and effect change. That is, we need to know more about the connections between knowledge, practice, action, application, and transformation. I have suggested some initial answers to these questions, but we need to know much more about practical theological know-how. We need to explore the shape

---

62. I thank James Nieman for his helpful response to my essay in Fall 2005 and, in particular, for his articulation of the general and specific moves of my analysis of the clerical paradigm and the proposals and questions it raises. I also thank other members of the Seminar on Practical Theology and Christian Ministry, sponsored by the Lilly Endowment, Inc., for their general comments and help in response to reading an earlier draft.

and practice of a pedagogy of know-how not only within seminary programs, but also in doctoral institutions that shape teachers of ministry students, as well as in congregations from which many of us come and go.

In Farley's repeated lament that theology is no longer "one thing," one cannot help but hear a kind of nostalgia for a bygone era. There is something almost mythic about this "historical archaeology" of "a time when 'theology' was a single thing," a time of "classical orthodoxy" when "a deposit of divinely revealed truths carried in ancient texts was the one ground of the one thing, theology."[63] Many other scholars have also assumed a largely negative view of specialization. Simply put, specialization equals fragmentation. It is inherently selfish, insular, and narrow.[64]

Instead of this curse on specialization and the nostalgia for theology as "one thing," what is needed is a clearer definition of the diverse kinds of theological engagement and their connection, as some scholars have already attempted. Roman Catholic theologian Robert Schreiter, for example, argues that "what has counted for theology since the thirteenth century in Western Christianity," a "university model" that emphasizes "clarity, precision, and relation to other bodies of knowledge," is no longer the whole of the discipline, if it ever was.[65] Other ways of doing theology deserve recognition, especially those that begin with the local context itself. Schreiter identifies three kinds of local theology (e.g., translation, adaptation, and contextual) and four different forms of theological expression (e.g., theology as sacred text, wisdom, sure knowledge, and praxis). In related fashion, systematic theologian Kathryn Tanner distinguishes between academic and everyday theologies. The former is not more theoretical and more abstract than the latter, as we usually assume. Instead, academic theology is itself a "material social practice among others" with different approaches and aims that include a greater interest in critical questions and ordering of religious practice. Rather than a "purely intellectual activity," it belongs on a "continuum with theological activity elsewhere as something that arises in an 'organic' way out of Christian practice."[66] Those who engage in everyday theology do

63. Farley, *Theologia*, p. 142.

64. For example, Kelsey and Wheeler, "New Ground," *Theology and the Interhuman*, ed. Williams, p. 186. They remark, "The subspecialties further splinter the already fragmented fourfold arrangement of studies."

65. Robert J. Schreiter, *Constructing Local Theologies* (Maryknoll, N.Y.: Orbis Books, 1985), p. 4.

66. Kathryn Tanner, *Theories of Culture: A New Agenda for Theology* (Minneapolis: Fortress Press, 1997), pp. 71, 72.

not need the kind of systematically consistent construction of beliefs that academic theologians desire. A more systematic theological inquiry is called for only when their faith practices break down and generate problems.[67] In other words, both Tanner and Schreiter illustrate alternative conceptualizations of theology as "many" rather than "one thing." They underscore the different ways of doing theology demanded by different contexts.

When I first started teaching pastoral care, I sometimes dealt with the challenge of teaching know-how by talking with students about the origin of the gap between what they study in seminary and their ministry. I found historical insights helpful. They allowed me to understand and describe the challenge as a long-standing problem that has been around at least since Schleiermacher, the rise of Enlightenment rationalism, and the growth of the modern university and the theological encyclopedia. I now realize that this post-dates the turning point. The medieval period *was* equally instrumental, as historian Randy Maddox demonstrates, in establishing theology as a theoretical or speculative university science and practical theology as just a "simplified version" of academic theology for the less educated. The social biases of theology were just as definitive then as they are today. The "debate divided roughly along the lines of those who were in the now independent universities," Maddox says, "versus those in schools with continuing monastery ties."[68] Universities covered theology proper, monasteries focused on practical theology, and neither made its way to the common folk.

This sounds incredibly, even comfortingly, familiar. The comfort of history, however, should not dampen our hope for a new day beyond intellectual elitism, prejudice, and nostalgia, a day when we are entrapped by neither the clerical nor the academic paradigm, and no longer view *thinking about faith critically* and *embodying it richly and effectively* as mutually exclusive enterprises of knowledge and wisdom.

---

67. Kathryn Tanner, "Theological Reflection and Christian Practices," in *Practicing Theology*, ed. Volf and Bass, p. 228.

68. Randy L. Maddox, "The Recovery of Theology as a Practical Discipline," *Theological Studies* 51 (1990): 653, 656.

Practical Theology, Pedagogy, and Theological Know-How

BACKGROUND AND INTRODUCTION

Chapter 8 was written in the light and aftermath of Chapter 7. If Chapter 7 is the dark side, Chapter 8 is the brighter, constructive side. Maybe I had to get one out of my system to move on to the other. And as is often the case in research, projects raise more questions than they answer. At the beginning of Chapter 7, I name two broad aims behind it — the desire to evaluate the 1980s literature on practical theology and an interest in learning more about practical knowledge. I make more headway on the first than the second. At the beginning, I say "Practical theology needs to learn a lot more about practical theological know-how," and I end not too far from there — with a battery of questions about practical know-how just waiting for answers. Chapter 8 takes a step in that direction.

    The Lilly seminar gave me the framework and the assignment. First, it re-oriented my theological understanding dramatically by underscoring that *telos* matters in theological education. This *telos* has received a wealth of definitions over time (e.g., love of God and neighbor, abundant life, social justice), and how one defines it is no frivolous matter. But I know now, as I had not understood before, that I should not teach a course without

---

This essay was originally published as "Practical Theology and Pedagogy: Embodying Theological Know-How," in *For Life Abundant: Practical Theology, Theological Education, and Christian Ministry*, ed. Dorothy C. Bass and Craig Dykstra (Grand Rapids: Wm. B. Eerdmans, 2008), pp. 170-90. Used by permission.

asking about the ultimate end for which I teach. In theological education, the *telos* extends beyond learning about a discipline or a subject matter.

Second, colleagues encouraged me to move from criticism to construction. If the academic paradigm has faults, how might they be remedied? Several colleagues presented syllabi, writing beautiful essays on the complex moves of teaching a particular practice. Along with them, I noticed a pattern. How we teach in practical theology says a great deal about the nature of the discipline, maybe more than conceptual or didactic definition. This is one of the chapter's basic contentions. If you want to understand practical theology, it argues, look at what we do as we teach, not (just) what we say.

A second thesis is related and more important. I argue that practical theologians have unique insight into a distinct kind of practical knowing that emerges from the practice of their discipline and approximates the kind of knowing needed to sustain Christian faith. This leads to a final conclusion. Those in disciplines beyond practical theology should have interest in what we have learned, just as practical theologians find knowledge in other fields important. I encourage scholars to "forage forth" and learn from their practical theological colleagues. My verb choice here echoes Robert Dykstra's and Valerie DeMarinis's redemption of a negative stereotype of pastoral theologians as "scavengers" who scrounge from other fields, and recommends scavenging as a positive practice for other scholars.

I have never been entirely satisfied with books that try to help us "think theologically" or with scholars who define theology mainly as "thinking" or "reflecting." This chapter starts to push past this. It benefits from other people's descriptions of what they do in specific courses on worship, liturgy, preaching, pastoral care, education, leadership, mission, and entrance and capstone divinity courses. I learned not just from the Lilly seminar but from participants who presented ideas on teaching in six practical theological subdisciplines at the 2006 Association of Practical Theology conference hosted at Vanderbilt University. (Participants' papers were later published by the *International Journal of Practical Theology*.) I step back from these materials and try to discern what practical theologians do when we teach the kind of knowledge particular to practice. What are the ingredients of practical theological teaching at its best? What counts for theological knowledge, and how do people participate in it?

In a way, this chapter is a summary or a synthesis of the individual essays and informal conversations about teaching on which it rests. My chapter, in other words, invites you to follow its footnotes if you want to understand more fully the wider case of which my chapter is a part. It also depends on the chapters in *For Life Abundant* to fill in the larger picture, such as where learning in faith and ministry begins and how it develops over a lifetime and through wider public efforts of social justice and care. Even though all chapters but one in *For Life Abundant* have single authors, the book was a community effort, and few chapters stand on their own.

In the otherwise vigorous academic revival of practical theology of the past few decades, little attention has been given to pedagogy.[1] Only rarely have scholars asked how those in the field actually teach — *qua* practical theologians — at least not as a primary question. Other significant conceptual matters of definition and method have naturally taken precedence.[2] Teaching largely remains secondary to scholarship.

Yet the lively national and international conversation about practical theology among scholars of theological education in recent decades has significantly affected how practical theologians teach. Invigorated by efforts to expand the scope and definition of the field and to revitalize theological education, many faculty in practical theology began to teach in new and valuable ways. But we have yet to explore how we are teaching differently and, more importantly, what it means.

On one level, questions about teaching are straightforward. What qualifies as a course in the area of practical theology? What must it include to be so named? How do such courses prepare divinity students for ministry? What distinguishes good teaching in the field? On another level, investigating practical theology in the classroom raises profound questions with far-reaching implications for Christian theology and faith. How are

1. A recent and important exception to this observation is Charles R. Foster, Lisa E. Dahill, Lawrence A. Golemon, and Barbara Wang Tolentino, *Educating Clergy: Teaching Practices and Pastoral Imagination* (San Francisco: Jossey-Bass, 2006), a comprehensive study of ways in which seminaries educate clergy and cultivate skills, habits, values, and insights. See also *Practical Wisdom: On Theological Teaching and Learning*, ed. Malcolm L. Warford (New York: Peter Lang, 2004). Nonetheless, there is still no major text that focuses entirely on practical theology and pedagogy.

2. For my own initial exploration of this problem, see Bonnie J. Miller-McLemore, "The 'Clerical Paradigm': A Fallacy of Misplaced Concreteness?" *International Journal of Practical Theology*, no. 1 (June 2007): 19-38.

practice and theology subtly intertwined and powerfully redefined in the practical theological classroom? How are distinctions between theological fields and between classroom and congregation both appreciated and transgressed? What is the place of self-examination in practical theology and theology generally? What is the place of proclamation and doxology in this (and potentially in other) academic work? Perhaps most importantly, what counts as theological knowledge, and how do teacher and student acquire it?

In response to such questions, this chapter makes a bold claim: Intrinsic to the practice of teaching in this field is a particular way of theological knowing that has important implications not only for the teaching of practical theology but also for the definition of the field and for the larger enterprise of theology itself. This way of knowing is a form of *phronesis* that, in this context, might be called "pastoral wisdom" or "theological know-how." This claim suggests that practical theologians, who among theological educators stand the closest to the juncture between church[3] and academy and thus must continually assert the relevance of their teaching in the theological academy, possess (or in order to be effective need to possess) pedagogical wisdom. This wisdom challenges common assumptions about the textual and interpretative knowledge needed to do ministry and suggests additional attributes, such as self-awareness, practice, action, exercise, accumulated trial-and-error experience, embodiment, and so forth. In short, how we teach says a great deal about the field, what unifies it, and what those who teach believe — not only about

3. I use "church" here for brevity and clarity. I actually mean something broader and more complex than the institutional church. I mean "lived experience" as pastoral theologians such as James Poling and Donald Miller describe it; "practice" and "religious practice" as Dorothy Bass and Craig Dykstra have described a faithful way of life; and "public" and "situation" as David Tracy and Edward Farley respectively describe the practical theological audience and subject matter. See James N. Poling and Donald E. Miller, *Foundations for a Practical Theology of Ministry* (Nashville: Abingdon Press, 1985); *Practicing Our Faith: A Way of Life for a Searching People*, ed. Dorothy C. Bass (San Francisco: Jossey-Bass, 1997), and Craig Dykstra and Dorothy C. Bass, "A Theological Understanding of Christian Practices," in *Practicing Theology: Beliefs and Practices in Christian Life*, ed. Miroslav Volf and Dorothy C. Bass (Grand Rapids: Wm. B. Eerdmans, 2002); David Tracy, "The Foundations of Practical Theology," in *Practical Theology: The Emerging Field in Theology, Church, and World*, ed. Don S. Browning (San Francisco: Harper & Row, 1983); and Edward Farley, "Interpreting Situations: An Inquiry into the Nature of Practical Theology," in *Practicing Gospel: Unconventional Thoughts on the Church's Ministry* (Louisville: Westminster John Knox Press, 2003).

the subject matter but also about Christian faith, theology, and life. It says more than any of us has yet dared to claim or fully articulate.

The classroom is only one piece of a much larger picture, to be sure. As other chapters in *For Life Abundant* demonstrate (notably those in the fourth section, "Practical Theology in Ministry"), not all that ministers need in order to learn to do their work well happens here.[4] In fact, despite its value, practical theologians are often especially attuned to the relative inadequacy of the classroom and to the need to reach both backward to where people come from and forward to where they are going in order to connect what is taught and learned in school to much broader contexts of learning and formation. But this recognition gets us a bit ahead of the story and into issues that this chapter hopes to spell out.

In naming general themes of practical theological pedagogy below, I mix concrete example with theoretical claim, exploring as I go an epistemological framework and theological rationale that explains and justifies what I think many practical theologians are doing in their courses. The themes mingle with one another, of course, and the act of extracting them necessarily reduces the complexity of pedagogy in action. What follows, then, is more circular than linear or hierarchical and more invitational than exhaustive or comprehensive. I hope this exploration will stimulate an expanding and clarifying conversation about pedagogy within practical theology and in theological education as a whole. Moreover, I believe that a close examination of how practical theologians teach will disclose a great deal about the field, its key commitments, and its central contributions to theological education, communities of faith, and the wider world.

Teaching a Practice

Although it seems obvious, it merits saying: Those who teach in the area of practical theology (e.g., care, homiletics, liturgics, education, leadership, evangelism, mission) teach a practice.[5] This explains a great deal about

---

4. *For Life Abundant: Practical Theology, Theological Education, and Christian Ministry*, ed. Dorothy C. Bass and Craig Dykstra (Grand Rapids: Wm. B. Eerdmans, 2008).

5. In this essay I use the phrase "a practice" to refer in most cases to a specific practice of ministry — something pastoral leaders do in the performance of their responsibilities. A "practice" in this sense is a part of and intimately related to the larger "practices of the Christian life" that Dorothy Bass and Craig Dykstra describe in their essays and also in *Practicing Our Faith*, but the meanings of the term are different in the two cases.

why teaching in practical theology is complicated and why the field faces a distinctive challenge. Those who come into the classroom must leave better prepared to do something, whether that be to listen, worship, preach, lead, form, teach, oversee, convert, transform, or pursue justice. They need theological know-how. They need more than just the capacity to "think theologically" (the focus of plenty of books on reflective practice[6] and the heart of many treatises on practical theology[7]); they need the capacity to "*practice* theology" by putting theology into action through one's body on the ground. Teachers of practical theology therefore must distill components of practice or a *theory* of theological practice *without losing sight of practicing* in our theorizing.

Orientation to teaching a practice to those who must not only *think* but also *do* (and do thoughtfully) fundamentally shapes those who teach in the practical areas. This stands in contrast to those who orient their teaching around the introduction of an academic discipline or area of study. It was not until retirement, for example, that systematic theologian Edward Farley recognized that his teaching had missed the mark. Rather than focusing on his students' "eventual use" of class materials, he taught it as an academic field of study, largely isolated from the various concrete situations with which students had concerns. He is not alone. According to an essay on teaching contained in a report by the Association of Theological Schools (ATS) on the qualities of a "good theological school," the drive to produce traditional scholarship often subverts exploration of alternative teaching practices geared more directly to the needs of students. Although the authors recommend that lecture no longer serve as the "sole pedagogy," most faculty arrive in schools with little background in "non-lecture pedagogical methods" and little incentive to change this.[8] "Even when we are aware of [the] gap between the requirements of our subject or field and the students' post-school interests and

6. See, for example, James O. Duke and Howard W. Stone, *How to Think Theologically* (Minneapolis: Fortress Press, 1996), and John B. Cobb, *Becoming a Thinking Christian* (Nashville: Abingdon Press, 1993).

7. See, for example, Edward Farley, *Theologia: The Fragmentation and Unity of Theological Education* (Philadelphia: Fortress Press, 1983), and Don S. Browning, *Fundamental Practical Theology: Descriptive and Strategic Proposals* (Minneapolis: Fortress Press, 1991).

8. Philip S. Keane and Melanie A. May, "What Is the Character of Teaching, Learning, and the Scholarly Task in the Good Theological School?" *Theological Education* 30, no. 2 (1994): 37.

pursuits," Farley confesses, "most of us teachers concentrate on the first and ignore the second."[9] This is less true for those who teach in practical theological areas.

Practical theologians confront questions of what it takes to shape the theologically wise practitioner the minute they cross the classroom threshold. Teaching worship as a course in practical theology is different from teaching an "introduction to the discipline of liturgical studies," says John Witvliet. It is a training camp for "full, conscious, active participation" in worship as an art of faithful Christian communal life. Its goal is insight into how theology works "with real people in all their social embeddedness" or, as Kathleen Cahalan puts it, with "real-life issues facing real people."[10] Few students will become worship professors or liturgical specialists, but nearly all will be worshipers, and some will plan and preside in worship. In teaching worship leadership and other practices of ministry, teachers must stay attuned to the use to which students put their learning.

Those who teach practical theology actually confront questions about wise practice the day they begin to search for a teaching job. How we practice what we teach is unavoidably an evaluative criterion for employment, and it also determines what we are asked to teach. When Cahalan arrived at her institution, she was immediately asked to take over two linchpins of the curriculum, perhaps the hardest classes to teach and sometimes the least appealing to other faculty — namely, the first-year and capstone courses. She must first introduce students to the curriculum as a whole and to the wider goal of maturation in the practice of ministry and then, before they leave, test their capacity for academic, ministerial, and vocational integration, ensuring that they have learned something transportable and valuable for their ministry. She cannot ignore what students will do after graduation with the texts they study, the papers they write, and the class lectures they hear. Inescapably she must keep an eye on the wider horizon of Christian practice.

---

9. Edward Farley, "Four Pedagogical Mistakes: A *Mea Culpa*," *Teaching Theology and Religion* 8, no. 4 (2005): 200.

10. See two essays in *For Life Abundant:* John D. Witvliet, "Teaching Worship as a Christian Practice," and Kathleen A. Cahalan, "Introducing Ministry and Fostering Integration: Teaching the Bookends of the Master of Divinity Program."

Those Who Teach *Can* Do

The fact that practical theologians teach the actual practice of practices implicates the teacher. "Everything we do in the classroom," observes religious education professor Katherine Turpin, "from how we establish the learning environment to how we . . . negotiate conflict," becomes subject to close examination.[11] Students notice if the candidate for the opening in homiletics cannot preach, if the pastoral theology professor does not listen to their questions, if the professor of religious education seldom leads students in creative exercises for learning, or if worship classes are not worshipful. The *teaching* of a teacher of teachers or the *preaching* of a teacher of preachers or the *caring* of a teacher of care is seen as witness and proof of the professor's embodied theology and real knowledge of the subject. In an odd twist of logic, as Turpin notes, "I teach about teaching by teaching." The classroom itself becomes a laboratory in which the mirror is turned back on the teacher.[12]

As a result, the position of the teacher is transformed. Witvliet becomes a "fellow-worshiper" alongside his students; James Nieman becomes a "fellow practitioner." Neither can fall back on the distance and comfort provided by disciplinary expertise. Both must engage what Nieman identifies as "daunting questions that required considerable self-examination."[13] How did *he* first come to distinguish the theological adequacy of the performance of particular rites? How did *he* learn how to reshape them or encourage congregants to reshape them accordingly? How will *he* move beyond historical and systematic theologies that he knows well to the practice-oriented guidance that will help ministers and congregants live their Christian convictions more fully?

In most cases, those in practical theology do not teach their subject matter without significant efforts to learn and do the practice they teach. This shapes their work in surprising ways. "My clinical supervision [as a pastoral counselor] taught me a new epistemology," pastoral care professor Pamela Couture declares, "that changed my life as a learner, a teacher, and

---

11. Katherine Turpin, "Distinctive Pedagogies in Religious Education," manuscript from the American Association of Practical Theology, April 2006, pp. 1-2, now published in *International Journal of Practical Theology* 12, no. 1 (2008).

12. Turpin, "Distinctive Pedagogies in Religious Education," p. 1.

13. See James Nieman, "Liturgy and Life: An Account of Teaching Ritual Practices," p. 154; and Witvliet, "Teaching Worship as a Christian Practice," p. 120, both in *For Life Abundant*, ed. Bass and Dykstra.

ultimately, as a scholar."[14] Her counseling training involved an embodied, full-sensory attending, a strategy for using theory without letting it swamp perception, and dexterity in responding to immediate pain and envisioning wider goals. An "avid note-taker," she eventually stopped taking notes; this knowledge was simply not easily translated into notes. Nor has she forgotten it. For her and many other pastoral care teachers, pedagogical schemas for incorporating practice rely heavily on these formative years in supervised counseling. Many pastoral theologians attempt to sustain a counseling practice as a key part of their vocation, just as those who teach preaching fill pulpits and those who teach religious education make their own pedagogical practice a regular part of class examination. Being engaged in actual practice "keeps us honest," my practical theological colleagues say.

A pedagogy that is developed and continually nourished in relation to clinical, congregational, or other non-academic practice engenders shifts in epistemological commitments. The modern academy, shaped by Western views of rationality, often assumes (or at least is dominated by teaching methods that seem to assume) that one thinks one's way into acting. It assumes, as Farley remarks, that "the primary mode of theology is thinking."[15] The question of how action transforms thinking has been submerged in the history of higher education in recent centuries. In the last three decades of scholarship in practical theology, however, many have argued that theory and practice "dialectically" influence each other.[16] Often drawing upon neglected but persistent strands in Western thought about the importance of practice, they have planted seeds for an alternative epistemology in the practical theological classroom. In how they teach, many practical theologians presume that practice engenders thinking as much as thinking enriches practice. For practical theologians, therefore, a (if not *the*) primary mode of theology is practicing the arts of ministry.

---

14. Pamela D. Couture, "Ritualized Play: Using Role Play to Teach Pastoral Care and Counseling," *Teaching Theology and Religion* 2, no. 2 (1999): 96.

15. Farley, "Four Pedagogical Mistakes," p. 202.

16. David Tracy, for example, depicts theology as a correlation between Christian fact and human situation; Farley talks about a "dialectic of interpretation" of truths and norms of the tradition and concrete situations of everyday life; Juan Luis Segundo decries imposition of doctrinal truth that ignores the "signs of the times." See Tracy, *Blessed Rage for Order: The New Pluralism in Theology* (New York: Seabury Press, 1975), p. 243, and *Analogical Imagination: Christianity and the Culture of Pluralism* (New York: Seabury Press, 1981); Farley, *Theologia*, pp. 165, 185; and Segundo, *Signs of the Times: Theological Reflections*, ed. Alfred T. Hennelly, trans. Robert R. Barr (Maryknoll, N.Y.: Orbis Books, 1993), p. 147.

It Takes Practice

As a result of new interest in practice and how practice shapes discourse, many now agree that the study of theology is itself a practice. Academic theology is "a form of cultural activity," says Kathryn Tanner. It does not stand over and above the everyday faith of religious communities as a distant intellectual storehouse of ideas, as second-order theoretical reflection reigning over first-order confession. Each discipline — and theological education as a whole — is "a cultural production," "something shaped by concrete social practice," "a material social process."[17]

What might we see, then, if we turn such claims back on academic culture itself by looking at one practice in particular — namely, the practice of teaching? Christian theology is shaped not only by the "way altar and pews are arranged," as Tanner acknowledges, but also, I would emphasize, by how chalkboards and desks are placed.[18] No good anthropologist walking into the hallowed halls of our institutions of theological education could possibly bypass close inspection of the patterns of our teaching activity — our rituals, daily gestures, expressive styles, and semester requirements — and how they manifest the distinctive, shaping commitments of each discipline.

In many practical theology courses, our anthropologist will discover desks and chairs oddly rearranged. On the first day of my pastoral care class, she would find us watching the film *Billy Elliott*. Billy loves to dance. He closes his bedroom door and bounces on his bed to music; he skips, hops, taps, and prances down the street; he leaps over fences. From the corner of the boxing ring, right before his opponent knocks him out, he eyes with envy the girls across the gym learning ballet. But in his corner of the world — a tough mining village in northeast England — eleven-year-old boys like Billy don't learn to dance. They learn to fight. So Billy must not only discover his hidden talent. He must also work extremely hard to realize it.

As the class watches Billy learn ballet, they notice that a great deal shapes the learning of a practice besides raw talent — familial and social prejudice and permission, money, friendship, study, apprenticeship with a demanding teacher, endless repetition of basic moves, repeated failure in

---

17. Kathryn Tanner, *Theories of Culture: A New Agenda for Theology* (Minneapolis: Augsburg Fortress Press, 1997), pp. 63, 67, 72.

18. Tanner, *Theories of Culture*, p. 70.

increasingly difficult moves, occasional success, emotional support, bodily memory, grit, perseverance, risk, passion, grace. I also show clips from another moving film, *Girl Fight,* about a teen from a black working-class family in Brooklyn who wants to box. She's good at it, and it relieves pent-up anger, but she too must work hard to prove her place. "I'll train you," says the coach she persuades to take her on, but, "If you don't sweat for me, you're out of my life."

Indirectly at least, I tell my students they'll sweat in my class. My deeper motive, however, is to open up discussion about what they think learning pastoral care involves. Why do I start my class here rather than with a lecture on the basics of pastoral care or the history of the field? Why does a colleague who teaches religious leadership start with a simulation game of a congregational conflict? Because we want our students to know that this course is about learning a practice and they will have to practice this practice as part of the class, something they may not have recognized or experienced in classes where the main task is learning history or theory. Practical theology courses also teach history and theory, to be sure, and other courses reflect on ministerial practice. But ultimately the primary focus in a practical theology classroom is a practice of ministry that aims to enhance the practice of faith.

Thus an unspoken rule or movement or litany guides practical theological pedagogy: Experience the practice, practice it, tell about it, ask questions about it, read about it, write about it, practice it, do it, empower others to do it. Turpin likens this movement to that of medical students learning a procedure: "see one, do one, teach one." Learning practical pastoral wisdom requires close observation of practitioners, doing the work of practitioners, and eventually teaching what one has learned to the faithful in congregations and at large. This litany or movement begins in but obviously extends well beyond the classroom, first in terms of classroom content and then in terms of the long-term vocational development of the practitioner and those she or he shapes.

Consequently, as Witvliet remarks, a "significant amount of energy should be reserved for encountering actual practices: concrete examples of gestures, symbols, sermons, songs, images, and environments."[19] Reliance on texts alone, Nieman says, would produce an impoverished view of the homiletical and liturgical practices he teaches.[20] An indispensable

---

19. Witvliet, "Teaching Worship as a Christian Practice," p. 130.
20. Nieman, "Liturgy and Life," p. 152.

addition to printed texts, as pastoral theology has argued for decades, is the "living human document," the "living human web," the situation in its fullness.[21]

So we send students to the field to interview, observe, and otherwise encounter the "real," as well as to witness, report on, and learn from actual practitioners. They counsel each other, interview someone in crisis, question someone who is an expert in a practice, compose case studies, assess each other's efforts to embody a practice, observe a congregation's practices of care, or work together on a community project. We also ask them to construct and participate in improvisational exercises that imitate the "real." Couture does this through alternating assigned reading with "ritualized playing" or role plays that put the entire class in action. This, she believes, "creates a learning environment that allows students to 'think on their feet' — to habituate themselves into good-enough practice in pastoral care situations."[22] Likewise, Nieman's course is built around a multilevel exploration and enactment of four particular worship rites.

This interest in show-and-tell has led some people to question the rigor of practical courses, as Cahalan acknowledges in a footnote.[23] If such exercises do no more than spark personal stories, if they do not connect students back to texts, theories, history, and intellectual ideas, such accusations would be correct. Practical theological pedagogy works hard, however, to make practice an avenue into fuller engagement with history and theory and to bring history and theory to bear in practice. Teachers who employ film, ask people to draw pictures, or experiment with singing use these means because they recognize that the knowledge intrinsic to the life of faith requires many avenues which cannot be accessed through conventional academic means alone.

---

21. See, for example, Charles V. Gerkin, *The Living Human Document: Revisioning Pastoral Counseling in a Hermeneutical Mode* (Nashville: Abingdon Press, 1973, 1984); Anton Boisen, *The Exploration of the Inner World* (New York: Harper Torchbooks, 1952); and Bonnie J. Miller-McLemore, "The Living Human Web: Pastoral Theology at the Turn of the Century," in *Through the Eyes of Women: Insights for Pastoral Care*, ed. Jeanne Stevenson-Moessner (Minneapolis: Fortress Press, 1996), pp. 9-26.

22. Couture, "Ritualized Play," p. 96.

23. Cahalan, "Introducing Ministry and Fostering Integration," pp. 93-94n.5.

Hints, Tips, and Rules of Thumb

Practical theologians teach a practice with the expectation that participation in that practice will cultivate the kind of knowledge, *phronesis,* that deepens students' capacities for further participation in the practice. But the path to theological wisdom is never quick or easy. At certain stages of learning, all sorts of hints, tips, and rules of thumb can be extremely helpful. In spite of criticism from those who worry about a presumed preoccupation in theological education with ministerial skills, many practical theologians, including myself, provide a constant stream of helps and hints to our students as valuable intervening steps toward pastoral competence. When rules of thumb are deeply connected to the beauty of richly embodied, theologically responsible practice, they play a needed (even if always limited) role in helping students move toward practical theological wisdom.

There are, after all, better and worse ways to stand when speaking from the front of a church or raising the bread and wine for praise and blessing. There are better and worse ways to enter a hospital room or to express care when a parishioner looks like she or he needs a hug. There are gestures in preaching that invite listening, and phrases in counseling that open up space. One may feel artificial and forced in making these moves at first, but over time, as one experiments with particular gestures and phrases, practices them over and over, and considers their theological implications, they can become a reliable and authentic part of one's own pastoral repertoire.[24] The development of such a repertoire, of course, only begins in the context of the theological school. It actually develops over a lifetime of the practice of ministry. So neither students nor faculty nor receiving churches should presume that seminary fully prepares students for ministry. Students should expect to be "caught by surprise" again and again, as Couture writes in her syllabus, until "after years of being surprised" they become "seasoned" pastors.[25] Such maturity rests on regular practice of disciplines of self-monitoring, dialogue with theory, and, of particular note here, facility with "rules of thumb."

Hints, tips, ground rules, and rules of thumb are not the whole game

24. I join Turpin in using the word *repertoire* intentionally here to refer to a range of skills and aptitudes, acquired over time, that one can perform. See Turpin, "Distinctive Pedagogies in Religious Education."

25. Pamela Couture, unpublished introduction to pastoral care syllabus, 1989.

or even a major part of it. They are small moves that are used strategically to improve enactment of a practice. They still have a place, however, and theological bearing. They shape and maintain "muscle memory," in Witvliet's words, and such memory comprises a needed, if overlooked, part of good pastoral ministry and faithful living. Like technique in the development of musicianship, skills are integral to theological maturation from the very beginning. Both Turpin and Witvliet liken rules of thumb to learning the scales so "one can begin to improvise in a particular key."[26] Just as you "can't be a musician without working on the scales" or "a good basketball player without practicing thousands of free-throws," so also, argues Witvliet, "effective improvisational ministry is impossible without excellent grounding (and constant rehearsal) in basic skills." The best practice embraces both "scales" *and* "artistry," "hard work *and* soaring vision."[27]

What we really need to know then, as Witvliet asks, is what "are the scales we need to practice in theological education?" As Christian Scharen points out, those in other fields, such as Patricia Benner in nursing education, have taken this question seriously. Drawing on applied mathematician Stuart E. Dreyfus's and philosopher Hubert Dreyfus's study of chess players, air force pilots, and army tank drivers and commanders, Benner breaks down the component parts and steps of "skill acquisition" in nursing care. Such skills "literally get sedimented" in the "embodied knowhow" of the mature practitioner. The expert nurse knows more "than he or she can tell or think to describe."[28] The challenge, as Nieman emphasizes, is that by contrast with the automatic expertise of masters, teachers of practitioners have to account "for how we first came to think and act as we did" and make this knowledge of "scales" available to students.[29]

Hints and helps need not be unsophisticated. The book of Proverbs

26. Turpin, "Distinctive Pedagogies in Religious Education."

27. John Witvliet, "Music/Practical Theology Comparison," unpublished manuscript, Seminar on Practical Theology and Christian Ministry, October 8-9, 2004, pp. 7-8, 13.

28. Patricia Benner, unpublished paper presented at the American Academy of Religion, 19 November 2006. See also Benner, "Using the Dreyfus Model of Skill Acquisition to Describe and Interpret Skill Acquisition and Clinical Judgment in Nursing Practice and Education," *Bulletin of Science, Technology, and Society* 24, no. 3 (June 2004): 188-99, and *From Novice to Expert: Excellence and Power in Clinical Nursing Practice* (Menlo Park, N.J.: Addison-Wesley, 1984). For further commentary on this research, see Christian Scharen's chapter in *For Life Abundant*, ed. Bass and Dykstra.

29. Nieman, "Liturgy and Life," p. 153.

and the long trial-and-error history that lies behind its pithy sayings of simple truth for living the life of faith — what one biblical dictionary describes as a "philosophy rooted in the soil of life" — models a similar kind of well-worn and reflected-on pragmatic guidance.[30] Our hints and helps sometimes reflect an analogous effort to distill the hard-earned history of therapeutic, relational, spiritual, and theological knowing that has given rise to the theological know-how embedded in the routines of the deeply knowledgeable faithful practitioner. So it is no surprise that Witvliet turns to the rich rhetoric of wisdom literature ("wise is the congregation that . . .") over the ultimatums and imperatives of legal language ("thou shalt not . . .") when he wants to model a way of theological knowing faithful to Christian worship and praise.[31]

Completing the Hermeneutical Circle

At the heart of the practical theological enterprise, then, stands a preferential option for practice. In the context of an intense focus on actual situations, the refrain "What then shall we do?" echoes through all areas of practical theology. To say this more theologically: an incarnational, prophetic, and eschatological theology marks our teaching. That is, convictions about the graced nature of embodied creation, the imperative to act on the gift of grace for goodness and justice, and the provisional incompleteness of all such activity stand behind teaching in the field. Theology is, in Nieman's words, less "a fixed set of direct, positive claims about divine being" and more "indirect gestures . . . to a sense of divine activity." Consequently, practical theologians often talk about theological messiness. "Our teaching," Nieman observes, "tended to highlight the contrasting elements within or opposing views about a rite so that all its messiness and complexity might become apparent."[32] In all three chapters in *For Life Abundant* on teaching particular subjects in practical theology, God's presence is described as iconic, metaphorical, paradoxical, mysterious, and "mystagogical"; it comes through shared action, through what practices already declare about what God is doing. As one colleague observed, Chris-

---

30. S. H. Blank, "Wisdom," in *The Interpreter's Dictionary of the Bible: An Illustrated Encyclopedia* (Nashville: Abingdon Press, 1962), p. 857.

31. Witvliet, "Teaching Worship as a Christian Practice," p. 145.

32. Nieman, "Liturgy and Life," pp. 159-60, 161-62.

tian practical theology searches for a "way of living up to the gospel we profess." Our courses are "trajectories," as Witvliet remarks, toward the lifelong exercise of faith.

Practical theological pedagogy strives for fluidity between theory and practice in various ways, but in any course in practical theology one should be able to find loops, circles, or spirals in the syllabus itself and in individual class sessions. That is, when those of us who teach in practical theology come up against the elusiveness of practice and the insufficiency of theology, we move. We jump onto the hermeneutical loop that Cahalan describes in her teaching of the front-end and capstone courses, moving among description, analysis, interpretation, decision, and action.[33] When students enter the program at the front end, she looks for the questions they bring, anticipates the resources they will need, and aims toward the capacities they will take with them when they leave. The structure of her penultimate assignment leads students through a similar circle of questions: "What is going on here? What does it mean theologically? What should we do?" Similarly, Nieman describes a "cycle" in his class on worship and preaching, repeated four times for each rite, around historical and structural description, formative experiences, theological encounter, scriptural examination, and actual enactment of the rite.

Much has been made and should be made of the first move — thick description and interpretation of the situation. Turpin talks about "reading" the specific and wider cultural context. Witvliet talks about training both "depth perception" and "peripheral vision" to enable people to see any given situation from a wide variety of angles.[34] Pastoral theologians talk about the living human person or web as "document" and "text." Some, such as Mary McClintock Fulkerson, define a "sort of 'phenomenology of situationality'" as the "larger frame" and the chief contribution of

33. Cahalan, "Introducing Ministry and Fostering Integration," p. 97. This method has received a variety of interpretations. See, for example, Juan Luis Segundo, *Liberation of Theology*, trans. John Drury (Maryknoll, N.Y.: Orbis Books, 1976); Poling and Miller, *Foundations for a Practical Theology of Ministry*; Browning, *Fundamental Practical Theology*; Evelyn and James Whitehead, *Method in Ministry: Theological Reflection and Christian Ministry* (Kansas City: Sheed & Ward, 1995); Thomas Groome, *Christian Religious Education: Sharing Our Story and Vision* (San Francisco: Jossey-Bass, 1999); and Roslyn Karaban, "Always an Outsider? Feminist, Female, Lay, and Roman Catholic," in *Feminist and Womanist Pastoral Theology*, ed. Bonnie J. Miller-McLemore and Brita L. Gill-Austern (Nashville: Abingdon Press, 1999), pp. 65-76.

34. Turpin, "Distinctive Pedagogies in Religious Education"; Witvliet, "Teaching Worship as a Christian Practice," p. 148.

practical theology.[35] I would agree with all of these claims but would add that the "larger frame" of practical theology is not satisfied until the loop is completed or until one moves from "interpreting situations" toward response. Students must engage in *phronetic* theological movement from "practice to theory and back again," as practical theologian Don Browning says, or, more specifically, from "theory-laden practice to a retrieval of normative theory-laden practice to the creation of more critically held theory-laden practices" (by which he means a movement from everyday practice to normative resources that themselves grow out of practices back to a more fully informed practice).[36] Many courses in practical theology adopt this movement as the implicit structure of the syllabus and the rationale behind specific assignments.

I would not expect those in other fields consistently to run this entire circle. There is place and need for disciplines that delve deeply in each of its specific moves. But practical theological pedagogy suggests that theological education needs more foraging forth by those in other fields than currently is the case. If those in practical theology find themselves drawing from every other discipline in the seminary curriculum, as Witvliet remarks; or appealing to areas as diverse as ritual studies, biblical scholarship, and ethnography, as Nieman observes; or requiring students to analyze demography, locate historical roots of a problem, and consider religious symbols, as Cahalan does, might those in other fields reach to practical theology?

Instruments of Peace

To "read" a community as a "theological text," one must, according to Fulkerson, take bodies seriously and all the "visceral, affective responses to different bodies," such as her own reaction to the "thin white man sitting twisted in a wheelchair" or "all the dark skin in the room" of the multi-racial church community in a working-class area of a small Southern city on which

---

35. Mary McClintock Fulkerson, "Ministry to Eunuchs and Other Ecclesial Practices: Toward a Theological Reading," unpublished manuscript, p. 13. These ideas now appear in her book, *Places of Redemption: Theology for a Worldly Church* (Oxford: Oxford University Press, 2007). Fulkerson relies on Farley's article, "Interpreting Situations," in which adequate framing of the contemporary situation is seen as the primary subject matter of practical theology and "situation" is defined as the "way various items, powers, and events in the environment gather to evoke response from participants" (p. 36).

36. Browning, *Fundamental Practical Theology*, p. 7.

she turned her anthropological-theological gaze.[37] A closer theological reading of the community requires attention to desire, fear, and aversion — affective responses — to counterbalance or correct the prevalent intellectualist leaning or cognitive focus of most systematic theological work.

Although Fulkerson does not say so, I would argue that to do accurate affective analysis — that is, to "read" and respond to a situation as a "theological text" with attention to affect — one needs not only ethnographical or other social-science tools and theological insight. One must also have a certain level of emotional and spiritual health — the much-maligned "therapeutic" vitality that contemporary psychology has often understood better than theology. If this were not true, then seminaries and judicatories would not bother to interview applicants, give them personality tests, or remark that this or that person is really not "cut out for" ministry or seminary teaching. Of course, a call from God or a religious community is not something any of us can be quick to judge, for premature and one-dimensional judgments are often in error. Nonetheless, those teaching care, education, preaching, leadership, and so forth know that personhood matters and find ways to work this into class discussion and assignments, as Cahalan's work with specific students makes most evident. The questions that students bring are intimately tied to questions of vocational discernment and identity confronted in "changing, ambiguous, and often contentious ecclesial" times.[38] If faith is not just a matter of beliefs, language, institutional structures, and practices, but also, as in Augustine, a matter of desire and its disorders, then healing ("therapy" in its broadest historical and classic meaning) of personal, relational, and social brokenness matters.

The know-how of practice is actually distinctly person-located. Practical reason or reason that orients action is "different from intellectual reason, reason that orients the mind," according to Couture. Drawing on Aristotle, she argues that practical reason is "necessarily imprecise and cannot cover all of the situations it governs." Only wise *persons*, then, "can make wise judgments in situations with variables for which theoretical reason cannot account." So, practical theological pedagogy has a particular aim: the formation of "wise persons" rather than "only intelligible theories."[39]

37. Fulkerson, "Ministry to Eunuchs and Other Ecclesial Practices," pp. 2-3.
38. Cahalan, "Introducing Ministry and Fostering Integration," p. 95.
39. Couture, "Ritualized Play," p. 97. Couture draws here on Aristotle's *Nicomachean Ethics* in *Introduction to Aristotle*, 2d ed., ed. Richard McKeon (Chicago: University of Chicago Press, 1973).

Perhaps one of the most important aspects of the final assignment that Cahalan requires in her culminating course has to do with what happens to the person him- or herself. Many are transformed, sometimes even in the moment of giving their public presentation. In the course of their degree programs, they change from naïve or terrified beginners to people with voice, presence, and emotional and spiritual integrity that will carry them over the threshold from classroom into ministry.[40]

This final element of engaging the learner holistically raises deep suspicions among some that practical theological courses are not intellectually rigorous or that they have simply succumbed to vagaries of modern psychology. Yet the focus on the person in practical theological pedagogy is not automatically a symptom of sloppy pietism or individualistic culture gone awry. Rather, it is a recognition that each person can become, as in the prayer of St. Francis, "an instrument of peace." Some would qualify Henri Nouwen's famous description of the minister as "wounded healer" by advocating for pastoral leaders that are "healed" or "recovering" wounded healers before they try to facilitate the healing and formation of others, whether through preaching, leading, educating, or other practices. Spiritual self-awareness is just as crucial today as it was for the likes of Augustine, Søren Kierkegaard, and other classic models of the Christian life. Education centered on students' formation can happen with "integrity and rigor," Cahalan insists. She uses means similar to those listed by Witvliet: "assigning challenging and compelling reading, asking probing questions about historical and cross-cultural examples, and requiring significant engagement within the classroom and with local worshiping communities."[41]

Other practical theologians ask students to do "genograms," plotting relational connections and disconnections as well as patterns of health and pathology over several generations, or to write in first-person singular about themselves with "experience-near analytical" rigor, as pastoral theologian Kathleen Greider remarks.[42] Such assignments point to the need to reach both backwards to where people come from and forward to where they are going. Students have a "history and future" with practices, Nieman acknowledges, that is "itself a resource for the course." When he

---

40. See Cahalan, "Introducing Ministry and Fostering Integration," pp. 92-93, 112-13.

41. Cahalan, "Introducing Ministry and Fostering Integration," pp. 93-94n.5; and Witvliet, "Teaching Worship as a Christian Practice," p. 120n.5.

42. Kathleen J. Greider, "Practical Theology, Pedagogy, and the Case of Pastoral Care," manuscript from the American Association of Practical Theology, April 2006, p. 9, now published in *International Journal of Practical Theology*.

asks students to describe in detail, "for good or for ill," the contextual history shaping their pre-understandings of particular liturgical rituals, he knows the class period might turn out to be "quite poignant and even emotion-laden." As Witvliet observes, just as a golf coach or singing instructor can make little progress without analyzing "persistent habits" that define a good swing or pitch, so also must seminary teachers begin by raising awareness of the "acquired habits" students bring to the classroom and to the practice of ministry.[43] Those who hope to lead religious communities and organizations need the kind of emotional intelligence obtained by therapists after years of intense training.

There is one additional dimension to this final element: Where theological education often aims at analyzing or deconstructing sacred texts and beliefs and rightfully encourages students to understand their complicated historical and cultural contexts and meanings, practical theological pedagogy takes up the task of post-deconstruction reconstruction. This, of course, is not a task that belongs exclusively to those who teach practical theological courses but raises common questions for all classes. Does this course only take apart, or does it also offer ways to put back together? Does it only promote disengagement from religion, or does it allow for fuller re-engagement? So, as Witvliet asserts, the "ethos" or the "undertone of fear, guilt, pride, or gratitude" of the classroom is important.[44] So also are sightings of grace. Practical theology pedagogy involves what Fulkerson identifies as a discernment of the "'theonomy' of a situation, its openings for God-dependence," or what she also calls "places of appearing," "signs" or "traces" of redemption. These can be theological even when we do not "use what are, strictly speaking, 'theological terms.'" The very act of analyzing the site of the "wound" where faith no longer works is "an indirect testimony to God" or to "that alone which can account for such a diminishing of social sin, the reality of God."[45]

Contributions to Curriculum and Theological Education

A closer look at how we teach discloses a great deal about the field of practical theology, its key commitments, and its central contributions to theo-

43. Nieman, "Liturgy and Life," p. 152; Witvliet, "Teaching Worship as a Christian Practice," p. 127.

44. Witvliet, "Teaching Worship as a Christian Practice," p. 143.

45. Fulkerson, "Ministry to Eunuchs and Other Ecclesial Practices," pp. 14, 16.

logical education, communities of faith, and the wider world. While practical theologians have searched in many directions for definition of the field, central conceptual and practical agreements have sprung up in our own backyards. We have not thought to look so close to home in part because we have been entranced with a particularly powerful diagnosis of the problems of theological education that discouraged attention to practical theological pedagogy.[46] But now we can see that courses in practical theology uphold a rich definition of theological know-how that recognizes the intelligence involved in practice and the teaching of practice. A closer look at practical theological pedagogy and the social enterprise of teaching provides an intriguing lens to understand theology anew, as it refracts the light of the practice of faith from which it comes and toward which it points.

Practical theologians emphasize not just learning about a discipline but also, as Witvliet says, "full, conscious, active participation" in it. Even courses introducing practical theological methods, as Cahalan observes, rarely discuss practical theology as a discipline. To learn about worship, one must engage in it; to understand care, one must try it out; one cannot learn to teach without teaching; one must engage concrete particular instances of ministry to do ministry. Ultimately, the teaching practices of practical theologians suggest one knows theology as one embodies it.

This has many pragmatic implications for the curriculum of theological education as a whole and for Christian faith more broadly. I will mention only a few of the more obvious. As I listened to colleagues share syllabi and delve into the strategies behind the readings, exercises, discussions, and requirements of their courses, I was surprised by the common elements that emerged. Clearer theoretical articulation of the features of practical theological teaching — the focus on practice, the interplay between scales and expert performance, the hermeneutic circle of description-interpretation-action, and the role of self-reflection and formation — provides resources to evaluate courses in practical theology. There are criteria that define a course in practical theology and make claims for or against one course or another.

In turn, this list of features provides a way for faculty in other areas to appreciate and incorporate into their own teaching the wisdom of learning a practice so central to the area of practical theology. Reaching across the curriculum should be less unilateral. If practical theology's ex-

46. Miller-McLemore, "The 'Clerical Paradigm.'"

pertise has been interpretation of and response to situations, should not faculty in other areas turn on occasion to resources in practical theology to understand more deeply particular issues and practices, such as ritual, marriage, suffering, anger, and so forth? Would it not be helpful if faculty in historical and systematic theology were to include good practical theology texts in their syllabi or require participant-observation of practitioners among their assignments? Those in practical theology might serve as guides.

Articulating the key features of practical theological pedagogy invites greater conversation across the disciplinary areas about the marks of excellence in theological education and the nature of doing theology for the sake of the Christian life. Those in practical theology often have insight into what is needed in introductory and capstone courses. But the auspicious aspiration harbored by many in practical theology is precisely what Cahalan names at the conclusion of her chapter: that integration is not something that students encounter only in courses in practical theology or only at the end of their course work. This is a task that must be shared by the whole faculty. Cahalan calls for a "culture of integration where all faculty members are intentional about how their teaching encourages a heightened sense of practical theological thinking in ministry."[47] In such a culture, few courses, if any, would be oriented around introduction to a discipline.

This inevitably requires greater proximity to practice on the part of all faculty. Practical theology confirms an epistemological truth elaborated by performance and ritual theory: performance "creates meaning that cannot be found elsewhere."[48] It is odd that facility in practice among faculty across the curriculum — so important in medical education, for instance — has received so little attention. Without practice of a wide variety of kinds, not only by those who teach in practical theology but by those in all fields of seminary education, can we understand the knowing needed by those we teach?

In short, some of the means and goals of practical theological pedagogy are worth wider emulation. Examination of the epistemological and

47. Cahalan, "Introducing Ministry and Fostering Integration," p. 14.
48. Charles J. Scalise, *Bridging the Gap: Connecting What You Learned in Seminary with What You Find in the Congregation* (Nashville: Abingdon Press, 2003), p. 120. He cites Jeremy S. Begbie, *Voicing Creation's Praise: Towards a Theology of the Arts* (Edinburgh: T&T Clark, 1991), and Frances Young, *Virtuoso Theology: The Bible and Interpretation* (Cleveland: Pilgrim Press, 1993).

theological commitments behind the goals and the ways various practical theologians strive to reach them validates teaching in practical theology as more complex, more theologically sound, and more fitting for ministry than has previously been recognized. Theoretically, theologically, and pragmatically, such teaching is a resource both for enriching seminary education as a whole and, perhaps more importantly, for understanding the ways of knowing intrinsic to ministry and faithful living.

PART III

GENDER: A KEY CATEGORY OF ANALYSIS

CHAPTER 9

Feminist Theory and Pastoral Theology

BACKGROUND AND INTRODUCTION

After publishing *Also a Mother* in 1994 and teaching courses on women, psychology, and religion for over five years, I became involved in two projects, a co-edited book, *Feminist and Womanist Pastoral Theology,* published in 1999, and a major Lilly Endowment grant directed by Don Browning on Christianity and the family that led to a co-authored book as its apex in 1997, *From Culture Wars to Common Ground: Religion and the American Family Debate.* Despite how much I learned from the multi-pronged family project, I remain ambivalent about the practical theology book that served as its capstone. Defying its title, we clashed as co-authors over the nature of the problem and our vision of the solution. The book's ultimate promotion of the "committed, intact, equal-regard, public-private family" was a compromise whose terms still bring back memories of difficulty. The book ultimately was not quite the culmination once imagined, and Browning himself went on to write a few more books on marriage that superseded it.

By contrast, working with friend and co-editor Brita Gill-Austern and other women on chapters for *Feminist and Womanist Pastoral Theology* was easy, despite typical editorial hassles, partly because the goal was

---

This essay was originally published as "Feminist Theory in Pastoral Theology," in *Feminist and Womanist Pastoral Theology,* ed. Bonnie J. Miller-McLemore and Brita L. Gill-Austern (Nashville: Abingdon Press, 1999), pp. 77-94. Used by permission.

almost the opposite — to represent a diversity of positions among new scholars in pastoral theology. We even invited diversity in definition of key terms, *feminism* and *womanism*.

In an introduction to its annual book issue in 2010, *The Christian Century* concludes, "attention to issues of race, class, gender, and sexual orientation may be less pronounced now than it was a generation ago" (19 October 2010, p. 7). Indeed, the academy and its constituencies, such as the *Century*, have incorporated concern for these issues to such an extent that attention may no longer seem necessary. The *Century* introduction notes the presence of diverse voices not "previously heard" among the "best theology books of the past 25 years" recommended by eight scholars solicited by the magazine. The scholars are themselves eclectic, likely chosen with care by the editors to represent diverse race, gender, and religious perspectives.

So, although problems of sexism and racism are by no means resolved, progress on inclusion has occurred. I would have less cause to label the academy "masculinist" today than I did in this chapter, written in 1999. And there is less need today than ten years ago to assess the impact of feminist theory on pastoral theology. But in the mid-1990s the need seemed urgent. A few collections on women and pastoral care and articles on feminism and pastoral counseling had been published. More women were teaching, attending seminary, and doing doctoral degrees in the field. But no one had attempted a full-fledged treatment of feminist and womanist pastoral theology as a new genre of scholarship.

Since it seems so common today, I am not sure people can fully appreciate what a change it was to include feminist theory as a significant dialogue partner at that time. Brita Gill-Austern and I agreed about the need to consider the implications. But as we say in our editors' introduction, neither of us had the desire or the time to write such a volume individually (while also raising three sons). We thought we could handle an edited book. And, as the chapter argues, collaboration is not an atypical feminist approach. Maxine Glaz and Jeanne Stevenson-Moessner had modeled this in their editorship of books on women and pastoral care. But, by contrast, Brita and I wanted to focus on wider questions of how feminist theory shapes not only *pastoral care* but also research and teaching in *pastoral theology* as a discipline. In a "field that necessarily remains focused on concrete topics of caregiving in congregations as its most central task," there is still a need for "concentrated reflection on the theories and concepts that inform these practices" (p. 14). The influence of feminist and womanist theory is at least partly responsible for the change in the field's subject matter from document to web and from private to public theology. So what does the inclusion of feminist theory promise for the "future of a discipline and our role in it," as we say in the preface? It seemed like a momentous time to raise the question.

Feminist and Womanist Pastoral Theology moves from history, definition, and method to implications for pedagogical and pastoral practice. The chapter that follows was my contribution and appears near the middle of the book. I presented a version of it at a 1997 Association of Practical Theology pre-session of the American Academy of Religion where British practical theologian Elaine Graham served as respondent. That she was working on a similar essay herself titled "Feminist Theory and Practical Theology," published in the *International Journal of Practical Theology* in 1999, the same year as my own chapter, reflects the wider interest in the question at that time.

This chapter moves methodically through definitions of feminist theory, feminist theology, and feminist practical and pastoral theology. The literature I chart and sort seems utterly familiar to me now, and my lists and definitions seem dry. Nonetheless, the chapter serves as an important marker in the evolution of a discipline, similar to Chapter 1. Its routine character results almost inevitably from its intent: it tries to describe the state of a field under the impact of feminist theory, define key terms and their development, and summarize or list some implications.

Because I first wrote this chapter for the Association of Practical Theology, I include another portrait of practical theology's disciplinary relationship to and distinction from pastoral theology, even though pastoral theology was my primary focus when I revised the essay for *Feminist and Womanist Pastoral Theology*. At that time I thought such distinctions between pastoral and practical theology were commonplace. I now realize that they are not universal. They are distinct to particular U.S. Protestant contexts. I also define practical theology so loosely that almost anyone could qualify. But at least I am beginning to see a conclusion that I reached recently in more extensive efforts to define the term: only a select group of people self-identify first and foremost as practical theologians in the disciplinary sense, even though others qualify when the term is used in ways that go beyond its reference to a scholarly discipline.

This chapter also repeats observations in Chapters 1 and 6, published a few years before it. I continue to rely on black feminist bell hooks to provide a baseline definition of feminism and on her insight that there is value in creating theory from the "location of pain and struggle." I add a few more sentences on my concern about the clerical paradigm as a narrow and overused diagnosis for all that ails theological education, naming for the first time the irony that its negative view of pastoral skills only made theological education "even more abstract and removed from Christian life, faith, and ministerial practice than before the critique," an idea to which I return later. My wariness about a theology removed from practice and "unnecessarily academic, obtuse, and abstract" remains a steady theme throughout this and other chapters. I caution practical theologians who see abstraction as a means to academic status *at the very same time* that I edit a book and contribute a chapter aimed largely at an academic and theoretical audience. I have to explain the value of the latter without falling prey to the former, a balancing act I do not always accomplish successfully.

Feminist theory has had a broad impact on the study of religion. When I did Ph.D. work more than a decade ago, few texts by women, much less feminists or womanists, were included on the exam bibliographies, and dissertation research on "women's issues" met with mixed reactions. Today, scholars in religion in the United States take feminist and womanist theory more seriously, even though they might not claim feminist or womanist identities *per se.* Certainly, wariness and outright hostility about the inclusion of power and gender analyses still abound, especially in conservative settings in the United States and on the international scene. But generally speaking, the study of religion, theology, and Scripture will never be quite the same again. Feminist and womanist thought has exposed the misogyny embedded in traditions and institutions that have characterized women as emotionally juvenile, morally and intellectually inferior, and spiritually evil. It has interrogated the very categories and customs that define religion.

Has the valley of genuine equality been lifted up and the mountain of sexism been made low? My rhetorical question suggests both the apocalyptic character of feminist hopes and the ongoing need for more analysis and transformation. What happens for feminists when mainstream scholars selectively use insights internal to feminist discourse? What are the issues distinct to the field of pastoral theology and its use of feminist discourse? Have feminist and womanist voices influenced pastoral theology to the same extent as other fields in religion, and if not, why not? What are some of the ways in which secular feminist theory itself has evolved, and how might feminist pastoral theologians make better, more critical use of it?

While I will not answer these questions comprehensively, I will begin the task of addressing them. I embark on this exploration by looking first at feminist theory itself, focusing primarily on definitions of feminism and their relationship to pastoral theology. I conclude by briefly identifying prominent characteristics of feminist pastoral theology and situating it within broader discussions of pastoral and practical theology as contemporary disciplines in search of clearer identities. Feminist theory in pastoral theology has seldom received clear articulation because of the precariousness of the practical disciplines and the difficulties of honoring in theoretical discussions the idiosyncrasies of ordinary lived experience — quotidian life with which women are often most familiar. Feminist analysis suggests that it is no accident that the closer one gets to practice, particular experiences, personal faith, emotions, and subjectivity, the lower the academic status of the field.

Feminist Theory: Working Definitions

The complaint of bell hooks about the careless use of the term *feminist* is a fitting corrective for current discussions in pastoral and practical theology.[1] Such carelessness characterizes literature on the pastoral care of women that assumes a great deal of feminist scholarship but avoids explicitly claiming or defining its feminist agenda. Closer to home, have I ever declared myself a feminist pastoral theologian? Probably not as forthrightly as I might have done. Refraining from such a declaration says something about the troubled meaning of the term in culture and congregations. Who knows what *feminist* means anymore? More often than not, many people associate the term with radical male-bashing politics. They reject feminism — all the while accepting, and sometimes even welcoming, a multitude of changes spawned by feminism.

On the other hand, are people justified in assuming, as is often the case, that I or any other woman in pastoral theology or ministry is a femi-

---

1. bell hooks, *Feminist Theory: From Margin to Center* (Boston: South End Press, 1984), p. 23.

nist simply by being a woman? Ironically, theories of liberation tend to create ontological categorizations in their very efforts to liberate particular groups. Such theories assign a person attributes because that person is a "woman," thereby perpetuating stereotypes that liberationists actually want to undo.[2] Automatic assumptions about sex identity fail to grasp the far-reaching implications of feminist theory itself.

A powerful definition of feminism comes from bell hooks. Simply put, feminism is a radical political movement. She writes, "Feminism is a struggle to end sexist oppression. Its aim is not to benefit solely any specific group of women, any particular race or class of women. It does not privilege women over men. It has the power to transform in a meaningful way all our lives."[3] As a black feminist, hooks is particularly concerned about the misuse of feminist theory in denying the realities and struggles of women of color. To call feminism simply a movement to make men and women equal reduces and even confuses its full intent. This is particularly true when an emphasis on sexual equality discounts the weight of other inequities and when sexual equality in the midst of sexual difference remains an elusive ideal. Feminism is far more than a movement to achieve equal rights, individual freedom, and economic and social equity for middle-class white women. A feminist perspective demands a critical analysis of structures and ideologies that rank people as inferior or superior according to various traits of human nature, including gender, sexual orientation, class, color, age, physical ability, and so forth. Feminism strives to eradicate sexism and related exploitative classificatory systems and to allow those silenced to join in the cultural activity of defining reality.

To think about the *study of religion* from this perspective demands an analysis of structures and ideologies that rank academic study as superior or inferior depending on its distance from or proximity to religious faith, concrete lives, emotions, and women's activities. Why, for example, are the complex thinking, acting, and teaching required to sustain viable practices of all kinds, and religious practices in particular (i.e., practical thinking), the most academically disregarded or disreputable? This disregard seems especially peculiar given the importance of healthy religious practices for human sustenance and survival — something the ecological movement has made most apparent in recent years.

2. See Victor Anderson, *Beyond Ontological Blackness: An Essay on African-American Religious and Cultural Criticism* (New York: Continuum, 1995).

3. hooks, *Feminist Theory*, p. 26.

As this example demonstrates, to think about *practical theology* from the vantage point of feminist theory requires prophetic, transformative challenge to systems of stratification and domination within the academy and to systems of power and authority within society and religious life, particularly those that rank men and male activities over women and female activities. Obviously, this is a huge agenda with multiple obligations, from challenging the assumed superiority of abstruse, highly theoretical forms of theological reflection, for example, to addressing the devaluing of women's lives or the ongoing resistance in congregations to making liturgy gender-inclusive.

More specifically, to think about *pastoral theology* from the feminist perspective defined above requires a fundamental re-orientation of the core functions of pastoral care. In place of or in addition to the conventional modes with which pastoral care has been routinely equated — healing, sustaining, guiding, and reconciling, articulated by Seward Hiltner and amended by William Clebsch and Charles Jaekle[4] — four other pastoral practices acquire particular importance: resisting, empowering, nurturing, and liberating.[5] Although not yet classified as four distinct typologies of pastoral care, these four practices have received extensive attention in many recent writings in pastoral theology. These activities are not exhaustive of new pastoral modalities sparked by feminism and womanism and do not offer a comprehensive picture of new definitions. But they need to be recognized and marked as fresh, prominent ways for re-organizing the functions of pastoral care.

While all or some of the four functions of resisting, empowering, nurturing, and liberating have operated during the historical periods described by Clebsch and Jaekle, they did not receive the kind of pre-eminence that has come recently as a result of feminist theory. For the moment I offer only rather terse definitions to give a general flavor of recent feminist- and womanist-influenced trends. *Compassionate resistance* re-

---

4. Seward Hiltner, *Preface to Pastoral Theology* (New York: Abingdon Press, 1958); and William Clebsch and Charles Jaekle, *Pastoral Care in Historical Perspective*, 2d ed. (New York: Aronson, 1983).

5. This is partially based on Carroll Watkins Ali's informal remarks during a panel at the American Academy of Religion, November 1996, drawing on her dissertation work on womanist pastoral theology. Since that time, she has published both a chapter — "A Womanist Search for Sources" — in the same volume in which this chapter appears (*Feminist and Womanist Pastoral Theology*), and a book: *Survival and Liberation: Pastoral Theology in African-American Context* (St. Louis: Chalice Press, 1999).

quires confrontation with evil, contesting violent, abusive behaviors that perpetuate undeserved suffering and false stereotypes that distort the realities of people's lives. Resistance includes a focused healing of wounds of abuse that have festered for generations.[6] *Empowerment* involves advocacy and tenderness on behalf of the vulnerable, giving resources and means to those previously stripped of authority, voice, and power. *Nurturance* is not sympathetic kindness or quiescent support but fierce, dedicated proclamation of love that makes a space for difficult changes and fosters solidarity among the vulnerable. *Liberation* entails both escape from unjust, unwarranted affliction and release into new life and wholeness as created, redeemed, and loved people of God. Resistance, empowerment, nurturance, and liberation all entail a deconstruction of limited definitions of reality and a reconstruction of new views of the world and one's valued place within it. Pastoral care in these modalities is not particularly "pastoral" or "nice" in the truncated ways in which it has been perceived. Pastoral care disturbs as well as comforts, provokes as well as guides. It breaks silences and calls for radical truth-telling; it names shame and guilt, calls for confession and repentance, and moves vigilantly toward forgiveness and reconciliation, knowing that both are even more difficult to effect than people have hoped. Indeed, if pastoral theology keeps the term *shepherd* as a central motif (and even that becomes questionable in a world where shepherding and shearing are no longer common experiences upon which to ground metaphor), a feminist perspective reminds us that sheep are not the warm, fuzzy, and clean creatures our storybook and Bible stories have portrayed.

By fostering redefinition in all three spheres of religious study, practical theology, and pastoral theology, feminist theory participates in undercutting primary assumptions of *modernism,* including the universality of certain pastoral "truths" and the inherent authority of male clerics, and ushers in a *postmodern* awareness of the influence of power in the formation of knowledge. Postmodernism signals the breaking up of the hegemony of modern Western culture and a receptivity to other perspectives. At the same time, this does not mean the absolute undoing of Western culture; feminist theory does not *de facto* mean the deconstruction of all knowledge.

6. See Nancy Ramsay, "Compassionate Resistance: An Ethic for Pastoral Care and Counseling," *Journal of Pastoral Care* 52, no. 3 (Fall 1998): 217-26; see also James N. Poling, *Deliver Us from Evil: Resisting Racial and Gender Oppression* (Minneapolis: Fortress Press, 1996).

Feminist arguments for shared, if not universal, assumptions about truth, justice, and many other matters can and must be made. Complete deconstruction is a final stage of later modernism rather than a stage beyond modernism. Maureen Kemeza remarks, "Nihilistic deconstructionism is a dead end, at best only descriptive of the current crises without any resource for creative response."[7] Some liberation theologies and feminist theories represent a more genuine *post*modernism in terms of constructing new theories *after* modernism.

Varieties of and Shifts in Feminist Theory

Such single-mindedness of purpose, however, has not been the nature of feminist thought. Perhaps one of the most common misperceptions is that feminism represents a monolithic movement. Entire books, such as Rosemarie Tong's *Feminist Thought,* are devoted to characterizing the various sorts of feminism, such as liberal, Marxist, radical, psychoanalytic, socialist, and postmodern feminism.[8]

In applying this typology to pastoral theology, we notice that because of the heavy reliance on psychology in pastoral theory, psychoanalytic feminists have influenced pastoral theology powerfully, perhaps more than other feminist views. In Tong's words, psychoanalytic feminists "find the root of woman's oppression embedded deep in her psyche."[9] This idea alone carries critical implications for pastoral theologians considering problems of individuals and families within congregations such as marital conflict, depression, abuse, and so forth. Psychoanalytic feminists such as Karen Horney have emphasized the role of a sexist social environment in shaping and distorting male and female development.[10] Others such as Nancy Chodorow have explored the prominent role of the mother in reproducing patterns of female fear of separation and male fear of relationship.[11] These ideas prove especially useful in rethinking pastoral care of

7. Maureen Dallison Kemeza, "Dante as Guide and Provocation," *The Christian Century,* 20-27 November 1996, p. 1148.

8. Rosemarie Tong, *Feminist Thought: A Comprehensive Introduction* (Boulder and San Francisco: Westview Press, 1989).

9. Tong, *Feminist Thought,* p. 5.

10. Karen Horney, *Feminine Psychology* (New York: W. W. Norton, 1930), and *Neurosis and Human Growth* (New York: W. W. Norton, 1973).

11. Nancy Chodorow, "Family Structure and Feminine Personality," in *Women, Cul-*

women and men. Moreover, psychoanalytic feminists provide a cultural critique of the implicit biases of psychology and therapeutic practice — a moral critique of values already familiar to theologians concerned about unreflective adoption of psychology by pastoral caregivers.[12]

However, I cannot think of any feminist pastoral theologian who would identify herself solely as a psychoanalytic feminist. More typically, pastoral theologians pick and choose from many schools of thought. Doing this becomes a problem only when done without sufficient statement of a rationale for selection.

At least one rationale for moving beyond psychoanalytic feminism lies in the broader moral and communal concerns of pastoral theology. This warrants employment of other forms of feminist thought, such as socialist feminism. Tong characterizes socialist feminism as a synthetic movement that attempts to interrelate the myriad forms of oppression in patterns of economic production (from Marxist feminists), in practices of reproduction and sexuality (from radical feminists), and in structures of domesticity and socialization of children (from liberal feminists). Socialist feminists contend that women are oppressed by both economic inequities and patriarchal devaluing of domestic and childbearing responsibilities. A woman's status and function "in all these structures must change if she is to achieve anything approximating full liberation."[13] Since pastoral theology is an integrative discipline that works at the intersection of personal experience, tradition, culture, and community, pastoral theologians should see a socialist feminist approach as particularly useful and appropriate.

Yet feminists in pastoral theology are not alone in resisting labels, and many feminists do not fall neatly into one or the other category. Although they serve a useful analytic function, labels retain an artificiality that distorts the heterogeneous character of feminist thought. The definition by bell hooks, which I have adopted and applied above, actually represents just such a blend of radical, socialist, and postmodern feminism. I have defined a type of pastoral theological feminism that builds on but slightly departs from the traditional liberal feminist emphasis on the logistical restraints that block women's entrance into the public sphere.

---

ture, and Society, ed. Michele Zimbalist Rosaldo and Louise Lamphere (Stanford, Calif.: Stanford University Press, 1974), and The Reproduction of Mothering (Berkeley and Los Angeles: University of California Press, 1978).

12. See Susan Sturdivant, Therapy with Women: A Feminist Philosophy of Treatment (New York: Springer, 1984).

13. Tong, Feminist Thought, p. 6.

My working definition actually represents a broader shift in the feminist discussion. A simpler and theologically relevant schema for depicting the development of feminist theory in pastoral theology can be borrowed from a classification developed by philosopher Iris Young.[14] She identifies a movement in the late twentieth century from what she calls humanist to gynocentric feminism. Despite the blending from time to time of these two forms of feminism in the women's movements of the nineteenth and twentieth centuries, liberal or humanist feminism predominated in the United States from the 1960s to the late 1970s. Humanist feminism captured the public imagination and is often the position with which feminism is identified. Humanist feminism also has a decidedly white, North American bias, shaped by democratic ideals of equal participation and self-sufficiency. In the 1960s, early second-wave feminist theory evolved in response to the particular problems of the isolated and disempowered white, middle-class, college-educated housewife. In response to views of women as inherently inferior to men, humanist feminism defined "femininity as the primary vehicle of women's oppression, and called upon male-dominated institutions to allow women the opportunity to participate fully in the public world-making activities."[15]

Several factors led to a shift from humanist to gynocentric feminism. Many women, especially women of color, working-class women, and mothers, felt disenfranchised by humanist feminist assumptions. African-American women, for example, did not see men or confinement in the home as the source of their problems and depended on solidarity between women and men to resist racism and its related problems. They recognized the multiple and destructive ways in which white feminists who sought liberation acted in turn as participants in the belittlement and disenfranchisement of black women and men, with little or no consciousness or concern. Women of color more generally did not aspire to the social status of the men they knew, who often did not have the same economic and social opportunities as the men of the dominant class. In addition, various injustices arose in treating women and men "alike" in the workplace or in divorce proceedings, for example, when reproductive and economic differences between men and women persisted and affected women's lives in distinct ways. In the late 1970s and 1980s, women began to recognize some

---

14. Iris Marian Young, "Humanism, Gynocentrism, and Feminist Politics," *Women's Studies International Forum* 8, no. 2 (1985): 173-83.

15. Young, "Humanism, Gynocentrism, and Feminist Politics," p. 173.

of the goals of humanist feminists as male-defined ideals that involved the repression of the body and relationality — power over others, competition and triumph, individual self-sufficiency, and personal fulfillment. Gynocentric feminists located women's oppression not in femininity *per se* but in a masculinist culture's denial of the female body, nature, and other modes of relational knowing and deciding, including maternal thinking, and in broader structures of oppression. Feminists still wanted equality with men but began to talk about an equality that encompassed sexual and other differences.

The outcome of this shift in feminist theory for the academy is still unclear. In some respects, a gynocentric feminism is less critical or overtly angry and hence represents a less visible attack on traditional scholarship and practices. Gynocentric feminism can actually perpetuate stereotypes of women as essentially more caring, relational, and maternal. It can accommodate too easily to existing structures and underestimate both the danger of conventional definitions of femininity and the value of male-associated activities. Alone it is not a sufficient base for an adequate feminist pastoral theology. Humanist feminists are partly justified in their accusations that gynocentric feminists have forsaken radical feminist politics. Yet gynocentric feminism asks for more fundamental changes in basic assumptions about gender, sexual difference, and power in Western thought. Political action that subverts conventional practices becomes less tied to women's oppression, more tied to social oppressions as a whole, and hence more complex and difficult.

In general, feminists and womanists in the academy walk a tightrope between acquiring the necessary tools of the master's house to survive and creating new tools for genuinely transformative work. True, as Audre Lorde first argued, one cannot dismantle the master's house using the master's tools.[16] One must break new ground and free oneself from portrayals of the world that obscure alternative realities. On the other hand, no one creates in a vacuum; dominant perceptions of the world must be confronted, and confrontation requires knowledge. Both moves, black feminist Patricia Hill Collins suggests, are ultimately more necessary than Audre Lorde first supposed.[17]

---

16. Audre Lorde, *Sister Outsider: Essays and Speeches* (Freedom, Calif.: Crossing Press, 1984), pp. 110-13.

17. Patricia Hill Collins, public lecture, Vanderbilt University, November 1997.

Feminist Theory and Feminist Theology

Feminist theory did not emerge out of thin air, and Christian ideas about freedom and human worth appear at least implicitly in hooks's definition. Although the history of the relationship of Christianity and women is far from simple and unambiguous, Christianity has influenced feminism and womanism as much as the reverse. Anne Carr, Elisabeth Schüssler Fiorenza, Rosemary Radford Ruether, and Delores Williams,[18] to mention only a few, have developed the thesis that Christianity has ideals internal to itself that are closely aligned with feminist and womanist ideals — justice, liberation of the oppressed, survival and well-being, radical mutuality, egalitarian community, and the inherent worth of women. Christianity and feminism, Carr argues, are not only compatible. They "are, in fact, integrally and firmly connected in the truth of the Christian vision." Feminist critique has served to reveal the "transcendent truth" within the symbols and traditions.[19]

Partially corresponding to developments in secular feminism, in theological circles feminist theory can be traced from (a) a humanist emphasis in early theological feminism to (b) a gynocentric religious feminism to (c) a nascent ecological religious feminism that combines elements of both. In the last two decades, feminist discussion has shifted from critical assessment of patriarchal traditions to inclusion of the history and knowledge of women and to new constructive projects in Scripture, ethics, and theology from a variety of diverse perspectives.

In contrast to both Tong's and Young's schema, however, feminist and womanist theologians are divided more along denominational or religious lines and according to conservative and progressive politics and less as socialist, psychoanalytic, radical, humanist, or gynocentric.[20] By and large, feminists in theology draw on more than one school of feminist the-

---

18. Anne E. Carr, *Transforming Grace: Christian Tradition and Women's Experience* (San Francisco: Harper & Row, 1988); Elisabeth Schüssler Fiorenza, *In Memory of Her: A Feminist Theological Reconstruction of Christian Origins* (New York: Crossroad, 1984); Rosemary Radford Ruether, *Sexism and God-Talk: Toward a Feminist Theology* (Boston: Beacon Press, 1983); and Delores Williams, *Sisters in the Wilderness: The Challenge of Womanist God-Talk* (Maryknoll, N.Y.: Orbis Books, 1993).

19. Carr, *Transforming Grace*, pp. 1-2.

20. For further development of this thesis, see Chapter Six in Don S. Browning et al., *From Culture Wars to Common Ground: Religion and the American Family Debate* (Louisville: Westminster John Knox Press, 1997).

ory and even subvert the divisions between schools. Indeed, Ruether grounds her classic work *Sexism and God-Talk* in the very attempt to avoid the dichotomies between radical, social, and liberal feminism.[21] Others, such as Judith Plaskow, suggest that a religious anthropology avoids the dualism between culture and nature typical of liberal and radical feminist theory. Plaskow observes, "Feminist theologians, perhaps because they have been forced to grapple with historical images of women, generally have not found rejection of women's body experience," as in Simone de Beauvoir or Shulamith Firestone, "an attractive path."[22] Nor have they indulged in exaltation of it. In general, feminist theorists in theology have not engaged in the bitter battles apparent among some secular feminists.

Powerful shared convictions among Jewish and Christian feminists lend at least a veneer of unity. Feminists and womanists of conservative and progressive religious backgrounds share the conviction that Christian and Jewish traditions are important sources of empowerment, despite their male-defined narratives and symbols. As part of this stance, religious thinkers share a list of theological affirmations. Feminist and womanist theologians emphasize the creation of women in the image of God and hence their inherent worth as partners and co-creators in life. They write about the imperative of egalitarian relationships of love, justice, and shared responsibility within families and society. The attempt to understand the religious and social grounds for radical mutuality is perhaps one of the most prominent common themes. They warn against the dangers and violence of patriarchy and racism, but contend that Judaism and Christianity when critically re-interpreted hold an array of anti-patriarchal, anti-racist values. They speak about the necessity of redefining religious doctrines of love, sexuality, sin, servanthood, and redemption. They seek a holistic view of creation and redemption that holds body and mind, material and spiritual needs in dialectical relation. Finally, they are sensitive to individuals and groups that have been relegated to the margins of social existence. These themes receive different interpretations, depending on the authority given to religious traditions and the extent of the critique of patriarchy, but their presence is pervasive among feminist and womanist theologians.

---

21. Ruether, *Sexism and God-Talk*.

22. Judith Plaskow, "Woman as Body: Motherhood and Dualism," *Anima* 8, no. 1 (1981): 57.

The Impact of Feminist Theory
on Practical and Pastoral Theology

Given these definitions of feminist theory and feminist theology, three general observations about the impact of feminist theory on practical and pastoral theology can be made. First, not surprisingly, there is sometimes a greater unity of method between feminists in practical theology and feminists in systematic theology than among feminists in practical theology and other practical theologians. Feminists and womanists in the other fields of study in religion have themselves become more interdisciplinary and anthropological in their approaches. Understanding lived subjective experience becomes an important means of mapping the making and un-making of culture in a variety of fields in religious studies.

Second, when feminist theory and women's studies become prominent dialogue partners for those in practical theology, the distinctions between different types of practical theology fade. For example, although the different chapters on religious education, pastoral theology, homiletics, and so forth in the edited collection *The Arts of Ministry: Feminist-Womanist Approaches* represent different foci in practical theology, they are united by commonalities in feminist resources and orientation. Across the board, a praxis method attempts to privilege marginalized perspectives, deconstruct dominant texts, resist evil, and promote justice.[23]

Third and related to my first point, sometimes the best pastoral and practical theology does not come from those who call themselves by such names. Church historian Roberta Bondi's work is a case in point. Her struggles with the repressive images of an authoritarian God in her confessional Baptist background and with the objective abstractions of higher education in religion led her to redefine "the primary stuff of theology." She rejects theology as "abstract, logical, propositional, and systematic" and the "hierarchy of truth" that does not "waste its time addressing the personal and the 'subjective,' the everyday or the particular"; she says theology is about the messy particularity of everyday lives examined with excruciating care and brought into conversation with the great doctrines of the Christian tradition.[24] While bell hooks would not identify herself as a

23. *The Arts of Ministry: Feminist-Womanist Approaches,* ed. Christie C. Neuger (Louisville: Westminster John Knox Press, 1996), p. 201.

24. Roberta C. Bondi, *Memories of God: Theological Reflections on a Life* (Nashville: Abingdon Press, 1995), pp. 9, 17.

pastoral theologian, when her efforts to address the sufferings and healing of African-American women lead her to emphasize the wisdom of the elders, the movement of the spirit, and the resources of religious traditions and communities, then she comes close to qualifying.[25] Womanists in general and liberation theologians in black, Hispanic, and Asian traditions almost always have a powerful pastoral intent and method behind their work in a variety of technically non-pastoral fields of study, such as Bible and ethics. Their work in particular cuts across and contests the traditional organization of the theological enterprise. This final observation raises two difficult questions: Is everyone who actually works as a practical theologian at the table in the formal academic discussion of practical theology? Is it even possible or realistic or wise to invite everyone?

Developments in Feminist Pastoral Theology

In contrast to progress made in other areas of systematic, biblical, and historical theology, explicit consideration of feminist and womanist theory in pastoral theology has taken longer to reach the table. There is a one-generational lag between the feminist and womanist publications in Bible, ethics, and systematic theology and those in pastoral theology. Unabashed feminist and womanist publications in practical theology are fairly recent.[26] Many persons pursue feminist ideas and methods without candid or straightforward advocacy of a feminist position.[27] Elsewhere I have speculated about one of the reasons.[28] Proximity to the more conserving structures of congregations, designed to preserve traditions, makes the introduction of the politically and spiritually disruptive ideas and practices of

25. See bell hooks, *Sisters of the Yam: Black Women and Self-Recovery* (Boston: South End Press, 1993).

26. *WomanistCare: How to Tend the Souls of Women,* ed. Linda Hollies (Joliet, Ill.: Woman to Woman Ministries Publications, 1992); Valerie M. DeMarinis, *Critical Caring: A Feminist Model for Pastoral Psychology* (Louisville: Westminster John Knox Press, 1993); Riet Bons-Storm, *The Incredible Woman: Listening to Women's Silences in Pastoral Care and Counseling* (Nashville: Abingdon Press, 1996); *The Arts of Ministry,* ed. Neuger; *Liberating Faith Practices: Feminist Practical Theology in Context,* ed. Denise Ackermann and Riet Bons-Storm (Leuven, the Netherlands: Peeters, 1998).

27. See, for example, *Women in Travail and Transition: A New Pastoral Care,* ed. Maxine Glaz and Jeanne Stevenson-Moessner (Minneapolis: Fortress Press, 1991).

28. Bonnie J. Miller-McLemore, "The Living Human Web: Pastoral Theology at the Turn of the Century," in *Through the Eyes of Women,* ed. Stevenson-Moessner.

feminism and womanism prohibitive and complicated. Perhaps, one might speculate, more conservative people are drawn to practical fields. Or on the other hand, when working with congregations, one temporarily suspends alien and disruptive notions until they can be well-received. Or perhaps it is only that practical fields attract more "doers" than "theorizers."

Other reasons for delayed reflection on a feminist pastoral theology might be adduced. The precariousness of the field itself and the potentially increased liabilities of adding feminism and womanism preclude discussion. To be a feminist is "to be perpetually aware of [one's] marginality," remarks English professor Gail Griffin; "indeed, it means on some level to choose it, to resist full belonging."[29] Why would one choose further marginalization in a field that already suffers that plight? Adding feminist theory to pastoral theology renders its position even more precarious as a discipline peculiarly poised between practice, person, confessional religious congregations, and the academy. Feminist and womanist scholars work within a still largely masculinist academy only mildly disturbed by our invasion of the sacred grove of intellectual pursuits.

Another factor contributes to a relative absence of explicit feminist discussion in the field. Certain methods in pastoral and practical theology already resemble elements in a feminist approach. One does not need feminist theory, for example, to justify engaging personal and marginalized experience as a source of theological reflection or to see the value of critical correlation between theology and life or the use of the social sciences. Finally, more recently, scholars in pastoral theology have recognized the ambiguities and limits of liberal European American feminism. Early humanist feminism cannot speak for all women. In addition, humanist feminism tended to ignore commitments to nurture, care, and relationship that remain central to pastoral theology. Underrepresented perspectives, including womanist views, are partly jeopardized by the sheer fact of fewer numbers. Only recently have more women of color entered programs, received academic degrees, and acquired teaching positions in pastoral theology.

I am not alone in my concern about the need for explicit examination of feminist practical and pastoral theology. Riet Bons-Storm and Denise Ackermann open their introduction to an edited collection of feminist practical theologies by observing that "practical theology is probably the theological discipline least influenced by feminist voices." In their ef-

---

29. Gail Griffin, *Calling: Essays on Teaching in the Mother Tongue* (Pasadena, Calif.: Trilogy Books, 1992).

fort to determine reasons, they go farther back and blame male scholarship itself. Practical theology remains "overwhelmingly a male-dominated discipline."[30] This is most apparent on the international scene but true in the United States as well. As a result, three additional factors lead to the paucity of feminist reflection. First, the modern prominence of a male clerical paradigm excluded women as actors and subjects. Second, male clerics learned to practice "feminine" emotional skills and had even less need for female input. Third, related to my observation above, an obsession with the identity crises of the field and men's insecurities about their own academic identity render the inclusion of the unfamiliar and the unexplored even more difficult and unsettling.[31]

Prominent Characteristics of Feminist Pastoral Theology

The generational lag or dearth of explicit reflection on feminism in pastoral theology might be characterized differently, however. Over the past three decades, feminist pastoral theology has generated a significant body of literature with three kinds of projects in mind: implicit critique of patriarchy; explicit critique and advocacy for women and other marginalized populations; and topical reconstruction.

The first project of implicit critique and unrest appears in the largely unpublished but compelling activities of women in the field, perhaps best exemplified by the work of Peggy Way. Since the 1960s, Way has mentored women in the field and used public speaking engagements to disturb the status quo on subjects such as violence in the family. She contested the conventional boundaries dictated by systematic theologians and demanded that pastoral theology grapple with the particularities of suffering and the ecclesial context of care.[32] Texts such as *Women in Travail and Transition* and *Life Cycles: Women and Pastoral Care*[33] also tend to focus on

30. *Liberating Faith Practices,* ed. Ackermann and Bons-Storm, pp. 1, 4.

31. *Liberating Faith Practices,* ed. Ackermann and Bons-Storm, pp. 1-3.

32. Peggy Ann Way, "An Authority of Possibility for Women in the Church," in *Women's Liberation and the Church: The New Demand for Freedom in the Life of the Christian Church,* ed. Sarah Bentley Doely (New York: Association Press, 1970), pp. 77-94, and "Pastoral Excellence and Pastoral Theology: A Slight Shift of Paradigm and a Modest Polemic," *Pastoral Psychology* 29, no. 1 (Fall 1980): 46-57.

33. *Women in Travail,* ed. Glaz and Stevenson-Moessner; and *Life Cycles: Women and Pastoral Care,* ed. Elaine Graham and Margaret Halsey (Cambridge: SPCK, 1993).

the experiences of women, assuming and promoting but not explicitly identifying, describing, and pursuing feminist theory or politics. The primary agenda is incorporating women's lives and voices into the traditions of reflection and practices of care, sometimes presuming that others have already completed the prior task of exposing androcentrism.

The second project of explicit critique of the classic texts and theories of pastoral theology has been more erratic. Articles on feminism and pastoral theology by Carrie Doehring and Christie Neuger and Valerie DeMarinis's *Critical Caring* suggest the importance of a hermeneutic of suspicion toward traditional scholarship and advocate active resistance to patriarchy, as does the more recent book by Riet Bons-Storm on breaking the silences that render women invisible and powerless.[34] Even in this body of literature, however, the primary goal usually remains pastoral. As in the introduction to *Through the Eyes of Women,* the overarching intent is to give "hope to women in the midst of despair."[35] Feminist critique is secondary or rather important primarily in its relationship to this central pastoral goal. Sexism is seen as contributing to but not as the fundamental source of conditions for women's despair.

The third project of reconstruction in feminist pastoral theology involves extensive engagement with particular thematic practices or topics, placing them within a broader panorama of psychological, cultural, and theological critique and reformulation. Several book-length treatments of important themes pertaining to women but also relevant to men and the field as a whole have appeared in just the last decade — books on poverty, self-esteem, anger, depression, aggression, violence, and work and family life.[36]

---

34. Carrie Doehring, "Developing Models of Feminist Pastoral Counseling," *Journal of Pastoral Care* 46, no. 1 (Spring 1992): 23-31; Christie C. Neuger, "Feminist Pastoral Theology and Pastoral Counseling: A Work in Progress," *Journal of Pastoral Theology* 2 (Summer 1992): 35-57; DeMarinis, *Critical Caring;* and Bons-Storm, *The Incredible Woman.*

35. *Through the Eyes of Women,* ed. Stevenson-Moessner, p. 4.

36. Pamela D. Couture, *Blessed Are the Poor? Women's Poverty, Family Policy, and Practical Theology* (Nashville: Abingdon Press, 1991); Carroll Saussy, *God Images and Self-Esteem: Empowering Women in a Patriarchal Society* (Louisville: Westminster John Knox Press, 1991), and *The Gift of Anger: A Call to Faithful Action* (Louisville: Westminster John Knox Press, 1995); Susan J. Dunlap, *Counseling Depressed Women* (Louisville: Westminster John Knox Press, 1997); Kathleen J. Greider, *Reckoning with Aggression: Theology, Violence, and Vitality* (Louisville: Westminster John Knox Press, 1997); Pamela Cooper-White, *The Cry of Tamar: Violence against Women and the Church's Response* (Minneapolis: Fortress Press, 1995); and Bonnie J. Miller-McLemore, *Also a Mother: Work and Family as Theological Dilemma* (Nashville: Abingdon Press, 1994).

These paradigmatic texts have not yet received adequate attention as a significant body of literature in feminist theory and theological practice. While diverse in specific focus, they establish a new example of pastoral theological research unified by at least five elements: revised correlational method; psychological and cultural sources; power analysis; feminist positioning; and pastoral intent.

Using Young's scheme, feminist pastoral theologians in all three projects have had a decidedly gynocentric, rather than humanist, flavor. Although concerned about rights and equality, they have focused on women-centered knowledge and relationships. This leaning toward a gynocentric approach accounts in part for the more oblique feminist critique.

Work in all three areas is also characterized by a threefold methodological emphasis on context, collaboration, and diversity. First, knowledge emerges within particular contexts and is defined by one's proximity to practices and not always along conventional academic lines. Clinical assessment involves social, contextual analysis. Psychological theory, though still important, plays a less commanding role. In using the social sciences, a feminist critique of the social and political biases of psychology is added as a second layer of analysis alongside moral and hermeneutical critiques of psychology. Other humanist and social sciences that contribute to understanding the broader cultural context, such as public policy, history, and sociology, have a place in pastoral analysis.

Second, adequate coverage of the issues requires a non-adversarial, even relational constructive interaction among colleagues. Several initial efforts to define a new pastoral care have involved collaborative efforts and edited collections rather than work by a single author. Finally, acknowledging the limits of one's vantage point becomes a common refrain and an invitation for further conversation. At the end of my preface of *Also a Mother,* I express a prevalent sentiment: "I, for one, want to hear other voices, voices different from my own."[37] The work of feminist pastoral theology is necessarily as limited as the range of its participants. In the past several decades, the participants have most often been European American Protestants. Under hooks's definition, this remains cause for concern and inspiration for corrective action. How can a richer diversity of perspectives, particularly womanist, Asian, and Hispanic, begin to reshape fundamental presuppositions of pastoral theology?

37. Miller-McLemore, *Also a Mother,* p. 15.

New Developments in Pastoral and Practical Theology:
Wariness and Appreciation

In an attempt to define how one studies religion in the field of pastoral theology, I have argued that anyone who wants to do constructive theoretical work in pastoral and practical theology must address and in some fashion dispel the persistent identity crisis of the fields or at least situate one's work in relation to this crisis.[38] David Tracy identifies three publics for which those in religion write: academy, society, and church. More than in any other area in the study of religion, those in pastoral and practical theology often attempt to speak and write for all three.[39] This cross-public audience is not new. Historically, theologians who worked in ways analogous to the field of practical theology today also addressed multiple publics. A chief difference today is the striking divisions among these three publics in terms of language, standards of truth, practices and rituals, and norms.

In some contexts — including this chapter itself — *pastoral theology* and *practical theology* are used as interchangeable terms. The two fields do have a close relationship. Those within *practical theology* share three elements: a common history within the evolution of the academy of religion and the division into biblical, historical, systematic, and practical theology; a common correlational method bringing together theology, the human sciences, and religious experiences; and a common concern with specific religious and congregational disciplines and practices.

Practical theologians differ in the United States, however, particularly within Protestant circles, according to the particular science with which they are most conversant and the specific religious practices in which they have interest. *Pastoral theology* focuses on care of persons and finds personality theories, particularly within psychology, primary resources for the enhancement of this practice. Distinct from other areas of religious study, the object of study in pastoral theology is *"the study of living human documents rather than books."*[40]

38. See Bonnie J. Miller-McLemore, "The Subject and Practice of Pastoral Theology as a Practical Theological Discipline: Pushing Past the Nagging Identity Crisis to the Poetics of Resistance," in *Liberating Faith Practices*, ed. Ackermann and Bons-Storm, p. 179.

39. David Tracy, *Blessed Rage for Order: The New Pluralism in Theology* (New York: Seabury Press, 1975), p. 5.

40. Boisen, cited by Charles V. Gerkin in *The Living Human Document: Revisioning Pastoral Counseling in a Hermeneutical Mode* (Nashville: Abingdon Press, 1984), p. 37; emphasis in the text.

In the past decade, several feminist pastoral theologians have modified the individualistic leanings of Anton Boisen's metaphor by turning to an alternative, related image of the living web.[41] The use of this metaphor, however, does not mean that the individual or the use of psychological sciences that provide insight into personal dynamics recedes in importance. It simply means that the individual is understood in inextricable relationship to the broader context. Psychology, as the primary cognate science for pastoral theology, is not inherently individualistic, having contributed to new understandings of connective selfhood in recent research.[42] The metaphor of web also affirms the important role of other social sciences and holds potential for practical theology.

One might argue that to study religion in *practical theology* is to study the living webs of congregational and social practices. *Pastoral care* is practical religious, spiritual, and congregational care for the suffering, involving the rich resources of religious traditions and communities, contemporary understandings of the human person in the social sciences, and ultimately, the movement of God's love and hope in the lives of individuals and communities. *Pastoral care from a liberation perspective* is about breaking silences, urging prophetic action, and liberating the oppressed. *Pastoral theology* is the critical reflection on this activity. In this schema, pastoral theology is located under the wider umbrella of practical theology, along with other disciplines that focus on other religious practices within the congregation, such as homiletics and religious education.

Yet in the mid-twentieth century, pastoral care and theology achieved a certain pre-eminence, however precarious and unstable, within the academic study of religion and in the congregation. This visibility resulted partly from the clarity that surrounded its disciplinary connections to psychology and theology. These connections established its place in the academy without negating its connection to congregational life. Prominent theologians such as Paul Tillich and Reinhold Niebuhr took develop-

41. See Larry Kent Graham, *Care of Persons, Care of Worlds: A Psychosystems Approach to Pastoral Care and Counseling* (Nashville: Abingdon Press, 1992); Bonnie J. Miller-McLemore, "The Human Web and the State of Pastoral Theology," *The Christian Century,* 7 April 1993, pp. 366-69, and "The Living Human Web"; Brita Gill-Austern, "Rediscovering Hidden Treasures for Pastoral Care," *Pastoral Psychology* 43, no. 4 (1995): 233-53; and Pamela D. Couture, "Weaving the Web: Pastoral Care in an Individualistic Society," in *Through the Eyes of Women,* ed. Stevenson-Moessner.

42. For further development of this thesis, see Chapter 7 in Browning et al., *From Culture Wars to Common Ground.*

ments in Freudian and Rogerian psychology seriously and, by extension, pastoral movements in the clinic and academy that engaged psychological theory. Pastoral theologians benefited from the popular acceptance, prominence, and rapid development of its primary secular science, psychology. And in contrast to religious education and homiletics, pastoral theology benefited from maintaining distinct connections to theology proper, even in the naming of its area of study itself as pastoral *theology*.

In the past several decades, those in the field of pastoral theology made notable contributions to the study of religion in the three areas of method, substance, and process in terms of (1) an emphasis on and exploration of a methodological focus on living persons rather than written doctrines or historical documents of the no-longer-living;[43] (2) a substantive use and critical analysis of psychology to expand previous religious understandings of human anthropology to include intrapsychic dynamics, developmental and life-cycle processes, and strategies of intersubjective communication;[44] and (3) a dynamic commitment to healing or change or "therapeutics" — what Rodney Hunter calls the "master metaphor" of the pastoral tradition.[45]

In addition, pastoral theology has operated not only within the sphere of practical theology. Pastoral theology is also one facet of a second arena often identified as "Religion and Personality" by several academic programs in the United States. Scholars of religion and personality can be roughly divided into three groups: those interested in pastoral theology, care, and counseling; those engaged in the critical correlation of religion and culture; and those involved in the empirical or hermeneutical social-scientific study of religious experience. While some European and U.S.

43. E.g., Anton Boisen, *The Exploration of the Inner World: A Study of Mental Disorder and Religious Experience* (New York: Willett, 1936); and John Patton, *From Ministry to Theology: Pastoral Action and Reflection* (Nashville: Abingdon Press, 1990).

44. E.g., Don Browning, *Religious Thought and the Modern Psychologies* (Minneapolis: Fortress Press, 1987); Donald Capps, *Life Cycle Theory and Pastoral Care* (Philadelphia: Fortress Press, 1983); Gerkin, *The Living Human Document*; and Hiltner, *Preface to Pastoral Theology*.

45. Rodney J. Hunter, "The Therapeutic Tradition of Pastoral Care and Counseling," in *Pastoral Care and Social Conflict*, ed. Pamela D. Couture and Rodney J. Hunter (Nashville: Abingdon Press, 1995), p. 17. For examples, see Wayne E. Oates, *Protestant Pastoral Counseling* (Philadelphia: Westminster Press, 1962); Carroll Wise, *The Meaning of Pastoral Care* (New York: Harper & Row, 1966); and Howard Clinebell, *Basic Types of Pastoral Care and Counseling: Resources for the Ministry of Healing and Growth* (Nashville: Abingdon Press, 1984).

scholars might legitimately see these three groups as subgroups of practical theology, secular scholars in religion and personality teaching in undergraduate programs in the United States would object to the classification of their research and teaching under the heading of theology.

The plethora of guilds in religion and personality and practical theology reflects both the richness of their manifold foci and the confusion over disciplinary boundaries. Some pastoral theologians, notably more of my women colleagues than men, for reasons worth considering, attempt to maintain an allegiance to several academic societies, however ambiguous and difficult. We might surmise that many women desire a more holistic approach to the study of religion, refuse conventional definitions of disciplinary boundaries, feel less bound by or less connected to ministry as it has been formally defined by men, and appreciate the freedom of thought and expression sometimes more characteristic of the academy and programs in religion and personality.

From the perspective of feminist pastoral theology, I am simultaneously wary and appreciative of new developments in practical theology. I am dedicated to a pastoral method that makes the immediate human experience of suffering and compassionate responses to it primary. In feminist pastoral theology, one studies religion at the point where human suffering evokes or calls for a religious response and sometimes at the point where a religious response is given and/or experienced. As bell hooks puts it, one dares "to create theory from the location of pain and struggle." Indeed, she expresses her gratitude to those who so risk, for "it is not easy to name our pain, to theorize from that location"; it takes courage to expose wounds and to lend one's experience as a "means to chart new theoretical journeys."[46] To a greater extent than other areas of religious studies, pastoral theology makes "limit situations," in Tracy's words, a central focus.[47] As I argue in another context, this requires a refusal of the pretense of pure objectivity; an invitation of face-to-face encounter, confrontation, and messiness; and a willingness to participate proactively in a revisionary project that changes the lives of the marginalized and of all the participants.[48]

A great deal of literature in the field of practical theology can be rightly faulted as unnecessarily academic, obtuse, and abstract. In contrast

---

46. bell hooks, *Teaching to Transgress: Education as the Practice of Freedom* (New York: Routledge & Kegan Paul, 1994), p. 74.

47. Tracy, *Blessed Rage for Order,* p. 93, pp. 104-8.

48. Miller-McLemore, "The Subject and Practice of Pastoral Theology as a Practical Theological Discipline," pp. 186-96.

to the practical intent and to other variations of practical theology around the globe, the primary audience and authors of practical theology in the United States mostly reside in the academy, not in the sanctuary or the kitchen.[49] At least two consequences emerge. First, some scholars in non-European American communities would not see their work included within the discipline as presently defined in the U.S. academy, even though they are engaged in important reflection in the midst of theological practices. Second, pressing questions are ignored. Discussions in practical theology and feminist theory remain far removed from faith practices. For example, most congregations have not considered inclusive language, much less the complex implications of new understandings of the Atonement and the Trinity, for the words said at the communion table, preached in the sermon, or sung in hymns.

Too often the problem with the "clerical paradigm" has been blamed on problems with conceptualizations in practical theology.[50] The focus on techniques of professional ministry as the main subject of modern practical theology is partially due to the limited horizons of the practical theological fields and the obsession with technical training in counseling skills. But the problem of the clerical paradigm is also a result of the movement of systematic and constructive theology away from the messiness of human suffering, the ambiguities and subjectivity of faith claims and spiritual experiences, and the complications of religious and ministerial practices of transformation. The complaints of Edward Farley and others about the clerical paradigm reflect an elitist academic failure to appreciate and to grapple with the work of ministry and the practice of Christian disciplines. Rather than grasping the pressing needs of those in the church and the reasons for the desirability of techniques and strategies, critics condescendingly portray the practical tasks necessary to maintain a local congregation as a healthy community and institution as non-theological or of little or no theological relevance. The final irony: the negative analysis of the clerical paradigm has resulted in a theological education even more abstract and removed from Christian life, faith, and ministerial practice than before the critique.

---

49. See Elaine Graham, "A View from a Room: Feminist Practical Theology from Academy, Kitchen, or Sanctuary?," in *Liberating Faith Practices,* ed. Ackermann and Bons-Storm, pp. 129-52.

50. Edward Farley, "Theology and Practice outside the Clerical Paradigm," in *Practical Theology: The Emerging Field in Theology, Church, and World,* ed. Don S. Browning (San Francisco: Harper & Row, 1983), pp. 21-41.

One goal behind the attempt to redefine practical theology in the past decade is the reclamation of its rightful place in the academy with clearer parameters, objectives, content, and foundations. On the one hand, one must wonder about the attempt to obtain scholarly validity by operating at a greater level of abstraction and theoretical generalization. In schemes in which the specific is less valued than the abstract, women, religious faith, and ministerial disciplines have more to lose, since they are often associated with the private or personal and automatically perceived as substandard. Postmodern thought has revealed the culture-bound nature of this value judgment, even if scholars have difficulty letting go of abstraction as superior.[51] Postmodernism suggests that those studying religion are seldom, if ever, able to extricate themselves from specific faith commitments of various kinds. All scholars, not just feminists, must assess the particular biases and advocacies that shape their understandings.

On the other hand, I am appreciative of new developments in practical theology as one means to retain a place in the academy. Practical theological reflection faces hard times in the current climate of university education. Even if it retains vitality within seminaries and congregations, the field will languish without university structures to sustain its theoretical development and refinement. Serious practical theology takes time, requires a rich variety of complex resources, and works best, despite the vast complications, with multiple authors.[52] Even when this kind of practical engagement of particular subject matter becomes impractical, the discipline and theory of practical theology remain critical to the theological curriculum, less in and of themselves than to suggest common methodologies shared by a variety of submovements in practical theology with different content and foci, such as pastoral care, religious education, and so forth. Of equal importance with the goal of academic integrity is the goal of recognizing the interconnections of the rich variety of specializations that have emerged in the practical arts of ministry of pastoral care, education, preaching, and so forth. In this respect, abstractions, generalizations, and meta-theorizing about practical theology have an important place — but not at the cost of disdaining the contingent, immediate questions and contexts of suffering and responsive practices of feminist pastoral theology.

51. See Susan Starr Sered, "Mother Love, Child Death, and Religious Innovation: A Feminist Perspective," *Journal of Feminist Studies in Religion* 12, no. 1 (Spring 1996): 22.

52. For an example of a more comprehensive practical theology, see Browning et al., *From Culture Wars to Common Ground,* written by five authors.

Examination of the impact of feminist theory on the development of feminist pastoral theology, as I attempted in this chapter, is important. Such codification partly goes against the grain of both a feminist method that prizes concrete, diverse experiences as the source of knowledge and a pastoral method that makes commitment to understanding suffering and compassionate response the primary focus. Reflection on developments of feminist and womanist pastoral theology is further complicated by the generational lag in feminist and womanist reflection in the field and the challenge of new problems of postmodernity. Scholars in other fields of systematic theology or theological ethics have already done some of the important work on pastoral issues. And other factors, besides the women's movement, will undoubtedly determine the future of pastoral theology.

Nonetheless, a sound grasp of the repercussions of new players in the pastoral theological discussion is absolutely critical to understanding developments in the conceptualization of pastoral care in theological education and in the ecclesiastical practice of caregiving. Following in the footsteps of those who have gone before them and yet making new paths, feminists and womanists in pastoral theology are hoping to prepare a way in the wilderness, making new highways for the entrance of God among us. Only ongoing reflective analysis will tell us when pastoral theologians have fallen far short of the hopes for transformation in justice and love and when we have genuinely made new possibilities happen.

CHAPTER 10

How Gender Studies Revolutionized
Pastoral Theology

BACKGROUND AND INTRODUCTION

This chapter was what the co-editors of *The Blackwell Reader in Pastoral and Practical Theology* describe in their introduction as "specially commissioned," written out of my particular expertise to their specifications and word limit for a book aimed at displaying succinctly the history, methods, and current issues in an evolving field. It appears in a middle section of the volume alongside pithy chapters on an eclectic range of issues, such as spirituality, race, sociology, political theory, and congregational studies. Like the other authors, I treat my assigned topic in a condensed fashion with minimal footnotes and a selected bibliography. The chapter represents a distillation rather than a development of ideas that I explore in greater detail in *Also a Mother* and a number of articles. Commentary on Freud's ambiguous legacy, New Testament household codes, love as mutuality, Valerie Saiving's work, new functions for feminist pastoral care, and so forth reappear here, but only in the most abbreviated form.

Despite this limitation, this chapter serves as a good companion to Chapter 9. Where Chapter 9 stands back and observes the general framework in which feminist pastoral theology operates, Chapter 10 gets closer to the ground. It fills in detail and adds color commentary on bodies, sexu-

---

This essay was originally published as "How Sexuality and Relationships Have Revolutionized Pastoral Theology," in *The Blackwell Reader in Pastoral and Practical Theology*, ed. James Woodward and Stephen Pattison (U.S. consultant, John Patton) (London: Blackwell, 1999), pp. 233-47. Used by permission.

ality, self-esteem, relationships, children, and love. Chapter 9 is like the skeleton; Chapter 10 puts flesh on the bone. Both chapters demonstrate the value of gender as a category of analysis in theology, just at different levels.

Compared to the chapters in Parts I and II, the chapters in Part III were written within a short time span. Published between 1999 and 2001, they reflect common influences. They reap the benefit of a decade of teaching classes on families and work; women, psychology, and religion; and pastoral care. They also come after the completion of *Also a Mother* and coincide with work on an edited volume, *Feminist and Womanist Pastoral Theology*, and a major Lilly-funded grant on Christianity and families led by Don Browning that culminated in a co-authored capstone volume, *From Culture Wars to Common Ground: Religion and the American Family Debate.*

Now that I have gathered all four chapters together in Part III, I see that they represent a kind of feminist period (so to speak) between 1990 and 2001. This is not to say I have left critical feminist theory behind today. I am just less preoccupied by it. In my preference for reading women authors, fiction and non-fiction alike, in my post-doctoral years, I was making up for years of reading books by men.

A better title for the original chapter might have been "Gender and Sexism and Its Impact on Women, Men, and Care." It is probably true to say that I had more interest in *sexism* than in *sexuality*, and the chapter reflects this. A chapter on sexuality today would need to devote considerably more attention to *heterosexism* and more space to changing sexual identities, patterns, and expectations in postmodernity. My interest at the time was challenging limited heterosexual gender ideals, especially as Christian theology perpetuated them. I wanted to know how sexism and the social construction of gender had distorted familial relationships as well as religious and secular views of suffering, illness, healing, and care.

Given my emphasis on sexism, I find it curious that I define *gender* and *sexuality* but leave *sexism* unspecified. Had I defined it, I would have distinguished, as Beverly Daniel Tatum does in her work on racism, between *personal bias*, which one may or may not possess or own up to, and the *systemic social structures* that hold everyone in their grip, making it impossible to grow up in the United States and escape participation in racism and sexism.

I also would not have put such an elusive term as *relationship* alongside *sexuality* unless given the title by the co-editors. But its inclusion in the chapter works out because distorted perceptions of gender and sexuality have had a huge impact on relationships in families, congregations, and society. Again, my main focus is the distorted patterns between men and women and between mothers, fathers, and their children in Christian contexts rather than the plurality of relationships about which we now know more through further research on lesbian parenting, gay marriage, blended families, intergenerational and interreligious families, and so on. Of all the chapters in the book, this one would require the greatest overhaul if rewritten today.

Nonetheless, the need to understand sexism remains a worthy project that we have yet to outgrow. Understanding sexism is not just a matter of acknowledging biases or confronting exploitation. It spawns "an entirely fresh way of perceiving reality" — one of the more important ideas in the chapter. One perceives anew at every level in pastoral theology — individual care and counseling, family, congregation, and wider society. Moreover, in pastoral care as distinct from secular care, it is essential to recognize the impact of religious images and practices on how people understand and act out gender and sexism in their daily lives. How Christians understand God, sacraments, Christ, love, authority, submission, and so on is not just a matter of theory, beliefs, or concepts. These ideas get enacted in the midst of everyday life. New understandings of sexuality and relationships cannot help but challenge the way that Christian theology is practiced and embodied.

In the past two decades, the study of gender and sexuality has become one of the most exciting areas in pastoral theology in the United States. Up until the middle of this century, men largely defined theology and ministry based on their own experiences and readings of religious traditions within ecclesiastical contexts that prized male knowledge and leadership. Few people even noticed that these experiences were gendered or that these readings were shaped by sexual biases against women. No one thought this influenced what one saw as important in pastoral thought and action. Gender simply did not factor into the equation as a category of analysis. "Mankind" included everyone. Women did not feel left out by the term, they said, since they assumed their own self-worth, even though few dared to suggest that "womankind" could include men or insisted on having a female senior minister. For the most part, women's public leadership was discouraged, and women's experiences and knowledge were largely ignored. No one noticed or cared.

A virtual explosion of literature on gender, sexuality, and relationships has occurred over the past two decades as women have gained public voice in both academy and congregation and as feminist theory has acquired recognition. This exponential growth of literature represents not just new ideas, experiences, and texts. It indicates an entirely fresh way of perceiving reality. No longer can one study pastoral theology without asking important questions about the role of the social and cultural context. Satisfactory pastoral response to a woman's depression, for example, requires consideration of political components, such as her subordinate position in family, church, and society, or her experience of authority or abuse within a patriarchal setting. Beyond the counseling office itself, pastoral care of women and men within the congregation includes considering the ways in which the participation of women in worship or the inclusion of gender-rich metaphors for God influence early development of children and the ongoing spiritual formation of adults. Beyond the confines of the congregation, pastoral theology concerns itself with the ways in which its public voice on gender and religion informs public policies that shape the lives of women, men, and children, such as divorce laws and sexual violence on television.

In this chapter I merely give a taste of some of the discussion of sexuality, gender, and relationships. I introduce some of the representative ideas that have emerged in psychology and pastoral theology and identify implications for pastoral theology in general. While gender is the central subject of this essay, it is important to acknowledge that gender is only one of a variety of fabrications, such as class, race, ethnicity, worldview, and so forth, that feed into the social construction of persons. Roughly speaking, I use the term *sexuality* to refer to the physiological, sensual dimensions of embodiment and *gender* to refer to socially constructed rather than biologically determined sexual identity. Sexuality in relationship always involves gender constructions or strategies of enacting sexuality. As both of these terms indicate, relationships among women and men have come under intense scrutiny. *Relationship* has been a central concept in feminist psychology and theology. This concern extends beyond specific considerations of sex and gender to matters as divergent as sexual harassment, inequitable domestic responsibilities, privileges in the congregation, household violence, and parental duties. Any one of these topics is deserving of a chapter unto itself. This chapter will accent, however, a feminist pastoral commitment that unites all of them — mutuality in relationship, or shared responsibility and equality of power and freedom. This commitment represents a fundamental re-orientation in gender and sexual relationships.

Psychological Revolutions in Gender, Sexuality, and Relationship

On my office door, I have a cartoon picturing Freud reclining on his couch with a balloon capturing his thoughts: "What does woman want?" Freud belonged to a broader movement of medical and scientific experts intent on solving "*the* women's problem." What was to become of middle-class women in an industrial era in which factory production and the emergence of professions had displaced them from prominent pre-industrial roles in the home and community? Behind him and out of his sight stands Mrs. Freud, sweeping. The cartoon bubble above her head shows her solution to the problem: she hopes that Mr. Freud will get himself off the couch and pick up the broom. In a word, Freud opened up new vistas of therapeutic intervention, radically altering common perceptions of human sexuality. But his view from the couch had its limits.

Freud contributed several key ideas that have become part of common conversation: (1) the hidden power of the unconscious over conscious thought and action, especially unconscious sexual desires; (2) the importance of early childhood sexual experiences and development; and (3) the powerful role of repressed and misdirected sexual desire in human pathology. These ideas have provoked invaluable reconsideration of human nature. On the other hand, Freud was unavoidably a man of his times, and he missed a few things about human sexuality. He capitulated to pressures to deny the reality of early sexual abuse and instead credited fantasies about sexual involvement with one's parents as the primal source of conflict in early development. Equally important, he discounted, misconstrued, and in some cases completely overlooked the particularities of growing up female in a male-dominated culture.

Freud had a mote in his eye: for all his attention to sexuality and the unconscious, he was unable, given the period in which he lived and worked, to see the importance of the cultural construction of womanhood, manhood, and sexuality. He mistook cultural envy of male power for an inevitable biological, psychological, and moral deficiency on the part of the woman. In his opinion, women have only three choices in their desire to compensate for their lack of a penis: (1) neurosis; (2) a masculinity complex — that is, the refusal to accept their castrated state; or (3) optimally "normal femininity." "Normal femininity" entails the passive acceptance of biological fate and even masochistic, narcissistic resignation to a secondary, dependent destiny as a vessel of male activity and a vicarious appendage of male offspring. In short, women can never emotionally, intellectually, or morally attain mature adulthood. In so arguing, Freud gave scientific support to age-old theological and philosophical premises about female inferiority and subordination.

Many recent studies of gender, sexuality, and relationship have contested these and other psychoanalytic "truths." Of particular interest are three prominent theorists: Karen Horney, Nancy Chodorow, and Carol Gilligan. All three make several claims that continue to shape psychological research. Although we still cannot determine the extent to which sexuality and gender are the result of body chemistry or social conditioning, feminist study of sexuality at least suggests that society constructs what it means to be a man or to be a woman to a greater extent than previously imagined. Prior constructions have made male experience the standard and have seen female experience as deviant, sick, bad, and immature. Seeing the world from a young girl's and a woman's eyes challenges this assumed pattern. The differences between theories of human development, or more exactly, *male* development and women's experience no longer signify a problem in women; they indicate an oversight or error in male theory. As pivotal, if sexuality is largely socially constructed, gender roles and identities can evolve and change. Horney is particularly interesting because she dared to protest Freudian ideas about female sexuality from inside the psychoanalytic movement during its earlier years of institutional consolidation. Partly as a result, until recently she was criticized, ostracized, and overlooked as an important analyst and theorist in her own right. She joined others like Alfred Adler in contending that penis envy, while a valid observation of female sentiment, results not from an ontological or natural female predisposition but from envy of male social domination and authority. Penis envy was in reality envy of male power in a world in which having a penis meant having economic, political, and social rank.

Slightly later, Helen Flanders Dunbar qualifies this further: penis envy is not an inevitable, automatic, or spontaneous reaction. Much more "truly spontaneous" is the remark quoted by Dunbar of a girl who, upon "seeing her baby brother in the nude for the first time," candidly observed,

"'Isn't it lucky that he hasn't got that on his face.'"[1] Horney also named the unnamable male envy of women: "men resent and fear women because they experience them as powerful mothers" — an idea that Chodorow picks up and develops in new directions.[2] Although seldom discussed and explored, the male inability to bear children is experienced as an inborn deficiency on a par with penis envy.[3]

Chodorow and Gilligan choose different entry points into the interior world of human sexuality and gender. An anthropologically interested sociologist who was later trained as a psychoanalyst, Chodorow shifts psychoanalytic attention from the importance of Oedipal struggles between father and child centered on the penis to pre-Oedipal dynamics between mother and child centered on separation and relationship. She proposes that motherhood and, more troubling, misogyny reproduce themselves precisely because women mother. When only women participate in the primary care of children, daughters have readily available the same-sex parent with whom they identify. While they struggle with enmeshment and self-differentiation in the consuming presence of a parent like them, they learn to value relationships and to fear separation. Boys, on the other hand, do not have the ease of gender identification with the mother and instead must actively disengage themselves and negate the value of connection and ultimately of the mother and women. While sons achieve greater autonomy and individuality, they tend to develop rigid, defensive ego boundaries and repress emotional needs. They struggle with attachment and intimacy. To counteract the devaluation of women and caregiving activities, Chodorow lends psychoanalytic support to a wider social, political premise that men and women should share primary parenting responsibilities.

As a scholar in education, Gilligan broadens the focus from emotional to moral development and significantly undermines the widely ac-

---

1. Helen Flanders Dunbar, *Mind and Body: Psychosomatic Medicine* (New York: Random House, 1947), p. 259, cited by Jeanne Stevenson-Moessner in "The Psychology of Women and Pastoral Care," in *Women in Travail and Transition: A New Pastoral Care,* ed. Maxine Glaz and Jeanne Stevenson-Moessner (Minneapolis: Fortress Press, 1991).

2. Nancy Chodorow, *Feminism and Psychoanalytic Theory* (New Haven: Yale University Press, 1989), p. 6.

3. See E. Jacobson, "Development of the Wish for a Child in Boys," *Psychoanalytic Study of the Child* 5 (1950): 139-52; John Munder Ross, "Beyond the Phallic Illusion: Notes on Man's Heterosexuality," in *The Psychology of Men,* ed. Gerald Fogel, Frederick Lane, and Robert Liebert (New York: Basic Books, 1986), pp. 50-51.

cepted stage theory established by Lawrence Kohlberg. In his theory, Kohlberg prizes abstract reasoning as the superior moral position and labels derogatorily decisions based on relationships as a lower stage of moral intelligence. Based on interview responses to ethical dilemmas, Gilligan persuasively argues that moral deliberation about relational connections requires comparably sophisticated, if not superior, reasoning of a different sort. Moral theory has unfortunately lost sight of this critical line of development of the capacity for intimacy, relationships, and care for both men and women.

In the short story "A Jury of Her Peers," a man has died while in his bed sleeping, a rope around his neck. As the mystery of his death unfolds, we witness powerfully alternative ways of seeing key evidence and interpreting the crime. The police inspector laboriously follows the linear lead of the rope, crossing back and forth from bedroom to barn; passing through the kitchen and giving orders, he entirely misses and dismisses central evidence as women's "trifles." Meanwhile, while waiting for the men in the kitchen, the wife of the inspector and a woman neighbor who came along to gather the jailed wife's belongings discover key clues by empathy, intuition, and attention to the domestic details of relationship. The wife, the women conclude, murdered her abusive husband in self-defense, self-preservation, even desperation. While they do not condone her action, they silently agree not to report the clues they have discovered, suggesting that justice cannot be served under the current circumstances of male-defined law. The crime is not just the killing in itself; the crime is their failure to reach out at an earlier stage; the crime is that domestic work of their own kept them from helping; the crime is that they did not want to visit the somber household or confront a harsh husband who abused his wife.

This story illustrates well central tenets of classic works of women scholars in psychology: if one-half of the population is omitted from research on human well-being and sexuality, whether in medicine, psychology, or theology, people cannot see the whole picture. If the measure of the most mature adult rests on male standards based on the study of men, women's reality disappears, and women appear deficient. If, however, alternative ways of knowing and deciding are honored, we may see anew. Among other contributions, studies of gender challenge male-defined interpretations of relational thinking as "pathological," identify other key developmental tasks, reclaim the values of dependency, endurance, connection, affectivity, and relationality, question the assigned parental roles of fatherly authority and motherly nurturance, and advance a critique of the dismissal of social and cultural considerations in psychodynamic therapy.

Pastoral Theological Revolutions in Gender, Sexuality, and Relationship

Pastoral theologian Emma Justes wrote one of the first essays on women and pastoral care. She boldly declares, "Pastoral counselors who find that they are unable to travel the route of hearing women's anger, of exploring with women the painful depths of experiences of incest and rape, or enabling women to break free from cultural stereotypes that define their existence, should not be doing pastoral counseling with women."[4] Good skills in pastoral counseling alone are not sufficient. Caregivers must deal with the impact of a variety of sexist attitudes and expectations, from economic matters of unequal pay in the workforce and the unequal second shift of domestic work; to identity issues of low self-confidence and esteem, conflicting roles of paid work and family, and changing lifestyles; to bodily struggles of bulimia, anorexia, rape, incest, and battering; to central religious notions of male headship, female submission, and self-sacrificing love.

Secular and pastoral counseling must connect internal psychic dynamics to "pathological" forces in the culture that uniquely damage women. Goals then encompass several new components: re-evaluation of female gender roles; a re-definition and valuing of female sexuality, embodiment, and sensuality; an emphasis on self-worth and on women defining themselves; differentiation between external conditions and internal feelings and reactions; recognition of anger, conflict, and pain as legitimate responses; social, political action as an integral part of healing; criticism of women's tendency to put themselves last; and awareness of abuse of power in relationships.

All of these components characterize new perspectives in both secular and pastoral intervention. Pastoral theology and care with men and women adds an important element: careful reconstruction of powerful operative religious ideas. Theologians have reconsidered a rich variety of themes, all of which demonstrate the necessity of dealing with religion

---

4. Emma J. Justes, "Women," in *Clinical Handbook of Pastoral Counseling*, ed. Robert J. Wicks and Richard D. Parsons (New York: Paulist Press, 1985), p. 298.

when considering questions of sexuality and relationship: the equation of women with Eve as the temptress and source of evil; the double standard that characterizes women's sexual desires as particularly unnatural and motherhood as asexual; doctrines equating love with self-sacrifice, selflessness, and suffering; fixed images of God as father and male; the elevation of men as closer to God in institutionalized religious practices and doctrines; scriptural and theological complicity in condoning male domination and female submission; and the related violation and abuse within families and congregations. Fortunately, contrary to the impression given by this laundry list of atrocities, Christianity has not just endorsed male domination and the patriarchal family as a religious norm; it has also acted to liberate people, including women, and has itself created precedent for radically inclusive justice and women's equal worth and participation as created in the image of God.

The power of reconstructing theological doctrines for pastoral purposes can be illustrated by looking at two of these themes — headship and Christian love as sacrifice. Without a doubt, Christianity has taught and continues to teach male headship. In fact, it is impossible to worship in the vast majority of Christian congregations today, even in the more liberal churches, without endorsing it, however subtly or indirectly. Nevertheless, many biblical scholars and feminist theologians now challenge religious sanction of male headship. Since at least the 1980s, feminist theologians have advocated the ideal of mutuality and shared responsibility as grounded in biblical, historical, contemporary, and practical studies in religion and theology.

The creation stories in Genesis do not establish male ascendancy as part of God's plan. Rather, recent biblical theologians demonstrate that Genesis 2–3 portray as normative a shared partnership of women and men in dominion and in fruitful propagation of the species. It is the fall into sin in Genesis 3, not God's intention in creation, that turns dominion into domination of male over female and turns companionship into social enmeshment of the female in human caregiving. The building of Christ's kingdom, then, calls us toward the renewal of the original creation of balanced alliance of women and men in work and love.

Perhaps the hardest texts to contend with, and the texts that have most influenced the ideal of male headship, are the household codes of the New Testament. "Household codes" is a term applied to scriptural passages that sought to order family relationships among early Christian converts in two Deutero-Pauline letters (letters attributed to but not authored by

Paul) of the New Testament, Colossians and Ephesians. Typically, family members are exhorted to certain behaviors in relation to one another, most specifically, subordinates (e.g., wives, slaves, children) to their superiors (e.g., husbands, masters, fathers). These texts are particularly problematic for feminist interpretations of mutuality. Regardless of their initial intention, from at least the Reformation to the nineteenth century they have given supernatural sanction to patriarchal family roles in which men lead and women follow.

There are sufficient grounds for arguing, however, that the codes were intended not to bolster but to reverse ancient heroic models of male authority in families.[5] In the household codes in Ephesians, for example, the author borrows and yet transmutes the metaphors of the surrounding male culture of strength, dominance, and conflict to suggest new virtues of peace, humility, patience, and gentleness. The husband is called to the self-giving love of Christ and to a kind of mutual subjection not found in similar Aristotelian codes. Over history, it is this accent on male subordination that has been most overlooked. Instead, women, more than men, have tended to absorb the message of sacrifice and submission. On occasion, when men have heard the Christian message, they have become less dominant and more giving. Nonetheless, as advocates of women, feminists in religion often deride the codes as a reversal of the more inclusive message within the early Christian community under the social and political pressures of the patriarchal society of that time. The passage ultimately obtains only a modified or benevolent patriarchy. Yet the hierarchical patterns of the Greco-Roman world, if not completely challenged, were at least mitigated in the household codes as well as in some important aspects of the Jesus movement and in some of the practices of the early church.

From early on, Christian feminists have contested the idealization of female self-sacrifice and claimed the centrality of radical mutuality in human relationships. In one of the earliest essays in feminist theology, Valerie Saiving suggests that women and men experience the Christian love command in the midst of different struggles. For a variety of anthropological, bio-sociological, and evolutionary reasons, men tend to face temptations of all-consuming power, prestige, self-assertion, pride, and self-centeredness. Male theologians have proposed the Christian solution of complete self-

5. See Chapter 5 in Don S. Browning, Bonnie J. Miller-McLemore, Pamela D. Couture, K. Brynolf Lyon, and Robert M. Franklin, *From Culture Wars to Common Ground: Religion and the American Family Debate* (Louisville: Westminster John Knox Press, 1997).

giving with no thought for one's own self. Women, Saiving argues, are more often engaged in the minutiae of daily care of others, including young children. As a result, they are more likely to struggle with distractibility, self-loss, dispersion, self-derogation, and fragmentation in the midst of multiple demands — that is, "underdevelopment or negation of the self."[6] Women have been expected to give up needs, desires, opportunities, and space to make way for others. They have been taught to suffer obediently and meekly, as Christ did.

However, Christian love modeled after the commandment to love the neighbor as oneself upholds the importance of God's love for each of us and of loving oneself as a source of love of others. A mother, for example, must balance the endless moments of responsive care of the infant with care for herself within a community supportive of the good of children and women. Sacrifice and suffering as ends in and of themselves are not only detrimental to subordinate groups; they are also misleading, since neither redemptive sacrifice nor suffering is the primary way to understanding Christ's death on the cross. The cross was an inevitable consequence of Jesus' political pursuit of care for the suffering, and upholds suffering as a standard of Christian commitment only when it serves to liberate the oppressed and free the captives. In short, adequate interpretations of Christian love recognize the dangers in making suffering a central Christian act and emphasize the secondary place of self-sacrifice as a means to the more encompassing end of mutual love.

Implications for the Field of Pastoral Theology

What do changes in understandings of sexuality, gender, and relationship mean for the field of pastoral theology more generally? Feminism is a radical political movement aimed at transforming categories of discrimination, especially but not restricted to categories of gender and sexual stereotype, that rank people as inferior or superior according to particular traits. To think about practical and pastoral theology from this vantage point requires prophetic, transformative challenge to systems of stratification and domination within society and religious life, particularly those that rank men and male activities over women and female activities.

6. Valerie Saiving, "The Human Situation: A Feminine View," *Journal of Religion* 40 (April 1960): 109.

Pastoral theology still focuses on care of persons and finds personality theories, particularly within psychology, primary resources for the enhancement of this practice. However, in the past decade, partly as a result of new studies of gender and sexuality, several feminist pastoral theologians have modified the individualistic leanings of Anton Boisen's metaphor of the living human document as the object of study in pastoral theology by turning to an alternative, related image of the living human web. The metaphor of web affirms the relevant role of other social sciences besides psychology in helping understand sexual roles and social relationships. But it does not mean that the individual or the use of psychology as the primary cognate science for pastoral theology recedes in importance. It simply means that the individual is understood in inextricable relationship to the broader context. And in contrast to popular characterizations of psychology as individualistic, psychology is not inherently so, having itself contributed to new understandings of connective selfhood in recent research. Feminist psychology in the different schools of psychoanalytic, self-in-relation, and family systems theory continues to shed light on the ways in which sexuality and gender are culturally determined by distorted patterns of male-female relationship and internalized perceptions of denigration and animosity.

This perspective requires a fundamental re-orientation of the core functions of pastoral care. Pastoral care still entails practical religious, spiritual, and congregational care for the suffering, involving the rich resources of religious traditions and communities, contemporary understandings of the human person in the social sciences, and ultimately the movement of God's love and hope in the lives of individuals and communities. However, pastoral care from a liberation perspective is about breaking silences, urging prophetic action, and liberating the oppressed. In place of the conventional modes with which pastoral care has been routinely equated with healing, sustaining, guiding, and reconciling, articulated by Seward Hiltner and amended by William Clebsch and Charles Jaekle, four pastoral practices acquire particular importance: resisting, empowering, nurturing, and liberating.[7] Pastoral theology and care oriented to the cry for gender justice disrupts and disturbs as much as it comforts and consoles.

One day in class, several students responded with mixed feelings to a

7. This is partially based on Carroll Weaver's informal remarks during a panel at the American Academy of Religion, November 1996, drawing on her dissertation work on womanist pastoral theology. [See also her book now published: Carroll Watkins Ali, *Survival and Liberation: Pastoral Theology in African American Context* (St. Louis: Chalice Press, 1999).]

book on women's struggles in a male-dominated society: an older woman denied gender and sexual oppression as a woman because she had loved mothering; a younger woman rejected the idea of oppression because changes had occurred and she felt equal rather than personally disadvantaged in her relationships; finally, a younger man disputed his role in the oppression of women, having done nothing he could see as exploitative. All three made appropriate claims. They personally did not belong either distinctly inside or outside the role of dominator and oppressed. No one wants to be falsely or rigidly labeled.

Nonetheless, all of these folks stand within a history and society in which social structures prize men more than women; and all of us reside in a context in which powerful religious practices, institutions, and doctrines about gender and sexual roles influence our behavior and beliefs about ourselves. Although none of the participants in the exchange above discussed their struggles publicly in the class, I knew from personal conversation with each of them that the older woman suffered in an exploitative, painful marriage; the younger woman came from a home in which her father had sexually abused her; and the young man benefited from the unseen economic and educational advantages of his male sex and white skin. Breaking silences about injustice and abuse leads to relief and fear, shame, even rage. Sometimes it is easier to avoid the kind of pastoral care and theology that surface such complex human sentiments. However, the benefits of entering into such conversation are multitudinous. Despite or even as a result of the turmoil created by changes in approaches to gender and sexuality, pastoral theology and its understanding of human relationships continues to evolve in ever new and exciting ways.

Selected Bibliography

Ackermann, D. M., and R. Bons-Storm, eds. *Liberating Faith Practices: Feminist Practical Theologies in Context.* Leuven, the Netherlands: Peeters, 1988.

Bons-Storm, R. *The Incredible Woman: Listening to Women's Silences in Pastoral Care and Counseling.* Nashville: Abingdon Press, 1996.

Browning, D. S., B. J. Miller-McLemore, P. D. Couture, K. B. Lyon, and R. M. Franklin. *From Culture Wars to Common Ground: Religion and the American Family Debate.* Louisville: Westminster John Knox Press, 1997.

Chodorow, N. "Family Structure and Feminine Personality." In *Women, Culture, and Society,* edited by M. Z. Rosaldo and L. Lamphere. Stanford, Calif.: Stanford University Press, 1974.

———. *Feminism and Psychoanalytic Theory.* New Haven: Yale University Press, 1989.

———. *The Reproduction of Mothering.* Berkeley and Los Angeles: University of California Press, 1978.

Clebsch, W., and C. Jaekle. *Pastoral Care in Historical Perspective.* 2d ed. New York: Aronson, 1983.

Cooper-White, P. *The Cry of Tamar: Violence against Women and the Church's Response.* Minneapolis: Fortress Press, 1995.

Couture, P. D. *Blessed Are the Poor? Women's Poverty, Family Policy, and Practical Theology.* Nashville: Abingdon Press, 1991.

Culbertson, P. L. *Counseling Men.* Minneapolis: Fortress Press, 1994.

De Marinis, V. M. *Critical Caring: A Feminist Model for Pastoral Psychology.* Louisville: Westminster John Knox Press, 1993.

Doehring, C. "Developing Models of Feminist Pastoral Counseling." *Journal of Pastoral Care* 46, no. 1 (Spring 1992): 23-31.

Dunlap, S. J. *Counseling Depressed Women.* Louisville: Westminster John Knox Press, 1997.

Ehrenreich, B., and D. English. *For Her Own Good: 150 Years of the Experts' Advice to Women.* New York: Doubleday, 1978.

Fiorenza, E. S. *In Memory of Her: A Feminist Theological Reconstruction of Christian Origins.* New York: Crossroad, 1984.

Freud, S. *Female Sexuality.* In *Standard Edition,* vol. 21, translated into English and edited by J. Strachey. London: Hogarth Press, 1953 (1931).

Freud, S. *Three Essays on the Theory of Sexuality.* In *Standard Edition,* vol. 7, translated into English and edited by J. Strachey. London: Hogarth Press, 1953 (1905).

Gilligan, C. *In a Different Voice: Psychological Theory and Women's Development.* Cambridge: Harvard University Press, 1982.

Glaz, M., and J. S. Moessner, eds. *Women in Travail and Transition: A New Pastoral Care.* Minneapolis: Fortress Press, 1991.

Graham, E., and M. Halsey, eds. *Life Cycles: Women and Pastoral Care.* Cambridge: SPCK, 1993.

Greenspan, M. *A New Approach to Women and Therapy.* New York: McGraw-Hill, 1983.

Greider, K. J. *Reckoning with Aggression: Theology, Violence, and Vitality.* Louisville: Westminster John Knox Press, 1997.

hooks, bell. *Feminist Theory: From Margin to Center.* Boston: South End Press, 1984.

Horney, K. *Feminine Psychology.* New York: W. W. Norton, 1967 (1930).

————. *Neurosis and Human Growth.* New York: W. W. Norton, 1973.

Justes, E. J. "Women." In *Clinical Handbook of Pastoral Counseling,* pp. 279-99, edited by R. J. Wicks and R. D. Parsons. New York: Paulist Press, 1985.

Lerman, H. *A Mote in Freud's Eye: From Psychoanalysis to the Psychology of Women.* New York: Springer, 1986.

Levant, R., and W. Pollack, eds. *A New Psychology of Men.* New York: Basic Books, 1995.

Miller-McLemore, B. J. *Also a Mother: Work and Family as Theological Dilemma.* Nashville: Abingdon Press, 1994.

————. "The Living Human Web: Pastoral Theology at the Turn of the Century." In *Through the Eyes of Women: Insights for Pastoral Care,* pp. 9-26, edited by J. S. Moessner. Philadelphia: Westminster John Knox Press, 1996.

————. "The Subject and Practice of Pastoral Theology as a Practical Theological Discipline: Pushing Past the Nagging Identity Crisis to the Poetics of Resistance." In *Liberating Faith Practices: Feminist Practical Theologies in Context,* pp. 175-98, edited by D. M. Ackermann and R. Bons-Storm. Leuven, the Netherlands: Peeters, 1998.

Miller-McLemore, B. J., and H. Anderson. "Pastoral Care and Gender." In *Pastoral Care and Social Conflict,* pp. 99-113, ed. P. D. Couture and R. Hunter. Nashville: Abingdon Press, 1995.

Miller-McLemore, B. J., and B. Gill-Austern, eds. *Feminist and Womanist Pastoral Theology.* Nashville: Abingdon Press, 1999.

Moessner, J. S., ed. *Through the Eyes of Women: Insights for Pastoral Care.* Minneapolis: Fortress Press, 1996.

Neuger, C. C., ed. *The Arts of Ministry: Feminist-Womanist Approaches.* Louisville: Westminster John Knox Press, 1996.

————. "Feminist Pastoral Theology and Pastoral Counseling: A Work in Progress." *Journal of Pastoral Theology* 2 (Summer 1992): 35-57.

Neuger, C. C., and J. N. Poling, eds. *The Care of Men.* Nashville: Abingdon Press, 1997.

Plaskow, J. *Sex, Sin, and Grace: Women's Experience and the Theologies of Reinhold Niebuhr and Paul Tillich.* Lanham, Md.: University Press of America, 1980.

Russell, L. M., and J. Shannon Clarkson, eds. *Dictionary of Feminist Theologies.* Louisville: Westminster John Knox Press, 1996.

Saiving, V. "The Human Situation: A Feminine View." *Journal of Religion* 40 (April 1960): 100-112. Reprinted in *Womanspirit Rising: A Feminist Reader in Religion,* pp. 25-42, ed. C. Christ and J. Plaskow. New York: Harper & Row, 1970.

Saussy, C. *The Gift of Anger: A Call to Faithful Action.* Louisville: Westminster John Knox Press, 1995.

————. *God Images and Self-Esteem: Empowering Women in a Patriarchal Society.* Louisville: Westminster John Knox Press, 1991.

Sturdivant, S. *Therapy with Women: A Feminist Philosophy of Treatment.* New York: Springer, 1984.

Westkott, M. *The Feminist Legacy of Karen Horney.* New Haven: Yale University Press, 1986.

CHAPTER 11

Feminist Studies in Psychology: A Resource

BACKGROUND AND INTRODUCTION

This chapter continues the project of understanding gender as an important category of analysis in theology. It fills in Chapter 9's broad portrait of feminist theory with more detail but in a different way than Chapter 10. It examines major scholars and movements in feminist psychology that have significant implications for understanding personhood and healing. It is among my favorite chapters, perhaps because of its careful coverage of a body of literature that I still find valuable. It seems useful, especially for those seeking a "research report," as the *International Journal of Practical Theology* calls them, on emerging areas of importance. I examine insights that took the U.S. imagination by storm in the 1980s and 1990s. Scholars in any number of disciplines, for example, could hardly stop talking about the "different voice" uncovered by education scholar Carol Gilligan in her empirical research on moral development, or the problematic gender patterns reproduced through mothering described by anthropologist and psychoanalyst Nancy Chodorow, or the ways of knowing studied by psychologists Mary Belenky and her peers. And if the wider public did not recognize these names, most knew about *Reviving Orphelia*, which basically adapted these feminist psychologies for popular consumption.

This essay was originally published as "Research Survey: Feminist Studies in Psychology: Implications for Practical Theology," *International Journal of Practical Theology* 4 (2000): 107-31. Used by permission.

In the late 1990s I received a request from Rick Osmer, then editor of the *International Journal of Practical Theology,* that appealed to me: to do a critical overview of scholarship in feminist psychology. I spent less time writing this chapter than almost anything else I have done because I had actually worked on it for years as I taught women, psychology, religion, and pastoral care. This chapter illustrates a truism (for me at least) that teaching can enrich writing. You know a subject matter in a fuller way if you have to figure out how to teach it. All I had to do was sit down and put in writing what I covered in class with a little more focus and analysis.

A colleague and student of retired Princeton pastoral theologian Don Capps once explained to me one reason for Capps's prolific publication record. In some of his work, he simply provides the service of review, figuring that people will appreciate his synopsis of books and articles that they may not know about or have time to read themselves. I do not often write with such an end in mind. But this chapter works in a similar fashion. However, I would want people to see this chapter as a fruitful *secondary* resource when set side by side with *primary* sources, which readers can trace through the footnotes. The footnotes themselves serve as a basic resource. I would not want readers to substitute this chapter for reading the primary materials. They might draw different conclusions or discover ideas, figures, and texts that I overlook. In fact, I hope that would happen. Such reader engagement is especially important because description bleeds into prescription even in the most objective reporting. Indeed, in my research report I attempt to model a certain genre of writing that positions and evaluates ideas even as it lays them out rather than simply summarizing them. Although developing a thesis was subsidiary in my mind to covering a wide-ranging body of research as comprehensively as possible, there is still an argument in the structure of the essay itself, albeit subtle. I claim that these five schools of thought and their key scholars — psychoanalytic, self-in-relation, developmental, family systems, and race theory — constitute the most influential sources in feminist psychology. Moreover, theologians should have some familiarity with their ideas if they want to speak adequately about human nature and aspiration.

The brief concluding section on the implications of these theories is actually packed full of big claims. I argue that feminist psychologists see selfhood as fundamentally relational and political. So they question the individualistic orientation and biological and psychological determinism that often characterize traditional psychoanalytic and psychological theory, and some theology too. Neither nature nor mothers alone account for human flourishing or failure. At the same time, psychology grasps an irreducible element or level of human functioning that cannot be known through sociology, political theory, or any other science. Feminist psychology in particular explains the psychological dynamics of gender oppression and misogyny that demean valuable human attributes such as vulnerability and emotional sensitivity and that make genuine love, mutual recognition, and justice difficult.

So, as unfashionable as psychology has grown since its mid-twentieth-century heyday, and as wary of feminism as some people may feel, theologians would do well to take feminist psychology more seriously. Psychology still has considerable cultural purchase. Feminist psychologists have criticized white, male, twentieth-century psychology for its moral biases and can aid theologians in uncovering and evaluating some of psychology's hidden values and normative assumptions. Their constructive proposals can also aid theologians in our efforts to comprehend human behavior and desire. But that is not all. The conversation could and should be two-way. Theologians have resources to enrich the moral evaluation of psychology. And we also have constructive insight into human nature and fulfillment that would benefit secular science.

For most of the history of modern psychology, men more than women speculated about the nature of human growth and fulfillment. Their subjects were most often other men. Even when women were subjects, conclusions ultimately rested upon male models and ideals. Psychologists became accustomed to seeing life "through men's eyes," as Carol Gilligan has said so well. Women were basically excluded "from critical theory-building studies," whether of human sexuality, cognitive development, or moral stages.[1] Likewise, in everyday life, "women's reality" or ideas and understandings commonly held by women were all too often labeled "sick, bad, crazy, stupid, ugly, or incompetent." The "White Male System," explains psychotherapist Anne Wilson Schaef, sets the normative agenda for human behavior and health.[2]

1. Francine Prose, "Confident at 11, Confused at 16," *New York Times Magazine*, 7 January 1990, p. 37.

2. Anne Wilson Schaef, *Women's Reality: An Emerging Female System in a White Male Society* (New York: Harper & Row, 1981).

Gilligan and Schaef are only a few of the people now churning out research in psychology that challenges the normativity of male experience and provides new understandings of gender, sexuality, selfhood, growth, and fulfillment. This research has only just begun to affect pastoral practice and theological language. Many clergy and other professionals now recognize that they must understand women and men within more inclusive psychological and theological frameworks. Ultimately these new frameworks have the power to transform divine imagery and devotional practices.

As requested by the editors of the *International Journal of Practical Theology,* my intent is to report on this relatively new and growing body of literature in the United States and to indicate some of its implications for practical theology. Since a research report such as this cannot cover all of the publications and trends of the past three decades, I will attempt to provide a taste of the major developments through attention to prominent works.[3] I will give more attention to early and pivotal works, in part because later works often build on and sometimes offer mostly minor variations on the revolutionary claims of the original texts.[4]

By necessity, I have chosen to exclude work on feminist spirituality and feminist therapy, although materials in both areas have also grown and have connections to and implications for feminist psychology and practical theology. I have also set aside popular or self-help books, even though these publications reach a wider public through bookstore chains and mass-media coverage. Such books often distill prominent ideas from the more academic works that I will discuss. Finally, an entire corpus of new literature in feminist practical theology has developed in the last two decades. Since a few pivotal papers have done a good job describing the contributions of feminist practical theology, I will not attempt to summarize this material or directly relate its growth to research in feminist psychology.[5] Of course, my interest in feminist psychology arises precisely out

3. A review article comments that "women's studies in the U.S. is in such a state of good health that it is currently producing at least 20 volumes of scholarly work a month" (*New Statesman and Society,* 16 February 1999, p. 32). For a useful anthology of pioneering and recent writings, see *Essential Papers on the Psychology of Women,* ed. Claudia Zandardi (New York: New York University Press, 1990).

4. For an example of such a book, see Ellyn Kaschak, *Engendered Lives: A New Psychology of Women's Experience* (New York: Basic Books, 1992).

5. See Bonnie J. Miller-McLemore, "Feminist Theory in Pastoral Theology," in *Feminist and Womanist Pastoral Theology,* ed. Bonnie J. Miller-McLemore and Brita L. Gill-Austern

of my own investment in practical theology, so I will make a few natural connections, even though this is not my main intent.[6]

On the part of my readers, I assume a certain level of unfamiliarity with feminist studies in psychology. I take the chance that I may both underestimate knowledge of feminist studies and overestimate acquaintance with general psychological concepts; I hope to strike a happy medium between these two extremes. In general, I want to show the high level of scholarship in the area of gender and psychology and encourage further exploration on the part of readers. In my teaching and writing on pastoral care and women, I have often quoted a maxim by Emma Justes: If clergy "are unable to travel the route of hearing women's anger, of exploring with women the painful depths of experiences of incest and rape, or enabling women to break free from cultural stereotypes that define their existence," they should not be doing pastoral counseling with women.[7] In like fashion: If scholars in practical theology are not willing to engage seriously a new body of scholarship on gender, sexuality, and women, then they ought not to theorize about the nature of human development and fulfillment in practical theology.

Locating Feminist Studies in Psychology

My own research and teaching history embodies the changes that have occurred in the last several years. In the early 1980s, when I considered a variety of topics for Ph.D. dissertation study, I refrained from writing on women, psychology, and religion. While publications by U.S. scholars in this area had grown exponentially during the 1970s, my hesitation reflected the ongoing lack of status and recognition of such research.

(Nashville: Abingdon Press, 1999); Kathleen J. Greider, Gloria A. Johnson, and Kristen J. Leslie, "Three Decades of Women Writing for Our Lives," in *Feminist and Womanist Pastoral Theology,* ed. Miller-McLemore and Gill-Austern (Nashville: Abingdon Press, 1999); and Bonnie J. Miller-McLemore, "The Living Human Web: Pastoral Theology at the Turn of the Century," in *Through the Eyes of Women: Insights for Pastoral Care,* ed. Jeanne Stevenson-Moessner (Philadelphia: Westminster John Knox Press, 1996), pp. 9-26.

6. For a review of some of this literature for a more general audience and in relation to practical theology, see Bonnie J. Miller-McLemore, "How Sexuality and Relationships Have Revolutionized Pastoral Theology," in *The Blackwell Reader in Pastoral and Practical Theology,* ed. James Woodward et al. (London: Blackwell, 1999), Chapter 10.

7. Emma J. Justes, "Women," in *Clinical Handbook of Pastoral Counseling,* ed. Robert J. Wicks et al. (New York: Paulist Press, 1985), p. 298.

Times have changed. By the time I began teaching in 1986, a few pivotal texts on women and psychology had begun to make a lasting impression on developmental and therapeutic theory. Ten years later, one can group and categorize this material into distinct movements and stages. In some cases, one can discern first, second, and third waves within particular schools of psychology. While recognizing that any such typology is partly artificial, I will organize my discussion of this evolution mostly in terms of schools of thought, covering the following five movements and prominent figures: psychoanalytic theory (Juliet Mitchell and Nancy Chodorow), self-in-relation theory (Jean Baker Miller), developmental theory (Carol Gilligan), family systems theory (Monica McGoldrick, Carol Anderson, and Froma Walsh), and ethnicity, women, and psychological theory (Lillian Comas-Diaz and Beverly Greene).

Again, this grouping is representative but far from exhaustive. Psychoanalytic feminism has had a longer history and greater influence than the other schools and hence will receive slightly more attention and space. Readers familiar with some of these movements and theorists know that the revolutionary ideas of only ten years ago now have their own problems. My exploration will attempt to identify some of this critique as well as to capture aspects of the initial impact and appreciation.

A brief word needs to be said on the preference for "feminist" rather than "gender" as a critical characteristic of the literature I will cover. A comprehensive definition of feminist theory in psychology is impracticable because each theorist and movement embodies slightly different interpretations of the dilemmas of women. Nonetheless, this literature as a whole does support *feminist* studies as distinct from *gender* studies in psychology. In a 1992 issue of *The Family Therapy Networker,* family systems therapist Betty Carter makes the case well and, at the same time, captures an important challenge of the evolving discussion in psychology. She is worth quoting at length:

> In spite of feminism's apparent impact on clinical thinking, I believe we have entered an ambiguous and slippery phase of change — that phase in which the system, having failed to intimidate the upstarts into giving up, now proceeds to water down, co-opt, and obfuscate the issues. The blurring begins, as always, with language, and so "feminist" becomes "gender sensitive," a men's movement is added to the women's movement, and *voila!* we are no longer talking about inequality, but simply about the unfortunate aspects of female socializa-

tion on the one hand, and male socialization on the other — the very juxtaposition suggesting an *equal,* though different, set of problems. The problems of most couples cannot be rationally addressed or resolved until the *core inequality* of their relationships is acknowledged.[8]

In a word, feminist studies in psychology assume a core inequality in the psychological dynamics and consequences of growing up female in a sexist society, even though individual scholars interpret this in different terms and with different emphases. Put a bit too colloquially, feminism is the radical notion that women are human. More formally, feminist theory repudiates the ranking of people as inferior or superior according to various traits of human nature, especially sexual traits. Such a definition locates women's specific struggles within a broader context of other sources of oppression (e.g., racism, classism). To differing extents, feminist theorists in psychology have located women's oppression in the psyche more than in economic disadvantage, cultural disempowerment, or political inequity, even though these other factors also receive varied attention.[9] Feminist theory is "an instance of critical theory" — in this case, theory that has a political purpose involving "a redistribution of power that will be emancipatory for women."[10]

Lest readers be tempted to forget or downplay the adversity and animosity that early feminist theorists in psychology faced, it is worth reviewing briefly some telling remarks about women by a few founding fathers of modern psychology. As Naomi Weisstein observes, these psychologists "set about describing the true nature of women with a certainty and a sense of their own infallibility rarely found in the secular world."[11] Of course,

8. Betty Carter, "Stonewalling Feminism," *The Family Therapy Networker,* January/February 1992, p. 66.

9. For amplification of different movements and emphases in feminist theory, see Rosemarie Tong, *Feminist Thought: A Comprehensive Introduction* (Boulder, Colo.: Westview Press, 1989), especially the introduction, and Josephine Donovan, *Feminist Theory: The Intellectual Traditions of American Feminism* (New York: Continuum, 1991).

10. Mary Ann Zimmer, "Stepping Stones in Feminist Theory," in *In the Embrace of God: Approaches to Theological Anthropology,* ed. Ann O'Hara Graff (New York: Orbis Books, 1995), p. 9.

11. Naomi Weisstein, "Psychology Constructs the Female," in *Women in Sexist Society: Studies in Power and Powerlessness,* ed. Vivian Gornick et al. (New York: Basic Books, 1971), pp. 133-46. For an early radical critique of the cultural construction of madness and the treatment of women in psychology, see Phyllis Chesler, *Women and Madness,* 25th anniversary edition (New York: Four Walls Eight Windows, 1972, 1997).

Sigmund Freud is most easily caricatured. He obstinately argued that women without question desire a penis "in spite of everything" and "refuse to accept the fact of being castrated." As a result, he declares,

> I cannot escape the notion (though I hesitate to give it expression) that for woman the level of what is ethically normal is different from what it is in man. . . . Character traits which critics of every epoch have brought up against women — that they show less sense of justice than men, that they are less ready to submit to the great necessities of life, that they are more often influenced in their judgments by feelings of affection or hostility — all these would be amply accounted for by the modification in the formation of their super-ego. We must not allow ourselves to be deflected from such conclusions by the denials of the feminists, who are anxious to force us to regard the two sexes as completely equal in position and worth.[12]

Elsewhere, he concludes that women's "social interests are weaker than those of men and . . . their capacity for the sublimation of their interests is less."[13] A few decades later, Erik Erikson moves away from penis envy and even postulates male envy of female reproductive powers but still finds himself entrapped in prejudices against women's independent self-development. He declares that "much of a young woman's identity is already defined in her kind of attractiveness and in the selectivity of her search for the man (or men) by whom she wishes to be sought."[14] In another example of male projection of women's desires, Bruno Bettelheim announces that "we must start with the realization that, as much as women want to be good scientists or engineers, they want first and foremost to be womanly companions of men and to be mothers."[15]

12. Sigmund Freud, "Some Psychological Consequences of the Anatomical Distinction between the Sexes," in *Sexuality and the Psychology of Love,* ed. Philip Rieff (New York: Macmillan, 1925, 1963), p. 193.

13. Sigmund Freud, *New Introductory Lectures in Psychoanalysis,* trans. and ed. James Strachey (New York: W. W. Norton, 1933, 1965), p. 119.

14. Erik H. Erikson, "Womanhood and the Inner Space," in *Identity, Youth, and Crisis* (New York: W. W. Norton, 1968), p. 283; reprinted in *Women and Analysis: Dialogues on Psychoanalytic Views of Femininity,* ed. Jean Strouse (Boston: G. K. Hall, 1974, 1985). See also Erikson's reply to his own work, "Once More the Inner Space," in *Women and Analysis,* ed. Strouse, pp. 320-40.

15. Bruno Bettelheim, "The Commitment Required of a Woman Entering a Scientific Profession in Present-Day American Society," in *Woman and the Scientific Professions* (Cam-

In general, these early psychological theorists promoted cultural consensus as biological and psychological fact. In establishing and justifying the inferiority of women, modern psychology nicely assumed a task previously performed by patriarchal religion. Women were again proven inferior by nature, but now in new and scientifically incriminating ways.

Nor were these purely theoretical speculations. A classic study in 1970 revealed that these assumptions spilled over into clinical practice and daily life. When asked to indicate traits of mature men, women, and adults, clinicians clearly held sexually differentiated standards of health. While the traits for healthy adults and healthy men correlate closely with one another, a woman cannot acquire the traits of a healthy adult (e.g., rational, independent) and the named traits of a healthy woman (e.g., emotional, cooperative) at the same time. In a classic double bind, a woman can be either a healthy adult or a healthy woman, but not both.[16]

Psychoanalytic Theory

Freud had his early dissenters. Helene Deutsch, Alfred Adler, and Clara Thompson discounted the import of the castration trauma in different ways. Without essentially disturbing the patriarchal status quo, Deutsch affirmed the positive role of "feminine" attributes, including the power to bear and nurture others.[17] Deviating more sharply than Deutsch, Adler and Thompson saw penis envy as envy of male social power and domination rather than as an ontological deficiency.[18]

---

bridge, Mass.: A MIT Symposium, 1965), cited by Phyllis Chesler, "Patient and Patriarch: Women in the Psychotherapeutic Relationship," in *Women in Sexist Society,* ed. Gornick et al., p. 264.

16. I. K. Broverman, D. M. Broverman, and F. E. Clarkson, "Sex Role Stereotypes and Clinical Judgments of Mental Health," *Journal of Consulting and Clinical Psychology* 34 (1970): 1-7; and I. K. Broverman, S. Vogel, D. M. Broverman, F. E. Clarkson, and P. Rosenkrantz, "Sex-role Stereotypes: A Current Appraisal," *Journal of Social Issues* 28 (1972): 59-78.

17. Helene Deutsch, *The Psychology of Women: A Psychoanalytic Interpretation* (New York: Collier Books, 1963). Deutsch's emphasis on normal femininity as requiring motherhood can also be read as only a further elaboration of Freud's limited theories. See Tong, *Feminist Thought,* pp. 24, 146, 257.

18. Alfred Adler, *Understanding Human Nature* (New York: Greenberg, 1927); Clara Thompson, "Problems of Womanhood," in *Interpersonal Psychoanalysis: The Selected Papers of Clara Thompson,* ed. M. P. Green (New York: Basic Books, 1964).

As a second-generation analyst, Karen Horney is especially notable because she dared to protest Freudian ideas about female sexuality from inside the psychoanalytic movement during its earlier years of institutional consolidation. We might consider her work a part of the first wave of feminist psychoanalytic theory.[19] In her eyes, Freud had simply projected his own little-boy view of girls onto women as a group. Trained at the Berlin Psychoanalytic Institute and eventually welcomed by both the Chicago and the New York Institutes in the 1930s, she joined a few others, including Adler and Thompson, in contending that penis envy, while a valid observation of female sentiment, results not from a natural female deficiency but from envy of male social status and authority. Penis envy is in reality envy of male power in a world in which having a penis means having economic, political, and social standing.

Horney also named the unnamable male envy of women: "Men resent and fear women because they experience them as powerful mothers" (an idea that Chodorow picks up later and develops in new directions).[20] Although seldom discussed or explored, the male inability to bear children is experienced as a sexual deficiency on par with penis envy.[21]

In her later writings, Horney captures powerfully the intense conflict for women between compliance with female devaluation through internalization of cultural expectations of femininity and the rage to triumph over and oppose these expectations. Domestic ideals of religious piety, sexual purity, wifely submission, and motherly domesticity led to inherent contradictions between responsibility for men and deference to them, self-reliance and dependence. In a powerful contemporary retrieval of the life and work of Horney, Marcia Westkott depicts the disharmony of the "feminine type" as understood by Horney:

19. See Karen Horney, *Feminine Psychology* (New York: W. W. Norton, 1930, 1967); and Karen Horney, "Flight from Womanhood," in *Psychoanalysis and Women,* ed. Jean Baker Miller (New York: Penguin Books, 1973), pp. 5-20. For recent attempts to situate Horney within psychoanalytic feminist history, see Marcia Westkott, *The Feminist Legacy of Karen Horney* (New Haven: Yale University Press, 1986); and Susan Quinn, *A Mind of Her Own: The Life of Karen Horney* (New York: Summit Books, 1987).

20. Nancy J. Chodorow, *Feminism and Psychoanalytic Theory* (New Haven: Yale University Press, 1989), p. 6.

21. See E. Jacobson, "Development of the Wish for a Child in Boys," *Psychoanalytic Study of the Child* 5 (1950): 139-52; and John Munder Ross, "Beyond the Phallic Illusion: Notes on Man's Heterosexuality," in *The Psychology of Men,* ed. Gerald Fogel et al. (New York: Basic Books, 1986), pp. 49-70.

Women were permitted to pursue education but expected to become mothers. They were encouraged to be sexually emancipated but supposed to limit sexual desire to monogamous marriage combined with asexual motherhood. They were told that they could have careers but were expected to defer to men at work and at home. They were enticed by ambition but taught to find salvation in love.[22]

It is no small wonder that many women suffered arrested energy and depression. What is surprising is that people like Horney were so quickly dismissed, in their own time and even recently, by clinic, academy, and church. Horney's work did little to alter the bias against women at the heart of culture. Until recently, Horney was criticized, ostracized, and overlooked as an important analyst and theorist in her own right, partly as a result of her dissent within the psychoanalytic movement.

With changes in the cultural climate of the United States in the 1970s, the work and ideas of Nancy Chodorow had a greater impact and more lasting influence. A sociologist with an interest in anthropology who later trained as a psychoanalyst, Chodorow is less interested in Oedipal struggles between father and child over sexual possession of the mother and more interested in pre-Oedipal dynamics between mother and child centered on emotional separation and relationship. Her lasting power may have something to do with her uncanny ability to crystallize and articulate a few rather remarkable theses that had been percolating throughout the writings of other social scientists at the time.

First, Chodorow argues forcefully that social constructions of motherhood and, more troubling, misogyny reproduce themselves culturally precisely because women mother. Second, and equally important, genderized, often opposing, and sometimes oppressive patterns of male independence and female dependence have their source in the distance of boys and the proximity of girls to the primary parent, normally the mother. These ideas first appeared in an article in 1974 and then in a pivotal text, *The Reproduction of Mothering*, in 1978.[23]

22. Westkott, *The Feminist Legacy of Karen Horney*, pp. 50-51.
23. Nancy J. Chodorow, "Family Structure and Feminine Personality," in *Woman, Culture, and Society*, ed. Michelle Zimbalist Rosaldo et al. (Stanford: Stanford University Press, 1974); Nancy J. Chodorow, *The Reproduction of Mothering: Psychoanalysis and the Sociology of Gender* (Berkeley and Los Angeles: University of California Press, 1978). See Chodorow's introduction to *Feminism and Psychoanalytic Theory*, pp. 1-19, for a helpful summary of the relationship between feminism and psychoanalysis over the past twenty years in terms of her work.

The article appeared the same year as another important text in academic psychoanalytic feminism, Juliet Mitchell's *Psychoanalysis and Feminism*. In striking opposition to the radical feminist denunciation of Freud,[24] she offered a defense of the relevance of psychoanalysis for feminist theory. Mitchell summarizes her argument on the opening page: "Psychoanalysis is not a recommendation for a patriarchal society, but an analysis of one. If we are interested in understanding and challenging the oppression of women, we cannot afford to neglect it."[25] The distinctive contribution of psychoanalysis is found in its attempt to decipher not the conscious but the unconscious motivations and ideations behind human cultural constructions, particularly the "law of the father" and a system that must by definition oppress women. For this, psychoanalysis is indispensable.

These two texts, along with a few others, constitute what might be characterized as a critical second stage of psychoanalytic feminism in the 1970s. They also reflect the influence of two developing traditions in psychoanalysis. Chodorow grounds her work in the British object relations school of D. W. Winnicott and its emphasis on the mother's role in pre-Oedipal development; Mitchell draws on the work of the French poststructuralist psychoanalyst Jacques Lacan and his emphasis on cultural constructions of language, the phallus, the law of the father, and sexual difference.[26] Chodorow's work represents a more popular and eclectic approach, while Mitchell has sometimes stood for psychoanalytic purism. I will focus on developments in the former school more than the latter because of their greater impact thus far on feminist studies in practical theology in the United States and because of their slightly greater proximity to clinical therapy.[27]

24. See, for example, Simone de Beauvoir, *The Second Sex*, trans. and ed. H. M. Parshley (New York: Vintage Books, 1949, 1974); Betty Friedan, *The Feminine Mystique* (New York: Dell, 1963, 1974); Kate Millett, *Sexual Politics* (Garden City, N.Y.: Doubleday, 1970); and Shulamith Firestone, *The Dialectic of Sex: The Case for Feminist Revolution* (New York: Bantam Books, 1970).

25. Juliet Mitchell, *Psychoanalysis and Feminism: Freud, Reich, Laing, and Women* (New York: Vintage Books, 1974), p. xiii.

26. Mitchell moves closer to Lacan in recent writings. See *Feminist Sexuality: Jacques Lacan and the École Freudienne*, ed. Juliet Mitchell and Jacqueline Rose, trans. Jacqueline Rose (New York: Pantheon and London: W. W. Norton, 1983).

27. For further discussion of feminists in the tradition of Lacan, see Helene Cixous, "The Laugh of the Medusa," in *New French Feminism*, ed. Elaine Marks et al. (New York: Schocken Books, 1981); Jane Gallop, *The Daughter's Seduction: Feminism and Psychoanalytic*

In an overview essay, Chodorow nicely summarizes the most recognized outcome of her early work: "I showed that the selves of women and men tend to be constructed differently — women's self more in relation and involved with boundary negotiations, separation and connection, men's self more distanced and based on defensively firm boundaries and denials of self-other connection." Or again, "women develop a self-in-relation, men a self that denies relatedness."[28]

When only women mother, daughters identify with the same-sex parent and struggle to establish a sufficiently individuated and autonomous self, while sons engage in defensive assertion of ego boundaries, repress emotional needs, and struggle instead with attachment and intimacy. Intrapsychically and cross-culturally, the more father-absence and distance, the more severe the boy's conflicts around fear of women and masculinity. In turn, women and mothers are devalued, and the very requirements of good parenting are lost. According to Chodorow, motherhood and fatherhood are not biologically or naturally determined roles, but biopsychologically reproduced. "Women come to mother because they have been mothered by women. By contrast, that men are mothered by women reduces their parenting capacities."[29]

Children of both sexes are subjected to the biases of the wider culture, which has conventionally limited the mother's power to the confines of the home, in contrast to the comparatively greater power of fathers in the public sphere. Woman's mothering generates, more or less universally, misogyny and sexism.[30] Almost exclusive female parenting leads to the de-

---

Theory (London: Macmillan, 1982), and Jane Gallop, *Reading Lacan* (Ithaca, N.Y.: Cornell University Press, 1985); Elizabeth Grosz, *Jacques Lacan: A Feminist Introduction* (New York: Routledge, 1990); Luce Irigaray, *Speculum of the Other Woman* (Ithaca, N.Y.: Cornell University Press, 1985), and Luce Irigaray, *This Sex Which Is Not One* (New York: Cornell University Press, 1985); Julia Kristeva, *The Kristeva Reader,* ed. Toril Moi (New York: Columbia University Press, 1986). For a nice discussion of this material, see Chris Weedon, *Feminism, Theory, and the Politics of Difference* (Oxford and Malden, Mass: Blackwell, 1999), ch. 4; and *Feminism and Psychoanalysis: A Critical Dictionary,* ed. Elizabeth Wright (Oxford: Blackwell, 1992). I also will not comment upon another branch of psychoanalytic work that has broken sharply from the clinical orientation and uses psychoanalysis as a cultural theory to read texts of various kinds. See, for example, Marianne Hirsch, *The Mother/Daughter Plot: Narrative, Psychoanalysis, Feminism* (Bloomington: Indiana University Press, 1989); and Elizabeth Abel, *Virginia Woolf and the Fictions of Psychoanalysis* (Chicago: University of Chicago Press, 1989).

28. Chodorow, *Feminism and Psychoanalytic Theory,* pp. 2, 15.

29. Chodorow, *The Reproduction of Mothering,* p. 211.

30. As an important source of this analysis, Chodorow credits the work of Philip Slat-

velopment of a defensive masculine identity, defined over against female attributes, and ultimately a compensatory psychology and ideology of male superiority that sustains male dominance.

To counteract the almost inevitable devaluation of women and care-giving activities, Chodorow lends psychoanalytic support to the wider so-cial and political premise that men and women should share primary parenting responsibilities. This analysis dramatically shifts the burden of family problems from the individual mother and her egotistic pursuits or possessive traits to the wider system of sexual inequalities. Primary parenting must be shared. Although Chodorow oversimplifies the ease with which this could come about and mostly ignores the biological com-plications of pregnancy, birth, and nursing, her argument is convincing that parenting or mothering qualities can and must be created in men. If they are not, families will continue to repeat patterns destructive to their very survival and the sustenance of community.

Feminists within and beyond psychoanalytic thought have debated whether joint parenting is an adequate solution to the gender asymmetries of patriarchal society.[31] In her later work, Chodorow acknowledges psy-choanalytic tendencies to universalize and discount cultural differences. She maintains the importance of psychoanalytic thought, nonetheless, as a source of knowledge of the unconscious and internal fantasies characteris-tic of all people in all societies, pointing out that the individual case study actually does a better job of respecting diversity than many other social science methods. She notes a "global shift" in her thinking from a mono-causal view of the source of women's oppression in women's mothering to a "multiplex" account of mothering as "one extremely important, and pre-viously largely unexamined, aspect of the relations of gender and the psy-chology of gender."[32] Still, she contends that she has yet to find an explana-

er, *The Glory of Hera: Greek Mythology and the Greek Family* (Boston: Beacon Press, 1968). See also Dorothy Dinnerstein, *The Mermaid and the Minotaur* (New York: Harper & Row, 1976).

31. For an early critical review, see Judith Lorber et al., "On the Reproduction of Mothering: A Methodological Debate," *Signs: Journal of Women in Culture and Society* 6, no. 3 (Spring 1981): 482-514. For a more recent exploration of issues of diversity, see Denise A. Segura and Jennifer L. Pierce, "Chicana/o Family Structure and Gender Personality: Chodorow, Familism, and Psychoanalytic Sociology Revisited," in *Signs: Journal of Women in Culture and Society* 19, no. 1 (Autumn 1993): 62-91.

32. Chodorow, *Feminism and Psychoanalytic Theory*, pp. 5-6. For another important psychoanalytic text, focused more on therapy, see Luise Eichenbaum and Susie Orbach, *Un-derstanding Women: A Feminist Psychoanalytic Approach* (New York: Basic Books, 1984).

tion of women's oppression that surpasses Horney's original suggestion about male resentment and fear of maternal power.

Since the 1978 publication of *The Reproduction of Mothering,* as Chodorow herself observes, the "psychoanalytic-feminist project has proliferated and become more intricate."[33] Jessica Benjamin's *Bonds of Love* further contests the genderized polarities of male and female parenting as a primary source of the perpetuation of domination and a key obstacle to the development of genuine mutuality. Mutual recognition of the other and the self are essential for satisfactory development. Yet when fathers excel in asserting themselves and mothers specialize in recognizing others, basic needs for recognition of oneself and for regard for the other are thwarted and distorted for both girls and boys. Like Chodorow, Benjamin points toward the need for shared parenting as a means to subvert patterns of male domination and female submission, so that mothers no longer symbolize engulfment and fathers no longer represent independence.[34]

Publishing in the 1990s, Jane Flax, Judith Butler, Madelon Sprengnether, Chris Weedon, and others turn to psychoanalysis as a secondary resource from their primary positions as political scientists, philosophers, literary critics, and so forth.[35] Bringing together feminism, psychoanalysis, and postmodernism and drawing upon her clinical work with borderline patients, Flax mounts a nice critique of the fashionable celebration of the "decentered" or "fragmented" self. By contrast, Butler further unsettles categories of selfhood by uncovering and contesting the heterosexism of

33. Chodorow, *Feminism and Psychoanalytic Theory,* p. 19. For a few good reviews of some of this literature, see Diane Jonte-Pace, "Psychoanalysis after Feminism," *Religious Studies Review* 19, no. 2 (April 1993): 110-15; Judith Kegan Gardiner, "Psychoanalysis and Feminism: An American Humanist's View," *Signs: Journal of Women in Culture and Society* 17, no. 2 (Winter 1992): 437-54; and Michele Barrett, "Psychoanalysis and Feminism: A British Sociologist's View," *Signs: Journal of Women in Culture and Society* 17, no. 2 (Winter 1992): 455-66.

34. Jessica Benjamin, *The Bonds of Love: Psychoanalysis, Feminism, and the Problem of Domination* (New York: Pantheon Books, 1988). See also Mariam M. Johnson, *Strong Mothers, Weak Wives: The Search for Gender Equality* (Berkeley and Los Angeles: University of California Press, 1988). This book combines psychoanalytic thought with sociology and cognitive psychology to explore the role of the father in perpetuating male dominance.

35. Jane Flax, *Thinking Fragments: Psychoanalysis, Feminism, and Postmodernism in the Contemporary West* (Berkeley and Los Angeles: University of California Press, 1990); Judith Butler, *Gender Trouble: Feminism and the Subversion of Identity* (New York: Routledge, 1990); Madelon Sprengnether, *The Spectral Mother: Freud, Feminism, and Psychoanalysis* (Ithaca, N.Y.: Cornell University Press, 1990); Weedon, *Feminism, Theory, and the Politics of Difference.*

psychoanalysis and the binary and constricting nature of sexual categories. Chodorow herself has also recently taken up the problem of monolithic portrayals of gender and heterosexuality and argues for a variety of sexualities.[36]

In different ways, these recent publications expand the dialogue between psychoanalysis and feminism to include postmodern theorists (Foucault, Rorty, Lyotard, Derrida), French feminists (Irigaray, Kristeva, Cixous), and, as already noted, other psychoanalytic theorists (Lacan in the French psychoanalytic tradition, Winnicott in the Anglo-American tradition). Together they form part of what might be seen as a third wave of psychoanalytic feminism.

Self-in-Relation Theory

Neo-Freudians, such as Erikson, Horney, and Harry Stack Sullivan, criticized the exclusive focus on intrapsychic causes of human behavior in orthodox Freudian psychoanalysis and attempted to re-order psychological exploration toward interpersonal and social aspects of selfhood. Jean Baker Miller, who was trained as a Sullivanian analyst, produced *Toward a New Psychology of Women* in 1976, the first book of its kind and now a classic. This acclaim results less from the specific contents of the book, written in nontechnical language for the general public, and more from its timing, its reclamation of devalued relational dimensions of human interaction, and its instigation of further clinical research. Miller's focus on the role of power, domination, and subordination in emotional development led to a new school and clinical approach identified with the Stone Center for Developmental Services and Studies at Wellesley College.

Miller begins *Toward a New Psychology of Women* by itemizing characteristics of dominants and subordinants in a stratified society. While dominants define "normal" human relationships, subordinants suppress their wisdom and capacities. With this claim as a basic premise, she sets about reclaiming the devalued qualities that women have perfected precisely as a result of their subordination. In a word, those characteristics seen as women's weakness actually qualify as great strengths when seen in a new light. Women have, indeed, functioned as "'carriers' for society of cer-

36. Nancy J. Chodorow, *Femininities, Masculinities, Sexualities: Freud and Beyond* (Lexington: University of Kentucky Press, 1994).

tain aspects of the total human experience."[37] Most centrally, women have valued affiliation rather than self-enhancement. In this, they have accepted the inevitability and naturalness of other qualities commonly devalued by society, such as vulnerability, dependence, weakness, helplessness, affectivity, cooperation, nurture, and emotionality.

More than just empirical or clinical observations, these comments suggest a re-definition of human nature. Humans are not driven by aggressive, destructive, sexual, or competitive needs. Humans are essentially cooperative: "there must be a bedrock modicum of cooperativeness for society to exist at all."[38] Rather than conceptualizing the self as ego mediating between instincts and reality, Miller hypothesized a "more complex" intersubjective structure and dynamic:

> We are suggesting then that the organizing principle in women's lives is not a *direct* relation to reality — as reality is culturally defined. Nor is it the mediation between one's own "drives" and that reality. Instead, women have been involved in a more complex mediation — the attempt to transform their drives into the service of another's drives; and the mediation is not directly with reality but with and through *the other person's purposes* in that reality.[39]

Miller makes an even more fundamental claim: Development itself proceeds "*only* by means of affiliation."[40] Assuming here an implicit ontological and moral foundation of reciprocity and harmony, she insists that one can and should meet one's needs as one meets the needs of others.

Where Miller's early work adopted a clear political stance challenging sexism and social inequality, contemporary colleagues have focused more on psychological issues and dynamics. Theoretical conceptions, first published as Works in Progress papers made available through the Stone Center,[41] have since partially appeared in two collected editions, *Women's*

---

37. Jean Baker Miller, *Toward a New Psychology of Women* (Boston: Beacon Press, 1976; 2d ed., 1986), pp. 22-23.

38. Miller, *Toward a New Psychology of Women*, p. 41.

39. Miller, *Toward a New Psychology of Women*, p. 72; emphasis in the text.

40. Miller, *Toward a New Psychology of Women*, p. 83; emphasis in the text.

41. See Works in Progress papers, available from the Stone Center Publications, Wellesley College, 106 Central Street, Wellesley, MA 02181-8259. For information on clinical training, contact the Jean Baker Miller Training Institute (JBMTI) at the same address or through the JBMTI Web site: www.wellesley.edu/JBMTI.

Growth in Connection and *Women's Growth in Diversity.*[42] These writings evolved primarily out of the clash between traditional therapeutic explanations and the experiences of clinicians in the privacy of therapeutic sessions. In their faithfulness to a collaborative process of intellectual exchange and encouragement at the Stone Center, the publications embody one of the main premises of connectivity of selfhood. Many of the ideas presented are said to have developed in community and are not attributed to any sole individual.

In this second wave of research, Miller, the first director of the Stone Center, and a growing number of other scholars at the Center, such as Judith Jordan, Alexandra G. Kaplan, Irene P. Stiver, and Janet L. Surrey, formalized the original interpersonal theory of *Toward a New Psychology of Women* into an approach now known as "self-in-relation theory," the "relational self" or the "Stone Center model" of development. While these titles stress the distinctive emphasis on relationship in this approach, they fail to acknowledge the extent to which this approach picked up and amplified ideas of others. Their contention that development proceeds not necessarily through stages of increasing distance, mastery, and independence but through increasing sophistication in relationship coincided with pioneering research by Daniel Stern, Gilligan, Chodorow, and self-psychological theorists.[43] By the time Jordan proclaims in 1997 that "we are suggesting a major paradigm shift in all of Western psychology . . . from a psychology of the separate self to a psychology of relational being," her assertion seems dated.[44] The shift is well underway by this time.

For this reason, and perhaps because the Center focuses on one primary theme and often replicates work done elsewhere, the Stone Center approach sometimes seems the least innovative and exciting of those in feminist studies in psychology. The introductions to both collections re-

42. Judith V. Jordan et al., *Women's Growth in Connection: Writings from the Stone Center* (New York: Guilford Press, 1991); *Women's Growth in Diversity: More Writings from the Stone Center,* ed. Judith V. Jordan (New York: Guilford Press, 1997). See also Jean Baker Miller and Irene Pierce Stiver, *The Healing Connection: How Women Form Relationships in Therapy and in Life* (Boston: Beacon Press, 1997).

43. See, for example, Daniel Stern, *The Interpersonal World of the Infant* (New York: Basic Books, 1986); Carol Gilligan, *In a Different Voice: Psychological Theory and Women's Development* (Cambridge: Harvard University Press, 1982); Chodorow, *The Reproduction of Mothering;* and Heinz Kohut, *How Does Analysis Cure?* (Chicago: University of Chicago Press, 1984).

44. Jordan, "Introduction," in *Women's Growth in Diversity,* ed. Jordan, p. 3.

peatedly state the in-process character of their claims. While this stance affirms a common postmodern caution about truth claims, it also leads to a weakened theoretical framework.

Chodorow identifies several key differences between object-relations feminists and interpersonal feminists. The latter have less interest in the inner object world, internalizations, unconscious desires and conflicts, and the early infantile and pre-Oedipal period, except as these influence relational dynamics — for example, between mother and daughter.[45] Interest lies instead in the investigation of interpersonal and social experience. Second, self-in-relation theorists adopt a more extreme gynocentric, woman-centered, or separate spheres position, focusing primarily on female psychology and displaying, almost without exception, a disregard for or disinterest in male psychology.[46] Essays focus on the mother-daughter relationship, women's anger, depression, empowerment, and sexuality, women's work inhibitions and eating patterns, late adolescent girls, minority women, lesbian relationships, and lesbians and their mothers. For the most part, perhaps as part of the original desire to reclaim devalued attributes, girls and women seem to be depicted as psychologically and developmentally healthier than boys and men. Comments on male development often enter the picture only as a foil or contrast to women.

Object-relations theorists more readily acknowledge the conflictual nature of all psychic life, including female development. Women's relationality has its own dangers of self-loss and self-demise. The close identification between mother and daughter can lead to psychological enmeshment and confusion, with the mother intolerant of her daughter's neediness (since she herself has had to learn to curtail her own desires) and the daughter losing a sense of what she wants. Merger with the mother can result in failure to achieve a sense of self-worth, self-entitlement, and separateness.[47]

45. See Irene P. Stiver, "Beyond the Oedipus Complex: Mothers and Daughters," in *Women's Growth in Connection*, pp. 97-121.

46. See Irene P. Stiver, "The Meanings of 'Dependency' in Female-Male Relationships," in *Women's Growth in Connection*, pp. 143-61; and Stephen J. Bergman and Janet L. Surrey, "The Woman-Man Relationship: Impasses and Possibilities," in *Women's Growth in Diversity*, ed. Jordan.

47. See Eichenbaum and Orbach, *Understanding Women*, chapter 2: "The Construction of Femininity."

Developmental Theory

All the theorists thus far suggest new ways of understanding human development. Gilligan, however, has a particular interest in developmental theory. A Harvard-educated clinical psychologist and later a Harvard professor of education, she returns to a nagging question about the role of gender in psychological maturation and women's absence from landmark developmental studies. Essentially, she broadens the focus from emotional to moral development and significantly undermines the widely accepted cognitive psychologies of Lawrence Kohlberg and, indirectly, Jean Piaget, and the life-cycle theories of Erikson and others. Influenced by Miller and Chodorow, her contribution centers on reclaiming women's voices and suggesting another line of development focused on relational concerns and care. Two important articles, appearing in *Harvard Educational Review* in 1977 and 1979, set the stage for *In a Different Voice,* a book published in 1982 that sold more than 360,000 copies by 1990.[48]

According to Gilligan, moral theory has mislabeled women's relational priorities derogatorily as deviations from a male norm, thereby losing sight of a critical line of development for both men and women: the development of intimacy, relationships, and care. When Kohlberg found girls and women more focused at a lower level of moral development centered on relationships, he was measuring women's development against a male standard. His theory prizes abstract reasoning as the superior moral position and labels negatively decisions based on relationships as a lower stage of moral intelligence. Based on interview responses to ethical dilemmas, Gilligan persuasively argues that moral deliberation about relational connections requires comparably sophisticated reasoning of a different sort.

Although Gilligan largely ignores social and political influences on morality, she draws on empirical research into women's perspectives on moral dilemmas to propose a reconception of moral development that recognizes for both sexes the importance throughout life of the connection between self and other. In rough terms, she outlines a three-stage movement in the development of an ethic of care from an initial focus on caring for the self in order to survive, to caring for others at the sacrifice of

48. Carol Gilligan, "In a Different Voice: Women's Conceptions of the Self and Morality," *Harvard Educational Review* 47 (1977): 481-518; "Woman's Place in Man's Life Cycle," *Harvard Educational Review* 49 (1979): 431-44; and *In a Different Voice.*

the self, to a third perspective in which "a new understanding of the interconnection between other and self" occurs.[49] In optimal adult moral development, an ethic of relationality overcomes the stark alternatives of
egoism and self-sacrifice. The most advanced moral self is neither egoisti-
cally concerned for itself nor lost in its concern for the other. Rather, the
moral imperative is "to act responsibly toward self and others and thus to
sustain connection."[50] To move to this more integrated stage of moral development that recognizes the mutual interdependency of self and other,
women often require powerful experiences of choice, such as meaningful
productive work or authority in reproductive decisions, to offset their pro-
pensity toward self-loss. Men need pivotal experiences of intimacy, such as
responsibility for the minutiae of daily child-care or acute sensitivity to a
partner's needs, to offset tendencies toward self-isolation.

Gilligan's initial research, like Miller's, has spawned waves of further
investigation. An edited collection, *Mapping the Moral Domain,* simply carries Gilligan's hypotheses about the gender-defined orientations of care and
justice in different directions.[51] Other more novel work has been under-
taken through the Harvard Project on the Psychology of Women and the
Development of Girls, founded in 1983. *Making Connections,* another collection of essays, contains innovative ideas grounded in a five-year study of
students at a private girls' school. Based on observations that morally articulate pre-adolescents become apologetic, hesitant teenagers, these studies
document ways in which girls "go underground" by age fifteen or sixteen in
response to cultural strictures that send them a message about their precarious position as women. This book was the first in a series of studies designed to "connect a psychology of women with girls' voices."[52] In the 1990s,
two more volumes have appeared, carrying the exploration of adolescent
girls further and bringing in other factors, such as race.[53]

---

49. Gilligan, *In a Different Voice,* p. 74. Earlier versions of Chapters 1 and 3 appeared
first in the *Harvard Educational Review.*

50. Gilligan, *In a Different Voice,* pp. 21, 149.

51. *Mapping the Moral Domain: A Contribution of Women's Thinking to Psychological
Theory and Education,* ed. Carol Gilligan, Janie Victoria Ward, and Jill McLean Taylor (Cambridge, Mass.: Harvard University Press, 1988).

52. Carol Gilligan, "Teaching Shakespeare's Sister: Notes from the Underground of
Female Adolescence," in *Making the Connections: The Relational Worlds of Adolescent Girls at
Emma Willard School,* ed. Carol Gilligan, Nona P. Lyons, and T. J. Hanmer (Cambridge,
Mass.: Harvard University Press, 1989), p. xiii.

53. See Lyn Mikel Brown and Carol Gilligan, *Meeting at the Crossroads: Women's Psy-*

A closely related project on development, education, and knowledge appeared in 1986. Building upon Gilligan and William Perry's theories of epistemological development, four women in the field of psychology — Mary Field Belenky, Blythe McVicker Clinchy, Nancy Rule Goldberger, and Jill Mattuck Tarule — spent five years interviewing 133 women in a variety of educational institutions. Not only do women define themselves relationally, they conclude, but the very ways that they learn differ significantly from male-defined epistemologies and conventional educational practice. Using the metaphor of voice as a unifying theme, they identify "five different perspectives" in women's engagement with knowledge, truth, and authority. While they claim that they do not intend these perspectives as developmental stages, the perspectives do represent a hierarchy of maturity and of complexity of thought. Women often move from phases of "silence" to "received" and "subjective knowledge" to modalities of "procedural" and "constructed knowledge" in which an integrated self participates in the creation of knowledge.[54]

The publication of *In a Different Voice* also led to a wide-ranging debate over the ethics of care, the ethics of justice, and their genderized connections in a host of other disciplines, such as social work, theology, and philosophy.[55] Theological ethicist Cynthia Crysdale helpfully divides responses to Gilligan's work into three categories: debate about empirical studies of moral orientation, debate about implications for moral philosophy, and feminist debate about dangers of relationality.[56]

Certainly one of the difficult issues for feminist studies is the rather apolitical cast of much of Gilligan's work and her reduction of differences

---

chology and Girls' Development (New York: Ballantine Books, 1993); Jill McLean Taylor, Carol Gilligan, and Amy M. Sullivan, *Between Voice and Silence: Women and Girls, Race and Relationship* (Cambridge, Mass.: Harvard/Belknap Press, 1996). Some of Gilligan's ideas have been more sensationally presented and publicly received through the work of Mary Pipher, *Reviving Ophelia: Saving the Selves of Adolescent Girls* (New York: Ballantine Books, 1994).

54. Mary Field Belenky et al., *Women's Ways of Knowing: The Development of Self, Voice, and Mind* (New York: Basic Books, 1986).

55. See, for example, *Women and Moral Theory,* ed. Eva F. Kittay and Diana T. Meyers (Totowa, N.J.: Rowman & Littlefield, 1987); and Susan J. Hekman, *Moral Voices, Moral Selves: Carol Gilligan and Feminist Moral Theory* (University Park: Pennsylvania State University Press, 1995). See also two journals that devoted issues to Gilligan's work in the 1980s: *Social Research* 50, no. 3 (1983) and *Signs: Journal of Women in Culture and Society* 11 (1986).

56. Cynthia Crysdale, "Gilligan and the Ethics of Care: An Update," *Religious Studies Review* 20, no. 1 (January 1994): 21-28. The review includes an extensive bibliography.

to gender.[57] Her advocacy of women's different voices left her open to criticism that she ignores the hazards of female socialization to care for others. She also displays a rather blind confidence that eventually over the life cycle, with the right kinds of provocation, female and male paths of development will complement one another. Finally, many scholars have accused Gilligan of an essentializing tendency in the naming of female traits. In her defense, she says she is astonished that she has been so "consistently misread." Care does not mean being "nice," nor is it defined only by gender; it is a radical ethic of mutuality or responsibility for oneself and others.[58]

Family Therapy and Theory

Like the women in psychoanalytic, developmental, and relational feminist circles in the 1970s, women in family therapy were also restless and active. In 1977, Peggy Papp, Olga Silverstein, Marianne Walters, and Betty Carter held their first meeting on the subject of "Women as Family Therapists" and constituted the Women's Project in Family Therapy.[59] Contrary to their expectation of a small attendance the next year, an audience of over 400 confirmed the importance of their work. This coincided with the publication of a groundbreaking article by Rachel Hare-Mustin, "A Feminist Approach to Family Therapy," in the journal *Family Process*.[60] In 1984, Monica McGoldrick, Carol M. Anderson, and Froma Walsh spearheaded the first major conference of family therapists with feminist interests and edited one of the best-known volumes on gender in family therapy, *Women in Families: A Framework for Family Therapy*, published in 1989. Several single-authored books also appeared in the 1980s as well.[61]

57. See Joan C. Tronto, "Beyond Gender Difference to a Theory of Care," *Signs: Journal of Women in Culture and Society* 12 (1987): 644-63; Ruth L. Smith, "Moral Transcendence and Moral Space in the Historical Experiences of Women," *Journal of Feminist Studies in Religion* 4 (1988): 21-37; J. Auerback, V. Blunt, and C. Williams, "Commentary on Gilligan's 'In a Different Voice,'" *Feminist Studies* 11 (1985): 149-61.

58. Prose, "Confident at 11, Confused at 16," pp. 38, 40.

59. Betty Carter, "Foreword," in *Women in Families: A Framework for Family Therapy*, ed. Monica McGoldrick et al. (New York: W. W. Norton, 1989).

60. Rachel Hare-Mustin, "A Feminist Approach to Family Therapy," *Family Process* 17 (1978): 181-94.

61. See Thelma Jean Goodrich, Cheryl Rampage, Barbara Ellman, and Kris Halstead, *Feminist Family Therapy: A Casebook* (New York: W. W. Norton, 1988); Harriet Lerner, *The Dance of Anger: A Woman's Guide to Changing the Patterns of Intimate Relationships* (New

These publications often build upon the massive literature on women produced in other areas in the 1970s. Different from the movements investigated above, many scholars have contributed, and no single pivotal scholar rises to the top. Hence, in this and the next section I will focus on a major edited collection rather than on any single theorist as representative of the discussion's breadth.

McGoldrick, Anderson, and Walsh identify Virginia Satir as the only widely recognized female voice among prominent family therapists until the 1970s. The first director of the Mental Research Institute, home of the brief therapy model, Satir used an experiential approach centered on feelings, intuition, and growth. While not overtly feminist, she sometimes represented a dissenting or different voice. Morris Taggart, however, reminds us that the *"founding mothers* of family therapy" do exist (Mary Richmond, Charlotte Towle, Emily H. Mudd), but they have been "largely ignored and consequently have fallen into oblivion."[62] In fact, women may have been more instrumental in the evolution of the new field of family therapy than in other therapeutic modalities. In general, *Women in Families* makes a good case that highlighting gender as a significant category of analysis is a natural next step in systems theory. Or, said inversely, "To ignore gender is, in fact, nonsystemic."[63]

Yet, oddly and sadly, major models of family therapy, such as the structural model of Minuchin or the Bowen method, have not attended to the power differentials between women and men in families. Indeed, these models have sometimes perpetuated sexist patterns. The Bowen Scale of Differentiation of Self, for example, rates "relatedness," "seeking love and approval," and "being-for-others" as characteristics of the poorly differentiated person, and "autonomous," "being-for-self," and

---

York: Harper & Row, 1985), *Women in Therapy* (London: Aronson, 1988), and *The Dance of Intimacy* (New York: Harper & Row, 1989); Debra Luepnitz, *The Family Interpreted* (New York: Basic Books, 1988); and Marianne Walters, Betty Carter, Peggy Papp, and Olga Silverstein, *The Invisible Web: Gender Patterns in Family Relationships* (New York: Guilford Press, 1988). The first edited collection was *Women and Family Therapy*, ed. Marianne Ault-Riche (Rockville, Md.: Aspen Systems Corporation, 1986), followed by *A Guide to Feminist Family Therapy*, ed. Lois Braverman (New York and London: Harrington Park Press, 1988), simultaneously issued by The Haworth Press under the title "Women, Feminism, and Family Therapy," *Journal of Psychotherapy and the Family* 3, no. 4 (Winter 1987).

62. Morris Taggart, "Epistemological Equality as the Fulfillment of Family Therapy," in *Women in Families*, ed. McGoldrick et al., pp. 102-3.

63. Froma Walsh and Michele Scheinkman, "(Fe)male: The Hidden Gender Dimension in Models of Family Therapy," in *Women in Families*, ed. McGoldrick et al., pp. 16-17.

"goal-directed" as healthy functioning.[64] Systems theory mechanistically establishes the rules of family functioning divorced from social, economic, and political factors. Lois Braverman believes that a fundamental reason that women themselves had their heads "buried in the sand" is the epistemological challenge of feminist theory. Acknowledging the impact of patriarchy threatens a major family therapy assumption that men and women are equal participants in family interactions and that marriage is only an interactional scene and not a political institution. Feminist theory challenges the viability of patriarchal families and hence of family therapy.

Still, for the most part the authors in *Women in Families* do not reject the family therapy movement itself. Instead, they demand a more politically sensitive and gender-informed family approach. Most important, the perception of gender as a "special issue" rather than a fundamental category deserves critique. Family systems theory cannot assume a gender-blind position when in reality women traditionally occupy a "one-down" position in families and in larger social systems.

Rather than assuming that all family members are interchangeable parts with equal control within the interaction of a family system, therapists must acknowledge the unequal division of power both within and beyond the confines of the home. In working with a couple in marital conflict, a therapist, for example, must consider such factors as economic dependency or the secondary status of a woman's life plans and personal goals in the family interaction. As Harriet Lerner notes, therapists must notice genderized patterns in families, such as the typical tendency of women toward "underfunctioning for the self while overfunctioning for others."[65] On the whole, *Women in Families* raises an ultimatum on par with those stated at the beginning of this essay:

> A therapist who fails to respond to a family's presentation of their problems with a framework that takes into account the inequities of the culture, and who attempts to maintain a so-called "neutrality" vis-à-vis the family, is necessarily doing sexist family therapy. . . . If the field cannot move to integrate current and developing information about gender and its impact, if it regards such criticism as simply rep-

64. Froma Walsh and Michele Scheinkman, "(Fe)male," p. 34. See M. Bowen, *Family Therapy in Clinical Practice* (New York: Jason Aronson, 1978).

65. Lerner, *Women in Therapy*, p. 153.

resenting only a few radical women, then none of us, male and female, will develop our abilities to the fullest.[66]

Ethnicity, Women, and Psychological Theory

As has become increasingly clear, gender is not the only critical category influencing self and knowledge. In the late 1980s and the 1990s, various psychoanalytic, self-in-relation, developmental, and family systems theorists all began to attend to the relevance of race and ethnicity in psychological theory and therapeutic practice.[67] In a variety of organizations such as the Feminist Therapy Institute, women of color called feminist psychology "on its racism and said 'Enough!'"[68]

Attention to race and ethnicity in psychology has not come about easily. Psychology is often seen as part of a medical world associated with the European-American middle class. At various times, modern medicine and psychology exemplified some of the racist prejudices of society at large. As a result, many people of color have had little, if any, confidence in either medical or psychological expertise on pathology and cure. Psychological analysis, with its focus on individuals and intrapsychic dynamics, seems to blame the victim and, sometimes worse, the victim's mother or the victim's ex-

66. McGoldrick et al., *Women in Families*, p. 13.

67. In psychoanalysis, see, for example, *Diversity and Complexity in Feminist Therapy*, ed. Laura S. Brown and Maria P. P. Root (New York: Haworth Press, 1999); *Female Subjects in Black and White: Race, Psychoanalysis, and Feminism*, ed. Elizabeth Abel, Barbara Christian, and Helene Moslem (Berkeley and Los Angeles: University of California Press, 1997); and Elizabeth Abel, "Race, Class, and Psychoanalysis? Opening Questions," in *Conflicts in Feminism*, ed. Marianne Hirsch and Evelyn Fox Keller (New York: Routledge, 1990), pp. 184-204. On self-in-relation theory, see *Women's Growth in Diversity*, ed. Jordan. In developmental theory, see Taylor, Gilligan, and Sullivan, *Between Voice and Silence*. In family therapy, see Monica McGoldrick, Nydia Garcia-Preto, Paulette Moore Hines, and Evelyn Lee, "Ethnicity and Women," in *Women in Families*, ed. McGoldrick et al., pp. 169-99; and Nancy Boyd-Franklin, "Recurrent Themes in the Treatment of African-American Women in Group Psychotherapy," *Women and Therapy* 11 (1991): 25-40. Other important books by feminist scholars on race and therapy more generally include Nancy Boyd-Franklin, *Black Families in Therapy: A Multisystems Approach* (New York: Guilford Press, 1989); Monica McGoldrick, John K. Pearce, and Joseph Giordano, *Ethnicity and Family Therapy* (New York and London: Guilford Press, 1982); and Elaine Pinderhughes, *Understanding Race, Ethnicity, and Power: The Key to Efficacy in Clinical Practice* (New York: Free Press, 1989).

68. Laura Brown, "Editorial Introduction," in *Diversity and Complexity in Feminist Therapy*, ed. Brown and Root.

tended family. In many ways, much of modern psychology has functioned as a rather elaborate ethnography of the white Western psyche.[69]

Publication of *Women of Color,* a collection co-edited by Lillian Comas-Díaz and Beverly Greene, represents a pioneering effort to integrate reflection on gender and ethnicity into mental health understandings and treatment of women. It is organized into three sections. The first explores the heterogeneity of women of color, with chapters on women who are African American, American Indian, Asian and Asian American, West Indian, and Latina. The second section evaluates a variety of theoretical and clinical frameworks for therapy, such as family therapy and psychodynamic approaches, and the final section treats special issues, such as mixed-race women, lesbian women of color, violence, and work. Throughout, the authors counter the tendency to subordinate race to gender. Comas-Díaz and Greene contend that failure to recognize the "combined influence and impact of racial and gender parameters can seriously compromise the effectiveness of mental health treatment."[70] In arbitrating multiple oppressive factors in their family and work lives, women of color find themselves in "double jeopardy."

Although not a psychologist, bell hooks argues that African-American women need both psychological self-actualization and political involvement, given patriarchy and racism. "We cannot," she contends, "create effective movements for social change if individuals struggling for that change are not also self-actualized."[71] Much like Miller, Gilligan, and others in feminist studies in religion, hooks argues that to move "ourselves from manipulable objects to self-empowered subjects," women of color must break with the ways "our reality is defined and shaped by the dominant culture" and assert "our understanding of that reality, of our own experience."[72] In her understanding of suffering and healing, she nicely combines a receptivity to psychology, self-help, and therapy, a view of self-actualization of oppressed groups as a political activity or "libera-

---

69. Elizabeth Abel, Barbara Christian, and Helene Moglen, "Introduction: The Dream of a Common Language," in *Female Subjects in Black and White,* ed. Abel et al., p. 1.

70. Lillian Comas-Díaz and Beverly Greene, "Overview: Gender and Ethnicity in the Healing Process," in *Women of Color: Integrating Ethnic and Gender Identities in Psychotherapy,* ed. Lillian Comas-Díaz and Beverly Greene (New York and London: Guilford Press, 1994), p. 187.

71. bell hooks, *Sisters of the Yam: Black Women and Self-Recovery* (Boston: South End Press, 1993), pp. 4-5.

72. hooks, *Sisters of the Yam,* pp. 1-2; see also pp. 9, 80-81.

tory political practice," and a sensitivity to the wisdom of the elders, the movement of the spirit, and the resources of religious traditions and communities. A first step in healing is breaking the silence and telling the stories of suffering, not unlike both the therapeutic talking cure and old traditions of storytelling.

Implications

What are some of the implications of this expanding body of literature for practical theology? This, of course, is a huge question that could conceivably occupy an entire article itself. Nonetheless, classic works of feminist scholars in psychology have dramatically and definitively reshaped thinking on women and men in several ways that must now be taken into account in all reflection on theological anthropology and religious practice. Beyond the specific achievements of particular schools of thought and individuals and by way of conclusion, it is worth listing a few of the more general contributions.

First and foremost, feminist theorists question biological and psychological determinism and bring to psychological theory and practical theology a serious exploration of the social construction of gender.[73] As is clear in the brief quotes from Freud, Erikson, and Bettelheim, early theorists in psychology made little distinction between sex and gender. The distinction arose in feminist theory as a way to depict the social and historical evolution of sex roles and categories. Feminist theorists in psychology emphasize the enormous plasticity of human sexuality from group to group and culture to culture, and the multiple ways in which social expectation and social contexts determine human behavior and personality. Gender and sexual differences are not absolute and irreducible. Time and place produce gender. The social, political, and economic context play an undeniable role in human pathology, and hence must receive serious consideration in any genuine therapeutic intervention.

Second, feminist studies in psychology uncover the genderized nature of family conflicts and the problems of sexual inequality in families. Simply put, not only is gender constructed, but the construction of gender is problematized. So also are sexual identity and desire. As Chodorow says

---

73. Many have, of course, turned to Michel Foucault, *The History of Sexuality, Volume I: An Introduction* (New York: Pantheon Books, 1978).

so well, "As long as women must live through their children, and men do not . . . provide easily accessible role models," the cycle of female devaluation will continue to the next generation and "neither boys nor girls [will] attain stable identity and meaningful roles."[74] Based on such assessments, many theorists argue for the centrality of an equal division of power and labor in families for healthy human development and family life. Theorists make not just an academic but a political case for significantly increased male parental involvement. In analogous fashion, women, particularly mothers, must have a valued role in families and, moreover, a clear sphere of public influence and legitimate social control that lies beyond intimate and family responsibilities and relationships.

Third, feminist psychologists identify ways in which female development of relationally grounded thinking and acting has been labeled "pathological" when judged according to male norms of adult development. Previously devalued personality attributes, such as dependence and sensitivity, are reclaimed as essential for full human development. Some schools, such as psychoanalytic feminism and self-in-relation feminism, actually stand previous theory on its head. These schools revalorize female development in connectivity while pointing out the problems of male development in opposition to the other, particularly the mother. Scholars, such as Gilligan, hope to make development a more complex and nuanced process, implying the validity of multiple lines of development. Moreover, many theorists advocate a fundamental revaluing of female subjectivity, including maternal subjectivity. They argue for psychological analysis of the mother as a subject and not just as an object in relation to the needs of the child.

Fourth, and related to this last point, feminist theorists advance a woman-centered critique of the individualism and solipsism of psychodynamic therapy and theory. Selfhood is fundamentally reconceived in more complex relational terms. Developmentally, infants do not begin life in a completely merged stage of symbiosis with a primary parent. Rather, selfhood is fundamentally intersubjective and fluid. Human development includes the maturation of other kinds of qualities, including connection, affectivity, endurance, and relationality. Autonomy depends on interconnection and differentiation rather than on complete independence and self-sufficiency. Therapy cannot focus on the individual alone. Neurosis and pathology do not evolve from genital conflict or intrapsychic dynam-

74. Chodorow, *Feminism and Psychoanalytic Theory,* p. 44.

ics alone. Rather, they evolve in the midst of problems of cultural valuation. The focus is on the experience of self with others and on critical social influences.

Fifth, feminist studies in psychology confirm the importance of psychology for theological scholarship in practical theology, particularly research focused on questions of theological anthropology, human nature, and fulfillment. In the first edited book on women and pastoral care, Maxine Glaz worried about the haste with which contemporary pastoral theologians were writing off psychology in their rush to become more theological.[75] Despite the contemporary movement away from psychology in practical theology, psychology remains essential to adequate understandings of human nature. Despite popular cultural stereotypes of psychology as a handmaiden to individualism, psychology has itself promoted relational and social understandings of selfhood and society. Despite early radical feminist condemnation of psychology as inherently oppressive, psychology has a primary place in understanding sexual oppression. As Chodorow contends, psychological theory "describes a significant level of relation that is not reducible to . . . social or cultural organization" and "is constitutive and determinative of human life."[76] Psychoanalytic feminists in particular argue convincingly that understanding the cultural construction of gender requires exploration of the power of the unconscious in sexual desire and formation. One must understand how fantasies and social realities interact. Psychology offers a means to understand the dynamics of patriarchy, even if it does not provide a fully adequate strategy for broader social transformations.[77]

Finally, feminist studies also help situate the science of psychology in its historical and political context and have made important contributions to the moral evaluation of psychology. Mitchell, for example, historicizes psychoanalysis; penis envy is not a theory for all people in all times and places, but embodies the height of a capitalistic, patriarchal edifice. Psychology, as Susan Sturdivant declared in 1980, is more a value-loaded philosophy than an objective science. Social and political beliefs have colored the questions raised and the answers given by scientific theories on the needs and abilities of women and men. If psychology is "related as much

75. Maxine Glaz, "A New Pastoral Understanding of Women," in *Women in Travail and Transition: A New Pastoral Care*, ed. Maxine Glaz and Jeanne Stevenson-Moessner (Minneapolis: Fortress Press, 1991), pp. 12, 29.

76. Chodorow, *Feminism and Psychoanalytic Theory*, p. 7.

77. Sprengnether, *The Spectral Mother*, p. 8.

to what we *believe* about people as to what we *know* about them,"[78] its claims about women and men deserve sustained critical moral and cultural analysis.

In the end, if the measure of the most mature adult rests on male standards based on the study of men, women's reality disappears, and women appear deficient. If one-half of the population is omitted from psychological and theological research on human well-being and sexuality, people will not be able to see the whole picture. If, however, clinicians and scholars attend to feminist studies in psychology, we may see human life anew.

78. Susan Sturdivant, *Therapy with Women: A Feminist Philosophy of Treatment* (New York: Springer, 1980), p. 4; emphasis in the text.

CHAPTER 12

Pastoral Theology and the Future of Religion and Psychological Studies

BACKGROUND AND INTRODUCTION

It seems fitting that this book end with definition, diagram, and words about the future of religion and psychological studies. One such paragraph comes near the beginning of the chapter:

> *Psychology* appears in at least two prominent ways [in pastoral theology]: as a tool for the enhancement of the faithful care of others and as a cultural force that shapes moral ideals and spiritual hopes and hence requires critical evaluation. *Religion* is also seen differently [by pastoral theology]: it is not simply an object of study but also a body of beliefs and practices about ultimate and mystical dimensions of life to be encountered, experienced, tried, and perhaps followed. *Theology* is the contemplation and testing of this endeavor of religious encounter and trial (emphasis added).

These are not formal or final definitions by any means. They are definitions specific to pastoral theology. For pastoral theologians, psychology is both a tool to be used and a creator of culture to be evaluated and influenced. Religion is a practice of life that includes experience of the holy,

This essay was originally published as "Shaping the Future of Religion and Psychology: Feminist Transformations in Pastoral Theology," in *Religion and Psychology: Mapping the Terrain,* ed. William B. Parsons and Diane Jonte-Pace (London and New York: Routledge, 2001), pp. 181-201. Used by permission.

perhaps even religious confession. This is also true for theology. Theology is not only cognitive or verbal knowledge of the divine; it also becomes available for understanding when those who perform it believe they have encountered the divine.

In a class on method in theology and the social sciences, I try to diagram the field of religion and psychological studies and its intersections with pastoral and practical theology. I have no problem drawing circles and lines of connections on the board. But students usually seem a bit lost in my multi-directional flow chart. As a kind of map key, I use books like *Religion and Psychology: Mapping the Terrain,* a valuable collection organized by Diane Jonte-Pace and William Parsons to assess the state of the field of religion and psychological studies, and *Pastoral Care and Counseling: Redefining the Paradigms,* Nancy Ramsay's edited update of the *Dictionary of Pastoral Care and Counseling.* The editor's introduction to *Religion and Psychology* provides a helpful portrait of different schools of thought. But it is clear that although they are familiar with undergraduate religious studies, they do not fully understand developments in pastoral and practical theology as well as they need to in order to ensure the vitality of the wider field.

Whereas most of the chapters so far came about as a result of solicitation, with this chapter, which appears in *Religion and Psychology,* I was asked but I also asked for it, so to speak. *Religion and Psychology* grew out of a panel at the American Academy of Religion (AAR) in 1997 designed to evaluate the prospects of sustaining the twentieth-century momentum of religion and psychological studies into the twenty-first century. At the session and in later conversation, I expressed frustration that an important voice was largely missing — scholars in pastoral theology. As I understand our shared history, the creation of doctoral programs in religion and psychology in major U.S. university divinity schools, such as the University of Chicago, Emory, and Vanderbilt, had as much to do with key *pastoral theologians,* such as Seward Hiltner, Charles Gerkin, and Wayne Oates, as with *psychologists of religion* in religious studies departments. These doctoral programs were as connected to seminary education as to undergraduate teaching. In essence, interest in the formation of Christian ministers allowed for the growth of doctoral programs in religion and psychological studies as a wider sphere of research and teaching.

This observation actually led to the heart of my argument in the chapter: Sustaining the complex relationships between pastoral theology in theological studies and psychology of religion in religious studies is critical to our future. We will rise or fall, or as I say in the chapter, "sink or swim" together. A second thesis follows from the first: Feminist pastoral theologians have an important role to play in insuring connection between the diverging specialties in the field of religion and psychology as a whole. I do not state this thesis clearly enough in the opening pages, but the chapter as a whole illustrates it.

This is the only chapter that touches on and tries to characterize the relationship between religious and theological studies. I should note that the division between them is less strident today than when I wrote the chapter. Postmodern recognition of the influence of power on knowledge, the contextual nature of truth, the impossibility of value-free study of religion, and the role of religious practice has continued to temper the tensions and led to fresh alliances.

This chapter also fits well at the end of the book because it circles back and adds material to rubrics in preceding chapters — the three phases of feminist pastoral literature, its five methodological moves, the three publics for which practical theologians write, the four new functions of pastoral care, and the subject matter of the web. In most cases, I expand and develop these ideas with the audience of those in the wider field of religion and psychological studies in mind. When I repeat the phases of feminist pastoral literature, for example, I spell them out in more detail with examples and explanations. Like the two preceding chapters on gender as a key category of analysis, this chapter also puts flesh on the bones of Chapter 9 that introduces the final section.

I also correct early arguments about the demise of the field and the silence of feminist scholarship within it, thus showing the evolving nature of my thought. I contend instead that crisis is a matter of perspective and women have shaped scholarship more than we realize. I now see other things that escaped me then. I am less confident today, for example, that the language of *first* and *second order* in this chapter clarifies adequately the different kinds of writing in pastoral theology. There are problems in opposing one body of knowledge as abstract and the other as concrete when, in fact, both represent certain cultures, languages, and practices that have complicated, interdependent relationships with one another. When I use *first order,* I mean writing that addresses care practices directly — what they look like and how one enhances them. *Second-order* writing takes a step back and considers the ideas that shape such practices. The distinction is fuzzy and maybe less useful than I once thought.

Ultimately, placing this chapter at the end makes sense because it is one of the more forward-looking chapters, even if not the most recent. Neither my essay nor the issue of *Religion and Psychology* in which it appeared have succeeded completely in shoring up doctoral programs in religion and psychological studies. But at least we have given our best effort to make the field's contributions apparent. This chapter has that purpose at its heart.

In an essay in *Religion and Psychology: Mapping the Terrain*, Diane Jonte-Pace argues that compared to the feminist advances in the "psychology *of* religion," feminist scholarship has had relatively little impact on the "psychology *and* religion" movement. The accuracy of her claim depends on how one understands the latter. Jonte-Pace is correct only if one employs a narrow definition of psychology and religion. While she is right to acknowledge the work still to be done in psychology and religion on the historical and cultural backgrounds of psychological theorists, I want to challenge and modify her claim that feminist scholarship has had little influence in the psychology and religion movement by characterizing the developments of the last two decades in pastoral and practical theology in the area of religion, psychology, and gender. An expanding body of literature in this domain should not be overlooked. This growth suggests interesting potential directions for the field's future evolution.

Defining the Field

In defining the field known as religion and psychological studies, scholars immediately run into problems. One of the easiest and perhaps clearest ways to delineate the field is unidirectionally — that is, as involving psychological attempts to understand religion. Of the various depictions, the "psychology of religion" definition is perhaps the simplest one. Given the academic climate of suspicion toward overt declarations of religious faith, it may also be the safest.

Scholars have had greater difficulty defining and defending the enterprise of "psychology and religion." The two-way interaction between psychology and theology as scholarly disciplines, therapy and pastoral intervention as practical endeavors, and psychoanalysis and religion as historical and cultural phenomena has made succinct outline of the field's agenda more complicated. It is in this second area that my interests lie — in the complex arena where secular science and faith-driven religious interpretation meet as analogous, albeit often divergent, partners in the scholarly enterprise of understanding human struggle, survival, and healing.

Scholars of psychology and religion include not only those interested in cultural and historical factors in the rise of psychology, as depicted by Jonte-Pace. From the beginning there have been others, such as Seward Hiltner and Paul Tillich, or more recently, Don Browning and Charles Gerkin, whose primary vocational identity remains theology and whose fundamental community often includes the congregation and related religious institutions. This offshoot might better be called the "psychology and *theology*" movement or psychology and theology "in dialogue." While interested in hermeneutical exploration of the foundations of psychology, these scholars see interpretation for the sheer sake of interpretation as an incomplete or arrested agenda. Instead, psychology is viewed as subordinate or propaedeutic to the aims of theological hermeneutics and religious practices. To a certain degree, psychology is employed in the service of shaping and preserving faithful, prophetic, caring religious practices and communities. The interest in psychology goes beyond psychological study of religious phenomena and cultural study of psychology to an understanding of psychology as an expansive, self-contained, culture-forming discipline, with a variety of theories besides psychoanalysis, and to therapy as a learned practice in its own right.

From this perspective, psychology appears in at least two prominent ways: as a tool for the enhancement of the faithful care of others, and as a cultural force that shapes moral ideals and spiritual hopes and hence requires critical evaluation. Religion is also seen differently: it is not simply an object of study but also a body of beliefs and practices about ultimate and mystical dimensions of life to be encountered, experienced, tried, and perhaps followed. Theology is the contemplation and testing of this endeavor of religious encounter and trial.

Recent History and the Future of the Field

As Freud himself contended, mapping the future requires remembering the past, not so that it may rule over us but so that we may respect it and hence steady its load. In the past two decades, scholars in the different areas of psychology of religion and psychology and religion have drifted apart, not only as a result of increased specialization and academic secularization but also as a corollary of current controversies over the place of religious studies in a free-standing university and the emerging, although controversial, distinction between religious and theological studies. Simply stated, religious studies asserts its validity as a university discipline by establishing itself over against the supposedly faith-driven biases of theological studies. Oddly enough, this gap widened alongside postmodern disclosure of the politically motivated prejudices behind the most objective scientific claims, a contention that would seem to weaken the so-called objectivity of religious studies. Nonetheless, the division persists in spite of the questionable claim that religious studies obtains a purer, less tainted rationality than theological studies.

Heightened divergence has also been a result of difference in location. Those in psychology *of* religion largely teach in universities and colleges. Those in psychology *and* religion often teach in seminaries and divinity schools. This division reflects the uncertainties of mainline Protestantism in an increasingly diverse society as well. Mainline Protestantism no longer defines mainstream U.S. culture or higher education as it did at the start of the twentieth century. At one time, the creation and sustenance of programs in religion and psychological studies depended in part on the financial and philosophical benevolence of mainline Protestant institutions and believers. With dwindling numbers and finances, this source of support carries less weight today.

Nonetheless, the two areas of psychology of religion and psychology and religion are historically intertwined. While distance and even defensiveness characterized relationships between psychiatry and religion during the heyday of the psychology of religion in the early part of the twentieth century, by mid-century, scholars and clinicians in both religion and psychology had entered into new phases of appropriation, affiliation, and critical assessment.[1] Such alliances helped strengthen the position of scholarly research and fostered the creation of doctoral programs in religion and psychology.

The success or failure of the field today and its survival as a whole, I would argue, rest on the ability to sustain the interconnections between

---

1. See E. Mansell Pattison, "Psychiatry and Religion Circa 1978: Analysis of a Decade, Part I," *Pastoral Psychology* 27, no. 1 (1978): 8-25, and "Psychiatry and Religion Circa 1978: Analysis of a Decade, Part II," *Pastoral Psychology* 27, no. 2 (1978): 119-41.

two otherwise largely distinct enterprises. In other words, wed initially in their attempts to make inroads into the academy, scholars in divergent branches shall sink or swim together. This strategic interdependence is particularly requisite in terms of sustaining strong doctoral programs, even if it is less pertinent for those who teach in professional schools or undergraduate programs. The associations between the areas have relevance in the latter two educational contexts as well, however. On college campuses, when young people arrive with particular faith experiences or alienated from specific religious communities, the connections between the scientific study of religion and theological debate can hardly be avoided. Inversely, seminaries ignore the contributions of reductionist studies of religion in the wider academy at their own intellectual risk.

I am more urgent about strategic interdependence in the context of this book, which continues a discussion begun by a panel on the future of the field at a 1997 American Academy of Religion (AAR) conference. The panel included only one person from a seminary context, and his paper contained a rather pessimistic forecast about the future of pastoral theology.[2] Another panelist was adamant about avoiding theology, ministry, and the quagmire of a "nonreductionist approach to religion" in which religion becomes more than a mere object of study.[3]

Granted, those in the field have good reason to be both pessimistic and cautious. Pastoral theology must continue to prove itself worthy of academic attention; and faith convictions can distort research. Nevertheless, these problems need not overshadow the importance of grappling with our stark differences, curious compatibilities, and contrasting contributions to the study of religion and psychology. We continue to have a good deal to learn from each other and to offer the academy at large. The panel discussion attracted an audience that included several divinity school and seminary faculty members, even though some pastoral theologians avoid the AAR entirely, ridiculing its ivory-tower pretensions and trivialities. Pastoral theologians need to become more willing to engage in the intellectual and political dealings of higher education; at the same time, the contributions of pastoral theology need to be taken more seriously by the academy.

2. Ian Evison, "The Dialogue between Psychology and Religion: Historical Considerations," presentation at the American Academy of Religion, 1997.

3. Susan Henking, "Religion and the Social Sciences: An Historical Perspective," presentation at the American Academy of Religion, 1997.

Scholars in religion and psychological studies would do well, then, to resist the centrifugal pull that spins us off in increasingly different directions. We would do well to stay our immediate biases against the specialized academic study of religion as an end in itself or, inversely, our biases against the incorporation of faith claims as a further aim shaping the scholarly vocation of religious study. For a variety of reasons, feminist scholars in religion and psychology may have the resources and the motivation to bridge the gap and soothe antagonisms between various branches of the field. By articulating the fresh parameters established through feminist scholarship in pastoral theology on both national and international levels,[4] I hope to further one of the goals identified in the introduction to *Religion and Psychology: Mapping the Terrain:* to challenge the segmentation currently dividing the field and to encourage awareness, communication, and even collaboration between participants in different areas. In the remainder of the chapter, I will draw on three recent research reviews of the state of feminist studies in pastoral theology and then will offer several observations about the nature of the contemporary transformations in religion, psychology, and gender and their implications for religion and psychological studies.

Developments in Feminist Scholarship in Pastoral Theology

Three essays by Kathleen Greider, Elaine Graham, and myself, each surveying the expansion of feminist theory and pastoral theology, have appeared in the last year. The fact that all three appeared in such a short span of time, with Greider's and my own in the same edited volume, and Graham's piece in an international journal but written after she took part in a panel responding to an earlier version of my essay, highlights several phenomena.[5]

---

4. While I speak specifically from a U.S. context, the international conversation on pastoral and practical theology has grown also. See, for example, *Liberating Faith Practices: Feminist Practical Theology in Context*, ed. Denise Ackermann and Riet Bons-Storm (Leuven, the Netherlands: Peeters, 1998); *Practical Theology: International Perspectives*, ed. Friedrich Schweitzer and Johannes van der Ven (New York: Peter Lang, 1999); and the Web site of the *International Journal of Practical Theology:* www.deGruyter.com/journals/ijpt.

5. *Feminist and Womanist Pastoral Theology*, ed. Bonnie J. Miller-McLemore and Brita L. Gill-Austern (Nashville: Abingdon Press, 1999); Elaine Graham, "From 'Terrible Silence' to 'Transforming Hope': The Impact of Feminist Theory on Practical Theology," *International Journal of Practical Theology* 6, no. 2 (1999): 185-212.

Scholars have reached a place where they believe they need to take stock of progress. A substantial body of feminist scholarship has accrued. Ultimately, distinct themes have arisen that point toward a shift in prominent models of study and practice in religion and psychology in the area of pastoral theology.

My own essay, "Feminist Theory in Pastoral Theology," was first delivered at a pre-session sponsored by the American Association of Practical Theology at the 1997 AAR and then revised for an edited book, *Feminist and Womanist Pastoral Theology.*[6] The book itself represents an attempt to attend to broader issues in the development and the future of the field. Although many of the authors have done other research on "first-order" matters of pastoral care and "second-order" use of psychology and theology to investigate women's experiences, this book's goal is to step back and offer "third-order" reflection on the methods and substance of the field.[7] More specifically, the collection articulates fresh directions resulting from the increased activity of feminist scholars:

> What does it mean that several significant edited collections in pastoral theology as well as single-authored volumes on numerous topics have appeared in the last decade, all done by feminist scholars? How will this influence pastoral ministry and care in congregations? And how will it shape theological schools and the academy of religion? Feminist work in pastoral theology is actually proceeding at a breakneck pace. . . . Pausing to consider what all this fresh activity means for the state of pastoral theology, care, and counseling, for congregations, and for the academy is absolutely requisite.[8]

The book identifies some of the major shifts in focus, subject, and method and their implications.

Until the past few years, I joined the crowd in lamenting the decline

---

6. Bonnie J. Miller-McLemore, "Feminist Theory in Pastoral Theology," the *Association of Practical Theology Occasional Papers* 2 (1998): 1-11; the revised version of this essay appeared in *Feminist and Womanist Pastoral Theology,* ed. Miller-McLemore and Gill-Austern.

7. See Theodore Jennings Jr., "Pastoral Theology Methodology," in *Dictionary of Pastoral Care and Counseling,* ed. R. Hunter (Nashville: Abingdon Press, 1990), p. 862, cited by Carrie Doehring in "A Method of Feminist Pastoral Theology," in *Feminist and Womanist Pastoral Theology,* ed. Miller-McLemore and Gill-Austern, p. 100.

8. Bonnie J. Miller-McLemore and Brita Gill-Austern, "Preface," in *Feminist and Womanist Pastoral Theology,* ed. Miller-McLemore and Gill-Austern, pp. 9-10.

of the field and the late arrival of feminist scholarship. On both counts, I have revised my thinking. In complaints on the demise of the field, I began to notice a pattern. Many of those worrying about the future of the "movement" are among the retiring generation who participated in the early rapid growth in the 1960s and 1970s but feel uneasy or slightly displaced by new developments. Addressing the Society for Pastoral Theology in 1994, James Lapsley identifies his fear that "pluralism and its advantages of inclusiveness . . . comes with [the] price" of conceptual incoherence and dismissal by the wider academy.[9] Liston Mills, Lapsley's close colleague, worries that next-generation pastoral theologians will misuse the increased responsibility that comes with the transition from an up-and-coming movement to an established discipline.[10]

Lapsley, Mills, and others, however, sometimes mistake change and difference for decline. The disturbing difference of the voices of women and minorities, the seemingly distracting fascination with inclusivity in the Society for Pastoral Theology, the dramatic decline in courses on counseling and the increase in courses on public policy, gender, and race, as well as spirituality, the move away from verbatims and role-play to other teaching tools, and the use of new feminist methods in research — all these changes have led to what I believe are false conclusions about the weakening of the field. The decline in the numbers of family therapy courses or even in the number of positions in the field (previously filled by white men) need not spell disaster.

In an important edited collection of international perspectives on practical theology, South African theologian Denise Ackermann and Dutch theologian Riet Bons-Storm complain that the "endless debates" at conferences about the identity of practical theology distract us from the "pressing concerns of practical theology in a world full of want."[11] There is an additional negative effect. Scholars who are anxious about their position and status in the academy "are not eager to let 'others' join them," because the "unfamiliar and the unexplored" seem to make the field even more precarious and vulnerable to dismissal and attack.[12]

But are such fears genuinely warranted? Might there be a less-than-

---

9. James Lapsley, "Remarks on a Panel at the Society for Pastoral Theology: Where We Have Been and Where We Are Going," *Journal of Pastoral Theology* 5 (1995): 502.

10. Liston Mills, "Background and Initiatives in Pastoral Care," unpublished panel remarks, the Society for Pastoral Theology, Denver, 17 June 1994.

11. *Liberating Faith Practices*, ed. Ackermann and Bons-Storm, p. 2.

12. *Liberating Faith Practices*, ed. Ackermann and Bons-Storm, p. 3.

benevolent association between doomsday forecasts of future demise and issues of gender? Is there an unhealthy relationship between predictions of decline and the arrival of the "other" on the scene?

The tendency to emphasize the generational lag in feminist scholarship in pastoral theology also needs reconsideration. In her recent article on the impact of feminist theory on the field, Graham concludes that feminist scholarship "only made an impression in the last ten years."[13] I have made similar observations a number of times over the past decade.[14] While perhaps this was an accurate claim in the early 1990s, I now believe these assessments to be dated and narrow. Patterns of feminist work need a more friendly reading, one that acknowledges the delays in scholarship caused by sexism and clericalism but also recognizes earlier contributions and applauds the progress made despite these impediments. While the 1990s do represent a distinct turning point, Graham's analysis is short-sighted with respect to prior developments and perhaps limited by her location in a British university.[15]

While I cannot judge well the evolution of feminist research in England, the so-called dearth of explicit reflection on feminism in pastoral theology in the United States needs to be characterized differently. Distinct patterns of growth have occurred. Over the past three decades, feminist pastoral theology has generated a steady body of literature with three projects in mind, somewhat analogous to Jonte-Pace's identification of moments of critique, analysis, and inclusivity in feminist scholarship: implicit critique of patriarchy; explicit critique and advocacy for women and other marginalized populations; and topical reconstruction.

---

13. Graham, "From 'Terrible Silence' to 'Transforming Hope,'" pp. 185, 193.

14. Bonnie Miller-McLemore, "The Human Web and the State of Pastoral Theology," *Christian Century*, 7 April 1993, p. 368; "The Living Human Web: Pastoral Theology at the Turn of the Century," in *Through the Eyes of Women: Insights for Pastoral Care*, ed. Jeanne Stevenson-Moessner (Minneapolis: Fortress Press, 1996), pp. 19-20; and "The Subject and Practice of Pastoral Theology as a Practical Theological Discipline: Pushing Past the Nagging Identity Crisis to the Poetics of Resistance," in *Liberating Faith Practices*, ed. Ackermann and Bons-Storm, pp. 5-6.

15. In an examination of the pastoral care literature in Europe and North America, Graham notes the deeply entrenched exclusion of women. See Elaine Graham, "The Pastoral Needs of Women," *Contact: The Interdisciplinary Journal of Pastoral Studies* 100 (1989): 23-25. See also Elaine Graham, "A View from a Room: Feminist Practical Theology from Academy, Kitchen, or Sanctuary?" in *Liberating Faith Practices*, ed. Ackermann and Bons-Storm; and Stephen Pattison, *Pastoral Care and Liberation Theology* (Cambridge: Cambridge University Press, 1994).

The first project — implicit critique and unrest — appears in the largely unpublished but compelling activities of women in the field, perhaps best exemplified by the work of Peggy Way and Sue Cardwell. Beginning in the 1960s and 1970s, Way mentored women in the field and used public speaking engagements to disturb the status quo on such subjects as violence in the family. She contested the conventional boundaries dictated by the study of religion and demanded that theology grapple with the particularities of suffering and the ecclesial context of care.[16] While most of Cardwell's publications focus on student success in theological education and ministry,[17] her own clinical and pedagogical expertise also functioned in an exemplary way for many women. Other, more recent texts focus on the experiences of women, assuming but not explicitly pursuing feminist and womanist theory and politics.[18] The primary agenda of this project is incorporating women's lives and voices into the traditions of practical theological reflection and practices of care.

In the first "official" book on women and pastoral care, *Women in Travail and Transition,* the critique of patriarchy, while still not overt, is woven between each line. Although the editors do not attempt to define feminist scholarship or require that individual authors identify with any particular feminist agenda, the book as a whole represents a "persistent methodological shift in that all contributors take seriously women's experiences, feelings, and formulations."[19] It includes chapters on such concerns as care of women in situations of violence and abuse, changes in women's roles and lifestyles, and women's bodily demands and needs. Emerging out of these subjects are a whole host of theological formulations to be com-

---

16. Peggy Ann Way, "An Authority of Possibility for Women in the Church," in *Women's Liberation and the Church: The New Demand for Freedom in the Life of the Christian Church,* ed. Sarah Bentley Doely (New York: Association Press, 1970); "Pastoral Excellence and Pastoral Theology: A Slight Shift of Paradigm and a Modest Polemic," *Pastoral Psychology* 29, no. 1 (1980): 46-57; and "Violence in the Family: A Theological Perspective," Disciples Lecture, Vanderbilt University, 1990.

17. See, for example, Sue Webb Cardwell, "Why Women Fail/Succeed in Ministry: Psychological Factors," *Pastoral Psychology* 30, no. 4 (1980): 153-62.

18. See Maxine Glaz and Jeanne Stevenson-Moessner, "Travail as Transition," in *Women in Travail and Transition: A New Pastoral Care,* ed. Maxine Glaz and Jeanne Stevenson-Moessner (Minneapolis: Fortress Press, 1991); *Womanist Care: How to Tend the Souls of Women,* ed. Linda Hollies (Joliet, Ill.: Woman to Woman Ministries Publications, 1992); *Life Cycles: Women and Pastoral Care,* ed. Elaine Graham and Margaret Halsey (Cambridge: SPCK, 1993).

19. Glaz and Stevenson-Moessner, "Travail as Transition," p. 195.

bated: the perception of woman as the source of evil or as temptress; the doctrine of original sin in which sin is communicated at conception; the deification of a Protestant work ethic that negates women's labor and jeopardizes children's lives; the double standards that deny female sexuality and bodily needs; doctrines that equate love with self-sacrifice and selfless suffering with godliness; rigid images of God as solely father or male; the institutional church's promotion of white male supremacy and an unquestioning stance toward religious authority; doctrines of condemnation that foster an immobilizing guilt; and complicity in condoning male domination, female submission, and the related violence in families. In a word, "unraveling the biblical injunction to love God, self, and neighbor in such a way that is not neurotic for women is surely a [critical] theological task."[20]

Criticism of psychology throughout this text focuses less on particular theories or classical theorists and more on the generic absorption of psychological "truths" in society and the church. One must combat psychological doctrines of female penis envy, masochism, the negative view of female dependency, and misrepresentations of women's development, and consider alternative theories that note "man's dread of women," "male fear and anxiety provoked by the mystery of motherhood," "envy of woman's essential creativity and centeredness in being," and women's experiences of connective selfhood.[21] In general, however, the authors make only a limited effort to construct an explicitly feminist theology and psychology. More important, perhaps, at this stage are their many pragmatic, programmatic suggestions that help clergy and counselors make a positive difference in women's lives.

The second project — explicit critique of the classic texts and theories of pastoral theology — has been more erratic but no less momentous. A constellation of articles by three different scholars — Christine Neuger, Carrie Doehring, and Nancy Ramsay — once again appears within the same year, marking an important historical moment.[22] All the articles be-

---

20. Glaz and Stevenson-Moessner, "Travail as Transition," p. 38.

21. Glaz and Stevenson-Moessner, "Travail as Transition," p. 38; and Bonnie J. Miller-McLemore, "Women Who Work and Love: Caught between Cultures," in *Women in Travail and Transition*, ed. Glaz and Stevenson-Moessner, pp. 75-79.

22. See also Valerie DeMarinis, *Critical Caring: A Feminist Model for Pastoral Psychology* (Louisville: Westminster John Knox Press, 1993); Christie Neuger, "A Feminist Perspective on Pastoral Counseling with Women," in *Clinical Handbook of Pastoral Counseling*, vol. 2, ed. Robert Wicks et al. (New York: Paulist Press, 1993); and Riet Bons-Storm, *The Incredible Woman: Listening to Women's Silences in Pastoral Care and Counseling* (Nashville: Abingdon Press, 1996).

gin with concise definitions of their feminist agenda. Ramsay asserts the demand to resist and transform "sexism and patriarchy toward an inclusive human community."[23] Doehring calls for "taking on the gods of patriarchy," those beliefs and structures that create "ecclesiastical, political, economic, and personal oppression for all peoples."[24] Neuger wastes little time on definitions, quickly claiming the "world in which women live" as her fundamental starting point and then moving right into a list of condemning statistics on oppression in all the areas that Doehring names in general.[25]

In all three essays, practical illustrations fill in the actualities and complexities of enacting this new approach to psychology and religion in the care of women. From case illustrations emerge fresh constructions of theological doctrines of God imagery, atonement, prevenient grace, community, Christology, and ultimately human empowerment — a prevalent theme in each essay. Conventional psychology and theology are considered limited and inept: as Neuger asserts, "I can rely on no personality theory or handbook of assessment" and no "adjustment oriented theological starting place" to understand adequately the fullness of women's lives and their plight. This means that in practice at least, if not in academic theory, "psychoanalytic, object relations, cognitive-behavioral, most forms of family systems, and humanistic [psychologies] must be held suspect" before the concreteness of lived experience.[26]

As in the first project, the primary goal in this body of literature remains pastoral and practical. For the most part, we find first-order language and scholarship describing practices of care. The focus in all three essays is on incorporating feminist theory into the clerical ministries of pastoral care and counseling. These and other texts in this second project suggest the importance of a hermeneutic of suspicion toward traditional scholarship and advocate active resistance to patriarchy. As in the introduction to *Through the Eyes of Women,* the overarching intent is to give "hope to women in the midst of despair."[27]

23. Nancy Ramsay, "Feminist Perspectives on Pastoral Care: Implications for Practice and Theory," *Pastoral Psychology* 40, no. 4 (1992): 245.

24. Carrie Doehring, "Developing Models of Feminist Pastoral Counseling," *Journal of Pastoral Care* 46, no. 1 (1992): 24.

25. Christie Neuger, "Feminist Pastoral Theology and Pastoral Counseling: A Work in Progress," *Journal of Pastoral Theology* 2 (1992): 37, 39-43.

26. Neuger, "Feminist Pastoral Theology and Pastoral Counseling," p. 49.

27. *Through the Eyes of Women,* ed. Stevenson-Moessner, p. 4; see also *The Arts of*

The third project — topical reconstruction — moves into second-order engagement in which the disciplines of psychology and theology are applied to specific subjects. Efforts in this area involve extensive engagement with particular thematic practices or topics, placing them within a broader panorama of psychological, cultural, and theological critique and reformulation. Several book-length treatments of important themes pertaining to women but also relevant to men and the field as a whole have appeared in just the last decade — books on poverty, self-esteem, anger, depression, aggression, violence, power dynamics in ministry, work and family life, loss in mid-life, and family.[28]

These are paradigmatic texts that have not yet received adequate attention as a significant body of literature in feminist theory, religion, and psychology. While diverse in specific focus, they establish a new example of pastoral theological method in religion and psychology unified by at least five elements: a cultural-political version of the revised correlational method; critical use of psychological and cultural resources; power analysis; explicit feminist positioning; and pastoral or transformative intent.

Drawing on Tillich, Hiltner, David Tracy, and others, these scholars understand the primary method in religion and psychology as involving the critical correlation of the Christian tradition and its contemporary reinterpretations with historical and contemporary cultural understandings, including psychology. In using this approach, however, feminist scholars in religion and psychology do not ignore its limits as a product of liberal

---

Ministry: Feminist-Womanist Approaches, ed. Christie Neuger (Louisville: Westminster John Knox Press, 1996).

28. Pamela D. Couture, *Blessed Are the Poor? Women's Poverty, Family Policy, and Practical Theology* (Nashville: Abingdon Press, 1991); Carroll Saussy, *God Images and Self-Esteem: Empowering Women in a Patriarchal Society* (Louisville: Westminster John Knox Press, 1991), and *The Gift of Anger: A Call to Faithful Action* (Louisville: Westminster John Knox Press, 1995); Susan Dunlap, *Counseling Depressed Women* (Louisville: Westminster John Knox Press, 1997); Kathleen Greider, *Reckoning with Aggression: Theology, Violence, and Vitality* (Louisville: Westminster John Knox Press, 1997); Pamela Cooper-White, *The Cry of Tamar: Violence against Women and the Church's Response* (Minneapolis: Fortress Press, 1995); Carrie Doehring, *Taking Care: Monitoring Power Dynamics and Relational Boundaries in Pastoral Care and Counseling* (Nashville: Abingdon Press, 1995); Bonnie J. Miller-McLemore, *Also a Mother: Work and Family as Theological Dilemma* (Nashville: Abingdon Press, 1994); Martha Robbins, *Midlife Women and Death of Mother: A Study of Psychohistorical and Spiritual Formation* (New York: Peter Lang, 1990); and Don S. Browning et al., *From Culture Wars to Common Ground: Religion and the American Family Debate* (Louisville: Westminster John Knox Press, 1997).

Christian theology. While feminist scholars in pastoral theology have not explicitly turned to "critical praxis" or "cultural-political" critiques of this method, such as those developed by Rebecca Chopp and Mark K. Taylor, they implicitly adopt many of their recommendations in unmasking the "compliancy of Christianity with . . . bourgeois existence" and speaking for the marginalized.[29] In other words, the two poles of tradition and experience are radically reformulated.

This reformation results in part from the other four elements — critical use of psychological and cultural resources; power analysis; explicit feminist positioning; and pastoral or transformative intent. First, psychology, while still foundational as an important cognate discipline, is now critiqued and supplemented by other disciplines in the social sciences. Theological analysis must grapple with the ways in which human agency and social systems co-constitute one another. Second, adequate analysis and understanding require attention to the dynamics, distribution, and distortions of power. Such analysis could occur from a number of vantage points, but in the case of this third project, the chosen position is feminist advocacy for women and women's experience as criteria of adequacy and truth.[30] Finally, the intent is empowerment and transformation through concrete pastoral practices.

This typology of the three partly sequential projects in religion, psychology, and gender still focuses primarily on the heyday of the 1990s. Kathleen Greider, Gloria Johnson, and Kristen Leslie also go back to the first published article by a self-identified woman pastoral theologian.[31] Then they trace a more complete trajectory of thirty years of feminist scholarship in the area of religion and psychology.[32] In terms of sheer numbers, they compile some interesting statistics:

29. Rebecca Chopp, "Practical Theology and Liberation," in *Formation and Reflection: The Promise of Practical Theology,* ed. Lewis S. Mudge and James Poling (Philadelphia: Fortress Press, 1987), p. 121. See also Rebecca Chopp, "When the Center Cannot Contain the Margins," in *The Education of the Practical Theologian: Responses to Joseph Hough and John Cobb's Christian Identity and Theological Education,* ed. Don S. Browning, David Polk, and Ian S. Evison (Atlanta: Scholars Press, 1989); and Mark Taylor, *Remembering Esperanza: A Cultural-Political Theology for North American Praxis* (Maryknoll, N.Y.: Orbis Books, 1990), pp. 26-28.

30. See Rosemary Radford Ruether, *Sexism and God-Talk: Toward a Feminist Theology* (Boston: Beacon Press, 1983).

31. See Peggy Ann Way, "What's Wrong with the Church: The Clergy," *Renewal* 3 (1963): 8-9.

32. Kathleen Greider, Gloria Johnson, and Kristen Leslie, "Three Decades of Women

From the 1960s through the late 1970s, books by women pastoral theologians were few in number — the majority of the literature and its impact is in journal articles. In the 1980s, the number of published books more than tripled. In the most recent period, 1990-97, the number of published books again nearly tripled. Women were barely represented in the academy at the beginning of the period and, for the first 17 years of the period under consideration, were rarely the authors of book-length publications. During the last 17 years, still statistically underrepresented on faculties and among professionals in ministry, women scholars have contributed [to pastoral theology, care, and counseling] 94 book-length publications.[33]

To organize the otherwise daunting task of summarizing the contributions of a 34-page, single-spaced bibliography, Greider et al. track the evolution of the field through seven loosely chronological themes or objectives in pastoral studies in religion, psychology, and gender: strengthening the *ekklesia;* attending to marginalized people and taboo topics; articulating female experiences; facilitating theological education; attending to the "needs of human souls searching"; countering violence against women and children; and building systems of care. Research and teaching in each of these categories have contributed significantly to a major movement in the field away from a clinical therapeutic paradigm toward the emergence of a "communal contextual paradigm" in method and practice.[34] For example, efforts to reclaim the biblically promised community or to understand the effects of marginalization have helped to foster an effective movement "away from the tendency to see therapy as the definitive act of pastoral care toward formulating theory and practice in and responsive to corporate human experience in its variety of cultural contexts."[35] Such documentation of the feminist contribution to this shift is invaluable, since recent introductory texts written by the old guard[36] acknowledge the importance of this change but tend to give feminist theory minimal credit.

Writing for Our Lives," in *Feminist and Womanist Pastoral Theology,* ed. Miller-McLemore and Gill-Austern.

33. Greider et al., "Three Decades of Women Writing for Our Lives," p. 24.

34. John Patton, *Pastoral Care in Context: An Introduction to Pastoral Care* (Louisville: Westminster John Knox Press, 1993).

35. Greider et al., "Three Decades of Women Writing for Our Lives," p. 22.

36. See Patton, *Pastoral Care in Context,* and Charles V. Gerkin, *An Introduction to Pastoral Care* (Nashville: Abingdon Press, 1993).

Conceptual Shifts in Religion, Psychology, and Gender Studies in Pastoral Theology

The Role of Psychology and Therapeutic Practice

Psychological theory alone is ultimately insufficient to the task of understanding gender and religion from the perspective of pastoral theology. Recognition of psychology's limits results from a commitment to both transformative praxis and a broader philosophical hermeneutics. Pastoral method requires a movement nicely described by Neuger from "culture to story to traditions for critique and reconstruction, back to story and pastoral strategy."[37] In many cases, such as the one Couture presents of a poor single mother, caring witness comes "through a practice more like social work than psychology."[38]

Knowledge in religion and psychology, then, is no longer defined along conventional psychological lines. Clinical assessment involves social, contextual analysis. Psychological theory, while still important, plays a less commanding role. Other humanistic and social-science disciplines that contribute to understanding the broader cultural context, such as public policy, history, and sociology, have a place. So do theological analysis and reconstruction. Doehring chooses the term "isomorphic" to describe the way in which intrapsychic, family, and larger cultural systems are nested together, giving as an example the parallel between an anorexic woman's self-distortions and the media's distortions of femininity.[39] This approach challenges the privatization and personalization characteristic of many psychological readings of religious beliefs and pastoral care. It calls for a careful philosophical, moral, and theological engagement and critique of psychology as a practice and a discipline.

Second, throughout recent developments in pastoral theology, few feminist scholars aligned themselves solely with one school of psychology, although psychoanalytic feminism has influenced pastoral theology powerfully, perhaps more than other psychological theories. Emphasis on the role of a sexist social environment in shaping and distorting male

37. Neuger, "Feminist Pastoral Theology and Pastoral Counseling," p. 48.

38. Pamela Couture, "Feminist, Wesleyan, Practical Theology and the Practice of Pastoral Care," in *Liberating Faith Practices*, ed. Ackermann and Bons-Storm, p. 36. See also Couture, "Weaving the Web: Pastoral Care in an Individualistic Society," in *Through the Eyes of Women*, ed. Stevenson-Moessner.

39. Doehring, "Developing Models of Feminist Pastoral Counseling," p. 24.

and female development[40] and on the prominent role of the mother in reproducing patterns of female fear of separation and male fear of relationship[41] have proven especially useful in rethinking pastoral care of women and men. Moreover, psychoanalytic feminists provide a cultural critique of the biases of psychology and therapeutic practice[42] — a moral critique already familiar to theologians concerned about the unreflective adoption of psychology by pastoral caregivers and the culture at large.[43]

Few pastoral theologians, however, would identify themselves solely as psychoanalytic feminists. More typically, people pick and choose from many schools of thought. At least one rationale for moving beyond psychoanalytic feminism lies in the broader moral and communal concerns of pastoral theology. Feminist theory itself warrants employment of other approaches, such as socialist feminism. Socialist feminists contend that women are also oppressed by economic inequities and patriarchal devaluing of domestic and childbearing responsibilities. Hence, a woman's status and function "in all these structures must change if she is to achieve anything approximating full liberation."[44]

The Role of Theology, Religious Symbols, and Religion

In many cases, feminist pastoral theologians are more adamant than their predecessors about both the importance of theological exploration and the articulation of religious commitments. As Graham argues, "Feminist pastoral care requires more than good therapeutic technique: it necessitates a critical engagement with theological language, church structures,

40. See, for example, Karen Horney, *Feminine Psychology* (New York: W. W. Norton, 1950), and *Neurosis and Human Growth* (New York: W. W. Norton, 1970).

41. See, for example, Nancy Chodorow, "Family Structure and Feminine Personality," in *Women, Culture, and Society,* ed. M. Zimbalist Rosaldo et al. (Stanford, Calif.: Stanford University Press, 1974); and *The Reproduction of Mothering* (Berkeley and Los Angeles: University of California Press, 1978).

42. See, for example, Juliet Mitchell, *Psychoanalysis and Feminism* (New York: Random House, 1974); and Susan Sturdivant, *Therapy with Women: A Feminist Philosophy of Treatment* (New York: Springer, 1980).

43. Don S. Browning, *Religious Thought and the Modern Psychologies: A Critical Conversation in the Theology of Culture* (Philadelphia: Fortress Press, 1987).

44. Rosemarie Tong, *Feminist Thought: A Comprehensive Introduction* (Boulder, Colo., and San Francisco: Westview Press, 1989), p. 6.

and ministerial practice as crucial arenas of feminist protest and reform."[45] Theology is not simply "an abstract series of philosophical propositions, but a performative discipline," known more through its impact on social relations and practical strategies than through its static properties and categorizations.[46] It is an active, life-shaping framework for making sense of the world. Like *gender, theology* is more of a verb than a noun.[47] Theology forms and deforms lives.

Hence, religious symbols are not merely items to be studied and described in their psychic function as transitional objects or collective archetypes; they are events to be met and embraced or rejected individually and communally, depending on whether, in Pamela Couture's words, they "exert the power of the status quo over women and the vulnerable" or "subversively strengthen women and the vulnerable in their quest to transform the status quo."[48]

In her recent work, Couture exemplifies a second shift in the role of theology and religion in pastoral scholarship. In two articles, she demonstrates with boldness and clarity the centrality of her own commitments.[49] She begins one essay, "I am a feminist, Wesleyan, practical theologian."[50] These are "lenses" through which she interacts with individuals, families, and society to promote love and justice in God's realm. These commitments require privileging women's experience, protecting the vulnerable, and insisting on the embeddedness of theory in practice in the creation of loving and just communities. Such a position has a precedent in the early work of Peggy Way in the 1970s. Way says her

45. Graham, "From 'Terrible Silence' to 'Transforming Hope,'" p. 198.

46. Graham, "From 'Terrible Silence' to 'Transforming Hope,'" p. 208.

47. See Judith Butler, *Gender Trouble: Feminism and the Subversion of Identity* (New York: Routledge, 1990), cited by Graham, "From 'Terrible Silence' to 'Transforming Hope,'" p. 205.

48. Pamela Couture, "Feminist Theological Commitments: Calling for New Modes of Care," p. 8, unpublished English version of a chapter published in Dutch in a festschrift for Riet Bons-Storm, "Vanuit een feministisch-theologisch engagement: Pleidooi voor nieuwe manieren van zorg," in *Geroepen om to spreken: Over verbeelding en creativiteit in theologie en pastoraat: Een bundel van vriendinnen, aangeboden aan Riet Bons-Storm* (Uitgeverij: Kok-Kampen).

49. Couture, "Feminist, Wesleyan, Practical Theology and the Practice of Pastoral Care," and Couture, "Feminist Theological Commitments." See also Couture, *Blessed Are the Poor?*

50. Couture, "Feminist, Wesleyan, Practical Theology and the Practice of Pastoral Care," p. 27.

identity as a minister carries more weight in her self-definition than her actual job description as teacher or administrator. Faith, rather than Scripture, tradition, or institution, grounds her ministerial authority, leading her to challenge the "masculine consciousness" that orders church and academy.[51]

Like Way, Couture readily acknowledges that her understanding of the scholarly vocation can spark discord with the "demands of scholarly guilds and the standards of scientific legitimacy."[52] Yet this clash does not ultimately deter the conviction that theological scholarship in religion, psychology, and gender requires participation in personal and social transformation and not just the investigation of it. Instead, the clash gives cause for critique of the academy of religion.

For the most part, the theological convictions of pastoral theologians have remained partially hidden behind philosophical claims. Browning, for example, has seldom located his partiality for Kantian ethics or communities of moral discourse as partly shaped by a particular Protestant denominational tradition that has emphasized rational, empirical, pragmatic reflection. While Couture does not argue for Wesleyan theology as *the* most appropriate foundation for scholarship in religion and psychology, she does claim it as instrumental in her understanding of experiences of God and the evolution of her scholarship. It clearly lies behind her predilection for a social ecological focus in pastoral theology and her view that academic pursuits in religion and psychology must be guided by a desire to contribute to a better world. The more clearly we can articulate the influence of our faith assumptions on our work, the better. If theological claims are to serve a practical purpose, how can one *not claim* one's faith commitments? If pastoral truth entails transformation and theological wisdom involves passionate engagement with knowledge, then how or even why would one bracket one's convictions?[53]

The Definition of Subject Matter

Couture declares, "Because of my theological commitments, I have specialized not in clinical pastoral counseling but in exploring the social and

51. Way, "An Authority of Possibility for Women in the Church," p. 88.
52. Couture, "Feminist Theological Commitments," p. 1.
53. See Ellen Charry, *By the Renewing of Your Minds: The Pastoral Function of Christian Doctrine* (New York: Oxford University Press, 1997).

cultural context in which pastoral care occurs."[54] This means judging the adequacy of pastoral care and, indeed, scholarship and teaching by their implications for the "treatment of the most poor and vulnerable, particularly children." Bons-Storm makes a similar declaration: her "canon" or "'measuring rod'" for effective scholarship is the following:

> Can [it] be heard as liberating, challenging, and inspiring for the most vulnerable, for the children? Do our thoughts and practices bring them further along the way to a world of faith and hope where they can grow up without violence, hunger, or refugee camps?[55]

Does a theology of praxis, asks Ackermann, contribute to the healing of her country and of women and children?[56] Healing, transformation, and social and individual holiness become criteria of adequate research and, in effect, define the necessary and appropriate subject matter.

As noted above, feminist scholarship in pastoral theology has sparked a shift in focus from the individual to the community, from personal distress to social injustice, from personal fulfillment to the common good, from an ontology of separative selfhood to an open web of relationality. Brita Gill-Austern talks about the importance of fostering an "ecology of care."[57] Couture uses a similar metaphor of a multi-tiered "social ecology" that includes consideration of individuals, families, and fictive kin, society, government-church relations, culture, economics, and nature. Particular individuals remain important but are now seen through the "wide-angled lens" that places them within the "nexus of a macrocosmic" system.[58]

A related and perhaps more prevalent metaphor for this shift in conceptualization of the subject of pastoral theology is that of the "living web." This image arose almost simultaneously in a number of places. Until re-

54. Couture, "Feminist Theological Commitments," p. 13. See also Pamela Couture and Robert Hunter, *Pastoral Care and Social Conflict* (Nashville: Abingdon Press, 1995).

55. Riet Bons-Storm, "Putting the Little Ones into the Dialogue: A Feminist Practical Theology," in *Liberating Faith Practices*, ed. Ackermann and Bons-Storm, p. 19.

56. Denise Ackermann, "'A Voice Was Heard in Ramah': A Feminist Theology of Praxis for Healing in South Africa," in *Liberating Faith Practices*, ed. Ackermann and Bons-Storm, p. 80.

57. Brita Gill-Austern, "Rediscovering Hidden Treasures for Pastoral Care," *Pastoral Psychology* 43, no. 4 (1996): 233-53.

58. Couture, "Feminist Theological Commitments," p. 8. See also Couture, "Feminist, Wesleyan, Practical Theology and the Practice of Pastoral Care," pp. 31-35.

cently, most scholars in pastoral theology looked to Anton Boisen's powerful foundational metaphor for the existential subject of pastoral theology — *"the study of living human documents rather than books."*[59] But when the "focus on care narrowly defined as counseling shifted to a focus on care understood as part of a wide cultural, social, and religious context," the "living human *web*" suggested itself as a better term for the appropriate subject of investigation, interpretation, and transformation.[60] Larry Graham, Gill-Austern, and Couture have also employed the metaphor of web or variations thereof, such as "matrix" or "psychosystemic view," to identify the interacting constellation of factors that foster or frustrate caregiving.[61]

The Definition of Primary Pastoral Functions[62]

To think about pastoral theology from a feminist perspective has led to a fundamental re-orientation of the core functions of pastoral care. In place of or in addition to the traditional pastoral modes — healing, sustaining, guiding, and reconciling — articulated by Hiltner and amended by William Clebsch and Charles Jaekle,[63] four practices acquire particular importance: resisting, empowering, nurturing, and liberating. Although not yet formally classified as four distinct typologies of pastoral care, these four practices have received extensive attention in many recent writings in pastoral theology. These activities are not exhaustive of new modalities sparked by feminism, but they need to be recognized and marked as prominent ways of re-organizing the functions of pastoral care.

While all or some of the four functions of resisting, empowering, nur-

59. Anton Boisen, *The Exploration of the Inner World: A Study of Mental Disorder and Religious Experience* (Chicago: Willett, Clark, 1950), cited by Charles V. Gerkin, *The Living Human Document: Revisioning Pastoral Counseling in a Hermeneutical Mode* (Nashville: Abingdon Press, 1984), p. 37.

60. Miller-McLemore, "The Human Web and the State of Pastoral Theology," p. 367, and "The Living Human Web," p. 16.

61. Larry Kent Graham, *Care of Persons, Care of Worlds: A Psychosystems Approach to Pastoral Care and Counseling* (Nashville: Abingdon Press, 1992); Gill-Austern, "Rediscovering Hidden Treasures for Pastoral Care"; Couture, "Weaving the Web."

62. This section appears in much the same form in Miller-McLemore, "Feminist Theory in Pastoral Theology," pp. 80-81 (used by permission).

63. Seward Hiltner, *Preface to Pastoral Theology* (New York: Abingdon Press, 1958); and William Clebsch and Charles Jaekle, *Pastoral Care in Historical Perspective*, 2d ed. (New York: Aronson, 1983).

turing, and liberating have operated during the historical periods described by Clebsch and Jaekle, they did not receive the kind of pre-eminence that has come recently as a result of feminist theory. For the moment, I offer rather terse definitions to give a general flavor of recent feminist-influenced trends. "Compassionate resistance" requires confrontation with evil and contesting violent, abusive behaviors that perpetuate undeserved suffering and false stereotypes that distort the realities of people's lives. Resistance includes a focused healing of wounds of abuse that have festered for generations.[64] Empowerment involves fierce advocacy and tenderness on behalf of the vulnerable, giving resources and means to those previously stripped of authority and power. Nurturance is not sympathetic kindness or quiescent support but passionate, dedicated proclamation of love that makes a space for difficult change and fosters solidarity among the vulnerable. Liberation entails both escape from unjust, unwarranted affliction and release into new life and wholeness as created, redeemed, and loved people of God. Resistance, empowerment, nurturance, and liberation all entail a deconstruction of unjustly limited definitions of reality and a reconstruction of new views of the world and one's valued place within it.

Pastoral care in these modalities is not particularly "pastoral" or "nice" in the truncated ways in which "pastoral" has sometimes been defined. As Neuger demands, "Isn't my role to engage in a pastoral therapy of *mal*adjustment" rather than to encourage adjustment to a crazy, sick society?[65] Pastoral care disturbs as well as comforts, provokes as well as guides. It breaks silences and calls for radical truth-telling; it names shame and guilt, calls for confession, and moves vigilantly toward forgiveness and reconciliation, knowing that both are more difficult to effect than people have hoped.

Indeed, if pastoral theology keeps the term *shepherd* as a central motif (and even that becomes questionable in a world where sheepherding and shearing are no longer common experiences upon which to ground metaphor), a feminist perspective reminds us that sheep are not the warm, fuzzy, clean creatures that our Sunday school books have portrayed. Womanist pastoral theologian Marsha Foster Boyd rejects "shepherd," "servant," and "wounded healer" as distorted and deforming images. She

64. Nancy J. Ramsay, "Compassionate Resistance: An Ethic for Pastoral Care and Counseling," *Journal of Pastoral Care* 52, no. 3 (Fall 1998): 217-26. See also James Newton Poling, *Deliver Us from Evil: Resisting Racial and Gender Oppression* (Minneapolis: Fortress Press, 1996).

65. Neuger, "Feminist Pastoral Theology and Pastoral Counseling," p. 49; emphasis in text.

suggests instead "empowered cojourner" as a better way to capture the nature of providing company and encouragement on life's pilgrimage.[66]

The Definition of Audiences and Publics

Paradigmatically, Graham titles her recent article "From 'Terrible Silence' to 'Transforming Hope,'"[67] referring to Bons-Storm's book on pastoral care that protests the deadly silence surrounding women in the church and making so many subjects taboo (the female body, gender roles, violence, etc.).[68] The use of gender as a category of analysis in pastoral theology renders visible the hidden assault of patriarchy in pastoral practice. Women write "for our lives," writing not just for enlightenment, but for survival, putting into words realities that seemed unreal when hidden.[69] Gaining a voice and "hearing into speech" bring the possibility of change.

In the move from silence to hope, feminist theologians assume a slightly different relationship than their predecessors to the three publics of society, church, and academy distinguished by David Tracy.[70] Historically, theologians addressed multiple publics. Today, pastoral and practical theologians are left trying to bridge the recent divisions among these publics in terms of language, standards of truth, practices and rituals, and norms. Feminist scholars are especially dedicated to addressing all three publics. Couture takes an even stronger normative stance, arguing that "it is incumbent upon the practical theologian to write for a variety of audiences." The practical theologian must obtain the "linguistic versatility" to speak to academic peers, church leadership, and social constituencies beyond faith communities.[71]

This position is embodied pragmatically in several ways. Many feminist scholars in pastoral theology attempt to function in both academic

66. Marsha Foster Boyd, "Some Reflections on the Pastoral Care and the Transformation of African-American Women," in *Embracing the Spirit: Womanist Perspectives on Hope, Salvation, and Transformation*, ed. E. M. Townes (Maryknoll, N.Y.: Orbis Books), pp. 199-200.

67. Graham, "From 'Terrible Silence' to 'Transforming Hope.'"

68. Bons-Storm, *The Incredible Woman*.

69. Greider et al., "Three Decades of Women Writing for Our Lives."

70. David Tracy, *The Analogical Imagination: Christian Theology and the Culture of Pluralism* (New York: Crossroad, 1981), p. 5. See Miller-McLemore, "Feminist Theory in Pastoral Theology," p. 90.

71. Couture, "Feminist, Wesleyan, Practical Theology and the Practice of Pastoral Care," p. 43.

and ecclesial capacities. Many maintain an allegiance to several different kinds of academic and clinical societies, however ambiguous and difficult. For example, they attend both the AAR and pastoral and practical theology societies as well as clinical organizations. From this, we might surmise that many women desire a more holistic approach to the study of religion. They refuse conventional definitions of disciplinary boundaries, feel less constrained by or less connected to traditional ministry and its institutions as formally defined by men, and appreciate the freedom of thought and expression sometimes more characteristic of the academy and programs in religion and personality.

Feminist scholarship in religion and psychology has also assumed a slightly different tactic for achieving academic standing. Early forerunners in the field, with Hiltner exemplifying the pattern, strove for recognition and legitimacy within the modern university. They hoped to move closer to the center of intellectual activity, arguing for pastoral theology as a new discipline that, alongside systematics, would become a fundamental form of theology.[72] More recently, Browning continued down this path. In *A Fundamental Practical Theology*, he argues that the hierarchy in theological study should be turned on its head, with practical theology as foundational, not merely a "subspecialty" but the "model for theology as such."[73] As well-received as these analyses have been, their impact on the actual organization of the academy itself is less apparent.

By contrast, as early as 1970, Way claimed her position of "historical exclusion" from the mainstream as an "unexpected source of insights" and did not seem to mind staying on the border. She refused to celebrate her appointment to a highly acclaimed divinity school out of acute awareness of the ongoing marginalization of women.[74] More recently, Couture observes, "When a theologian constructs her scholarship from commitments which may place her at the margins of the academy and the church," she does not fight against such marginalization. Other women such as Bons-Storm have been her "allies" in this process. Speaking from the position of "other" requires the use of "imagination to create scholarship" out of the rich potentialities of the context in which one finds oneself.[75]

Many feminist scholars acknowledge and even welcome the position

72. Hiltner, *Preface to Pastoral Theology*, pp. 15, 24-29.

73. Don S. Browning, *A Fundamental Practical Theology: Descriptive and Strategic Proposals* (Minneapolis: Fortress Press, 1991), pp. 7-8.

74. Way, "An Authority of Possibility for Women in the Church," pp. 77, 88.

75. Couture, "Feminist Theological Commitments," p. 1.

of marginality. As Luce Irigaray and others contend, it is from the position of "other" or even "lack" that rich knowledge emerges.[76] Rebecca Chopp provides a strong theoretical argument for the value of this position:

> To preserve the differences [liberal theology] negates through its ordering of discourses and practices, feminism must acknowledge its own discourse as marginal. *From the space of marginality* feminism must declare the unthinkable in terms of the liberal strategy: the liberal assumption that the center can hold all is not a principle of inclusion but a strategy of containment.[77]

The intent, then, is not to move into the center but to transform an ordering of academic status that rests on the oppression of certain persons and disciplines. External standards that determine academic status and theological standards that define the "orthodox" tradition need radical reconception. Like Ackermann and Bons-Storm with their petition that we cease lamenting our identity crisis as a field and get on with addressing life's pressing needs, Chopp argues that feminist theologians ought to celebrate our decentered context, for "it is only by looking away from our . . . preservation and our own identity that we have any hope in offering the world what it so desperately needs."[78]

In all five of these areas — the role of theology, the role of psychology, the definition of subject matter, pastoral function, and public responsibilities — the use of gender as a key category of analysis in pastoral theology has made significant contributions in method and substance. General observations about these contributions may exaggerate their importance and distinctiveness. But at this point in the history of the field, it is best to risk overstating the case, if only to get a fair hearing that will lead others to pay attention to this growing body of feminist literature in pastoral theology and to develop fresh and critical assessments of their own. Only through this kind of ongoing dialogue and debate will the future of the study of religion and psychology be well-secured.

76. See Luce Irigaray, *This Sex Which Is Not One,* trans. A. Sheridan (New York: W. W. Norton, 1977).

77. Chopp, "When the Center Cannot Contain the Margins," in *The Education of the Practical Theologian,* ed. Browning et al., p. 66; emphasis added. For a further elaboration of the processes of containment of feminism, see Rebecca Chopp, *The Power to Speak: Feminism, Language, God* (New York: Crossroad, 1989).

78. Chopp, "When the Center Cannot Contain the Margins," p. 76.

Index

academic paradigm, 53-54, 139, 162, 164, 170-74, 180n.57, 182, 184, 186
academic theology, 2, 194
Academy of Homiletics, 62n.49
Ackermann, Denise, 89, 137, 227, 295, 307, 312
activity of faith, practical theology as, 101, 103, 106-7
Adler, Alfred, 243, 263, 264
advocacy, 157, 301
African-American women, 144, 151, 221, 226
aggression, 229, 300
aging, 6, 21
Ali, Carroll Watkins, 97, 217n.5
American Academy of Religion, 5, 102, 141, 213, 287, 292, 311
American Association of Christian Counselors, 92
American Association of Pastoral Counselors (AAPC), 59, 85, 92-93, 96, 141
American Association of Practical Theology, 294
Anderson, Carol, 260, 277
Anderson, Herbert, 114
Anderson, Victor, 77-78
androcentrism, 229
anger, 229, 300

Anglicanism, 105
application, 162, 163, 173-74
approach to theology, practical theology as, 106, 107-9
Aristotle, 105, 202
Armistead, Kathy, 70
Association of Clinical Pastoral Educators, 94, 96
Association of Practical Theology, 62n.49, 102, 109, 140, 186, 213
Association of Professional Education for Ministry, 141
Association of Professors and Researchers in Religious Education, 62n.49
Association of Seminary Professors in the Practical Fields, 140
Association of Theological Field Education, 62n.49
Association of Theological Schools, 190
attentive love, 131-32
Augsburger, David, 39
Augustine, 141, 146, 147, 202, 203

Bart, Pauline, 125
Bass, Dorothy, 5-6, 101, 175, 188n.3
Bateson, Gregory, 125
behavioral sciences, 55-57

Belenky, Mary Field, 115, 116, 131, 255, 276

Bellah, Robert, 174n.34

Benjamin, Jessica, 38, 269

Benner, Patricia, 198

Bettelheim, Bruno, 13, 262, 282

biology, and knowledge, 130-31

black theology, 106

Boisen, Anton, 4, 26, 36, 42-43, 49, 52, 55, 60, 73, 104, 105, 139-40, 145, 146, 147, 157, 232, 250, 308

Bondi, Roberta, 144, 145, 225

Bonhoeffer, Dietrich, 157

Bons-Storm, Riet, 89, 137, 227, 229, 295, 307, 310, 311, 312

Boston University, 102

Bourdieu, Pierre, 106, 175

Boyd, Marsha Foster, 309

Braverman, Lois, 279

breaking the silence, 218, 229, 251, 282

Brock, Rita Nakashima, 145

Browning, Don, 9, 33, 58, 71, 78, 86-87, 91, 101, 115, 140, 146, 154-55, 173, 175, 201, 211, 239, 290, 306, 311

Bucchino, John, 47

Buckley, William Joseph, 77

Butler, Judith, 269

Cabot, Richard, 55

Cahalan, Kathleen, 10, 11-12, 101, 191, 196, 200, 202-3, 205, 206

Campbell, Alastair, 166

Campbell, Alexander, 4

Campbell, Thomas, 4

capitalism, 90, 284

Capps, Don, 256

Cardwell, Sue, 40, 114, 297

care, 33, 124, 132, 135, 142

caregivers, 51, 53, 95, 105, 108, 109, 232, 258, 316

Carr, Anne, 118, 223

Carter, Betty, 260, 277

case study, 57, 109

castration theory, 262, 263

chaplaincy, 31, 93-94

Chicago Theological Seminary, 113

child rearing, 133-34

Chodorow, Nancy, 115, 134, 219, 243-44, 255, 260, 264, 265-69, 272, 273, 274, 282-83, 284

Chopp, Rebecca, 79, 301, 312

Christian Century, 25, 122, 212

Christian Church (Disciples of Christ), 16-17

Christianity
on family, 92
and feminism, 223-24, 247

Christian life, 54, 171, 175, 177, 189n.5, 203, 206, 235

Christian Right, 78

church, 188n.3
and academy, 28, 162
as community of moral discourse, 86-87
and pastoral counseling, 85

civil religion, 74, 78

Cixous, Hélène, 270

class, 28, 38-39, 216

Clebsch, William, 97, 144, 217, 250, 308-9

clergy burnout, 48

clerical paradigm, 5-6, 53-54, 87, 139, 155, 161-62, 163-71, 177, 182-84, 214, 235

Clinchy, Blythe McVicker, 116, 276

Clinebell, Howard, 29, 32, 39, 85

Clinical Pastoral Education (CPE), 47, 48-53, 62
and congregations, 66-67
and diversity, 65
history of, 55-60

clinical-pastoral paradigm, 80

clinical therapeutic paradigm, 302

clinical training, 86

Clinton, Bill, 93

Cobb, John B., Jr., 36, 167n.9

Cobb, Kelton, 19

Collegeville Institute for Ecumenical and Cultural Research, 6

Collins, Patricia Hill, 222

colonialism, 79

Comas-Diaz, Lillian, 260, 281

communal contextual paradigm, 80-81, 302
community, 50, 103, 307
  and caregiving, 61, 81
compassionate resistance, 217-18, 309
congregation, as community, 46, 61
congregational care, 250
contextual theology, 104
Cooper-White, Pamela, 15-16
Copernicus, 157
counseling, 96, 142
Couture, Pamela, 3, 61, 78, 82, 85, 90-91, 192, 196, 197, 202, 303, 305-7, 310-11
creation, 20, 91, 224, 247
crisis intervention, 29
cross, 19, 20, 249
Crysdale, Cynthia, 276
cultural anthropology, 14, 106, 152
culture, 87, 143, 145
curricular area, practical theology as, 101, 103, 106, 107

Darwin, Charles, 147
de Beauvoir, Simone, 224
de Certeau, Michel, 106
deconstruction, of knowledge, 218-19
DeMarinis, Valerie, 40, 186, 229
depression, 97-98, 229, 300
Derrida, Jacques, 131, 270
descriptive knowledge, 176
DeShazer, Mary K., 150, 153, 156
Deutsch, Helene, 263
developmental theory, 256, 260, 274-77
Dinnerstein, Dorothy, 134
discipline, practical theology as, 11-13, 101, 103, 106, 109
disembodied knowing, 129, 138
divinity schools, 142
Doehring, Carrie, 40, 229, 298-99, 303
domesticity, 264
domestic violence, 97-98
domination, 81-82, 249, 270
Dreyfus, Hubert, 198
Dreyfus, Stuart E., 198
Duke University, 102
Dunbar, Helen Flanders, 243

Dykstra, Craig, 6, 101, 172-73, 174-76, 188n.3
Dykstra, Robert, 47, 186

early childhood development, 242
Eastern Orthodoxy, 105
ecological movement, 216
ecological religious feminism, 223
ecology of care, 61, 81
ecumenism, 81, 83-84
egalitarianism, 224
Eichenbaum, Luise, 38
ekklesia, 302
embodiment, 101, 103, 201
  and knowing, 130, 132
  and practice, 196
  and theology, 192-93
Emory University, 102
empathy, 151-52
empowerment, 97, 144, 217, 218, 250, 301, 308-9
Engel, Mary Potter, 157
Enlightenment, 53, 169, 184
epistemological development, 276
epistemology, 114, 117-18, 120, 126, 134, 192-93
equality, 242
Erikson, Erik, 262, 270, 274, 282
Estadt, Barry, 42
ethnicity, women, and psychological theory, 260, 280-82
Eve, 247
existential-anthropological mode, 82

faith-based organizations, 76
family, 89, 90-92, 282-83
family systems theory, 82, 250, 256, 260, 277-79
Farley, Edward, 2, 3, 56, 87, 138, 160-62, 164, 166-74, 179-81, 182-83, 188n.3, 190-91, 193, 235
fatherhood, 267
female anatomy, and knowledge, 130-31
feminism, 34-35, 44, 79, 81, 212, 214, 215, 224, 261
feminist epistemology, 117-22, 129, 135

feminist pastoral theology, 226-30, 288, 293-302
feminist psychoanalytic theory, 219-20, 250, 263-70, 284, 303-4
feminist psychology, 28, 257
feminist studies, 260-63
feminist theology, 106, 144, 223-24
feminist theory
  and pastoral theology, 212-13, 217, 225-26
  and practical theology, 217, 225-26
  varieties of, 219-22
Feminist Therapy Institute, 280
Firestone, Shulamith, 224
Flax, Jane, 123, 269
Fortune, Marie, 90
Foucault, Michel, 270
Francis, Saint, 203
Frankfort School of social theory, 58-59, 84, 145
French feminists, 270
Freud, Sigmund, 32, 38, 47, 58, 129, 142, 157, 233, 238, 242-43, 262, 282, 290
Fromm, Erich, 145
Fulkerson, Mary McClintock, 200, 201-2, 204
"fundamental practical theology," 155

Gadamer, Hans-Georg, 155, 173, 174n.34
Gardner, Howard, 173
Garlid, Kitty, 47
Geertz, Clifford, 13-14, 15, 106
gender, 1, 28, 38-39, 118-19, 216, 240-42, 255, 258, 260, 270, 295, 305, 312
  and knowledge, 120-21, 136
  new scholarship on, 259
  social construction of, 239, 241, 282
generativity, 135, 149
Gerkin, Charles, 30, 48, 287, 290
Gibbons, Jim, 51
Gilkes, Cheryl Townsend, 151
Gill-Austern, Brita, 61, 81, 211, 212, 307, 308
Gilligan, Carol, 115, 116, 124, 243, 244-45, 255, 257-58, 260, 272, 274-77, 281, 283
Gilpin, Clark, 78

Glaz, Maxine, 38, 40, 212, 284
God
  as father, 247, 298
  love of, 249
  as mother, 115, 117
Goldberger, Nancy Rule, 116, 276
Gordon, Mary, 128, 149
Graham, Elaine, 175, 176, 213, 293, 296, 304-5, 310
Graham, Larry, 35, 61, 82, 159, 308
Grant, Jacquelyn, 151
Greenberg Quinlan Research, 93
Greene, Beverly, 260, 281
Greider, Kathleen, 88, 203, 293, 301, 302
Griffin, Gail, 227
Groome, Thomasa, 146
Gudorf, Christine, 156
Gustafson, James, 78, 86
gynocentric feminism, 221-22, 223, 230

Habermas, Jürgen, 106
habitus, 169, 174-75
Haraway, Donna, 119
Hare-Mustin, Rachel, 277
Harrison, Beverly Wildung, 113, 129, 132
Harvey, Van, 170-71
Hauerwas, Stanley, 77, 174n.34
headship, 247
healing, 20, 64, 68, 97, 144, 202-3, 217, 250, 281-82, 307, 308
health care, 92-93
hegemony, of Western culture, 218
Henry R. Luce Foundation, 76
hermeneutical circle, 109, 199-201, 205
hermeneutics, 173, 175
hermeneutics of suspicion, 138, 150, 229, 299
Hess, Carol, 152, 153
heterosexism, 79, 239, 269, 270
hierarchy, 3-5
Hiltner, Seward, 1, 2, 3, 4, 9, 30, 59, 78, 85, 92, 104, 105, 140, 145, 176, 217, 250, 287, 290, 300, 308, 311
historical-critical method, 169
Holiday, Billie, 19

Index

Holifield, E. Brooks, 29, 38-39, 55, 56, 83-84
hooks, bell, 34-35, 143, 144, 153, 213, 215, 216, 220, 223, 225-26, 230, 234, 281-82
Horney, Karen, 219, 243-44, 264-65, 269, 270
hospital chaplaincy, 51-52
Hough, Joseph C., Jr., 167n.9
house-church movements, 141
household codes, 247-48
Howard, V. A., 178
humanist feminism, 221-22, 223, 227
human suffering, 31, 57, 143, 146, 150
Hunter, Rodney, 47, 58, 74, 80, 83-84, 176-78, 233

individualism, 38, 56, 74, 81, 83, 140, 203, 232, 250, 283, 284
inequality, 271
injustice, 97, 307
interdisciplinary study, 159
International Academy of Practical Theology, 62n.49, 70, 102, 109, 141
International Journal of Practical Theology, 255, 256, 258
interpersonal feminists, 273
Iraq war, 72
Irigaray, Luce, 131, 270, 312

Jaekle, Charles, 97, 144, 217, 250, 308-9
James, William, 142
Johnson, Gloria, 88, 301
Joint Commission on the Accreditation of Healthcare Organizations, 94
Jones, Serene, 101
Jonte-Pace, Diane, 287, 289, 290, 296
Jordan, Judith, 272
Journal of Pastoral Care, 94
Jung, Carl, 142
Justes, Emma, 41, 246, 259

Kaplan, Alexandra G., 272
Keller, Catherine, 36-37, 145
Keller, William, 55, 58
Kelsey, David, 78, 165, 167n.9, 179
Kemeza, Maureen, 219

Kierkegaard, Søren, 141, 203
Kohlberg, Lawrence, 245, 274
Kohut, Heinz, 32, 125
Kristeva, Julia, 124, 127, 270
Kübler-Ross, Elisabeth, 32

Lacan, Jacques, 266, 270
lactation, 129-30, 133, 149
Lapsley, James, 49n.5, 140, 295
Lartey, Emmanuel, 96
Lerner, Harriet, 279
Leslie, Kristen, 88, 301
Lewis, C. S., 147
liberal feminists, 220
liberal Protestantism, 52-53
liberation theology, 4, 73, 79-80, 81, 82, 87-88, 106, 144-45, 154, 155, 157, 158, 216, 226
Liebert, Elizabeth, 34
Lilly Endowment, 76, 100-101, 211
"limit situations," 147, 234
Lindbeck, George, 77
lived experience, 188n.3, 299
living human documents, 42, 48-49, 55, 59, 60, 73, 105, 140, 196, 231, 250, 308
living human web, 1, 26, 36, 42, 50, 60-62, 63, 73, 81, 95, 140, 196, 250, 307-8
local theology, 104, 109, 183
Lorde, Audre, 157, 222
love
   for neighbor, 249
   as sacrificial, 151, 247
Lovin, Robin, 78
Luther, Martin, 3, 4, 141

MacIntyre, Alasdair, 106, 174n.34, 175
Maddox, Randy, 161, 184
Maduro, Otto, 154
mainline Protestantism, 291
   social activism of, 76
   on theological education, 167
male clerics, 218, 228
male envy, 262
male experience, as normative, 243, 257-58, 285
male headship, 247

male social power, 263-64
the marginalized, 42-43, 45, 99, 227, 301, 302, 311
Marsh, Charles, 4
Marty, Martin, 25, 78
Marxist feminists, 220
maternal knowing, 115-16, 117, 119, 123-28, 132-136, 149
Mathews, Shailer, 78
McCarthy, Mary, 59
McClure, Barbara, 64n.54
McDannell, Colleen, 181
McFague, Sallie, 115, 134
McGoldrick, Monica, 260, 277
Miller, Donald, 188n.3
Miller, Jean Baker, 115, 260, 270-72, 274, 275, 281
Mills, Liston, 32, 49n.5, 63, 140, 295
misogyny, 214, 244, 257, 265
Mitchell, Juliet, 260, 266, 284
modernism, 218
Moseley, Romney, 87-88
motherhood, 114-15, 118, 123-36, 244, 247, 251, 265, 267, 268, 283
Mudd, Emily H., 278
Mud Flower Collective, 121
multiple publics, 158, 231, 310
mutuality, 91, 224, 242, 248

narrative theory, 109
Neuger, Christie, 40, 229, 298-99, 303, 309
Niebuhr, Reinhold, 232
Nieman, James, 4, 101, 182n.62, 192, 195, 196, 199, 200, 201, 203
Noddings, Nel, 125, 131
North American Academy of Liturgy, 62n.49
Nouwen, Henri, 34, 203
nurturing, 144, 217, 218, 250, 263, 308-9

Oates, Wayne, 59, 85, 86, 287
objectivity, pretense of, 150
object-relations feminists, 273
occasional theology, 13-14
Oduyoye, Mercy Amba, 133

Oedipal struggle, 244, 265
Oglesby, William, 56
Olsen, Tillie, 127
oppression, 79, 216, 249, 220, 222, 250, 251, 257, 265, 268-69
Orbach, Susie, 38
original sin, 298
Ortner, Sherry, 6, 13
Osmer, Rick, 62, 256
Ottenhoff, Don, 11

paideia, 169, 172
Papp, Penny, 277
Parish Nursing, 95
Parsons, William, 287
pastoral care, 55-60, 232
    communal and public nature of, 84
    dimensions of, 97, 144, 217, 250, 308-9
    disturbs and provokes, 218
pastoral counseling, 25-26, 34, 85
pastoral psychotherapy, 27, 31, 33-34
pastoral theological feminists, 220
pastoral theology, 9-10, 27-28, 142
    developments within, 80-95, 231-37
    as modern discipline, 138, 141-42
    political imperative of, 144-45
    and practical theology, 104, 138-39, 145-46
    as public theology, 70-99
    and social sciences, 28, 29-32
    strengths of, 158-59
    vs. pastoral psychology, 32
patriarchy, 124, 136, 220, 224, 229, 247, 248, 263, 265, 268, 284, 296-99
Pattison, Stephen, 89
Patton, John, 61, 80-81
Peck, M. Scott, 32
pedagogy, of practical theology, 187-89, 196, 200-201, 203-5
Pellauer, Mary, 154
penis envy, 243, 262, 263-64, 284
Perry, William, 276
person, personhood, 202
    as document, 68
    social construction of, 241
    and web, 63-65

personal formation, 57
personality, 145, 233-34
Peterson, Eugene, 34
Pew Charitable Trusts, 76
phronesis, 188, 197
Piaget, Jean, 274
Placher, William, 78
Plaskow, Judith, 224
pluralism, 65
poems of resistance, 150, 153, 156
Poling, James, 35, 90, 188n.3
post-deconstruction reconstruction,
204
postmodernism, 79, 138, 145-46, 152, 218-
19, 236, 270, 288
post-structuralism, 79
poverty, 79, 229, 300
power, 79, 89, 90, 99, 106, 150, 158, 261,
270, 283, 300, 301, 309
and epistemology, 126
and knowledge, 218, 288
practical knowledge, 177, 185, 186
practical language, 17
practical theology, 2, 142
in the academy, 235-36
as bridge between disciplines, 62
definition of, 100-110
developments within, 231-37
identity of, 295
messiness of, 153-56
and pastoral theology, 104, 138-39,
145-46
as method, 101, 103
as theology for the masses, 18
practical wisdom, 1
practice, 171-79, 181, 190, 194-96, 199,
205, 214
pragmatism, 155, 175
pre-Oedipal period, 244, 265, 273
process theology, 82
Protestantism. *See* mainline Protestantism
Proverbs, 198-99
psychoanalytic theory, 256, 260, 263-70.
See also feminist psychoanalytic theory

psychology, 30, 37-38, 68, 83-84, 87, 96,
105, 138, 232, 250, 257
importance of, 284
and pastoral theology, 29-32, 303
and religion, 289-90, 291-93
psychology of religion, 287, 289, 291-93
psychosystems approach, 82, 308
public theology, 74-80

race, 28, 38-39, 256, 280-82, 295
racism, 74, 79, 84, 88, 90, 97, 212, 239
radical feminists, 220
Rahner, Karl, 10, 18, 108
Ramsay, Nancy, 70, 96, 287, 298-99
rationalism, 169, 184
Rauschenbusch, Walter, 85
Redwood, John, 89
Reform Judaism, 105
relationships, 239-40, 241, 247, 272, 307
religion
and culture, 143
and psychology, 289-90
religious diversity, 50, 65
religious idolatries, 66
religious pluralism, 75, 106
religious studies, 287, 291
Richmond, Mary, 278
ritual theory, 206
Rogers, Carl, 29, 41, 151, 233
Roman Catholics, 105, 155
on contextual theology, 104
on pastoral ministry, 10
on pastoral theology, 12
on theological education, 167
Rorty, Richard, 270
Rossi, Alice, 128
Ruddick, Sara, 117, 128, 131
Ruether, Rosemary Radford, 39-40, 113,
223, 224

sacrifice, 247, 248-49
Saiving, Valerie, 151, 238, 248-49
Satir, Virginia, 278
Saussy, Carol, 114
Schaef, Anne Wilson, 32, 115, 257-58
Scharen, Christian, 198

Schechter, Patricia, 121
Schleiermacher, Friedrich, 2-3, 9, 19, 53, 98, 104, 155, 166, 167, 168, 172-73, 184
Schlüssler Fiorenza, Elisabeth, 40, 113, 118, 150, 223
Schneiders, Sandra, 11-12
Schreiter, Robert, 162, 183-84
Schweitzer, Friedrich, 15
Seaman, Barbara, 143
secular feminism, 223
Segundo, Juan Luis, 193n.16
the self:
  self-actualization, 281
  self-esteem, 229, 300
  self-examination, 188
  selfhood, 37, 38, 46, 68, 80, 83, 99, 232, 250, 256, 258, 269, 270, 283-84, 298, 307
  selflessness, 247
  self-love, 151
  self-realization, 83
self-in-relation theory, 250, 256, 260, 270-73
seminaries, 8, 142. *See also* academic paradigm; clerical paradigm and Clinical Pastoral Education (CPE), 50, 52-54, 56, 66-69
servanthood, 151, 309
sexism, 74, 79, 88, 212, 214, 216, 229, 239-40, 271
sexual abuse, 41, 97-98, 242
sexual equality, 216
sexual ethics, 156
sexuality, 220, 239-42, 247, 258, 282
  new scholarship on, 259
  repressed or misdirected, 242
  social construction of, 118
shared parenting, 267-69
Shinn, Roger, 77
Silverstein, Olga, 277
sin, 32, 64, 92, 151, 163, 189, 216, 236, 259
slavery, 151
Smith, Archie, 40, 84
Smith, Christine, 150, 152, 157
Smith, Roy Steinhoff, 33
Smith, Ted, 101

Snorton, Teresa, 94
Snyder, Ross, 140
social activism, 76, 84
social gospel, 85
socialist feminism, 220, 304
social sciences, 105, 202, 250, 301
social-scientific study of religion, 142
social solidarity, 89
social transformation, 96
society, 71, 76-77, 103
Society for Pastoral Theology, 45, 49n.5, 62n.49, 113-14, 140
Spencer, John, 36
spirituality, 94-95, 295
spiritual practices, 12
Sprengnether, Madelon, 269
Stephen Ministries, 95
Stern, Daniel, 272
Stevenson-Moessner, Jeanne, 2, 26, 40-41, 212
Stiver, Irene P., 272
"Stone Center model" for development, 270, 272
Stout, Jeffrey, 174n.34
strategic practical theology, 155
Streck, Danilo and Valburga, 89
Sturdivant, Susan, 284
Suchocki, Marjorie, 145
suffering, 18, 43, 68, 157-58, 247, 249, 281-82
Suleiman, Susan Rubin, 125
Sullivan, Harry Stack, 270
Surrey, Janet L, 272
systematic theology, 169-70, 182

Taggart, Morris, 122
Tanner, Kathryn, 163, 183-84, 194
Tarule, Jill Mattuck, 116, 276
Tatum, Beverly Daniel, 239
Taylor, Mark K., 301
teaching practice, 189-91, 192-93, 205
theological education. *See also* academic paradigm; clerical paradigm problems of, 205
  as social enterprise, 179
  telos of, 185-86

theological encyclopedia, 167-68, 179
theology
  cognitive captivity of, 162
  democratization of, 3
  and experience, 105
  fresh construction of, 299
  as local, 4
  marginalization of, 169-71
  messy particularity of, 225
  as multivalent, 2
  as performative discipline, 305
  plurality of contexts and purposes,
    162, 183-84
  as practice, 194
  and psychology, 25-26
  and religious studies, 291
  as scientific discipline, 104-5
  and social sciences, 142
  as "thinking" or "reflecting," 186
theology of culture, 87
theory and practice, 32, 52, 57, 155, 173,
  181, 190, 193, 200-201
therapeutic, 33, 84, 202, 233
thick description, 45, 106, 159
Thiemann, Ronald, 77
Thistlethwaite, Susan, 154, 157
Thomas Aquinas, 129
Thompson, Clara, 263, 264
Thornton, Edward, 56-58, 66-67
Tillich, Paul, 30, 65, 78-79, 232, 290, 300
Tong, Rosemarie, 219-20, 223
Towle, Charlotte, 278
Townes, Emilie, 40, 156
Tracy, David, 30, 71, 77, 78, 79, 147, 152,
  154, 158, 188n.3, 193n.16, 231, 234, 300,
  310
transformation, 15-16, 301, 307
tree metaphor, 2-3, 19-20
truth
  contextual nature of, 288
  universal assumptions about, 218-19
truth-telling, 156-57, 218
Turpin, Katherine, 192, 195, 198, 200

University of Chicago, 71, 73, 77-78, 80,
  87, 161

University of Manchester, 102
Unterberger, Gail, 113

Vanderbilt University, 137, 140, 160
Vatican II, 81
violence, 89-90, 154, 218, 228, 229, 298,
  300, 302

Walsh, Froma, 260, 277
Walters, Marianne, 277
Way, Peggy, 40, 113-14, 228, 297, 305-6,
  311
web metaphor, 37, 46-47, 58, 60, 62, 81,
  232, 250, 308
Weedon, Chris, 269
Weisstein, Naomi, 261
Wesleyan theology, 306
Westkott, Marcia, 264
Wheeler, Barbara, 165, 167n.9, 179
Whitehead, Alfred North, 164
Whitehead, James and Evelyn, 146
Wicks, Robert, 42
Wilkerson, Mary, 51
Williams, Delores, 223
Williamson, Clark, 17
Wimberly, Edward, 40, 59, 84, 97
Winnicott, D. W., 266, 270
wisdom, 20, 177, 182
Wise, Carroll, 85
Wissenschaft, 104
Witvliet, John, 177, 191, 192, 195, 198-99,
  200, 201, 203-4, 205
womanism, 40, 212, 214, 217, 224, 226
womanly discourse, 120-21
women
  and care, 249, 297, 299
  in the church, 44, 113
  experiences of, 241, 243, 305
  Freud on, 242-43
  and pastoral care, 246, 297
  in pastoral theology, 38-43, 88-89, 113,
    212, 215-16
  sexual desires of, 247
  submission of, 247, 248, 264, 298
women of color, 123, 216, 221, 227, 280,
  281

Woodruff, Roy, 92
Woolf, Virginia, 127
wounded healer, 203, 309
Wuthnow, Robert, 77

Yale Divinity School, 77-78
Young, Iris, 221, 223, 230